The George Seldes Reader

Randolph T. Holhut

BARRICADE BOOKS INC.

New York

Published by Barricade Books Inc.
61 Fourth Avenue
New York, NY 10003

Printed in the United States of America.

Library of Congress Cataloging-in-Publication Data

Holhut, Randolph T.
    The George Seldes reader/by Randolph T. Holhut.
        p. cm.
    ISBN 1-56980-007-3: $17.00
    I. Seldes, George, 1890–   . II. Title.
AC8.H35 1994
081—dc20   93-48816
                                                CIP

First printing

Table of Contents

PART THREE: PRESS CRITIC

Notes and Acknowledgements

THE PIECES that appear in this book are as George Seldes wrote them. Certain passages have been deleted due to redundancy and spelling and usage has been changed in spots to conform to modern style, but I left his writing alone for the most part.

I selected the pieces with an eye to their historical significance. A lot of what I chose consists of the history of the Twentieth Century that most of us never learned in school.

In his 21 books, Seldes often repeated himself. When I had several versions of a particular episode in his life, I chose the one from his older, out-of-print books.

This book is divided into three sections: Foreign Correspondent, Freedom Fighter and Press Critic. I began each section with an introductory essay by Seldes. The introduction to this book originally appeared as a series of columns in the *Brattleboro* (Vt.) *Reformer* in July and August of 1992.

The Foreign Correspondent section contains the European adventures of Seldes during his years with the *Chicago Tribune,* he and his wife's trip to Madrid to report on the Spanish Civil War and his travels in Eastern Europe after the end of World War II.

Fighting fascism was Seldes' main occupation in the 1930's and 1940's and the Freedom Fighter section of this book covers the rise of Redbaiting, how big business subsidized fascism prior to and during World War II, and the origins of the Cold War among other topics. Seldes' sharp insights on the workings of the media through this century make up the final section of this book.

Almost all of Seldes' books are out-of-print and difficult to find. Three booksellers in particular have been a great help to me: Al Fullerton of Bernardston Books in Bernardston, Mass; Eugene Povirk of Southpaw Books in Conway, Mass.; and John Durham of Bolerium Books in San Francisco, Calif. Bernardston Books is where this book was conceived, I found the first few books that got me interested in Seldes' life and work there. Southpaw and Bolerium managed to come up with the rarer volumes and an obsessive personal search of other old bookstores in New England located the rest.

Peter Stein and his computer service—AllWrite! of Northampton, Mass.—saved me months of retyping by scanning the text I selected for this book onto computer discs and also assisted in preparing the final manuscript.

My partner, Joyce Marcel, assisted with the initial editing and helped me learn to master the Macintosh. Her support and love were invaluable in the making of this book.

Finally, I'd like to thank my family for believing in me even when it seemed like I was wasting my time trying to become a journalist. My late father always told me that I could do anything I wanted to do if I wanted to do it bad enough. I wanted to be a journalist and suffered through a lot of disappointments and lean times before I succeeded. Their encouragement helped me stay the course and realize my dreams.

Randolph T. Holhut
Townshend, Vermont
August 1993

The Forgotten Man of American Journalism

THERE HAVE been three great independent journalists in this century—Lincoln Steffens, I.F. Stone and George Seldes.

Steffens and Stone are the best known of the three. With his magazine articles and books like *The Shame of the Cities*, Steffens, along with fellow muckrakers like Will Irwin, Ida Tarbell and Upton Sinclair, helped to invent the art of investigative journalism in the first decade of this century.

Stone, a veteran Washington reporter, published *I.F. Stone's Weekly* from 1953 to 1971, a newsletter that printed the news that was overlooked in the mainstream press. His work almost single-handedly revived investigative reporting and inspired a new generation of writers on the Left.

The lives and work of Steffens and Stone are well-known to journalists and historians. Unfortunately, Seldes is not. History has overlooked his life and career, but he is the living link between Steffens and Stone. His life and work deserve to be reconsidered.

The story of George Seldes is the story of the Twentieth Century. He has written 21 books and is the archetype of the independent and crusading journalist. He was a witness to and occasional participant in some of the most important events of this century. There is scarcely a person still alive who has seen the things that he has seen.

Seldes was one of a group of four journalists who snuck into Germany at the end of World War I to get an exclusive interview with Field Marshall Paul von Hindenburg, the supreme commander of the German Army. The interview might have changed the course of history had it not been censored by the Allies.

In 1922, Seldes was in Russia to cover the meeting of the Third International, a gathering of the world's communist leaders. There he met Lenin, Trotsky and the founders of the Soviet Union. He spent a year reporting from that country and was eventually expelled by the Soviet government for not bowing to its censorship of the news.

He chronicled the rise of Benito Mussolini in Italy in the 1920's and was also expelled from that country when he refused to write what the Fascisti wanted him to write.

He and his wife Helen Larkin went to Spain in the mid-1930's when General Francisco Franco, aided by Germany and Italy, overthrew the democratically elected government and established a fascist dictatorship. The Seldeses reported on how the dress rehearsal for World War II was being played out on Spanish soil as the world impassively watched.

Disatisfied with censorship and the Right-wing bias of the American media, the Seldeses started *In fact,* the first publication in America solely devoted to press criticism. It was published from 1940 to 1950 and had a peak circulation of 176,000 before being Red-baited out of existence.

Because of his insistence upon writing the truth, George Seldes has been ignored by the mainstream media and has been denied his rightful place in the history of American journalism. But he harbors no bitterness toward the media establishment. "One of the greatest sources of comfort to me is knowing that I have lived long enough to be vindicated. I've outlived all of my enemies, but I've also outlived all of my friends," Seldes told me during my first meeting with him in the summer of 1992.

I came across Seldes' last book, *Witness to a Century,* in the spring of 1992. He completed it when he was 96, a valedictory on his life and the people who populated it. Reading it was like sitting on the front porch, listening to your grandparents tell you stories about the old days, only in this case, the old days are merely the biggest events of the twentieth century. As a journalist and amateur historian, I had to meet this man.

Seldes was born in Alliance, New Jersey on November 19, 1890. His rise to the top echelons of journalism was rapid. He started as a cub reporter on the *Pittsburgh Leader* in 1909; five years later he was the night editor at the *Pittsburgh Post.* After taking a year off to attend Harvard (at the insistence of his brother Gilbert, who would later write "The Seven Lively Arts" and become a prominent commentator on the American cultural scene), he went to London in 1916 to work as a reporter for the United Press.

A year later, upon America's entry into World War I, he went to Paris and became the managing editor of the Army edition of the *Chicago Tribune*. He soon left that job to join G-2-D, General John J. Pershing's press section, as an accredited war correspondent for the Marshall Syndicate. It was in that role that Seldes got the story that he believes was the most important of his career: the exclusive interview with Hindenburg.

In the interview, Hindenburg acknowledged the role that America played in defeating Germany. "The American infantry," said Hindenburg, "won the World War in battle in the Argonne." But American newspaper readers never read those words. Seldes and the others were accused of breaking the Armistice and were court martialed. They were also forbidden to write anything about the interview.

Seldes believes that the suppression of the interview proved to be costly to the world. Instead of hearing straight from the mouth of Germany's supreme commander that they were beaten fair and square on the battlefield, another story took hold: the Dolchstoss, or "stab-in-the-back." This myth held that Germany did not lose in battle, but was betrayed at home by "the socialists, the Communists and the Jews." This was the central lie upon which Nazism was founded.

"If the Hindenburg interview had been passed by Pershing's (stupid) censors at the time, it would have been headlined in every country civilized enough to have newspapers and undoubtedly would have made an impression on millions of people and became an important page in history," wrote Seldes in *Witness to a Century*. "I believe it would have destroyed the main planks on which Hitler rose to power, it would have prevented World War II, the greatest and worst war in all history, and it would have changed the future of all mankind."

The episode also played an important role in Seldes' life. He would spend the next 10 years in Europe reporting for the *Chicago Tribune*. He would be in on some major events in that tumultuous decade, like his trip to the Soviet Union.

Lenin was already on his way out when Seldes went to Russia, as the power of the secret police and the Communist Party bureaucrats overshadowed that of the leader of the Russian Revolution. Seldes still remembers the day when Lenin had to talk his way past the guards to address the Third International.

"He'd been missing for about a year, and there were all kinds of rumors about his disappearance," said Seldes. "The hall was crowded with people (for the Third International, a select gathering of Communist leaders, orators, debators and parliamentarians who were in Moscow in 1922 to celebrate the fifth anniversary of the Russian Revolution) when we heard a commotion at the entrance. There, we saw a little man arguing with the guards to come in. It was Lenin, and he apparently didn't have the right pass to get in."

Lenin got in and received a thunderous ovation. After he addressed the gathering and the congress adjourned, Seldes and the other American reporters in attendance then crowded in to try and get an interview.

"Someone hollered to ask if Lenin spoke English," Seldes said. "He replied, 'I speak her, ze English, not zo ver goot.' He then started speaking in German, which I did understand." Lenin told Seldes and the other reporters that he occupied "a large portion of my time with American affairs." He added: "Your American newspapers frequently report me dead. Let them fool themselves. Don't take away the last hope of a dying bourgeoisie by saying you spoke to me."

Seldes spent a year in the Soviet Union covering the American Relief Administration's efforts to help famine victims. Every news report that came out was cleared by Soviet censors. But Seldes and other reporters who were interested in reporting the truth found a way around the censorship. "We put our dispatches in the ARA diplomatic courier pouches, where the Russians weren't allowed to look," said Seldes. "We'd write them like letters, start them off with 'Dear so-and-so,' then write our story and close with 'Cordially yours' and mailed them to London."

Eventually, Seldes was found out and expelled by the Soviet authorities in August 1923. Other reporters, like Walter Duranty of the *New York Times,* went along with the censorship and stayed on. "Duranty told me that the highest job in America is to be a *Times* reporter," Seldes said. "Nobody wanted to lose the privileges that came with it."

Seldes told me that he still could not believe that the Soviet Union no longer exists. "I never thought I'd see Russia break apart. The things that (Russian president Boris) Yeltsin said and did would have got him executed in Red Square back in the Twenties. I always expected to see a big socialist movement around the world, especially in the United States. It seems to have disappeared entirely."

Seldes was among the first American journalists who dared to write truthfully about fascism. In 1925, the *Chicago Tribune* assigned him to Italy, where Mussolini had recently come to power. Seldes said that the foreign journalists working in Italy were too timid to print the truth about Il Duce.

"Everyone had copies of the confessions of the men who killed (Giacomo) Matteotti (the head of the Italian Socialist Party and Mussolini's chief political rival). The documents clearly implicated Mussolini in the killing, but not one person wanted to write about it. They thought Rome was too nice a posting to give up to risk publishing them. They didn't want to, but I did."

The story ran on the front page of the Paris edition of the *Chicago Tribune* and it resulted in Seldes' immediate expulsion from Italy, and a narrow escape from a group of Blackshirts who wanted to kill him. The major American newspapers at the time supported fascism as a legitimate political movement. "They loved Mussolini because they thought he restored order to Italy and businesses there were doing well. It got more and more difficult to report on what was really happening there," said Seldes.

Seldes was sent to Mexico in 1927, when the United States came close to invading that country when the Mexican government threatened to take back the mineral rights from the American corporations that stole them from the Mexican people.

He wrote a series of stories for the *Tribune* that were censored to fit the political views of Colonel Robert McCormack, the reactionary owner and publisher of the paper. While he usually allowed his European reporters freedom to write truthfully, McCormack did not extend this freedom to his domestic editorial staff. This experience convinced Seldes that he would not be able to write freely until he left the *Tribune* and wrote on his own.

Seldes quit the *Tribune* in 1929 and continued as an independent journalist and author. His first two books, *You Can't Print That!*, in 1929 and *Can These Things Be!*, in 1931, attempted to set the historical record straight as Seldes told the stories that he could not tell in the *Tribune*. His next book, *World Panorama*, in 1933, was a narrative history of the post-World War I years.

In 1932, he married Helen Larkin. They met at a party in 1929 in Paris, where Larkin was a student studying physics at the Sorbonne. When the conversation turned to the Soviet Union, where Larkin wanted to go after graduation to work for the physiologist Ivan Pavlov, Seldes told Larkin about his trip to the Soviet Union "and the many difficulties of ordinary daily life. I went on to attack the Soviet Communist dictators and the regime's denial of civil liberties to the masses and Miss Larkin, who obviously was getting angrier and angrier, cut me short with the remark, 'I don't think I ever want to see you again, Mr. Seldes,'" George recalled in *Witness to a Century.*

When they unexpectedly met again in Paris three years later, George said "it was without question 'love at second sight.'" After a three-week courtship in Paris, they were married. With a loan of $5,000 from Sinclair Lewis, the Seldeses bought a home in Woodstock, Vermont, where they would spend their summers for the next four decades. Helen would assist George on all of his writing projects until her death in 1979.

After writing an objective history of the Catholic Church, *The Vatican: Yesterday-Today-Tomorrow,* and an exposé of the world armaments industry, *Iron, Blood and Profits,* in 1934; Seldes wrote the most complete account of the life of Mussolini and how he came to power, *Sawdust Caesar,* in 1935. He then turned his attention to the transgressions of the American press with *Freedom of the Press* in 1935 and *Lords of the Press* in 1938. In between writing those two books, the Seldeses went to Spain in 1937 to cover the Spanish Civil War for the *New York Post.*

General Franco's forces were well equipped by Germany and Italy, who used Spain as a proving ground for their weapons and tactics. The Republicans, the people who were fighting to take back their country, were outnumbered and outgunned. "They had no guns, food or medicines and the world press published falsehoods about them, called them 'Reds' and let them die," Seldes said.

The major American newspapers of the time took the side of Franco, who was portrayed as ridding Spain of communism. They similarly lauded Mussolini and Hitler for ridding their countries of "the Red menace." The *New York Post* was at the time among the few liberal dailies in America which would report the truth about the Spanish War but even they succumbed to the pressure of the American Right and the Catholic Church, both of whom supported Franco and threatened boycotts and economic ruin to any paper that criticized him.

The whole Spanish experience left Seldes and others on the American Left embittered and angry. Evil had triumphed, no thanks to the press lords who refused or were to afraid to print the truth about fascism. It also inspired three more books by Seldes, *You Can't Do That!,* in 1938 discussed attacks by the Right upon civil liberties in America; *The Catholic Crisis* in 1940 examined the Church's ties to fascist organizations and *Witch Hunt,* also in 1940, which looked at Red-baiting in America.

Spain also proved to be the catalyst for Seldes to start his own newsletter that would crusade against against the lies of the times, *In fact.*

The newsletter's mission was clearly stated on its masthead: "An Antidote for Falsehood in the Daily Press."

"He's about as subtle as a house falling in," wrote fellow press critic A.J. Liebling in his classic 1947 book, *The Wayward Pressman.* "He makes too much of the failure of newspapers to print exactly what George Seldes would have printed if he were the managing editor. But he is a useful citizen. *(In fact)* is a fine little gadfly, representing an enormous effort for one man and his wife."

The first alarms on the link between cigarette smoking and cancer appeared in the pages of *In fact.* "The tobacco stories were suppressed by every major newspaper," Seldes said. *"The Nation, The New Republic, The Progressive...*none of those magazines were writing about it. For 10 years, we pounded on tobacco as being one of the only legal poisons you could buy in America."

But what really made Seldes a pariah in the world of journalism was his stories on the frauds and falsehoods in the American media. Reporters who could not get their stories published in the papers they worked for gave their information to Seldes on the sly.

In fact was a success. It proved that there were a lot of people in America who believed, like Seldes, that they were not getting the truth from their newspapers. The *"In fact* Decade" as Seldes called it, also produced four of Seldes' most pointed books, *The Facts Are...* in 1942 dissected how and why the American media misleads the people; *Facts and Fascism* in 1943 exposed the big money interests behind fascism in Europe and America; *1000 Americans* in 1947 detailed the people and corporations that control America and *The People Don't Know* in 1949 discussed the origins of the Cold War.

A combination of incessant Red-baiting from the big newspaper chains and major business organizations forced Seldes to close down *In fact* in October 1950. "The word got around that I was a communist," Seldes said. "I never, never, never was a communist, even though Earl Browder (then the head of the Communist Party of the United States of America) kept asking me to join." J. Edgar Hoover's FBI compiled lists of people who subscribed to *In fact* as well as other liberal publications. Many of Seldes' subscribers cancelled their subscriptions for fear of being branded "subversives."

Three newspaper columnists in particular, Westbrook Pegler, George Sokolsky and Fulton Lewis Jr., frequently slandered Seldes. "They were bastards," Seldes said. "They would write that a Russian agent stopped by my office each week to pay my salary. I didn't have the money to sue them for libel. My lawyer told me it would take years to reach a settlement and even if I won I would never see a dime. There was no way I could fight them."

Seldes devoted the post-*In fact* years to summing up his life, his career and his views on the American media in four different books, *Tell the Truth and Run* in 1953, *Never Tire of Protesting* in 1968, *Even The Gods Can't Change History* in 1976 and *Witness to a Century* in 1987. He also compiled the best ideas and quotations of the world's great thinkers in two books, *The Great Quotations* in 1960 and *The Great Thoughts* in 1985.

A stroke a few years ago has slowed Seldes somewhat. He can't remember much of the present but his memory of the past is marvelous. He is under round-the-clock care and can't walk without assistance. His eyesight is still pretty good, but his hearing is about gone. He tires easily and he spends much of each day sleeping. But people still find their way to his home in Hartland-Four-Corners, Vermont to visit a man who has seen so much history. He is always ready to talk.

"A lot of people call here and say 'I didn't know you were still alive,'" he said. "For the longest time, my name never appeared in the papers. People thought 'this guy is a troublemaker, the hell with him.' I never had it easy, but I never missed a meal and I've never been broke."

Seldes' place in the history of journalism is secure, as the living link between Steffens and Stone. "Lincoln Steffens was the godfather of us all," said Seldes. "He was an older man when I first met him (in 1919). He was the first of the muckrakers. As he once said, 'where there's muck, I'll rake it.' He often warned me that I was starting to get a bad reputation for myself. I guess I never worried about that."

Steffens inspired Seldes to become an crusading journalist. In turn, Seldes inspired Stone to start his own newspaper. "He wanted to restart *In fact* after I stopped publishing it," Seldes said. "I warned him about how badly I was Red-baited and suggested he start up his own paper. I gave him my subscription list, the 'Five Dollar Liberals' we called them, and he got his paper going."

For someone who has seen and been involved in so much history, Seldes is a modest man. He isn't nostalgic for the good old days for he knows that they were not always good, especially in his chosen profession.

"It's hard to understand how lousy newspapers were in my time," he said. "There is no comparison, the quality of the press today is much better. Things were pretty crude in my time, but it's a new world now."

Many of the dragons that Seldes battled are still with us, under different aliases. Instead of Father Charles Coughlin, we have Reverend Pat Robertson and the Christian Coalition to represent religious reaction. Pegler, Sokolsky and Lewis no longer walk the earth, but people like Rush Limbaugh and Pat Buchanan carry on their tradition. Is Ross Perot nothing more than Huey Long with a bigger bank account? The children and grandchildren of the "1000 Americans" that Seldes said control America still rule today. The press lords like William Randolph Hearst, Colonel Robert McCormack, Roy Howard and Frank Gannett have been dead for years, but the media empires they created have grown more immense and still control what America reads, hears and views. Advertising has become even more pervasive and powerful.

This is not to say that Seldes labored in vain. He was one of the first to write about the dangers of tobacco, now there are few if any Americans who do not know that cigarette smoking is harmful. Seldes was an early booster of consumer reporting. Consumers Union, once Red-baited, is now an American institution and more media outlets do objective reporting that benefits the consumer. *In fact* pioneered press criticism, now it has become a staple in publications of all political stripes. The Liberal media is still is the minority in America, but the stalwarts like *The Nation* and *The Progressive* have been joined by vibrant voices like *Mother Jones, Tikkun, Utne Reader, In These Times, Z,* the *Village Voice* and others.

In short, there have been victories, stalemates and defeats for the Left in America in this century. George Seldes was involved in many of the battles. He did not conform to any rigid ideology other than that of finding the truth and letting the facts speak for themselves. More often than not, that put him on the Left, but he disdained the Left's political orthodoxy and sectarianism. His writing was open-minded and fair, but it also took a stand.

"The middle of the road is a crowded place (and many on it are crushed by the cars of Juggernaut, radicalism and reaction, pushing inevitably to the Right and the Left)," wrote Seldes in *Tell the Truth and Run.* "During all these years of work and talk I had had a fine contempt for the frightened majority which traveled the middle road. I had thought of myself as one of the non-conformists along the less-traveled and rather lonely individual path of my choosing."

Seldes said that "tell the truth and run" was an old Yugoslav proverb. "People didn't like that as a book title," he told me. "They said I should've called that book, 'Tell the Truth and Stay.' Stay and get killed! Sometimes its better to run and get another chance to tell to the truth."

When asked the inevitable question of how he made it past the century mark, Seldes credits three things. "I never got drunk, I was married and stayed faithful to one woman for almost 50 years and I stopped smoking in 1931.

"I'm the only person in my family who has lived past 100, and I really don't know why. All I feel like doing now is laying in bed all day. I like to say that I'm the biggest lie-r in America. I miss getting out, because the doctors don't want me outside without accompaniment. I've thought about writing a book. I'd call it 'To Hell with the Joys of Old Age.' My publisher said I'd sell 20,000 copies just on the title alone. But I don't think I've got that much time left."

Seldes believes in the words that Abraham Lincoln said during the Civil War, words that guided Seldes throughout his career. "I am a firm believer in the people," said Lincoln. "If given the truth, they can be depended upon to meet any national crisis. The great point is to bring them the real facts."

Every honest journalist in America owes Seldes a great debt. The abuse he endured to write the truth has made it easier for his progeny to do the same. This collection of his work is a small attempt to give him the recognition that is due him.

PART ONE

Foreign Correspondent

Nations in
Straightjackets

In 1937, Eugene Lyons put together a book of essays from 16 foreign correspondents, the best in the business in his view (as editor, he also included himself.) The book was called We Cover The World. *In those days, foreign correspondence still was considered glamourous, but Seldes' contribution to the book showed the frustrations and hardships as well as the glamour. It is the condensed version of his decade as a reporter in Europe for the* Chicago Tribune, *and his constant battles with the authorities to get the truth out.*

WE COVER the world. But year by year, ever since the War, ever since America became conscious of Europe, ever since foreign correspondents became important figures in international affairs, the dictators have preceded them in covering Europe. They painted Russia Red, Italy Black, Germany Brown, Hungary and Poland White, Bulgaria Green; they established a whole spectrum of censorship and terror, and they made honest news reporting a gay, sometimes romantic, but perpetual battle with suppressive and repressive forces.

At least, it was so for me.

I did not go round defying the dictators. But neither did I trim my sails or make compromises, or sign false names to my dispatches, as the brilliant William Bolitho was forced to do. So naturally everywhere I went—to Russia under Lenin (and Felix Dzherjinsky, the head of the dread Cheka); to Fiume, where the fantastic poet d'Annunzio ruled in fantastic ways; to Marie's corrupt Romania; to Eternal Rome, where a fellow-journalist knew better than any man living how to suppress the news; to Mesopotamia, and Syria, and Arabia, where Oriental guile and Occidental imperialism contended for oil and prestige and face-saving; on occasions such as the Kapp Putsch, the Ruhr-Rhineland republic, the Hitler beer-hall revolution in 1923; the Damascus bombardment; the Vienna revolution—it was just fifteen years of contention with the dictators.

We, the 20 members of the Press section of the American Expeditionary Force in France, believed on Armistice morning that the bugles which sang peace also piped journalistic freedom; we knew, of course, that military censorship in wartime was a matter of life or death, but we expected the triumph of Woodrow Wilson's policy. I remember attending the first meeting of the Supreme Council on the 12th of January, 1919, when the world believed that Lloyd George's program ("a new deal for every one") and Wilson's thesis ("open covenants openly arrived at" and "pitiless publicity") were on their way to realization. But on the fifteenth of that same peace-happy January in Paris, Georges Clemenceau supported by Japan and Italy, ruined the American President by making the real peace conference sessions secret.

Nobly the 400 or more American journalists rose to the support of Wilson and Lloyd George, and we saved the plenary sessions for the public, but the vast intrigue which made the Versailles Treaty the crime it is was conducted behind censorship walls. Georges Clemenceau was the virtual dictator. He corrupted the Press then as thoroughly as any Hitler or Mussolini did later. And the Anglo-American newspapermen could do very little, because the Espionage Act and the Defense of the Realm Act still prevailed. Clemenceau had actually sent a communication to all the editors of France which contained these three items:

> *First: to emphasize the opposition to Mr Wilson in America by giving all the news possible regarding the speeches of Republican Senators and other American critics.*
>
> *Second: to emphasize the disorder and anarchy in Russia, thereby stimulating the movement towards Allied military intervention.*
>
> *Third: to publish articles showing the ability of Germany to pay a large indemnity.*

We begged permission of Wilson to publish the story of Clemenceau's dictatorship and corruption of the French press, but the President, who never did like and never fully trusted newspapermen, thought secrecy and diplomacy, rather than open action, was the way to break the conspiracy. Versailles became a battle of censorship versus publicity, and when censorship and Clemenceau won Wilson and the American journalists lost a just peace for the world.

With the refusal of the Conference to deal with Russia that country withdrew into itself, disdaining the kind offers of the "bourgeois" press to send "impartial" men to report the course Bolshevism was taking. And as the difficulties of censorship increased in Europe the passion for getting the news, reborn Armistice morning, burned with a fiercer flame, became a roaring fire, despite the dictators who arose everywhere.

My first dictator was Gàbriele d'Annunzio.

In 1919 Tom Morgan, then with the Associated Press, got to Fiume just after the poet drove the Allied forces out of the town. He hid in the coal-bunker of the little train which kept up haphazard communications between the new "principality" and Italian Trieste. But, while it was not easy to enter the blockaded city, the censorship within was one of the worst in history. It grew even more stringent as the outside world, the poet-tyrant, the Yugoslavs, the Allies, the hungering black-fezzed Arditi legion, the disgruntled citizens, became more desperate, and reinforcements in supplies, men, and money which a journalist named B. Mussolini was gathering in Milan failed to arrive. These promised "troops" had been "diverted" to create a Blackshirt militia in Italy, yet the morally cynical but politically naive poet suspected no treason then.

When I found that d'Annunzio had a secretary named Henry Furst, an American citizen who had volunteered and become a lieutenant in the Dalmatian Legion, who spoke Italian beautifully, and was willing to help me to get through the guards and the bars of secrecy which the poet had erected, I was overwhelmed by the unexpected kindness. In the fortnight in which Lieutenant Furst was assuring me he was doing his best to obtain an interview for me I naively told him the names of persons I was meeting, the temper of the population, the stories I was smuggling out with passengers on the daily train and through bribed officials. I told him I thought the fair thing to do was get both sides of the story, letting a Yugoslav leader speak for his people and d'Annunzio for Italy. Lieutenant Furst agreed.

Two weeks passed. Every day I smuggled a story out of Fiume, and although I received no word from Paris or Chicago, I had reason to believe that my work was satisfactory. But I still had no interview with d'Annunzio. Then one morning in the hall of the royal palace I met an Italian writer named Prezzolini, who asked me what I wanted. I replied that I had been trying to get word to d'Annunzio for a fortnight. Prezzolini laughed. "Via Signor Furst?" he asked. I nodded.

"Signor Furst's functions are not to expedite," continued Prezzolini, with a wink, and at the same moment he knocked on the door opposite us. It opened. And there stood d'Annunzio.

A minute later the poet-dictator was cursing Woodrow Wilson in the most beautiful language I have ever heard a man utter.

On my way back to Trieste d'Annunzio guards stopped the train at a little village which passed as a frontier between the "free state" and the mainland of Italy. They demanded my passport, said it was not in order, despite a special rubber stamp applied at the poet's headquarters, and insisted that I must spend the night in the frontier jail. I refused the invitation. It finally got down to a tug of war, three soldiers armed with bayonets and rifles versus one reporter clinging desperately to a portable typewriter and the baggage shelf.

In the railway station I insisted on sending telegrams to President Wilson, the American Ambassador in Paris, the consul in Trieste, Colonel McCormick, and other impressive names, and as a result I was kept under guard instead of behind bars. My baggage was searched, and typewritten material and letters removed. An officer who could speak a little French arrived, but we came to no friendly understanding, and when the next train came in—24 hours later—I was released minus printed and written matter.

At Trieste I found that all my stories had been confiscated. I had been incommunicado for a fortnight. And the first news out of Fiume was that d'Annunzio had arrested the Yugoslav spokesman whom I had interviewed "so as to present both sides of the Fiume question." As for my fellow-American and volunteer assistant, Mr. Furst, the American vice-consuls who had been expelled from Fiume gave me the information that they had cancelled his passport when he had joined a foreign army. There was plenty of trouble ahead for d'Annunzio's boastful American secretary.

The Fiume incident, my first experience with a living dictator, taught me never to trust those who have usurped power, and to beware especially of the fanatical converts to a foreign cause.

Of the censorship in Russia lengthy volumes could be written. A paramount fact, it seems to me, is that the world, and naturally the journalists of the world, were, thanks to propaganda spread by the Allies, antagonistic to Bolshevism from the first days of the Kerensky revolution in March 1917.

Because we already hated the Germans the propagandists told us that it was Ludendorff who arranged for Lenin to come to Russia from his Swiss exile via Germany for the purpose of spreading Communistic defeatism among the Russian troops, thus eliminating the Eastern front and making a swift German victory possible on the Western. It was Allied propaganda that distorted the whole Brest-Litovsk Treaty, and it was Allied propaganda that made inhuman monsters of the Bolsheviki. For example, it took Lincoln Eyre, of the *New York World,* two years to trace the myth of the nationalization of women, a myth which is now supposed to have died many years ago, but which still appears occasionally, the last revival being in an American magazine in May 1933.

The majority of newspapermen who went to Russia between 1918 and 1921 either were sympathetic to the Communistic experiment or were prejudiced against it. Few were really neutral. In many instances representatives of each class underwent a change of heart. Even Emma Goldman, who, when she was being deported to Soviet Russia in 1920, told reporters that "This is the greatest day of my life—I do not consider it a punishment, I consider it an honor," after working for the Communist Government a year said that Lenin's was a "blood and murder regime...Our comrades have been arrested and shot as bandits by the Cheka." Russia did queer things to passionate persons.

One case of "conversion" I must mention in detail. It concerns the representative of a reactionary American newspaper who was sent with instructions to get a series of articles against Bolshevism. This elderly man, with a wife and children and a salary of 75 dollars a week, at first obtained material about the Red terror, the suppression of public and private liberties, the Cheka prisons, all the usual and expected items. But as the weeks went on he began to change his mind: he admitted the terror, but found reasons for it, such as treason within the ranks during a blockade and invasion by the Allies, the shooting of Lenin by a girl member of his Social Revolutionary Party, and the claim that a continual civil war was in progress. He was impressed by statements from the leaders of the Soviets that the militant phase of Communism was temporary—temporary in the historical sense, that is—and would end when opposition ended, and he was made to see that the ultimate goal of Communism was an idealistic Utopian State where the French idea of *Liberte, Egalite, et Fraternite,* and the American ideal of all men born free and equal, would actually, and for the first time in history, become a reality. He was taught to take the "long view." So he came out of Moscow and began writing a series of articles mentioning the terror, but explaining it, apologizing and stressing ultimate ideals.

The result was a cable from America saying in effect, "Change your bias or resign."

This correspondent considered his family, his three children, his whole future, the fact he would be boycotted among newspapers if he were fired for "going Bolo." He obligingly changed his viewpoint and wrote, from his imagination, a more stirring series of anti-Bolshevik editorials than his paper had ever printed. He was given a bonus.

Russia was opened to the "bourgeois" press by the treaty between Walter Lyman Brown, representing Herbert Hoover, and Litvinov, representing the Soviets, signed in Riga in 1921. Permission for all correspondents, regardless of their own or their newspaper's political color, to visit Russia was the result of an interview between Soviet diplomatic officials and Albert Boni, the New York book publisher, who was in Berlin attempting to get a visa for Moscow for the purpose of obtaining memoirs or historical works from Lenin, Trotsky, and other leaders. The Russian insisted that only American journalists whose papers or who themselves were sympathetic to Bolshevism would be given visas.

"In that way you would ruin everything," said Mr. Boni, "because no one would trust the news."

"But," the Soviet representative exploded, "you wouldn't expect us to let the *New York Times* in—or their Paris man Duranty—after all those terrible stories of the past three years."

"Exactly that," replied Mr. Boni. "Let them come into Russia, and you will see that the fake news will stop." After hours of argument the Russian said, "I will take this up with Radek."

A few days later many of us were on the way to Riga.

Floyd Gibbons, chief of the *Chicago Tribune* foreign news, headed our delegation. All we knew at that time was that the Bolsheviki said that there was a famine, and that there were two journalists somewhere in the famine district who might scoop the world with their stories. Haste was imperative. Floyd was on the first train to Moscow, leaving me behind to relieve him later and to handle his telegrams. There was then no direct communication between Russia and the rest of the world, but telegrams addressed to Riga could be forwarded to Chicago.

How Floyd scooped the world is one of the grand stories of American journalism. With three colleagues he went from Moscow to the dying heart of the famine zone; he saw horrors unparalleled in war, suffering indescribable. As he walked through the streets of dead houses in a stricken town he had to step over the bodies of men, women, and children, dying where they fell. But instead of returning to Moscow with his colleagues to write the great story of the famine—it had not entered their heads that there was a possibility of a post office being open in a dead town—he kept on walking towards the post office. It was a stroke of genius. He found an emaciated telegraph operator, and with his usual nonchalant Midwestern manner shoved him a sheaf of typewritten copy addressed to me in Riga and said, "Send that."

When the train arrived in Moscow four days later each of Floyd's three colleagues found awaiting them angry and explosive cables from America, telling them they had been scooped badly on the biggest story since the Armistice.

In 1922 I relieved Gibbons in Moscow. The third day after my arrival I realized I was being shadowed by agents of the Cheka. The head clerk at the official Soviet hotel, the Savoy, turned out to be a spy also—we spotted him in a Cheka parade in uniform, but whether his marching there was stupidity or astuteness I can only guess—and from our bedroom windows all of us could see our spies conferring in dark passages across the street. At first it was amusing. It soon got to be nerve racking.

I laid all my papers, all my letters, all my notes—everything—on the table, figuratively and literally, in Moscow, so that the Chekists had no difficulty in making their reports, but I never forgot that I was working for an American newspaper which liked scoops, expected you to beat the censorship, and enjoyed a fight with any and all dictators, color immaterial.

I am not quite sure which item got me into trouble with the ruling powers, but it is probably the first in the following list:

(1) The Butchkavitch execution following the trial of two Roman Catholic prelates charged with treason.

(2) Secret visit to the Red Army. Trotsky had dallied with my request for months. One day Sam Spewack, of the *World*, met the colonel who had shown him the Tsarist jewels. This officer was now back with the troops.

Without informing Trotsky we went secretly to the cavalry, infantry, and artillery headquarters and were the first to see Trotsky's new Red Army. I smuggled the story out in the diplomatic mail-bag.

(3) Discovery of a secret army in the Ukraine. One day the European edition of the *Tribune* published a big story about my discovery of a secret military organization numbering something up to 50,000 armed men, Jewish youths of the Ukraine, whose Communist or anti-Communist politics was immaterial, but who were banded together to prevent another massacre of Jews by the Soviet troops. It was probably the first reliable report that there had been a massacre of Jews by Soviet soldiers.

The story so far was authentic, but unfortunately for its Moscow correspondent the Paris edition not only dated it from Kiev and printed it under my name, but also added the following words: "By courier from Moscow to London to escape Soviet censor." I had, of course, smuggled the story to London in the diplomatic mailbag, and had suggested that it should appear dated from London, but in no circumstance be credited to me.

I will not here repeat the story of the trial of Archbishops Butchkavitch and Zepliak, nor can I pass judgment on the case. The priests were charged with being agents of the Polish Government during the Russo-Polish war, of giving aid and comfort to fellow nationals, of counter-revolutionary activities in the interests of a foreign state. What I do want to point out is the fact that the Soviet Government made a complete volte-face as regards the newspapermen and their reports on the famous trial. At the beginning we were encouraged to tell the story fully. The result was that Protestants and Jews, as well as Catholics, throughout the world rose as a body in protest. Religious fervor, not the question of justice, was the international answer to our telegrams. Poland threatened a new war. Immediately the Soviets resorted to the most stringent censorship exercised for years. The Cheka took charge of the situation and managed it so completely that neither Kursky, the Minister of Justice, nor Foreign Minister Chicherin knew that Monsignor Butchkavitch, who they assured us would be pardoned, had been executed secretly in the Lubyanka Prison.

Thanks to the censorship, there was again a deluge of false and hysterical dispatches emanating from Helsingfors, Berlin, and other centers of anti-Russian news. Even the Liberal *World* expressed doubt concerning correspondents in Moscow, saying that it was "very doubtful whether correspondents in Moscow are in a position to get any perspective on events so stupendous as those involved in the religious revolt now occurring in Russia."

But in this case the only persons, it seems to me, who had the perspective were the correspondents in Moscow. They were among those Americans who remained objective in a time of mass hysteria; they saw the "anti-God crusade," atheism advancing with banner, for what it was: a movement led by children, inspired by elders who hoped in two or three generations to free the Russian mind from the degradation of the Russian Orthodox Church, which had scores of Rasputins, whose priests lived in sin, and whose Patriarch had, for bribes, betrayed his associates to the Tsar on every occasion when the reigning plutocracy had need of mass suppressions. The correspondents reported the atheistic movement fairly—i.e., factually; they did not approve of the verdict of death in the trial of the Polish priests, and told the Soviet officials, hoping that this warning would save the lives of the condemned, that they would arouse world hatred by executions. But the correspondents realized that the trial was a fair one, and that, although the priests would be martyrs in the eyes of the Church, they were evidently political traitors in the eyes of the established Government.

The correspondents were also fair in reporting the establishment of the new Living Church with Bishop Vedensky as its Patriarch. The latter had opened his new career by a sermon in which he said, "The Soviet Government is Christian because it is trying to bring about the evangelical brotherhood of man.... Capitalism is one of the seven deadly sins.... In Western countries capitalism has caused Christianity to elect Rockefeller, not Christ, its leader." The correspondents agreed with the reports from outside that the Soviet Government was subsidizing this new Church. Of course it was, because it was good policy for any Government to divide and conquer, and the old Russian Church had been a Tsarist tool, a bloody instrument for oppression. But the correspondents denied that the new Church was a hypocritical mask for the Bolsheviki. They found that no more sincere religious leader existed than Bishop Vedensky and so reported. The fairness of the newspapermen in Moscow can be judged from the fact that after cabling a report on the sincerity of Vedensky they followed it the next day with the story of how Bishop Blake, who had given the blessing of American Methodism to the Living Church, had had his pocket picked at its latest conference of bishops! Could anything be more impartial?

However, it was the Catholic trials which confirmed the suspicion of the Bolshevik Foreign Office that the majority of American correspondents were not friendly, and when, some time later, it was found that several of us had been sending out censorable news items via the diplomatic mailbag four of us were expelled from Russia. First to go was Francis McCullough, of the *New York Herald,* whose cables, after the Catholic trials, had taken on an anti-Russian color. Percy Noel, of the *Philadelphia Ledger,* Samuel Spewack, of the *World,* and I were expelled within the next week. I cannot for the life of me see how we three could be accused of sending news which was false or colored or prejudiced. But it is true that we had sent news secretly—uncensored news which was fact, and fact which was probably not pleasant to the Soviet Government.

One of the features of the Moscow censorship was that incoming mail and telegrams were read as well as outgoing, a fact I did not know until one morning when I had climbed the six weary flights of steps of the Narcomindel, Mr. Chicherin's Foreign Office, I was received with ironic laughter by the censorship officials, who talked about my paper sending an "ultimatum" to Russia. I did not know what they were talking about. Apparently there had been a communication from Colonel McCormick addressed to me which every one in the Foreign Office had read, but which was never delivered to me. Amid the general and derisive laughter I was informed, "Chicherin wants to see you; come at two-thirty."

Promptly at two-thirty I climbed the six flights again.

"What do you want now?" the censors asked.

"That interview with Chicherin at two-thirty . . ."

"Two-thirty?" Everyone shouted and laughed. "Chicherin never sees anyone in the afternoon. He sleeps all day. Come again at two-thirty A.M."

It's an old revolutionary custom. Foreign Minister Georges Chicherin, and many other former enemies of the Tsar, did all their sleeping by day because once, in Switzerland and London and New York, they had done all their plotting and planning by night. It became a mode of living, a habit which Chicherin could not break, and the Foreign Office was conducted, as far as possible, on a turn-night-into-day basis.

So I had to keep awake, and at half-past two in the morning I climbed the terrible six flights and was shown into Chicherin's office. He greeted me in a friendly way, and then shoved this cablegram across the desk:

SELDES, HOTEL SAVOY, MOSCOW

Inform Chicherin Tribune *will withdraw correspondent and get other papers do likewise unless censorship stopped.*

MCCORMICK

"Who is your McCormick?" thundered Chicherin in his small way. "Is he a nation? Is he a Foreign Office? Is he a Government? What is this?"—pointing to the cablegram. "He sends me an ultimatum! He addresses me as an equal power!"

I attempted to point out the fact that the cablegram was actually addressed to me, and that if the Cheka had not intercepted it I might have presented the "ultimatum" in a less-ultimatumly fashion.

"You can cable your McCormick," continued Chicherin, "that until he can prove to me that he is a Foreign Office I cannot accept ultimatums from him."

Which I did.

The next day I was asked to leave Russia.

Rereading the series of articles I wrote when I "came out," I find that, while I did not make a fool of myself by publishing the rumors and propaganda against the Soviets which in 1923 still filled the world, I protested vehemently against the Cheka system of espionage, surveillance, and imprisonment of political dissidents, the maintenance of the Red Terror, the absence of democracy. I find that I did not believe for a moment the Soviet claim that the censorship and Cheka, or the terror system, were necessary because Russia was in a state of war with the bourgeois nations which surround her. I did not then believe the Russian statement that Japan was planning aggressions in the East, with Poland, France, and German imperialists (led by General Hoffmann) to come from the West. I realize now that I placed no faith in anything the Bolsheviki said—at a time when the world press was telling the world not to place any faith in anything the Bolsheviki said—and that I returned from Russia with exactly the same views I took there. I was still the democrat, still the Liberal, the middle-of-the-road man (who is usually run down by the traffic on both the Right and Left), still the champion of a free press, individual liberty—in short, the libertarian I was brought up to be.

It took me about 10 years to realize that Russia was then, is now, and will for a long time be, in a state of war.

In a state of war a nation is seized by the throat by madmen and assassins. In fighting to extricate itself all weapons are used, and all moral and ethical means are used, abused, discarded, in a blind fury for survival. No one should expect anything that is good or true to survive in time of war. My strictures therefore had been naive and unwarranted.

When I came to Rome "permanently" in 1925, I was told by Baron Valentino, head of the press bureau, that there was no censorship. Mussolini has said so many times. So has Dino Grandi. Of course, it would be presumptuous for a mere reporter to call dictators liars, so their statements may be dismissed as merely diplomatic. Was it not Sir Henry Wotton who said that an ambassador is a man sent abroad to lie for his masters? It is a fact that no official censorship exists—that is, no one cuts words out of telegrams, as they did in Russia—but it is also a fact that the person who sends out words, even be they one hundred percent true, will in turn be sent out of the country if these words are unfavorable to the Fascist regime.

And that, I believe, is what happened to me.

One point I must emphasize here is that the Anglo-American press corps in Rome, supported by German, French, and other journalists, protested against my expulsion to Mussolini. Only two men broke that unity. I mention this with no feeling of resentment. The two men were Italians, and their action was therefore logical.

In 1925 Italy was not the so-called totalitarian State of today. As recently as August 1924 there had been a revolutionary surge against Fascism (following the discovery of the dismembered body of the opposition leader Giacomo Matteotti) which might easily have been converted into a civil war if Giovanni Amendola, the new leader, had cared to play the role of a Trotsky instead of choosing that of a Kerensky. The nation still seethed. The vast majority were non- if not anti-Fascist. The Matteotti case was still untried. Sensational documents came to light frequently— confessions by members of Mussolini's political household, telling of crimes and the part the Duce had played in them.

Was that news? I thought it was. While one day I might report a Mussolini "victory" in increasing the grain acreage or birth rate, or defying some defeated nation, another day there would be a document written in his own fine Italian hand saying, "Make life unbearable for Signor X..." And soon after we should hear of the murder of Signor X. I did not hesitate to send both kinds of news. Once I reported that the Fascisti had coerced an American Consul. Foolishly, perhaps, I took their word for it that there was no censorship.

On page five of the *New York Times* of 28 July 1925, there is the following item from the man who still represents that paper in Rome:

> *Signor Grandi . . . formally requested Ambassador Fletcher on Friday last to use his influence to "make George Seldes understand that his stay in Italy is no longer advisable...." Officials of the Foreign Ministry explain this measure against an American correspondent by asserting that Mr. Seldes has cabled to his paper a series of misleading, exaggerated, and alarmist dispatches during the several months of his sojourn in Rome....*
>
> *Signor Grandi received a delegation of American newspapermen,... refusing to reconsider Mr. Seldes' case.... "There is no form of censorship existing," he said. "No newspapermen need fear to cable any facts, even if damaging to the Government, or need fear to express any honestly professed opinion."...*
>
> *Signor Grandi in his letter to the American Ambassador asserted that Mr. Seldes had "become the mouthpiece exclusively of small groups and political minorities in whose hands he is a passive instrument."*

My own paper had reported—and, in all fairness to the *Times*, it must be said that it reprinted this report—that my last dispatch "was so garbled or so stringently censored that its meaning was lost," and that "on Wednesday a group of other American correspondents in Rome, including representatives of the *New York World, Christian Science Monitor, Chicago Daily News, Philadelphia Public Ledger,* and the United Press" had protested against my treatment as "unfair and high-handed." "And," continued the *Times* dispatch from Chicago,

> *The Tribune adds that it telegraphed to the State Department in Washington that it has reason to fear, in connection with the threatened expulsion of its correspondent, that his life or physical safety is imperilled, and asking that the American Embassy intercede to protect Mr. Seldes from threatened violence.*

The fact is that Grandi, who received the American press corps, minus the *Times* and Associated Press representatives, at the same time that Mussolini was receiving Ambassador Fletcher, informed the delegation, headed by Thomas B. Morgan, of the United Press, that Premier Mussolini had reconsidered my case, and that I could remain in Rome.

This called for a celebration. We had a grand banquet. For the occasion Hiram Motherwell, of the *Chicago Daily News*, composed a song, and we sang it to the tune of Old Man Moses:

Dino Grandi, fine and dandy,
He's as sweet as a stick of candy.
Ain't it grand he is so handy;
That kid's candy, the dandy Grandi.
(Refrain) Mister Grandi, how we love YOUUU.

Some are naughty—Grandi's not, see?
Goes to church with his friend Regazzi.
Says his prayers, and is never snotty;
The guy that was naughty was Matteotti.
(Refrain.)

Every evening, just at seven,
He goes to call on the Lord in Heaven.
"Walk right in, you're welcome, very,
Specially to Christ and the Virgin Mary."
(Refrain.)

The Chicago Tribune's molto sporco (very bad),
Gets its stuff from a grosso porco. (fat pig)
A newspaper-man should write what's vero (true)
Just like us in the Rome Impero.
(Refrain.)

The merrymaking was interrupted melodramatically by a knock on the door. A secret agent entered and walked over to me. "You have 24 hours in which to leave the country."

On the train to France I felt scared for the first time since the War. I had that morning received from Chicago a copy of that telegram addressed to the State Department saying, "We have reason to fear that in connection with the threatened explusion or deportation . . . Mr. Seldes' life or physical safety is imperilled . . . Respectfully request you ask American Embassy to intercede to protect Mr Seldes from threatened violence," and the reply from Secretary of State Kellogg that "no violence had yet been shown him." That "yet" got me.

On the train there was a compartment in which sat three men, two in the uniforms of officers of His Britannic Majesty's Navy. The third, in civilian clothes, was also an officer, he informed me later, and all were on leave from their squadron in Malta. I explained my case. They insisted that I should sit with them.

Just before we got to Modena the train made its usual stop. Down the platform we could see a crowd of Blackshirts armed with sticks and clubs. They were shouting. As they came closer we heard the words, "Dove Sel-des? Dove Sel-des?" ("Where is Seldes?") The officers understood. The Blackshirts barged into our carriage, banging on every door. They came to the one in which I was sitting.

"Dove Sel-des?" they shouted.

"You get the devil out of here!" the superior British officer replied. "We are four British officers."

One look at the uniforms was enough for the Fascisti. They went to the next carriage.

The *Manchester Guardian*, the *New York World*, and some seven hundred other newspapers of which I have seen clippings called the expulsion stupid. *The Nation* added an important point for questioning: "The European correspondents of the American press have more than once demonstrated their loyalty to the principle of the freedom of the press, and we hope that their home offices will boldly sustain them."

Mine sustained me. And neither did I then nor do I now resent the events of the aftermath. All they do is to recall my first city editor's words, "Rats, this isn't a profession; it's prostitution."

This is what happened. No sooner did I land in Paris than I began a series of articles on Fascist Italy which appeared in the *Chicago Tribune* and the many papers which subscribe to its service. But these articles were suppressed in the Paris edition of the *Tribune* by order of the local business department which stood to lose some Italian hotel advertising. Nor was that all. While the editorial office at home was supporting its correspondents everywhere in a demand for press freedom, the business office in Paris was sending slick gentlemen to apologize to all the hotel-keepers and steamship and tourist bureaus for the late unpleasantness for which I was guilty.

And in addition to this, and surely without the knowledge of the editor of the *Tribune* in Chicago, a member of the Paris editorial staff was sent to apologize to Mussolini, and to ask for the restoration of the Governmental advertising.

In the long series of articles which I wrote on Mussolini and Fascism I tried objectively to present the whole picture. I compared the Fascist Cheka to the Russian Cheka; Mussolini's Press censorship to Trotsky's—the former, secret, sly, hypocritical, the latter, honest and open, but none the less drastic; the Fascist terrorism to the Bolshevik terrorism; the political prisoners on the Liparian isles to those at Solovyetsky, in the Arctic Circle; and the fate of democracy and freedom under dictatorship in the two countries. Generally speaking, I concluded that the two systems had much in common.

If, therefore, I am one of the many who is responsible for the myth that all dictatorships are alike in action, that Bolshevism and Fascism and Naziism are angles of the same triangle, all I can do now is make public penance. But I can produce the evidence that I was among the first to see that Mussolini and his self-announced philosophy and ideology were nothing but frauds. In that midsummer of 1925 I published not only the official evidence of the complicity of the Duce in the murder of his chief political rival, but also the evidence which other correspondents had given me (it was useless to them unless they wanted to be expelled) and which proved that Fascism had no philosophy or even a program. It was, rather, merely the Lega Industriale and the Chambers of Commerce of Milan and Turin, the bankers of these cities and Naples and Rome, the manufacturers of steel and iron and munitions, automobiles and tires, and shipbuilding. Mussolini was the condottiere, Fascism the fighting power, of big business.

"All the rest," wrote that grand reporter William Bolitho, the colleague who had worked with me to break through the censorship in the Ruhr in 1923 "is merely word-spinning." Mussolini's definition of Fascism in the official encyclopedia is mere falsehood—except for the statement that it prepares for and glorifies war as an ideal human expression.

Eleven years have passed since I wrote the first articles of what I considered the whole truth about Fascism, and during all that time I have continued to assemble evidence. With a few exceptions, all the journalists stationed in Rome have, during all these years, assisted this collection, and I have never been forced to change my main conclusions. In 1931 I wrote in Scribner's Magazine on "Twilight of Dictators," showing how they were going down in economic disaster and wars in South America, and predicting that wars and disaster were their fate in the rest of the world.

Within a few months the Spanish dictatorship which Primo de Rivera had bequeathed to General Berenguer collapsed, and it took four more years before Mussolini resorted to war. But it was in 1925 that I showed (from the charts prepared by Hiram Motherwell, my Chicago rival) that Fascism was making no headway economically and socially, and in 1929 I claimed that the budgets were fraudulent, that the standard of living had gone down desperately, and that Mussolini would either collapse or go to war. Collapse and war were inherent in a programless dictatorship whose one aim was to preserve the banker-manufacturer group in political power.

So, while I had come to Rome after an unfortunate experience with the Bolsheviki, I was never for a moment fooled by the pretenses and frauds and charming manners of Fascism, nor could I, after seeing what it really was, recommend Fascism as an alternate philosophy, program, or ideology. As such, Fascism does not exist. Even Hitlerism, perverted as it is, wrong as the civilized world may consider it, is much more a philosophy, a program, and an ideology than Fascism. Italian Fascism substitutes bayonets for ideas.

Is the choice in America today really between Fascism or Communism? I do not know. Unlike so many of my colleagues in Russia who first embraced the Bolshevik philosophy (and then turned against it), I am unable now, although my general attitude is changed, to accept the dilemma. The mistake I acknowledge is attacking Communism for Russia. It was there; it should have been reported honestly. The honest reporter must neither attack nor defend. Beating the Bolshevik censor was all very well—it was the game my employers expected me to play; but reporting on the Bolshevik experiment should be left neither to the enthusiasts who went to Moscow determined to see nothing but the rosy color of things, nor to the police reporters who were out to "get the goods on the Bolos." Interpretation should be the exclusive domain of journalists capable of diplomatic objectivity. Russia was no place for prejudiced cynics or naive idealists.

There is really no choice between Communism and Fascism, because Fascism is nothing. Communism is an assertion, Fascism is a negation. Communism is an attempt to hasten the ideal future; Fascism at its best is an attempt to return to the serfdom of the medieval past. The choice, it seems to me, is not between Communism and Fascism, but the choice of means, program, philosophy, or weapons if necessary, in achieving the ultimate goal, the cooperative commonwealth which I once heard Lenin describe, and which is not different from the dream of every humanitarian since civilization began.

"In the Darwinian progress from an ape to a commissar," I heard Lenin say at the fifth anniversary session of the Comintern celebrating the October revolution, "it may be necessary to pass through the phase known as a labor Government." Perhaps the political labor movement which is now beginning to stir in the United States is the necessary phase for America on the road to the ideal cooperative commonwealth.

But to continue with the dictators.

In May 1928 the Duce was inadvertently named a member of the National Press Club in Washington. The Board of Governors cabled Mussolini notifying him of the honor, expressing the pleasure of the American organization in having so distinguished a member. This telegram was given to the Press of Italy with instructions that it should be played up as indicating the feelings of the Press of America towards the dictator of Italy. The Fascists made a Roman holiday out of the cablegram.

But it was also posted on the club's bulletin board. The by-laws of the club provide a period of several days for protest, and in this case it was more than a protest. It was a mass uprising, led by Charles G. Ross, head of the Washington bureau of the *St. Louis Post-Dispatch.* The reader will find little or no mention of this event in the daily press, but *Editor and Publisher* said:

> The stand of the National Press Club for freedom of the press and against any actions to abrogate that freedom was made definite and final on 1 June, when the board of governors, "assigning reasonable cause," withdrew from further consideration the nomination of Benito Mussolini for non-resident membership....
>
> Mussolini, he [Mr. Ross] pointed out, had since 1917 been engaging in the suppression of newspapers opposed to him, and had carried on his campaign of suppression of the press....
>
> The expulsion of foreign correspondents, including George Seldes, of the Chicago Tribune, was also cited by Mr. Ross as another evidence of Mussolini's opposition to the freedom of the press.

Altogether there were 25 newspapermen's names attached to the protest, although only 10 were required, and there was no opposition, except from some movie operators and other non-journalists.

When notice was sent to Mussolini that he was persona non grata in American journalism naturally not a word of this "insult" was printed in the press of Italy. Of course, Mussolini earned the disgust and enmity of the civilized world in 1935 when he attacked Ethiopia. But the evidence is clear that he had already been discounted by the intelligent journalists of the world years earlier.

In 1925, when the Druse rebellion spread to the Syrian Nationalists, and the two joined forces and sacked the town of Kaukaba, the French military and the French censorship not only suppressed parts of my telegrams, but called me into headquarters and requested my aid in corroborating a lying statement they had made. In wartime lies are always necessary, and in this instance it was vitally so. From the first days of the Druse uprising the French command had continually used every power to keep Syrians from joining the pagans, and, failing to do so, to keep the pagans and Mohammedans from turning revolution into holy war. War was war, but massacre was still worse, and had to be prevented by all means, by blood and money.

The Christians of Lebanon, however, found they could not rely on the small French army which was being driven crazy by the fantastic Druse plan—which was to sack a town, then ride off in another direction, mislead the heavy-moving French expedition, appear suddenly in another part of the country, and sack another town. Only airplanes could have prevented these tactics, but, with some two thousand airplanes in France, France had less than a good dozen at the war front. That was military bureaucracy for you. The Christians not only organized a secular army under command of Patras Bey and Joseph Karam, descendants of the national hero, but they went into battle, and after considerable bloodshed took back their lost towns.

For me this was purely a good human-interest, melodramatic adventure story; but for the French it was a disastrous item if it became generally known. The arming of Christian civilians would result in Mohammedan arming; the fact that Mohammedans had already killed Christians, and that the first battle of a religious war had been fought, would most likely result in civil war and great massacre.

"We do not deny your facts," said the commandant who had charge of intelligence and the foreign press, "but military necessity requires our changing them. We cut out all references to a Christian army, and we denied that any Mohammedans had joined in the Druse attacks. We ask you as a favor not to mention such things in future dispatches. You understand the delicacy of the situation, I hope."

I did. I told the officer, moreover, that I had forwarded carbon copies of my telegrams via Haifa and Cairo to London. These would pass uncensored through British hands.

This altered the situation. It was now beyond the French military command to suppress the news. (Not that I would not have willingly omitted references to Christian-Mohammedan bloodshed if I had known of the French fears of a general religious war.) The commandant realized that I had no intention to complicate the situation. "If we issue a statement to the local Arab press, saying that you now admit that no Mohammedans were in the attack on Christian towns, will you oblige us by not denying it?" the commandant asked. I agreed.

I certainly did not want to be the cause of more bloodshed—no press scoop was worth that—and I was more than willing to get the French into my debt after all the difficulties I had had with military bureaucracy, censorship, suspicion, and insults.

The war in Lebanon was covered from Beirut, the war against the Druses from Damascus; for two of the three events which were important enough to make the front pages in America I was the only war correspondent present. The bombardment of Damascus was a world scoop; the capture of the Druse capital, Soueida, with the subsequent desertion by an American from the Foreign Legion, his capture and trial, was another scoop. But at the time of the Kaukaba massacre seven or eight Americans and a few British and French correspondents had arrived.

In Beirut and Damascus both the French and the natives were very angry with me. Both sides thought me unfair. The military were exceedingly annoyed with my telegrams since they betrayed the fact that the French were committing tragic strategic errors, that they were sacrificing men in badly prepared weak attacks instead of reinforcing their army, that they had no airplane service, although they knew how the British in Iraq had quelled native disturbances, and that, in general, the military situation was unfavorable. The stupid censors believed they could have kept the Damascus bombardment from the world if I had not been present: they could not get it into their bureaucratic heads that other rumors and dispatches exaggerating the incident ten to a hundred times had done them that many times as much harm as my factual dispatches.

The Syrian nationalists, on the other hand, at first accused me of sympathy for the French, and later of being in their pay. A secretly printed

Arab publication mentioned a million francs as my price. When the
French civilian administrator, M. Lapierre, arrived in Damascus I met him
at the Hotel Victoria and showed him the cutting.

"Will you compromise for a cocktail?" he asked.

"If you buy me a drink it will be the first thing I've had from the
French since I've been here," I said, and we drank a cocktail.

It was not until a French journalist, M. Brochier, arrived that I was
able to get the French command to do something for me. The army had
captured Soueida, but did not hold all the intervening ground. I wanted
to go to the capital of the Druses. I still had at that time my credentials as
World War correspondent, signed by General Pershing, and his letter of
1919 thanking me for my work. I translated them to the French general.
He was not impressed. But M. Brochier was a schoolboy friend of the new
French commander, Andrea, and he got a message through to the front.
When Damascus headquarters issued a permit for Brochier they could not
well refuse me, and so we went to the aviation base and got permission to
sit in the back cockpits of the first airplanes flying into Soueida.

I flew with Captain Pittault, who had been commissioned by
Commandant Wauthier. Five years later, when I went to Le Bourget to
welcome Willie Seabrook and Marjorie Worthington home from flying
adventures in Timbuctoo and the Sahara Desert, their pilot, descending
from the plane, looked at me and said, "*Tiens,* if it isn't *monsieur le journal-
iste* whom we almost killed that day at Soueida!" The fact was that Pittault
forgot all about me, sitting in the back cockpit wedged among hundreds
of Lewis-gun ammunition drums. He had spotted some Druses in the
fields, and let loose with his machine-guns; the latter returned the fire,
and Pittault began a series of acrobatics in which he several times almost
spilled me. On landing on the improvised flying field at Soueida, moreover, the aviator hit a rough bit, and the old 1918 Spad, which I could
swear had its struts tied with string, crashed and tangled us both pretty
badly.

General Andrea was the embodiment of friendliness. He shared his
meager meal, the bad water, the thin pinard, and the abominable sleeping
quarters with me. It was a night of fleas. Not Roman fleas, the two per visit
one must expect at the Costanza Opera House, the one per trip in a
Roman cab, but fleas by millions, all the descendants of the King of the
Fleas which mythology has reigning in Tiberiad. So I left at dawn, by the
first plane out.

But I took with me the second scoop, the story of the man who said his name was Gilbert Clare, and who was in reality Bennett J. Doty, of Memphis, Tennessee. He was the only American in the Foreign Legion, and what a story he had!

This story became even better when, a few days later, my friend Brochier arrived in Beirut with the news that Doty, several Germans, and Harvey, the Legion's lone Englishman, had deserted, fought their way through Bedouin ambush, engaged in battle with French gendarmes, and had been finally captured, tried, and condemned to death.

"And," added M. Brochier, "General Andrea is very angry with you; he accuses you of starting this revolt in the Foreign Legion."

It was Sunday morning. I got Consul-General Knabenshue; we went to the Beirut authorities, and telegraphed Consul Keeley in Damascus. Our intervention postponed all talk of execution. Later Doty was retried, sentenced, pardoned, and shipped home. At the same time I wrote to General Andrea explaining that the worst I could possibly have done to instigate a "mutiny" was to discuss America with a homesick soldier.

It was at this time that I was threatened with disembowelment by the Arab nationalists.

For years the native Syrian press named me as a propagandist for the French. But the truth was I thought the French were stupid, and the religious hatred between Christian and Mohammedan stupid, and intense nationalism stupid. I had had sympathy only for old General Sarrail, who had tried to break up feudalism, ruin the power of the emirs and other exploiters of the poor Druses, poor Arabs, poor Christians—and who reaped rebellion and dismissal as a result of his socialistic ideals. He died soon after, a broken man.

The Romanian censorship is slippery, secret, and arbitrary—on a par, in fact, with the national politics, which are the most corrupt in Europe. I wrote the story of a session of the Romanian Parliament, where the Bratianu boys put through a law giving themselves control of the oil-wells of the nation, and how, although there were only 86 members in the chamber after the Opposition had walked out, the Bratianus announced a vote of "a hundred and twenty-six in favor, two opposed." Business and graft are synonymous terms in this country, as the various American representatives of railway and oil companies have found out; the agent for a Philadelphia railway company was able to get an instalment on his bill paid only because he had prepared for the American newspapermen in

Bucharest one of the most amazing stories of national corruption in history. I saw part of it, and really regretted that the Bratianus paid, because I had been promised the story if they didn't.

Naturally the correspondent who tries to tell even a small part of the crookedness of the Romanian situation lands in jail or is expelled. Warned in advance, I made arrangements with the porter of my hotel, to whom I gave a larger bribe than his monthly bribe instalment from the Government, so I escaped arrest after cabling items of the character indicated above. But at least a dozen colleagues have been arrested or expelled, or both. The most notable of them is Clarence Streit, of the *New York Times*, and I mention him because he is one of the fairest and most objective correspondents in Europe today. His newspaper requires no sensationalism from him.

Mr. Streit made arrangements to go electioneering with the two leading opponents in a Romanian general election. The first day he witnessed Government agents intimidating and terrorizing Opposition voters, and the next day he was refused permission to accompany Government candidates. Instead he received a letter charging him with "gross exaggerations and insults addressed to the Romanian Crown and country."

He was asked by General Nicoleanu, Prefect of Police, to leave the country, and when the American charge' d'affaires, Benjamin Riggs, protested to the Foreign Office the Minister of the Interior hinted that Streit had better leave in a hurry—otherwise he might be attacked in the streets of Bucharest.

Threats and intimidation are part of the Romanian Press censorship. Even blackmail is not beyond Romanian diplomacy. Thus in 1932 the Crown Prince and ex-King Mihai of Romania, who was taught English by his British grandmother, Queen Marie, read with great interest in the Paris edition of the *Daily Mail* that Papa Carol had a beautiful red-headed mistress named Magda Lupescu; the youngster did not know what the word "mistress" meant, and addressed an inquiry to Colonel Grigorescu. The colonel reported to the Embassy, and the Embassy sent a diplomat to the offices of the *Daily Mail* with a royal demand for an apology and a promise that Carol's mistress should remain unmentioned in the future. The *Daily Mail* refused to listen.

"If you don't retract," the Romanian Ambassador threatened, "I will have stories about the affairs of the Prince of Wales published in the Romanian papers."

Whereupon the blackmailing diplomat was thrown out.

Romania was a country where the King, the Bratianu dictators, the Queen's friends, a few generals, and a few of the leading businessmen seemed, in my time, interested only in dividing the natural wealth of the nation among themselves. Carol has been implicated in more than one graft case; the recent bribing of high officials by the Skoda armament works is one of the many instances which was exposed in the foreign press. Years ago Gregory Phillipescu, who in his Epoca wrote of Queen Marie and of Prince Stirbey as the "man behind the portieres," had to flee to Paris, and Jon Bratianu handed journalists cigars with thousand-lei notes as bands. Romania muzzles its own press and attempts to muzzle the press of the world. The correspondents who break the censorship invariably are hounded by the police and expelled. But it is significant that they keep on.

But not all of them, and not everywhere. Because wherever there is a dictatorship American correspondents must make one of three choices: they can defy the dictator, as dozens of us have done; or they can embrace the regime, as a few of the best-known journalists have done; or they can accept certain compromises which make work possible and delay or elimi- nate expulsion.

Those who defy the dictators, whose latest recruits are Edgar Ansell Mowrer, Dorothy Thompson, and David Darrah, expelled by Hitler and Mussolini, are lucky if they have the support of their home offices behind them. I do not want any applause for my activities, because I was fortunate in having an employer who was defiant of Europe in general, and who glo- ried in the fact that his men were always getting into trouble with foreign dictators.

On the other hand, the few who go over to the dictators are generally accepted as gentlemen. When a correspondent writes for years in a liberal and intelligent manner from many countries, then suddenly becomes biased and obscurant, it is quite likely that the dictator of either the country to which he is assigned or in his home office has made his influ- ence felt.

There are many other things than the bribe which the Fascist Foreign Office and the chancelleries of several Balkan states—notably Yugoslavia and Bulgaria, in my time—give in the form of free telegram, radio, or cable tolls. Even a great newspaper publisher sometimes never quite gets over the fact that he has had the honor of shaking hands with the demigod-like Duce. Mussolini's autographs, smiles, frowns, interviews, and commendatore ribbons have worked more miracles for Fascism than Fascist money.

Newspapermen can no more escape psychological imperatives than common mortals. Among them there are also power and success worshippers, good republicans at home, and democratic in all things American, who bow and tremble before success and power personified in humanitarians or tyrants. They do not question; they abase themselves from inner necessity. Generally when one talks of "prostitutes of the Press" the inference naturally is that the reporter is good, the employer evil, that the good is debased by the bad. But I am sad to record that there are instances of voluntary, happy prostitution by noted foreign correspondents. For anonymous example, my colleague who wrote to Mussolini for an interview in these words:

> *I beg thy face to see,*
> *Thy hand to clasp,*
> *Thy mighty voice to hear,*
> *For thou art Rome,*
> *And more than Rome to me !*

The majority of men assigned to Russia after 1921 have always been anti-Communist, but some embrace Communism; others merely recognize the regime as de facto and try to assume a machiavellian, if not a neutral, attitude in describing its progress; while still others let their enmity get into their dispatches and soon find themselves outside. One thing that must not be forgotten about all dictatorships, reactionary or radical, is that they hold to the old maxim that who is not for us is against us. "Objectivity" to them consists of giving one view of affairs—their view alone.

Many foreign correspondents are not too well paid, although their salaries are higher than those of the average newspaperman at home; the result is that economic pressure sometimes encourages friendship for dictators. If you are inimical things are hard for you, and if you succeed in the miracle of being objective they are not easier; but there are ways and means of making life more livable in the hard times of dictatorships. The problem of housing, of foreign exchange and inflated money, of bringing in foreign food or clothes, and many other things, are solved for those who accept the aid of regimes they do not defy.

The ideal situation, of course, would be for American correspondents to maintain an Olympian aloofness from the problems of the peoples and dictators of Europe; to report, if they were able, on the successes or failures, Utopian progress or hellish terrorism, of life under the dictators. And in order to do so they would not necessarily have to be supermen. It is quite possible for a reporter to voyage to Mexico and write a truthful account of the conflicts of Fascism with Communism, the Government and the Catholic Church, the patriots and the interventionists, the people and the exploiting land- and mine- and concession-owners, at a time when a large part of the American people, for religious or financial reasons, have a biased interest in Mexico; it should be even easier to treat of the same conflict of philosophies, religions, social, and economic forces in European countries, where our moral and financial investment is comparatively smaller.

One of the reasons why American correspondents abroad can be divided into three classes—the defiers, the foot-kissers, and the sail-trimmers—is the failure of the newspaper publishers and the press services they directly or indirectly control to unite in the common cause of a free press. After all the shouting for freedom of the press, after all the orations about the press being the foundation, the keystone, the main bulwark, and the last ditch of all our liberties, the newspaper owners do nothing to clear the poison from the springs of European news. The publishers and owners have never yet united in supporting their correspondents abroad. They have never united in protesting against the expulsion of honest and conservative correspondents, let alone taken common action when the representative of a dictator-defying newspaper gets what was perhaps coming to him.

I have given dramatic personal examples of what the business of European news reporting has become. I must add that daily journalism is not always running to a fire—or a revolution. Yet between the high spots and the daily routine it is a very important work in these days when the United States, unentangled, has to watch the great movements of Communism, Fascism, Democracy, Reaction, fighting for world control. We may remain as we are for a long time, but sooner or later we also shall have to choose. We should therefore be informed. The chief means of information is the newspaper, and the representatives of the American press abroad ever since the War have been bound and gagged by the dictators. How, then, are they to inform the American people?

Why should not the American Newspaper Publishers Association at its next convention plan united action in supporting the correspondents abroad? Not even Hitler will dare to fire the American press corps if the united newspaper publishers support such persons as future Edgar Mowrers and Dorothy Thompsons, whose truthfulness and integrity cannot be questioned, and whose only crime has been telling facts which Hitler could not bear to have told.

Perhaps more important, the correspondents themselves would do well to stop playing local police reporter or the lone-wolf game abroad, and to cooperate and fight unitedly against the dictators, the corrupting forces, and for a free and a clean flow of world news for the enlightenment of the millions at home who are at present lost in the no-man's-land of warring political, social, and economic philosophies.

How I Captured
St. Mihiel

The First World War was Seldes' first encounter with the capriciousness of the history books. After months of slogging through the front lines with the infantry of the famed Rainbow Division, Seldes got a tip that St. Mihiel, a small town in France, was about to be abandoned by the Germans. He managed to be the first American to reach the town after the German retreat, beating Generals Pershing and Petain by several hours. Seldes received a hero's welcome by the townspeople of St. Mihiel, but Pershing and Petain got the credit as the liberators. The story of the adventure comes from Seldes' 1931 book, Can These Things Be!

12 September 1918

AFTER LONG and careful preparation, the St. Mihiel salient was attacked.... The capture of St. Mihiel and the surrounding country although of great importance to the Allies, presented no serious difficulties, and Generals Petain and Pershing entered the town as victors the following day. (From a historical summary.)

Our one "triumphal entry."

We had come into the war late but decisively. Foch, Ludendorff and Hindenburg himself have given the American army credit for winning the war. In this way: our one hundred thousand casualties in the total of twenty million killed, wounded, disabled, was just enough of a sacrifice to break the balance of power, prevent a stalemate, bring victory to the Allied side.

This story of St. Mihiel therefore is no attempt to belittle the American effort.

It had been a war without heroics. At least not since the first days of open warfare when the Germans marched into Brussels with flags flying. Since then trench and mud warfare, gains by yards, almost every yard covered with blood. Never a clean victory.

But on the 13th of September 1918 the Allied armies had a chance to be spectacular, dramatic. They had liberated St. Mihiel, the key to Verdun, the one town that had remained in German hands since 1914, and all the possible generals got ready for a triumphal entry. It also celebrated the first All-American show. Pershing was to lead the famous into the town. This is the story of how an American newspaper correspondent entered St. Mihiel three hours before the generals and got the cream of the ovation, unwillingly enough.

St. Mihiel is the apex of a triangle which also rests upon Haudiomont and Pont-a-Mousson. It was the weakest link in the great German chain from Calais to Switzerland, and for that reason there had always been a newer and better chain in readiness connecting the two latter towns.

The Germans held on to St. Mihiel so long as they had hopes of winning the war. Weak as it was, it was a dagger in the heart of France, the fangs of a lion, or to use a third figure, the doorway into the enemy country. Through this postern gate Germany always hoped for a sortie to cut off Verdun.

On the morning of 18 July 1918 Foch made the attack which is now generally admitted the decisive battle of the World War. The Germans had launched their last desperate offensive on the 14th, ironically the French national holiday, and it had only partly succeeded. Foch mobilized his best troops, placing the Moroccan division between the American First and Second Divisions, the Foreign Legion of the French in liaison with the Marines of America. At the end of the 18 July offensive there was a bulge in the line, but this time it bulged towards Germany. At the apex of this bulge were the Foreign Legion and the Marines. They had 50 or 60 percent casualties in three days. The dead negroes of the Moroccan division, I remember seeing thrown into the ditches along the roadside; after all, they would have no fathers or mothers to worry about them.

No sooner was the battle ended that also ended Germany's hope of victory or stalemate, than it was known that General Pershing would reach the ambition of a lifetime, lead an All-American army into a battle. The Germans knew that also. Complete plans for the evacuation of the St. Mihiel salient had been worked out by General Ludendorff and his staff, and the work was almost complete when the Americans attacked on 12 September. General Otto von Ledebur, who commanded, writes:

"As early as 1916 the Michel position was laid out. Eight days were allowed for the removal of war material and the destruction of the defensive works. (On 1 September a bulletin was issued by the Germans stating: The supreme command has reported that the Americans intend to advance along both sides of the Moselle towards Metz.) We started the removal of war material from the St. Mihiel salient on 2 September."

The secret had not been kept by the American army. General Eugene Savatier, who says the American officers and men spoke too freely, also reports that Foch said to him when he issued the order on 24 July for the attack on St. Mihiel: "A quarter of a million Americans every month! The superiority is now on our side. This superiority may be small, but it is definite; it will soon be decisive."

Foch's order, paragraph C, was: "Liberation of the Paris-Avicourt track in the region of Commercy, by a reduction of the salient of St. Mihiel. Preparations are to be made without delay and the operation is to be undertaken by the American troops as soon as they have the necessary means."

On the day before each big American operation it was the custom of General Pershing to appear personally at press headquarters or to send General Nolan or General Fox Connor to us, or sometimes two of them would come together, and take us completely into the confidence of the general staff. They would bring out the secret maps of the battle and tell us the position of our troops, the enemy troops, the objective of each attack and the greatest secret of all, the zero hour. I do not think in the history of the world that newspaper men were ever given such confidence.

But in the case of St. Mihiel there was no surprise, and little news for us in this secret conclave.

Not only had we seen the preparation for the St. Mihiel battle, but we had had intelligence reports posted in press headquarters translating German secret orders and news. On more than one occasion we had posted German orders for the evacuation of St. Mihiel, news of how it was succeeding, and German reports as to the zero hour. That point alone was in dispute.

"We are going over the top at 5 o'clock," said General Fox Connor that day when we were locked in the small dining room of press headquarters, with soldiers at the doors and windows keeping people away; "each of you can attach yourself to a regiment if you like and go over the top."

I went with the Rainbow Division. Colonel Ben Hough of the 166th Infantry, and the intelligence officer, Lieutenant Alison Reppy, now professor of law at New York University, were my especial friends in the Army, so I joined this division, and at break of day, after a night of considerable fear and trembling, we went over to find that the Germans had gone home before the battle. Or at least to their good Michel line.

On the morning, Friday the Thirteenth, September 1918 General Petain said to General Pershing: "You have cut the Brute's throat." Petain was using the figure of the beast with the fangs, which the St. Mihiel line also resembled. Petain proposed a triumphal entry to Pershing.

The throat had been cut by the Rainbow and the First American divisions. Up north, where I was to go later, the Yankee Division had dealt the Brute a piledriver blow between the eyes. It was the force of the two American offensives on the north and south which had gone beyond the reckoning of the German staff, so that despite the fact they had evacuated the town itself, they were forced to lose 3,000 guns and many prisoners in that week's fighting.

On the morning of the 13th, when Petain had got word that some of his French colonial troops were throwing a footbridge across the Moselle, and had communicated with Pershing, I got up very early because I had figured out the night before that the great success on the two flanks would necessarily drive the Germans out of the apex.

It was a day of pale sunshine and chilly rainbursts. As it was also the most thrilling day of my life, I can remember that very well.

As one of the 20 accredited war correspondents—G-2-D, GHQ, AEF, advanced section—I rated a big car, in fact, a general's car. We wore an officer's uniform without insignia of rank, but a red C on a green, or intelligence section, brassard. In the British army the press section had the rank of captain, but this was all very confusing; it required the saluting of general officers and the taking of salutes from soldiers, all of which was most embarrassing.

As there were never enough cars to go around, it was our custom to go out by twos and threes. It so happened that for some time six artists, each with the rank of captain, had been attached to our section, and as artists were not news rivals, we frequently took them in our cars.

I asked Captain Wallace Morgan and Captain Ernest Peixotto if they would care to go with me that morning. I had a hunch I could get into St. Mihiel. Apparently no one else did. I told them in secret and they joined with enthusiasm.

We left about 8 in the morning and headed for Chauvoncourt, the last town on our side of the river, opposite St. Mihiel. Nothing much happened on the trip. When we got near our objective, however, we saw a sight which I will never forget.

Everywhere, from Belgium to Belfort, I had seen smashed villages. I had previously been at Bapaume and Fricourt, at least I had been assured by British soldiers that I had been in those towns, but all I had seen outside the few wooden signs, freshly painted, saying, "This is Fricourt" and "This is Bapaume," were a few battered bricks in a large field, and some dust of wooden houses. Those villages had been churned up a dozen times and all the stone and iron and brick and blood had mingled in a universal debris.

Here on the road to St. Mihiel was a town that had died on its feet. It was dead, and yet it was intact. Not a wisp of smoke came from a chimney, not a stone had been touched by a shell, not a window broken. It was all there, but dead. Apparently the French had evacuated it the first days of the war and the natives had not been allowed to return. There had never been any use of it as a military base, and so, although it was in a sort of No Man's Land, it was intact, and yet dead. It gave us all the creeps. It was a really horrible place to go through.

We did not realize what luck we had. We rode straight into Chauvoncourt. It was only late that afternoon that we heard what difficulties Petain and Pershing had in finding roads over the old trenches and the old battlefields, and how the signal corps got lost. The latter fact accounts for there being no official pictures of Pershing's entry, except the amateur set I made.

At Chauvoncourt we were stopped by an enormous German tank trap. It stretched across the only road, from house to house, and there was no chance of riding farther. We abandoned our car and walked to the river. As we got our first view of St. Mihiel the ruined walls of the old Roman camp above the city glistened with rainbow colors as the sun burst through the rain.

Approaching the plank bridge we were met by a gesture which was the symbol of immortal France—the Tricolor, carried by a little crowd of French boys and girls, flags hidden for years, now in the hands of sad-faced children who had lived in hunger and terror and knew that *le jour de gloire est arrive.*

At the sight of Morgan, Peixotto and myself clambering up the wooden planks which led us up the other bank of the river, the children began to shout.

They had never seen Americans before.

From out of the town a great crowd advanced upon us. An old man in a cracked voice began yelling, "*Vive l'Amerique. Vive l'Amerique,*" and the children echoed him.

The French colonial sentry at the St. Mihiel side of the improvised bridge came to a smart salute. We snapped a return in our triply unmartial manner.

The children and the few villagers, shouting for joy, led us to the central square of the town. Here the whole population was gathered. And here they hailed us as the conquerors, the victors of St. Mihiel.

We got the big ovation.

When the great generals arrived, hours later, the reception given them could not equal that given us. We were the first Americans in the first town liberated from the Germans after four years, and without ever desiring to, we just about spoiled the only triumphal entry of the last years of the war.

An old Frenchman, clad in rags and a discarded German round cap pushed his way through the cheering mob and insisted on kissing us. A child came running up with flowers. They all cheered for the American army and they embarrassed Morgan, Peixotto and myself some more.

For a long time they encircled us, and old women wept. The men wanted to know everything. For four years they had been hearing nothing but the Germans talking about how they were winning the war; now they wanted to know the truth.

"They told us only a few of you Americans had arrived in France, and that not a single American soldier was at the front," one old man said, "and that is why when we first saw three officers in a strange uniform approaching we did not know to what nation you belonged."

An old woman came up to me and said, "Oh, monsieur, you will never realize how we have suffered," and went away.

Another old man said: "Yesterday I was a hundred years old. Today I am twenty years young. I thank *le bon Dieu* I have lived to see you."

A girl, pretty despite privations, dressed in mended and discolored clothing came up.

"*Mon officier*," she said, "will you bring back my brother? The Germans took him yesterday. He was a frail weak child just a few days over 16 but they took all the boys from 16 up and all the men up to 45. We have heard that your wonderful American soldiers have trapped the Germans up there and that our men will be restored. Is this true?"

As if in answer there was another dull crash of shellfire miles away.

Men and women were crying. Children were boisterous. It was holiday amidst the ruins. Always a heavy boom told us that the war was still on, north and east but far away from St. Mihiel now.

A man on crutches told us about the Roman camp. "That stone to the left," he said, "we used to call the Devil's Table because there was a flat stone on top. Only this morning we noticed that that stone was gone. Now I put it that the devil"—he pointed northward to the new German line—"has gone and taken his table with him, not so?"

Willing guides took me to the untouched parts of the town. In the movie house there were stacks of 50 pfennig tickets at the window. In the German officers' casino we found glasses half-filled with beer and fresh cigar butts in the laden ashtrays. A cucumber salad remained on the bar. A barrel of beer which had not been consumed the night before had been opened this morning and spilled on the floor. There was a pool of dark, sour-smelling stuff.

All the French houses had been looted of linen, feather beds and things of value. All that the Germans left behind were lithographs of the Kaiser and the Kronprinz which the inhabitants were busy dislodging with brooms. There was not a dog in the village—the inhabitants said they had been gathered and slaughtered the day before and the carcasses taken for food.

When we returned to the public square the crowd there had been increased by several hundred, practically all the able-bodied. They burst out again with cheers for us and thanks to heaven because the Americans had liberated their town. Despite our protests that we were only one corre-spondent and two artists, they treated us as the representatives of the American army and made speeches to us.

I noticed that two girls did not participate in all this excitement. They stood aside, just the two of them, eyeing us and being eyed by the whole town.

"Why do those two stand apart?" I asked a guide.

"They are now ostracized," he replied. "They lived with German officers. They are our own people, French women and they lived with German officers during the years of occupation. Well, they had it good for a time. If there was food and drink and clothing around, they got it. They were the queens of the town then. They looked down upon us. But now we look down upon them. We will drive them out soon."

It was twelve o'clock. We had been in St. Mihiel more than two hours and hunger was drowning whatever satisfactions we might have been enjoying in the applause of the city which hailed us as its captors and liberators. As it was not much use trying to buy a meal in that looted town, and as the inhabitants had about shouted and cried themselves out with joy, we started for the bridge. Scores of the natives determined to accompany us to the edge of the town. "*Vive les Americains,*" they shouted.

We crossed back to Chauvoncourt and found my car. Before we could turn around, we saw, coming up the main street, a long string of cars. We waited. General Petain, General Pershing, General McAndrew and Colonel Carl Boyd, the first aide of our commander in chief, various other French and American generals, and the French mayor and French prefect, the latter two in black and silver uniforms and kepis, the more splendid by contrast with khaki and horizon blue, came piling out of the new cars. But no new correspondents, and no members of the signal corps to immortalize the moment in movies.

We shook hands. General Pershing asked me what I had seen in the town and I told him. We joined and the whole party came back to the plank bridge.

There were no fanfares, no fireworks, no Kaiser on a milk-white charger brazenly entering a conquered city. Our impassioned democracy was never better personified. Whatever was triumphant and exultant remained in the quickened hearts beneath drab brown and drab blue uniforms. The French sentry again snapped a salute and General Pershing snapped one back, glanced quickly up and down the shattered facade of the town and turned to regard the shaky little bridge.

General Petain stepped aside. General Pershing hesitated. Then urged by a gesture from the French commander he stepped first across the quiet stream. This was the Frenchman's salute to the American as the real victor although it had been Petain's own colonials who had actually been first in St. Mihiel that morning.

In the public square the crowd reassembled, recognizing the importance of their visitors by the stars on their sleeves or shoulders, and their own mayor and prefect.

"But who is this general in brown, with the frown and the German-like cropped moustache?" the townspeople asked.

"*Le* General Pershing."

The name got around. I heard them trying it on their tongues and finally it rippled through that pool of pale faces.

"*Pairshang. Pairshang. C'est le general Pairshang.*"

They had never heard the name before. The Germans had said there were no American soldiers on the fighting line.

Of course they cheered again. But there was now not that spontaneous outburst which had greeted the first Americans in the city square. The French colonial band then struck up the anthem rarely heard since 1914:

> "*Allons enfants de la patrie,*
> *Le jour de gloire est arrive.*"

The day of glory had indeed arrived for them. It was soon to arrive for more towns and for all of France.

Out in the occasional sun flashed the curved blades of the colonial cavalry. The foot soldiers stood at attention some 15 feet away. The visiting officers stood at the salute. The civilian population, the men and boys hatless, without advice or order, formed into a double row and General Petain and General Pershing passed between, as if reviewing a regiment. The little girl who had first brought a bouquet of wildflowers to me, now brought another one. As the two commanders halted, she hesitated between them, then turned to the better known uniform of blue and presented the flowers to Petain. Petain immediately bowed and gave the flowers to Pershing and in this graceful act the inhabitants again saw the significance of the victory being American.

"*Vive l'Amerique. Vive la France. Vive Petain. Vive Pairshang. Vive Foch.*"

It began to rain. The liberators moved towards the town hall, the high officers entered, the 3,000 natives dispersed.

"You have restored me my office, and this time for good," said the prefect to Pershing. "Mine, too," said the mayor.

"It has been my honor to be the first French general to work under an American command," said the French colonial officer.

Pershing and his entourage then returned to the bridge. There was some handshaking with civilian officials and French officers who were staying behind. That was all there was to the American triumphal entry of St. Mihiel.

On the Chauvoncourt side some French soldiers came up with three German prisoners. Pershing stopped to cross-examine them through an interpreter. One German said he was pleased to be taken by the Americans. The talk lasted five minutes. Pershing moved on.

Suddenly there was an explosion about 50 feet down the road. Cries of men in agony and a cloud of smoke. We thought a German shell had fallen. Everyone stopped dead still. But Pershing pushed on.

We found a little group of French soldiers carrying two others whose hands and faces were streaming with blood.

The retiring Germans had laid a grenade trap across the road. If General Pershing had not stopped to talk with the prisoners it might have been his foot which would have caught the wire and ended the triumphal day in tragedy.

When we got to our autos, beyond the tank trap, Secretary of War Baker and his party, accompanied by a British and two American correspondents, arrived. While Baker and Pershing were exchanging congratulations and regrets at not having been able to meet at Chauvoncourt earlier, my colleagues pumped me. I was not a "cable" man, I wrote only mail articles, and they were chagrined they had not been able to witness the entry. (To make up for that, however, they cabled they had.)

"Can you come to dinner with me tonight?" said Baker to Pershing.

"I am sorry," replied the American commander, "but I am going to be busy tonight and tomorrow too."

It was that tomorrow which saw the two American divisions meet across the neck of the Brute, and from that day on they marched on towards Germany.

Before St. Mihiel we showed the world we had soldiers. 18 July proved that amply. September, however, proved we also had an American army.

As for me, I always feel a little bit sorry that I got to St. Mihiel ahead of Pershing.

U. S. Infantry Won
the War—Hindenburg

This is the story of one of Seldes' greatest scoops, his trip into Germany after the Armistice with fellow reporters Cal Lyon, Lincoln Eyre and Herbert Corey to interview Field Marshall Paul von Hindenburg. This account comes from his 1929 book, You Can't Print That. *This interview is nothing more than a footnote in the history of World War I, something that still rankles Seldes more than seven decades later.*

THE CHARGE against us was simply: first violation of the Armistice; crossing into Germany; passing through the Great German Retreat; and interviewing Hindenburg the week the war ended. We made no defense.

General Dennis Nolan, under special orders of General Pershing, conducted our trial at Chaumont. The verdict put us into an awkward position—either resign from the Press Section, lose our army standing, and depart for home, or remain in the AEF under technical arrest and refrain from writing the greatest story of our lives. Thus spoke army discipline and military press censorship.

Today we are proud of our crime, if crime it was. We can afford to forget the humiliation of arrest, the discomfiture of the trial, but we remember the thrill of that day we left Luxembourg, the sudden terror of being caught (in the midst of his marching men) by a furious Prussian colonel, and the great climax, the meeting with Hindenburg.

For it was then that the commander of the enemy, the one man in the world who could best make a historical judgment, made an admission in the honesty of tears, an admission which for political reasons he can never repeat: "The American infantry," said Hindenburg, "won the World War in battle in the Argonne."

First, a word on the nature of our "crime." We were all members of the Advance Section, G-2-D, GHQ, AEF. In other words, in that part of the Intelligence Corps of the American army known as the Press Section. We were given the uniforms of officers without insignia of rank and entitled to the privileges of generals. We ranked with the doughboys when we were in the trenches and just below Pershing on our visit to Chaumont. We found the question of saluting and getting saluted difficult because we had refused to take the two bars of a captaincy which our British colleagues wore.

But more important, we considered ourselves more free than a ranked and placed person in uniform the day the eager doughboys, still hoping for laurels, fired cannon five minutes after eleven and the Armistice hushed the thundering front.

That minute we felt ourselves civilians again. Again we felt free to use our wits in getting scoops—to think up some big stunt which would rattle the morale of our competitors and amaze the world.

"Let's cross into Germany."

Spoken as a joke—hiding a mighty desire—needing only a seconding motion to light an enthusiasm which would carry us over that yesterday's horror which was No Man's Land and that yesterday's hatred which was Enemy Land—and to a tomorrow which was grand and thrilling and perhaps laden with death.

But someone must have suspected such a plan even before it was born. We had already heard our sergeant and corporal chauffeurs whispering instructions received either from Pershing's headquarters or through the major commanding us that there must be no violation of the Armistice, that while we might drive into No Man's Land, we must never drive across the Armistice line.

"Youse guys can boss us anywhere you want to go," Sergeant Jack Cooper, one of the best drivers in the army, told me, "but dere's one thing you can't make us do and dat's cross over. We got superior orders, see?"

I still believe the two chauffeurs innocent, but I do not credit it altogether to our superior guile, for the spirit of adventure must have blinded their eyes too, to the many false roads and wrong turns we methodically took. They did protest at first.

"The map shows to the right—"

"The map is wrong. Take the turn to the left."

Every half hour a similar conversation.

And so we rode out of gay Luxembourg, that lovely city on a cliff where our doughboys had had the time of their lives what with being treated as a quarter million heroes and dragged by squads and companies from the open peaceful highways into the homes of happy and rich Luxembourgeoises where champagne and song lasted a full seven days.

It was still Armistice week when we started, dull and early, towards Germany. Well, it didn't take long to cross that tiny "Grand-Duchy," and as there was no longer an organized German frontier, we must have ridden into Enemy Land with no more excitement than the noise automobiles make on hard military roads.

But excitement, which was to hold us breathless for a week and more, began almost immediately. As we flew into the first German village we passed a triumphal arch, if you please, all decked out with flowers and laurel and bearing on its keystone the legend "Welcome Our Undefeated Heroes." And then we saw the flag we had never dreamed we would ever see, the red, white and black of the Kaiser's monarchy, waving in ignorant pride from many windows.

They say the civilians have the most hate and fear. At the front, Heaven knows, we had had our share of both. But certainly the civilians across the sea felt the war was over when the Armistice was signed while on the other hand so many at the front who had been in or watched the slaughter and the mud day by day, unchanging, unceasing, had felt there must be a catch in it somewhere, that it wasn't really true, that it didn't mean what it seemed. So when the chauffeurs of both cars put on the brakes bringing us to a crunching, huddled halt, we too had forgotten the Armistice and felt civilians' hate and fear pointing at us in the snake-ends of the wind-snapping enemy banners.

The chauffeurs argued perhaps half-heartedly. Army discipline had never really existed in our outfit. Adventure lay ahead and nothing but explanations behind. "You might as well go on, we are ten miles inside Germany already," was someone's conclusive statement, and ahead we went.

In this town of Borg we found the German army in full retreat. We came up behind it, noting immediately the splendid discipline of the defeated. Their lines were right and their step firm: even in facial expression there was no sign of a collapsed morale. Their uniforms and equipment seemed shoddy.

"*Amerikaner—Amerikaner.*"

Without hatred or passion the surprised soldiers passed the word along the undulating ranks.

We rode slowly alongside, our hearts beating high.

Soon we were in the town square, a triangle between streets, where the German colonel on a horse was directing operations.

He saw us at a distance and rode forward.

"Halt!" he commanded with a mean voice and uplifted hand.

We halted.

"What in thunder and lightning are you doing here?"

Our spokesman stammered an answer.

"You are interfering with our military movements—you must go back to the American line," the colonel said decisively.

"But—"

"I forbid an answer!"

At our left, meanwhile, hundreds of German soldiers with rifles on their shoulders, an occasional 77, and a frequent "goulash cannon" were thudding and clanking onward.

We all began to talk at once. The colonel became furious.

"I tell you to get out, and immediately, or I take the lot of you prisoner. You are in great danger. Your lives are at stake here. You are the enemy—the men might shoot you all—or the civilians attack you—any moment. I tell you to return—"

At this black moment there was a civilian flurry in the square from which a sailor emerged, running towards us. He had that universality of blue serge and seaworn face which make the sailors of all lands alike.

"What's the trouble here?" he asked.

We were immediately amazed by the daring of an enlisted man in the presence of high officers. But we noticed also there was something different about this sailor's uniform—a red band on his left arm. Later we read the black print on it: "*Arbeiter—und Soldaten—Rat,*" or Workers and Soldiers Council, or Soviet.

Seeing sympathetic ears, we poured a broken German explanation into them. We noted, too, a change in the behavior of our swell colonel. His starch and bluster were gone. He sat on his horse, looking disgusted and arguing less vehemently than ourselves.

"They're in danger here," he repeated.

"Not while I'm in command in this area," replied the sailor cockily.

"They must leave at once I tell you," said the colonel.

But the colonel's antagonism reflexed the sailor's sympathy for us.

"You go and mind your own business," he ordered.

The colonel went.

"My name is Fritz Harris," the sailor beamed. "Does any one of you know my uncle in Cleveland?"

"But what does all this mean?" we asked, shaking negative heads.

"Well, I'm in control," replied the sailor, jumping on the running board and shooing away the old men and women who now dared crowd our automobiles. "We started the revolution in Kiel. On the ships. Just before the Armistice. Everything is going in good order. Don't worry. We did everything with shipshape discipline. Each sailor was assigned a city, his own city usually, and went with orders to proclaim the German revolution there. This is my home. Not a drop of blood was shed here. It was different in Trier and Frankfurt. Now, honored gentlemen, what is it you want?"

This piece of diplomacy we left to our spokesman. He had considerable hold of the language but I still believe it was a slight error that made the rest of our adventure possible. He had tried to say we were a part of the press section which had come to see how Germany had lived during the war, what the food situation was, and all that, and sailor Fritz Harris interrupted him with:

"Ah, the American Food Commission—yah, yah, we had heard you would send us food. *Willkommen, willkommen.*"

(This promise of white bread had been probably our most effective propaganda. For months our aviators had dropped cards over the German lines saying every prisoner, and everyone who surrendered voluntarily, was getting two pounds of white bread a day—and many a German came to claim his portion.)

We let Fritz's mistake go unchallenged and were conducted with rejoicing to the Rathaus, where we were welcomed by the soldier and civilian Soviet of the town. At our request they telephoned to Trier asking that everything be done to insure safety for our lives and means for getting the information we wanted.

On the road out of Borg we had a great panorama of the German forces endlessly flowing eastward. Despite the seeming discipline peasants told us how they had bought artillery horses for 50 marks and exchanged a goose for a brace of rifles and an egg for a parabellum pistol. No bloodshed was reported in the countryside.

In Trier a reception committee met us and wanted to entertain us but we pressed on to Frankfurt which we reached the next day.

Up to now we had no thought of Hindenburg. Our secret ambition had been to be the first Americans in Berlin. We confided it to our host at Frankfurt, the usual *Arbiter-undoldatendrat*, who agreed to help us, but first we had to be given a banquet.

We sat in the spacious hall of the *Frankfurterhof*, now revolutionary headquarters, and ate as bad a meal as one can imagine, thin soup whose only distinguishing taste was salt, some goose, the only meat we found anywhere, potatoes and very soggy black bread. The wine was excellent.

Our hosts held long discourses and our spokesman replied. My own contribution was a one line speech: *"Es lebe die Republik"*—long live the Republic—which was an excuse for draining another green decanter of Rhine.

During prolonged arrangements for continuing our journey, one of the council said timidly:

"We would like you to see Hindenburg first."

Hindenburg!

It was almost as amazing as the Armistice itself. The latter was a bit unreal, but this was a dream desire—to call on and interview the leader of the enemy, the second best-hated man in the world then, the general whose men were killing our men, the apotheosis of German frightfulness, the incarnation of that which six days before was all the evil in the world— such a thought was beyond our still khaki-clad minds.

"It can be arranged," said the Rat.

Two German cars were given us, so we could release the doughboys who were becoming indignantly mutinous—perhaps through ignorance of what was to come—and with tires exploding every hour and engines going wrong every three, we managed to arrive in Cassel, where Hindenburg had removed his grand headquarters from Aix-la-Chapelle.

We came to the Rathaus confident all was well. But it wasn't.

Hindenburg politely refused to see us. He said he would meet no one in the uniform of the enemy.

That day and the next we spent in conferences with members of the Rat at City Hall and sulking at our hotel, where, by the way, our presence was objectionable. The owner was surly and the help mean. Our finances were low. I still have a grudge against that hotel man who gave me 60 paper marks for my reserve $20 gold piece.

We decided to go to Berlin at once. We went to the Rathaus to say good-bye. Then a sergeant-major member of the council took up the telephone and insisted on speaking to Hindenburg himself.

It was a long conversation in which our sergeant-major, an ugly, emaciated person with protruding yellow teeth, very much the "Hun" of British war cartoons, became more and more exasperated. Finally he shouted:

"This is an order to you, Excellency, not a request."

A moment of silence for Hindenburg's reaction.

"Then at three o'clock, you will send one of your cars."

He hung up the telephone and a proud smile came over his distorted face.

"At three this afternoon he will send his car."

The car came on the stroke. Our hotel keeper with almost oriental obeisances directed seven employees who grovelled us into Hindenburg's grey monogrammed limousine.

In the marble castle of Wilhelmshohe an aide-de-camp took us upstairs. A squat, stoutish man in a regulation general's uniform with an additional white cloth around his head, received us.

"General Groener," he said to each, snapping his feet.

We shook hands.

"The general hasn't been wounded?" queried our spokesman.

"No," he smiled, "but I have a terrible headache."

Our spokesman interpreted. "He has a terrible headache."

"He should have," whispered the roughneck among us. "He has just lost a world war."

General Groener bowed us into the next room, marvellous, rococo, pale blue and gold and palatially uncomfortable.

Hindenburg arose.

He was dressed in field grey-blue. Tall, red-faced, broad shouldered. The usual officer's decorations on the wide chest were absent. Around his neck, unbuttoned for comfort, was the small blue cross of the *Pour le merite*. His head was covered with stiff toothbrush-like white hairs, cropped to about a half-inch, and revealing, by their scarcity, a very pink scalp.

But what I thought was funny, was the famous Hindenburg moustache. It looked theatrical. It looked false, and stuck on, and it certainly curved itself along the cheeks as no non-Thespian moustache has ever done.

"*Die Herrschaften sprechen Deutsch, nicht wahr?*" said Hindenburg in a kindly smiling voice, shaking hands for the first time since the war with men in the uniform of his enemies.

Three disclaimed speaking German so Hindenburg fixed on our spokesman, motioned us to a circle of chairs, and began:

"I will answer any military questions. I am a soldier. But I refuse to answer any political questions." He shrugged his shoulders. "I am a soldier."

We had previously discussed no questions for this interview; it was one of those cases where any word given us, on any subject, was precious.

"Is the demobilization proceeding satisfactorily—we have heard of some fighting and bloodshed." Our first question.

"Yes," he replied, "although there is some trouble when the men come to the cities, the return from the front is fully disciplined. Men and officers remain in their usual relationship. The troubles are not serious among the troops, officers and civilians, except when there is an attempt to disregard the present change in government."

"What is your position at present?"

"I have given my pledge to Mr. (Friedrich) Ebert (the first president of the Weimar Republic), who is in control of the government in Berlin, that I will stay in command until all the troops are safely returned from the front and to their home barracks. My functions then cease. I have finished my duties. I mean to retire into private life."

"Do you think the present socialist government will remain or will fall soon?"

"I cannot answer that. I am not a politician. I am a soldier."

Several questions followed. Either of minor importance or of a political nature.

"I cannot answer. I am a soldier," was the inevitable reply to the latter category.

All these minutes undoubtedly each of us was steeling himself for another question—a question we were burning to ask, and which was merely "Who won the war?" heavily muffled in diplomatic garments. We fell to debating "the next question" among ourselves, and finally someone said:

"Go ahead—ask him—you know what."

So the spokesman with considerable throat clearing and much redundancy, asked it.

When we asked "Who won the war?" we were ignorant of what our home papers had said. Our American papers in France, like the Entente press, from October to 10 November reported nothing but French, British, Italian, Belgian victories. "British troops advance 20 miles," "Brussels captured," "Lille entered," "Italians cross three rivers." The three armies northwest of us had advanced many miles each day. City after city was captured by them. But what was the American army doing all this time? Merely fighting. Yes, fighting. In the Argonne. Through dense, almost impassable forests, over cliffs and hills, wading in ravines, struggling through mud thick as boiling rubber, bombing, hand-grenading, machine-gunning, bayonetting their way northward towards the jugular of the German armies, the Metz-Longuyon railroad, the one means of retreat of the enemy.

Hindenburg was shortening his lines. He was quitting northern France and Belgium. But he was holding the Argonne. Day by day the representative of our GHQ had shown us the map with every enemy division and reserve force marked. Hindenburg had 32 reserve divisions at the beginning of our Argonne drive. When November began two or three remained. What had become of an army of German reserves?

Very few had appeared on the French or British front almost all were thrown against us. We were doing almost all the fighting while the Allies were marching unhindered into famous cities and famous battle fields of 1914 and capturing the headlines of the world. We were losing men and taking prisoners and trenches—fighting most of the war then and getting no credit from the press because our work was not spectacular. Hindenburg and Pershing knew what we were doing. What would Hindenburg say?

"I will reply with the same frankness," said Hindenburg, faintly amused at our diplomacy. "The American infantry in the Argonne won the war."

He paused and we sat thrilled.

"I say this," continued Hindenburg, "as a soldier, and soldiers will understand me best.

"To begin with I must confess that Germany could not have won the war—that is, after 1917. We might have won on land. We might have taken Paris. But after the failure of the world food crops of 1916 the British food blockade reached its greatest effectiveness in 1917. So I must really say that the British food blockade of 1917 and the American blow in the Argonne of 1918 decided the war for the Allies.

"But without American troops against us and despite a food blockade which was undermining the civilian population of Germany and curtailing

the rations in the field, we could still have had a peace without victory.
The war could have ended in a sort of stalemate.

"And even if we had not had the better of the fighting in the end, as
we had until 18 July 1918 we could have had an acceptable peace. We
were still a great force and we had divisions in reserve always which the
enemy attacks could never use up completely.

"Even the attack of 18 July which Allied generals may consider the
turning point in the war, did not use up a very important part of the
German army or smash all our positions. To win a war it is necessary, as
you know, to place the enemy forces *hors de combat*. In such a manner of
warfare which began when Japan and Russia met in the wheat fields of the
Far East, you must engage and defeat hundreds of thousands, millions of
men.

"In the summer of 1918 the German army was able to launch offensive after offensive—almost one a month. We had the men, the munitions
and the morale, and we were not overbalanced. But the balance was
broken by the American troops.

"The Argonne battle was slow and difficult. But it was strategic. It was
bitter and it used up division after division. We had to hold the Metz-
Longuyon roads and railroad and we had hoped to stop all American
attacks until the entire army was out of northern France. We were passing
through the neck of a vast bottle. But the neck was narrow. German and
American divisions fought each other to a standstill in the Argonne. They
met and shattered each other's strength. The Americans are splendid soldiers. But when I replaced a division it was weak in numbers and unrested,
while each American division came in fresh and fit and on the offensive.

"The day came when the American command sent new divisions into
the battle and when I had not even a broken division to plug up the gaps.
There was nothing left to do but ask terms.

"Until the American attack our positions had been comparatively satisfactory. We had counted on holding the Argonne longer. The advantage
of terrain was with us. The American troops were unseasoned. We had
also counted on their impetuosity. There was great wastage in your army
due to carelessness, impetuosity and the disregard of the conditions of
modern warfare.

"Yet from a military point of view the Argonne battle as conceived and
carried out by the American Command was the climax of the war and its
deciding factor. The American attack was furious—it continued from day
to day with increasing power, but when two opposing divisions had broken

each other, yours was replaced with 27,000 eager for battle, ours with decimated, ill-equipped, ill-fed men suffering from contact with a gloomy and despairing civilian population.

"I do not mean to discredit your fighting forces—I repeat, without the American blow in the Argonne, we could have made a satisfactory peace at the end of a stalemate or at least held our last positions on our own frontier indefinitely—undefeated. The American attack decided the war."

A moment of silence.

"*Ach, mein armes Vaterland—mein armes Vaterland—*"

Hindenburg bowed his head and tears flooded his pale, watery eyes. His huge bulk was shaken. He wept for his "poor fatherland."

We sat and wondered over so much emotion in a military leader supposedly devoid of sentiment and sentimentality.

Thus the interview terminated with a strange human spectacle and in an uncomfortable silence. A fallen Colossus. A broken Superman. Blood and iron suddenly tears and clay.

There was no more to ask. Here we were with the biggest story in the world, and even before Hindenburg was through speaking, our thoughts were searching cable ends or messengers or some new means of communication with our papers.

There came the usual anticlimax. "Where do you go from here?" asked Hindenburg. "Ach, Berlin, so? Well, *gluckliche Reise.*"

"*Auf Wiedersehen.*" A loose handclasp. We were ushered out by the snappy aide-de-camp.

My colleagues started for Berlin; I got up at four the next morning to make the 5 a.m. train for Luxembourg. As I reached the station I saw part of the real German revolution.

Mingled with the monarchist flags and drapery over the Cassel railroad station and triumphal arches were red streamers and bunting placed by the revolutionary sailors and town Soviet. The troops coming by train knew nothing of the Kaiser's cowardice or the change to a republic.

A regiment was detraining. As the colonel led his men from the station into the public square he seemed lightning-struck when he beheld the revolutionary color mingling with his Kaiser's.

"Tear the red rags down!" he ordered his captains.

A captain in turn spoke to his men, who refused to move.

"I'll do it myself," said the captain, and grabbing a red streamer from the triumphal arch, he pulled.

Two soldiers with red arm-bands approached threateningly, and I stopped too.

"Pardon, captain," said one, "but we have had a revolution."

"Revolution, to the devil—" replied the captain, pulling.

The two soldiers raised their rifles.

The captain drew his pistol.

Click!—Crack!

At this precise moment the little experience I had had in the Luneville-Baccaret section with the Rainbow Division, pulled my habit muscles. I dropped flat.

A dozen rifles and a pair of revolvers snapped. A man fell partly on me. I turned cautiously on my left side. His face was in pain, and his hands were at his middle, and blood was flowing from his stomach. He was the captain who had pulled the red flag. The soldiers had shot him.

Men ran over us, around us. Lying flat, I had a panorama of flying feet in the semi-darkness. Shooting was spasmodic, now near, now at a distance. I wondered what I could do for the man lying over my feet. I pulled myself up. I think he died without a groan.

Bodies were writhing in the open square. One wounded man was shrieking. But the troops were gone and scared civilians were appearing from hiding places and the station.

"Too bad," they murmured, "but these officers won't believe the guards who tell them there has been a revolution—and a republic."

In three days and three nights the train meandered a hundred miles. It was crowded with German officers who mistook me for a returning prisoner of war and who were kindlier than any German civilians and who gave me their precious bad bread.

At Wasserbillig, the Luxembourg frontier, was the most welcome sight in the universe: a doughboy. He got me a car to Luxembourg. I was promptly arrested. Pershing insisted the German government return my colleagues from Berlin, and our trial at Chaumont followed.

I have seen Hindenburg since. No longer the broken old man weeping. Nor quite Hindenburg of the iron-nailed statue. But times had changed in Germany. Seven or eleven political parties were bitterly fighting for power, and the old monarchists and the old militarists were spreading the myth that the war was lost, not by Wilhelm's armies, but by the republican Dolchstoss—the civilian "stab in the back."

I recalled the Cassel meeting. Hindenburg shook his head in acknowledgment.

But for political reasons he can never again repeat his confession of Armistice week.

Long Armistice

The blunders made in 1919 by the men who drafted the Versailles Treaty that officially ended the First World War led directly to the start of the Second World War two decades later. Seldes was there and saw the betrayal of the common people through the avarice and stupidity of the Allies and their desire to crush Germany and carve up the spoils from victory in the "War To End All Wars." Seldes wrote about it in his 1933 book, World Panorama.

MR. WOODROW WILSON came to Paris to complete the regeneration of mankind; M. Saionji wanted only a small slice of China and Signor Orlando came to get a piece of Yugoslavia. As for M. Clemenceau . . .

At lunch with George Adam, the "father of victory" was asked by the journalist what he thought of the Fourteen Points. The reply will bear repeating. "*Le bon Dieu,*" said M. Clemenceau; "the good God had only Ten."

That was Georges Clemenceau's attitude, which made the treaty of Versailles and "broke the heart of the world." As a young man he had been a socialist, had given himself to this just cause and that, had fought for Dreyfus, suffered ostracism, loss of public life. In due time he became a realist, dropped his ideals, turned into the fiercest patriot France had ever had. He was not angered by Mr. Wilson's idealism. He looked upon the American President as a little child.

When Woodrow Wilson sailed for France on 4 December 1918, not quite a month after the Armistice made on his terms, a war ended by an enemy which had had a revolution because it believed everything he said, he was hailed around the world as the greatest man of our time. Some people called him the greatest man of all time, some compared him to the Man who had become God. In Italy he was soon to be worshiped as the Prince of Peace—for a few weeks at least.

In recorded history there had never been an instance of one statesman speaking for the people of the world as Woodrow Wilson spoke in those days. The greatest religious leaders at the greatest day of their lives had never appealed to so many and diverse nations and races. At that moment he could have given the signal in all lands, he could have said to millions and millions, "Arise and follow me to Utopian times, shake off the tyrants, destroy the oppressors, down the politicians, the feudal land barons, the exploiters." He could have achieved some sort of Wilsonian revolution, saved humanity academically by merely uttering a few words.

He did, in fact, try to utter those words. But too late. From the first day of the Peace Conference, when he let M. Clemenceau fool him into agreeing that sessions should be secret, until that day in April when he ordered steam up in his private liner as a threat to return to America, he had so deeply compromised himself that the faith of the world in him was shaken, and his followers were fighting among themselves. M. Saionji was now trading a strip of mainland for a fort and an island, Signor Orlando was drawing lines around Fiume, and M. Clemenceau, being told that Ignace Paderewski, the greatest pianist in the world, was now premier of Poland, remarked laughingly, "What a fall!" M. Clemenceau had much to laugh about in the spring and summer of 1919.

On the second of the three days in which the American Army clanked across the Rhine bridge, magnificently alarming the military Germans, the President of the United States arrived in Paris, where he was described as "the King of Humanity." The night of 13 December saw greater rejoicing than the night of the Armistice, if one believes certain enthusiastic reports. Certainly the Place de la Concorde equaled the madness of the month before. It was one vast illuminated dance hall with no room to dance but enough for embraces and close confetti throwing. The memory of bloodshed was now a bit dimmed. The people of France too joined the people of Germany in the hope and belief that the tall, thin, ascetic messiah had come to announce the new great age.

To M. Poincare, the President promised a permanent peace and punishment of the guilty. To the socialists he said that from now on the world must cooperate through the instrumentality of a league of nations.

Two days later the victorious French Government refused the social-ists and labor unions a permit to march by Mr. Wilson's home. The President remained at his window, waiting to salute the workingmen of France. He did not know of the governmental action. MM. Poincare and Clemenceau had not told him.

They sent the police and the military to frighten and subdue the "pacifists." There was no parade, although several thousand, unorganized, straggled through the cordons. The next morning the victorious French press denounced the workmen of France for bowing to Wilson "like sup-plicants at the passage of a King."

British labor too held a meeting and announced simply, "We are behind the President." The reactionary Northcliffe press was duly alarmed. British and French journals of the Right agreed that Mr. Wilson, whenever he chose, could upset the premiers of both governments by merely expressing a wish for more liberal regimes.

Meanwhile the President was seeing the Italians Orlando and Sonnino, asking them to reduce their exaggerated claims for more terri-tory in Europe. At the Sorbonne he received a degree and said, "My con-ception of the League of Nations is just this—that it shall operate as the organized moral force of men throughout the world."

All the oppressed nations sent kings, princes, premiers and delega-tions to Mr. Wilson and called him the sole arbiter of the New World. President Masaryk came with thanks for the new nation of Czechoslovakia. The Poles did the same. In colorful robes the Sherif of Mecca touched his head and his heart and bowed to the ground. General Skoropadski, hetman of the Ukraine, presented his claims. For anti-Bolshevik Russia, Professor Paul Miliukoff gave advice. From America came word of the lifting of the food ban, of "open hostility to liquidating loans to France"-of resentment of the soldiers in having no say in the making of peace and their "hostility to a bone-dry law passed without the soldier vote."

For Christmas morning Mr. Wilson cabled that "the certainty of lasting peace is our Christmas gift."

The President spent the day with the army. "It must be a people's peace," he said.

Very faintly the sniping of Messrs. Roosevelt, Knox and Lodge began to be heard in Europe; very faintly European politicians began asking whether or not the American people were behind their representative, or only his own party, or that party divided.

Accompanied by several hundred journalists, Mr. and Mrs. Woodrow Wilson crossed the Channel escorted by three British destroyers, starboard and larboard, which cut patterns in the quiet waters. In London the President received "the greatest welcome given a foreigner in British history, a people's welcome."

King George himself provided the visitors with ration cards for butter, sugar, jam, oleomargarine, lard, meat. A neat gesture! While the heads of the English-speaking nations dined in Buckingham Palace, the press was given a banquet in the Savoy. Sir George (now Lord) Riddell presided. Anglo-American friendship was cemented in oratory. A Virginia editor, fortified by port and champagne, made the following speech:

"Gent'men: Before the war I used to think the British were a godamned lot of sons of bitches, but now . . ."

He was dragged down, and the next day's big event, the luncheon by Lord Northcliffe, was divided into two parts, many of the cementers of international bonds eating at a second table, about a mile away.

Nineteen-eighteen came to an end. Mr. Wilson returned to Paris to fall out with M. Clemenceau before continuing his Mohammedlike hegira to Rome. M. Clemenceau openly declared himself for old diplomacy, the balance of power.... "If such a balance had preceded the war, if England, the United States, France and Italy had agreed, say, that whoever attacked one of than attacked the whole world, the war could not have occurred. the system of alliances, which I do not renounce, will be my guiding thought at the peace conference...."

Mr. Wilson did not take this seriously. "If the future had nothing for us but a new attempt to keep the world at the right poise by a balance of power, the United States would take no interest in it," he said and believed all he would have to do was to explain to his brother idealist and all would be well.

He went to Rome to receive the homage due to a messiah. He paid no attention to the news that an American attack on the Archangel Front "with light casualties" had resulted in Bolshevik villages and blockhouses being captured, that France had issued her claim for Armenia, Lebanon, Syria—the word "protectorate" dared not be used and the word "mandatory" had not yet been suggested. The American Army of Occupation had ordered the burgomasters to refrain from celebrating the New Year with customary noise, with conventional firecrackers, and all enemy citizens had to be indoors by eleven o'clock. American soldiers, previously ordered to refrain from talking to German citizens, were additionally

warned "not to fraternize with German children." The press viewed with
its daily alarm Italy's seizure of territory along the Adriatic. France now
claimed more purely German territory beyond Alsace and Lorraine, and
poor little outraged Belgium proposed the annexation of Luxembourg
and pieces of Holland, while "Poland is threatening and perhaps actually
has occupied Danzig, a German city, with a mere sprinkling of Poles, thus
to cut off East Prussia and West Prussia." It was unjust, alarming, said the
Allied press; it was a new *casus belli* with which to open the Peace Year.

The "most powerful figure in the history of the world" arrived in
Rome. Pope Benedict sent a New Year's message to the American people
"as the champions of these same principles which have been proclaimed
by both President Wilson and the Holy See, insuring the world justice,
peace and Christian love." The President visited the King and the Pope.
The Pope presented him with a mosaic judged to be worth $40,000. It was
placed in the trunk with the gifts of King George, King Victor Emmanuel,
and the presents in gold and silver and precious stones from lesser and
greater men.

Long, long afterwards, Mr. Wilson learned the truth about this visit to
Italy. To a committee of notable citizens which included a prince and
many officers decorated for heroism, he said he had chosen Rome for his
great appeal to all the peoples of Europe to join the American people in a
friendship which would never again be broken by dissensions and wars.
He did not know that this committee was repudiated as "Red" and that the
government had sent regiments of soldiers to threaten and club the
100,000 Romans who had come to the Palazzo Venezia Square. President
Wilson was not allowed to talk to the European public. The monarchy was
sacred.

In Genoa batteries from the hills thundered welcome and workingmen knelt behind the lines of soldiers and prayed to Wilson as to their
favorite saints.

In Milan he said, "The social structure rests upon the great working
classes of the world; these working classes in several countries of the world
have by their consciousness of community of interest, by their consciousness of community of spirit, done perhaps more than any other influence
to establish a world which is not a nation, which is not a continent, but is
the opinion, one might say, of mankind."

The socialists and the labor unions dominated the celebrations. They
were joined by the Liberal Party, the Catholic Party, the Union of
Reformed Socialists and the Republican Party. For one day the govern-

ment's censorship was lifted from press, speech and thought. The people of Milan were free—for one day.

They called upon Wilson to smash imperialism, the enemy's and also their own. Forty socialist mayors carrying red flags, appealed to him to help Italy in the appalling industrial situation. He replied that the League of Nations would surely do something. The government was angry.

A certain Milanese editor, whose name was later to cause a shiver throughout the Continent, wrote a headline: "Welcome to President Wilson in the name of the traditional ties of democracy." A typographical error crept in. It read "traditional lies of democracy." It was a portent. The writer of the headline was Benito Mussolini.

Mr. Wilson returned to Paris and the serious business of saving the world. He read with some concern the speech of Senator Lewis saying that "a conspiracy existed of Republican senators, for political purposes, to belittle the President and make his mission for world peace a failure."

On the 12th of January, 1919, the Peace Conference opened informally in Paris; on the 18th formally in Versailles. Just halfway between these dates it became apparent that it had already failed in one of its main points. Mr. Wilson's proclamation of a peace of the people, not of governments, a peace made with pitiless publicity, was completely negatived by the announcement that the Supreme Council of the Associated Nations would meet in secret and that a bulletin of accomplished facts only would be published. The world was thus banished from advising, debating, criticizing, participating, in the peace.

M. Clemenceau had urged secrecy. He had won. The battle for publicity was in reality the battle for a just peace. It was waged by the American Government and the American press. It failed. After the American protest to President Wilson, the British press protested to Lloyd George. What had become of "open covenants openly arrived at?" There was no answer.

Today the reason for this black diplomacy is only too apparent. It is not the "sharp and not diminishing discords" among the premiers, as officially announced by Reuters, but the fear these premiers had that the workingmen, the peasants and the soldiers back home would destroy them when they learned the truth about what was happening in Paris.

On Saturday afternoon, 18 January, at three o'clock, the Peace Conference opened under the presidency of Premier Clemenceau. Fanfares of trumpets greeted the delegations. Mr. Wilson additionally was cheered. A ruffle of drums announced M. Poincare. M. Clemenceau declared that the first subject to be discussed was the proposal of a league of nations. Not a king was present, not a prince, and every man there had a beard or was bald, except the American representative, the only clean-shaven diplomat. There were no women present.

To the arsenal which M. Clemenceau had prepared for fighting Mr. Wilson there was added at that last moment a report from his jurists that the Kaiser could be punished for the war. The report quoted Wilhelm as having written to the Emperor of Austria:

> *My soul is torn asunder, but everything must be put to fire and blood.*
> *The throats of men and women, children and the aged, must be cut, and not a tree left standing.*
>
> *With such methods of terror, which alone can strike so degenerate a people as the French, the war will finish before two months, while if I use humanitarian methods, it may prolong for years. Despite all my repugnance, I have had to choose the first system.*

M. Clemenceau kept his hand on the report, ready to answer any wild Wilsonian claim for leniency with the Germans. Interpreting Lloyd George's speech, Lieutenant Mantoux referred to M. Clemenceau as "a grand youth."

"No, no," interrupted the British Prime Minister; "I said 'grand young man'; that's different."

The congress laughed. It was the only note of humor in a grave afternoon.

The victory in placing the League first on the agenda was followed in Versailles by another victory for President Wilson. Russia would be recognized. All factions, Bolshevik and anti-Bolshevik and monarchist and emigre, would be invited to a truce conference on the island of Prinkipo, where Mr. Wilson would help them form a true government of all the people.

"They [the Associated Powers]," read the official announcement, "recognize the absolute right of the Russian people to direct their own affairs without reservation...."

Bolshevik Russia at first was willing. But Serghei Saonoff, the Tsarist Minister who was later disclosed as not having stopped the mobilization of Russia when the Tsar himself was willing to postpone the war, speaking for his people, informed the congress that "I refuse to sit at the table with assassins." Other Russian factions did likewise. The plan was forgotten.

Mr. Wilson proposed to sink all submarines and to forbid building new ones. That little plan too was soon forgotten.

On the 25th of January the League of Nations was unanimously adopted. Three days later President Wilson could report another victory; all annexation of colonies was dropped by the winning nations. Instead, the League would own them and would distribute mandates, here and there. Mr. Wilson was having victories all along the front. Soon he proposed that the blockade against Germany be lifted so food could be sold. But the French objected, saying the Germans might spend money on eating which they should save up to pay war reparations. The French won.

The French won, the Japanese won, the British won, the Poles won, everybody won; and Mr. Wilson either did not realize his defeats or, as the majority of his critics now agree, hoped to win everything back through his League of Nations. What Mr. Wilson did not realize was that the people of Europe had begun by backing him, would have backed him, had he fought through the conference without a single compromise, and that their faith in him was going, was gone; it was now too late to regain their confidence with his high words.

The vicious Continental European press was again in power. One who saw clearly, Mr. Wilson's delegate to the impossible Prinkipo conference, William Allen White, did tell the American people what was happening. He noted that Wilson was being attacked by the reactionary press of the world, that he was no longer in February of that fatal year, the "Christ come again" of January, whom Italian peasants worshiped. Now only the social democrats of the world were in unflinching support. The labor unions were sympathetic but already suspicious. In Italy the scandal caused the monarchy by the Wilson visit was being stilled by the monarchist newspapers. In Paris the press made constant attacks on the President: he was personally ambitious, an egotist, a seeker of power, and he was of course pro-German. M. Clemenceau deliberately used his venal press to poison Franco-American relations. The only nation permitted to receive uncensored reports of the negotiations was the United States, but the French censor tore up the best part of the two American newspapers printed in Paris. The Army Edition of the *Chicago Tribune* and the Paris Edition of the *New York Herald*, for example, tried to report the plan to remove the Peace Conference to a neutral country and they had reported the desperation of the American delegation in the face of the continued propaganda attacks from the French press.

Le Figaro, La Liberte, Le Journal des Debats, then turned on the press in America, even to accusing the *New York Times* and the *New York World* of being pro-German and the several hundred correspondents at the conference of carrying on German propaganda. They deplored the fact that American news was not censored. As usual, one of those "better Americans," those expatriates who are always apologizing for their own dear country, was given an opportunity to speak. Thus the pro-French bunkum of Walter Berry, president of the Chamber of Commerce in Paris was headlined, "Boche propaganda is inexhaustible" in *La Liberte's* attack on the newspapers of America.

The day came when President Wilson read the covenant establishing a league of nations. 15 February was gray and misty outside. Mr. Wilson's voice was as gray and misty as the day. He droned. He read without accent, color, human feeling, in a tired, middle-aged voice. Once or twice he exchanged small smiles with his wife.

The gentlemen of the press were the first to realize that some great event was taking place behind these tired words, that some new Magna Carta was being announced, some new declaration of independence of all the nations of the world.

There was no applause. A dull translation into French followed.

The next morning it was hailed throughout the world as marking a new stage in the social and political progress of mankind!

Mr. Wilson cabled every member of the House and Senate Foreign Affairs Committees to wait silently until he returned. He sailed for home. Most Senators, regardless of party, were of the opinion he had violated the Monroe Doctrine. He was soon to learn how true were the angry words of former President Theodore Roosevelt, who had addressed the nations of Europe a fortnight after the Armistice: "Wilson has no authority whatever to speak for the American people at this time. His leadership has been emphatically repudiated by them."

The German national assembly in Weimar listened "in agonized silence" to Matthias Erzberger, delegate to the new armistice conference in Trier, giving General Foch's new terms. Erzberger had protested. General Foch, he said, replied that, "These are purely military measures in accordance with Wilson's Fourteen Points." They were nothing of the sort. Foch, said Erzberger, had told him that the terms had "the unqualified approval of President Wilson." Mr. Wilson was on his ship and could not be questioned.

Kurt Eisner, Red Premier of Bavaria, was assassinated by Count Arco-Valley.

An anarchist named Emile Cottin fired seven times at M. Clemenceau, wounding the premier slightly.

"Why did I do it?" he replied to the police. "Because Clemenceau is the greatest enemy of humanity.

"I wished the man who is preparing for another war to disappear.

"I am a friend of man, not excepting the Germans, a friend of humanity, of fraternity. This is my red-letter day."

Aged Clemenceau, agile despite his eighty years, a little man with a very large head, round and bald, a man with sad blue eyes, lay in bed fighting for his life. He had been fighting for the life of France. He must not be misunderstood. For him there was nothing in the world but France, no league of nations, no brotherhood of man, nothing but his own people, his own land; and this conference was the turning point in the history of his nation, and he would die rather than have it turn the wrong way. To Italy, for instance, which was demanding the domination of Southern Europe, which wanted to replace Austro-Hungary as dictator of Balkan destinies. To England, for instance, who wanted her old privilege maintained, domination of the Seven Seas for at least another century and arbiter of Continental balances.

Landing in Boston, Mr. Wilson said, "No nation now suspects the motives of the United States." He addressed Governor Calvin Coolidge and the American people. "I have fighting blood in me and it is sometimes a delight to let it have scope, but if it is a challenge on this occasion, it will be an indulgence." And more of like rhetoric.

M. Clemenceau recovered, Mr. Lloyd George waged Mr. Wilson's battle until his return. The French thesis that Germany must starve and keep its money for reparations was nullified when the British premier read a telegram from General Plumer, commanding the Army of Occupation, saying "The British soldier would revolt rather than continue to be compelled to see starving children and women on the streets of the German towns." The Allies sent a communication to Weimar offering food until August—also insisting the German merchant fleet be delivered at once.

President Wilson returned to France and to secret conferences, where his Allies continued to destroy the Fourteen Points, leaving him only the League. The traditional spoils of war were being divided traditionally. One day the President revolted. He would make no more concessions. At last his American eyes had been opened. All his principles were involved. He ordered steam up in the *George Washington*, which was to come to Brest and take him away from France forever.

Wily Lloyd George called in the editor of *Le Matin* and gave him a long interview denying there was "divergence among the negotiators." *Not a word appeared in the French press of Mr. Wilson's threatened withdrawal; for three days, from the seventh to the tenth of April, the crisis was suppressed in the newspapers in Paris.* Meanwhile Wilson was pacified. The Monroe Doctrine was written into the League. Negotiations proceeded. On the 20th of April there was a crisis in Italy's claim for Fiume. Italy produced her secret treaty, the infamous corpse of secret diplomacy which the Bolsheviki had exposed in November 1917. The treaty had been printed everywhere and every one in the world but Mr. Wilson knew about it. Italy had sold her support to the Allies for a definite price. Paragraph Number IV gave her "Trentino, the whole of Southern Tyrol, as far as its natural and geographical frontiers, the Brenner"; Paragraph Number V gave her Dalmatia; Paragraph Number VII gave her "the right to conduct the foreign relations of Albania," etc. On the 21st Italy bolted. President Wilson, the "New Saviour of democratic Italy," had become the abomination of nationalistic Italy in just 15 weeks.

Then Japan struck. While Messrs. Clemenceau and Lloyd George were begging Wilson's concessions for Italy to restore the conference, the Japanese decided to ruin it completely unless their secret desire to seize parts of China were publicly gratified. With the world falling down, the Allies surrendered to Japan. Japan received more in Kiaochow and Shantung than Germany had ever had. The Chinese delegation cabled home, "We have failed in our mission to the peace conference. Shall we stay?"

But they did not leave. Then a conciliatory note, with terms about Fiume kept secret, was despatched to Italy, and on 7 May:

In the main hall of the Trianon Palace Hotel at Versailles, at tables which almost formed a square, the most drastic peace terms ever imposed upon a great nation were given to Germany in the solemn French hope that Germany was forever crushed.

The Chasseur Alpin guard of honor had blown fanfares at the arrival of all the notables. It was withdrawn just before the Germans rolled up slowly in French military limousines, noteworthy "prisoners of war." Instead of a military salute, they faced a rattle of camera shutters.

M. Clemenceau sat at the center of the head table with President Wilson at his right, Lloyd George at his left. When the German delegation filed in, there was the tension, which a notable journalist, Herbert Bayard Swope, described as "the same feeling as in court when the judge pronounces sentence of death on a murderer."

M. Clemenceau said:

"Gentlemen, Plenipotentiaries of the German Empire: "It is neither the time nor the place for superfluous words. . . The time has come when we must settle our account.

"You have asked for peace. We are ready to give you the peace....

"We must say at the same time that this second Treaty of Versailles has cost us too much not to take on our side all the necessary precautions and guarantees that the peace shall be a lasting one...."

All present noted that M. Clemenceau addressed the losers as representatives of the German Empire, not Republic. It was deliberate. France had no faith in the change of government reported from Weimar and Berlin. For the coming four or five years it was to show no belief in republican sincerity. M. Clemenceau continued for a few minutes. He had sentenced the criminal to death. A secretary tiptoed across the hollow square and laid a copy of the treaty in front of Count von Brockdorff-Rantzau. It was as simple as all that.

To the anger of M. Clemenceau and the surprise of the diplomats of the world, the German delegate asked to be heard. There followed an incident unequaled in the history of the century. Count Brockdorff-Rantzau did not rise. He had been so ill he could hardly walk into the hotel. Starving Germany could not have sent a better picture to the Allies. To give himself Dutch courage, Count Brockdorff-Rantzau had also taken several small drinks of brandy. Not only did he not rise but he did not ask permission to sit while speaking. He spoke:

"Gentlemen: We are deeply impressed with the sublime task which has brought us here to give a durable peace to the world. We are under no illusion as to the extent of our defeat and the degree of our want of power. We know that the power of the German army is broken. We know the power of the hatred which we encounter here....

"It is demanded of us that we shall confess ourselves to be the only ones guilty of the war. Such a confession in my mouth would be a lie.... We energetically deny that Germany and its people, who were convinced that they were making a war of defense, were alone guilty....

"In the past fifty years the imperialism of all European States has chronically poisoned the international situation . . . the disregard of the rights of peoples to determine their own destiny contributed to the illness of Europe, which saw its crisis in the World War....

"Crimes in war may not be excusable.... The hundreds of thousands of noncombatants who have perished since 11 November by reason of the [food] blockade were killed with cold deliberation after our adversaries had conquered and victory had been assured to them. Think of that when you speak of guilt and of punishment."

As Count Brockdorff spoke, those who understood him looked at M. Clemenceau. When the interpreters began translating, the Tiger squirmed, frowned; it was feared he would forget himself and let his anger silence his enemy. But he merely kept on repeating "Louder, louder" in a pained, angry, exasperated voice. He leaned over to President Wilson, kept whispering during the translation, then subsided into his chair as if bored by such useless talk.

The delegates were shocked, electrified, knocked breathless. They could not believe their ears; their eyes were reserved for M. Clemenceau, the father of victory. And when the German in conclusion accused the Allies of murdering hundreds of thousands of innocent people by the food blockade, dignified diplomats gasped heavily.

The next morning the French press tore its hair in anger. What! The Germans had dared ask for Justice instead of Clemency! Unheard-of arrogance! The French and the Allies had been insulted. Not once, but three times. As Count Brockdorff was being helped up the steps of the hotel "he threw a cigarette among the Allied officers"; moreover, sitting at the conference table, "he broke a paper cutter placed before him"; moreover, "he showed no respect for the treaty because he placed his gloves on it."

Impotent rage could go no further. One may well wonder today whether the recorders of this insolence and arrogance might not smile a little over their own brave words. Perhaps they might also admit that old Count Brockdorff that day was just as heroic a figure as those machine-gunners who had chained themselves voluntarily to their guns to hold up the enemy while their brothers retreated in safety.

On the 28th of June—the French chose that day because it was the anniversary of the shot that started the World War—in the Hall of Mirrors of the Palace of Versailles—the French chose that place because the Germans in their foolish pride had used it to proclaim their Reich—the treaty of peace was signed without any noteworthy incident.

The Prince of Peace returned to a land which knew him no more.

Though Wilson suffered defeat at home, his magnificent phrases did not cease to echo throughout the world. Slick gentlemen like Lloyd George, Poincare, Clemenceau, Mussolini; idealists like Masaryk and Pilsudski, De Valera and Griffith; bombastic D'Annunzios, crafty Feisuls, humanitarians, patriots, and crooks were repeating noble promises to the people and coining new ones.

The two elements that were to contribute most to the making of the new age, which might even establish a poetic parliament of man, a federation of the world, were the men in uniform, the 50 or 60 millions, and the laboring masses. It was not forgotten that the Russian revolution had been started by workers and soldiers, committees later called soviets, and that the German revolution was the act of the sailors, soldiers and workingmen who had organized their Arbeiter-und-Soldatenrat. The leaders of all nations promised:

A new world. (Do not be content, said Lloyd George addressing labor, with anything less than a new world.)

A land fit for heroes.

Freedom and justice for labor (Resolution of the Pan-American Labor Conference meeting in Laredo, Texas, Samuel Gompers presiding, in 1918).

End of conflict between capital and labor; workingmen's cooperation in industry (promises of Schwab, Giolitti and others) .

Land for the returned soldiers (in America, Britain, Italy, Bulgaria, etc.).

A new deal for everybody (Lloyd George).

Industrial Democracy (Wilson).

The problem that faced the world of peace was the returned soldier, the workman, and the soldier turned workman again. In America every Sunday the newspapers and every month the magazines blazed forth with beautiful and inspiring stories of the new freedom and the great result of the war: friendship, cooperation between capital and labor. "Partners in the Future of America."—"We have entered upon a social era," predicted Mr. Schwab, "in which the aristocracy of the future will be men who have done something for humanity and their nation. There will be no rich and no poor."

When New Year's Day, 1919, dawned it was believed in Anglo-Saxon lands and in the new republics of Europe that the voice of Labor would dominate the peace conference, which having arranged the political problems to the satisfaction of every one, would provide a decent standard of living throughout the world. Gompers came to Paris not merely to advise the President, but to organize the International Labor Federation which would supersede the Second Internationale, the Third Internationale, a score of national labor organizations, and work with kings and premiers in organizing the promised world cooperation of capital and labor which would approach Utopia. In January, Mr. Gompers had the blessings of America.

But in February, or March, or April? As the Versailles meeting turned into a conspiracy for national ambitions, the hopelessness of international action became apparent. The labor movement in every country was denounced in the same press which was encouraging the politicians to more land and commerce grabbing, as radicals, Reds, socialists, Bolsheviki. Even the mild support of Mr. Gompers to certain unionizing attempts was termed an attack on the traditional individualism of America.

The labor problem was met in all countries with suppression and bloodshed. The soldier problem proved easier in one land, harder in another. In Italy, the capitalization of soldier discontent and the organization of jobless privates and officers gave one group of crafty farseeing industrialists control of a government and raised one man to unparalleled powers.

Soldiers throughout the world were disgusted, angry, disillusioned. The second Grenadiers, the first regiment to return London, marched the streets to the tune "Hail the Conquering Hero Comes" from massed bands. Twelve men of one original battalion and not a single officer who went with it to France survived. The press reported that the men laughed and smiled. They did not. They marched in gloom and sadness. Other soldiers came back and found no work. Some went into the Strand and Piccadilly, selling their war medals. The politicians feared a bad time was coming.

In the spring of the first year of peace, numerous veterans' associations appeared in the United States, including one which was not only socialistic but almost openly communistic. To put an end to all individualistic movements, Lieutenant Colonel Theodore Roosevelt, Jr., in April 1919 issued a call for a convention in May in St. Louis for the purpose of organizing the American Legion.

The American soldier had not shown himself as articulate as the British, the German, the Italian. Nor had he yet found leadership. Most important still was the fact that the majority was civilian, despite the uniform, and civilians were the best haters in the world. On the day following the Armistice the march of socialists to celebrate the German republic was attacked by soldiers in New York. A crowd leaving a hall where speakers had said Tom Mooney's trial had been unfair was assaulted by uniformed men who beat women to the ground, while policemen stood by, refusing to use their clubs on heads covered with military caps. In Utica, some time later, American Legion lads cut electric-light wires, leaving Fritz Kreisler to play 40 minutes in the thrilling dark, but in New York City the Legion gave the same Austrian a testimonial. In Bogalusa, Louisiana, three were killed in a fight between the Legion and a miscellaneous mob. Soldiers led a crowd of good citizens of Washington County, Texas, which took Anton Pawlosku, whipped him in the public square, painted him yellow, and forced him to march through the streets carrying an American flag and shouting at each prod of the club, "To hell with the Kaiser" and "Hurrah for Uncle Sam" at the alternate prod. That was on 12 November 1918.

Hatred and intolerance had been organized better in America than anywhere in Europe. The rioting, the violence, the brutality blamed on soldiers just following the Armistice and for a long time afterwards was generally the exhibition of civilian emotion clad in khaki. Soldiers did not hate. At least, not until they had been absorbed in new movements, new hysterias.

When serious American war films were shown in Europe, soldiers frequently collapsed with laughter; when "Shoulder Arms" went the rounds of camps and troopships, there were sometimes tears. For such a contribution to patriotism as the Fox film, "The Prussian Cur," there could be nothing but disgust. The scene showing a soldier crucified by the Germans was "vouched for by a Baltimore clergyman who gives instances where four Canadians were crucified in one room."

Fifteen years of investigation have failed to find any proof of this or thousands of other reported German atrocities. The real soldiers did not need refutation. They knew that the war was made up of individual and mass murders and not atrocities. Such films were for civilians. It went on, up to the Armistice and after. Chancellor Day of Syracuse had decreed that "it is religious to hate the Kaiser" and the leader of the Chicago Ethical Culture Society in an article, "The Duty of Hatred," spoke of the time soon coming "when the wild beast has been caged so that he can no longer burn, poison, rape and destroy," and the press was printing letters from "A Soldier Boy's Mother," protesting, after the war, against the sending of food to the starving children of Vienna and Berlin, mentioning atrocities, adding, "I think the mother of every other American soldier boy will agree with me in saying that no mercy should be given to them."

The returning soldiers, not the first to come back and get the ovations, but the men who had been in the trenches, were amazed at this envenomed spectacle in America. Even the prize-winning ship-building poster with "Build to Kill" was a shock to many. Those who had suffered in the Villers-Cotterets drive, had seen the fields strewn with their own dead outside Thiaucourt, had gone through the Argonne hell, did not come back to join in the hysteria of hatred. Frequently the men in uniform preaching revenge for atrocities were none other than the heroes of battles with sardine cases and cartons of cigarettes of Brest, Bordeaux and St. Nazaire.

Long before the Armistice, Philip Gibbs had found that the Germans were human beings. He saw them frequently in the middle of a battle as the British line advanced. "Truth was on their lips when I met them, for men do not lie when they are still trembling with horror and when their life is a miracle of escape.... They cursed the war as an outrage against God and men."

At the beginning, in France, Gibbs had found that in this one European country there were no pacifists, no conscientious objectors, and all men said, "This is the war to end war. By our death we shall overthrow militarism and win peace for the world."

But as the bloody years dragged on without peace, Gibbs heard these same soldiers say "to the statesmen and diplomats, to the newspaper men and commercial men, to the jingoes and breeders of hate, and exploiters of world markets, and financiers of wealth produced by labor": "You also are guilty. We, who are going to die, accuse you also as our murderers. Your villainy, your stupidity, your poisonous philosophy, your betrayal of Christian ethics, and the old spell words of falsity which you put upon those who were ignorant as we were ignorant, have helped to bring about this beastliness. You are only a little less to blame than those Germans who were more efficient in the same evil use of power and in their hold over the minds of their people. We shall go on to the end, but after the end there will be a beginning, and a new democracy enlightened by the revelation of this war will sweep away the old frontiers of hatred, the old spell words, the old diplomacy, and arrange new relations between civilized peoples based upon mutual interests instead of fear and force."

The Russian soldiers had walked home from the Front in 1917. Before leaving the trenches they had fraternized with the Germans. It was not

Bolshevism then, it was fraternization, the very same thing that had occurred the first Christmas of the World War on the Western Front when the British, French and Germans shook hands and traded food. The Russian soldiers had been betrayed by their Tsar, their generals, their munition profiteers; they were driven in dumb herds to the front and their dead bodies covered fields two and three deep. There had been no slaughter like that in history. Those who at last walked away from the Eastern Front had spoken of peace and tyranny to their German friends. This is what Ludendorff calls the Bolshevik virus which ruined his army's morale.

These real soldiers were the men who came home hating the war.

The longer they were in it, the more certain they were. The battle-fields of Rupert Brooke of the early days of fighting became the battle-fields of Siegfried Sassoon of later time.

> *"The place . . . rotten with dead; green clumsy legs*
> *High booted, sprawled and gravelled along the saps;*
> *And trunks, face downward, in the sucking mud,*
> *Wallowed like sandbags loosely filled;*
> *And naked sodden buttocks, mats of hair,*
> *Bulged, clotted heads slept in the plastering slime."*

The soldiers, the real soldiers of Flanders and the Chemin de Dames and the Argonne and Verdun, were sick of the war and sick of the civilians who made the war, and sick of everything civilian, including civilian gloating in enemy suffering and enemy dead. Sassoon saw these hate-filled civilians in the London theater, watching one of the many war plays, heard some one say, "We're sure the Kaiser loves the dear old Tanks."

> *"I'd like to see a Tank come down the Stalls,*
> *Lurching to ragtime tunes, or 'Home, sweet Home'*
> *And there'd be no more jokes in Music-Halls*
> *To mock the riddled corpses round Bapaume."*

A French poet, Marcel Martinet, addresses "the civilians of unshrinking courage, around their writing desks, their dining tables," urges the soldiers to

> *"Come, come with outstretched hands,*

You with burnt eyes, with eyes thrust out,
With noses gone, with stinking wounds,
You, hideous without lips, without jaws even;
Your faces are a terrible scar; approach,
And closing in, and pressing all around,
Stare at them with your dark and sightless sockets—
At these fine folk who don't believe in pity!
... The non-combatants who stand so firm...."

Songs of hate were written by civilians in training camps, perhaps, or in Tin Pan Alley. They were heard only at home. Marching around the front the Americans once sang, "I didn't raise my boy to be a soldier" or sentimental ditties of peace years, while British Tommies had "Keep your head down, Allemand," a friendly advice on how to avoid a bullet in the head, or more often,

"Take me down to the sea,
Where the Allemand can't get at me;
Oh, my, I don't want to die,
I want to go home."

Which the British army did not find treasonable. Seeger and Kilmer wrote poems of the Rupert Brooke era, heroic and sentimental. After the Armistice, high dispute raged in the American ranks over the authorship of the army's newest and most popular ballad:

"Darling, I am coming back;
Silver threads among the black;
Now that peace is drawing near,
I'll be home in seven years.
When the next war comes around,
In the front ranks I'll be found,
I'll rush into war, pell mell,
Yes I will—like hell, like hell."

No, they would never go to war again, these Sassoons and Martinets who had seen the riddled corpses at Bapaume and the hideous faces of their comrades or the legs of their brothers sticking out of shallow graves. They would never go to war and they would never hate the Germans, who had turned out to be human beings and who probably never did cut off children's hands or turn soldiers' bodies into axle grease. Probably nothing but propaganda to all those stories. They were coming home to live in the lands fit for heroes. But if danger threatened those lands, if the Bolsheviki were destroying, burning killing, raping—if, as the papers said, they were nationalizing women and property, destroying the church . . . reaching out into the labor unions in London, Lancashire, the coal mines of Pennsylvania—if they had already gained most of Germany and were preparing to invade France—if the Labor Party was already tainted and likewise the American Federation of Labor and the Confederation Generale du Travail, if—if—

In the first few months of 1919, the universal craving for a new world, political and industrial democracy, lands fit for heroes, and all that sort of idealistic ballyhoo was diverted into Red hysteria, lynchings, supernational adventures, patriotic intolerance, civil wars, bloodshed and violence throughout the world.

The same soldiers who swore "This must never happen again," the same shouters of "*Nie wieder Krieg*" and "*Jamais plus de guerre*" were marching in the Rhineland and the Ruhr, fighting in Archangel and Siberia, erupting into Vilna and Fiume. Hatred and intolerance were remobilized; redirected. Morally and militarily. The new crusades led into many lands and many continents of the universal emotions.

How far and over what road had the world traveled since that day in December 1918, when the French Foreign Minister in the Chamber of Deputies, after announcing his peace terms, heard the shout, "The war is beginning anew," and the day in December 1932, when Colonel House wrote that the aim of new Roosevelt administration would be "to liquidate the war and liquidate it finally!"

It had traveled the road of war—war with other weapons. It had at least proved that the Versailles treaty was only a prolongation of an armistice—an armistice now in its 15th year. It had brought about its own economic collapse through its refusal to solve its problems in an international cooperative way. And finally, in February 1933, it had to listen to the Japanese delegate to the League of Nations, Yosuko Matsuoka, threaten a second world war if the nations attempted to enforce any sanctions against Japan's plan for Prussianizing the Far East.

The economic war begun Armistice Day had resulted in defeat for every one. The reparations war against Germany had resulted in defeat for every one. The armament race had drained the budgets of the world and helped on the economic debacle. The causes for war written into the Treaty of Versailles remained unchanged in the 15 years of armistice. The situation in Europe summed up by an Allied general (Fuller, of Britain) sounds hopelessly true. "The hegemony established by France," he concludes, "is intolerable. The pre-war diplomat were *escrocs* . . . those of today are bandits. They speak without ceasing of peace but do nothing to permit its establishment. The present Austria is an anomaly. The Polish frontiers cannot be maintained. The Corridor is a veritable anachronism. The Baltic States cannot continue to live. The situation in Hungary is a crying injustice. The vanquished nations are disarmed; the conquerors increase their armament each year. These are the results of the French panic.... War itself would be preferable to the present situation."

Against the resumption of armed conflict, the League of Nations, after five years of preparation, adopted at the close of the first part of the Disarmament Conference, 23 July 1932, the Benes Plan for a substantial reduction of world armament to include naval, air and land arms. Airplane attacks against civilian were forbidden, bacteriological and chemical warfare were forbidden, the reduction of national defense budgets was recommended and an armament truce extended four months! "Wars will be able to continue, but they will be humanized." That was the progress made.

It had been written in Versailles that the world was to follow Germany in disarming but all nations had forgotten that clause "The immense land armaments of France," Lloyd George mourned in 1932, "are a glaring and arrogant breach of the undertakings."

Yet France also had a case to present to the court of world opinion. In 1870 she had realized she would never regain her lost provinces without outside aid. She signed treaties, indulged in foreign friendships, plotted with Russia. Nineteen Eighteen taught her she would never retain her gains without outside aid. She lost America, then Britain, then Italy. She was forced to join with Poland, Yugoslavia, Rumania and other minor countries. Her one program became Security. But no great nation was willing to countersign it, surely not faraway America. Economic destruction of Germany therefore became the implement of the policy of security.

The League of Nations did not make up for the Anglo-American failure to guarantee France. But the League could be made into a weapon. So France, after deriding it, accepted it and sought to dominate it. She built up the French hegemony of the Continent, defeating all diplomatic and financial efforts of England and other nations, sabotaging the peace and disarmament conferences when need be, and laughing realistically at the Utopian demand of her public enemy Number 2, Russia, that the nations of Europe cease talking disarmament and actually disarm.

The only great step towards peace was the destruction of the reparations war against Germany—at a time when the imininent German national bankruptcy threatened to bring Bolshevism to the Rhine and to the threshold of France. Like the Versailles Treaty, the end of reparations was acknowledged in the lengthening shadow of the Red Kremlin. The Lausanne conference of 9 July 1932, fixed the total amount due at 714 million dollars—Germany was ordered to pay just one cent on the original dollar the victor nations had asked.

"We have reached, I believe, the best conclusion that could be reached for world peace," exclaimed Premier MacDonald, while the German chancellor chafed because the "war guilt lie" was not erased from the Versailles Treaty.

In 1918, some 15 million minority peoples were under Pan-German dictatorship; in 1933 of 80 million Germans, no less than 15 million were under the rule of foreign nations.

In 1918, Lenin quoted Marx to the effect that a class war is inevitable, once a socialistic State becomes successful. In 1933, Stalin quoted Lenin to the effect a war between Communist Russia and its capitalist neighbors was inevitable.

1919 saw the Japanese defeating the treaty makers by threatening to quit the conference unless their spoils were legalized; in 1933 they were defying the world on account of Manchuria.

1918 saw the Kaiser fleeing to Holland in fear and trembling; 1933 reported him packing his baggage for a return to emperorship.

1918 found the world not only fighting for peace but insisting on international disarmament as its best guaranty; 1932 heard the renewed demand of Germany for a larger army.

1919 found all the victor nations girding themselves for a great commercial recovery; 1933 found such stagnation in international trade— there had been a 60 percent decrease in four years due to economic nationalism and tariff barriers— that an official American observer on the preparatory committee of the 1933 world economic conference predicted that all international trade would cease by May 1934.

1919 saw Clemenceau chopping off the political heads of generals who might want to ride into the Quai d'Orsay on horseback; in 1933 the Duc de Guise, pretender to the throne of France, issued a proclamation of monarchy to save the country from "the oppression of socialistic anarchy."

1919 saw the beginning of Fascism in Italy. Raids, riots, street fights, reprisals, burning and looting, the Fascists armed, the labor organizations and socialist clubs practically disarmed, finally victory by a private militia and a strong leader; 1933 found Fascism triumphant in Germany in the very same manner, with Hitler proclaimed dictator for four years.

In 1919 some 20 million were demobilized; 1933 found new standing armies of five million men (France with her reserves included had more than that number)—the largest known in times of "peace." Five billion dollars a year was the price of war preparations in 1931, 1932, 1933 (provisionally).

"While millions are on the verge of starvation, growing restless and ugly," broadcast Senator Borah, "from 80 to 85 percent of all taxes extorted from the people go for war purposes. All this is another name for slow and inevitable suicide." His words were "magnificently and justly howled down" by the Fascist Jeunesses Patriotes at the Trocadero, Paris, peace congress.

1919 found all the world emerging from a great catastrophe with a spirit of idealism it thought justified the slaughter of a generation; 1933 finds it hoping it will emerge from hunger and suffering, once more to enjoy radios and automobiles and the materialistic comforts of a scientific civilization.

1918 saw several hundred million men stirred by a vision of a noble world; in 1933, 30 million had their bread taken away and many times that number thought of nothing but jobs.

For 15 years the stale phrase about making the world safe for democracy had been mouldering in its grave with its creator—the reaction to the World War had been the inevitable and opposite one. Democracy appeared to be in a decline. Revolutions, it is true, had come out of the war and some people had been liberated, but almost always the victor nations plunged backward into tyranny. The movements of progress, individual liberty, public liberty, private emancipation, collectivism, international cooperation, Wells' Cosmopolitanism, the religious and political soap-box idea of the brotherhood of man, had been overwhelmed by nationalism, conservatism, super-patriotism, dictatorial egotism and the wild scramble for spoils, wheat fields, African and Asiatic mines, for naked races to exploit with calico sheets, for land and more land for surplus populations.

"Men who remember the last war seem to be preparing for the next," wrote Sir Phillip Gibbs. "Nothing was learned, nothing was settled by that monsterous struggle. The ruin of it still exists. The economic downfall of civilization is due to that and to nothing else, because of the heritage that was left in men's minds and the destruction of intelligence."

1918-1933: On all fronts, military, economic and spiritual, there was not one day of peace. The panorama changed: the world moved on, no one could predict whither.

Lenin

In this piece from You Can't Print That, *Seldes shows the human side of Lenin that the history books have forgotten. He has often said that Lenin was one of the few revolutionaries he had known that had a sense of humor. In contrast to the other great leaders of his time, Lenin did not encourage any cult of personality and talked about the failures of Soviet communism in equal measure with its successes. By the time of his death, the Soviet bureaucracy wielded more power than Lenin did. Still, Seldes ranks Lenin among the most important figures in human history.*

LENIN HIMSELF was not stronger than the censorship and the Cheka.

Many people trembled when the name of the dictator was mentioned. But in dirty little offices sat little grey bureaucrats who changed Lenin's speeches when they feared he had spoken too dangerously, and in other dirty little offices sat military political police officials who bragged that they would arrest the man if he acted too dangerously.

When we said to the censors, "Lenin himself said this," they laughed. When it served their purposes they added or deleted, and sometimes they suppressed Lenin entirely. When it pleased them they arranged interviews, but for years they did their best to keep the "capitalist" journalists out of Lenin's sight.

We heard him, however, at all the big congresses.

He spoke with a thick, throaty, wet voice. He was in very good humor, always smiling, his face never was hard. All his pictures are hard but he was always twinkling with laughter. Eyes bright, crows feet, a real, unserious face. He had a clever motion of the hand by which he could emphasize a point and yet steal a look at the time on his wrist watch. Frequently he pointed with both index fingers, upwards, shoulder high, like the conventional picture of a Chinese dancer.

When he announced the occupation of Vladivostok and added imperialistically, "We will never give up a single conquest we have won," he seemed surprised by the sudden burst of nationalistic applause which followed. Frequently he dropped his voice, stuck both hands into his coat pocket, threw back his head, and said something ironic. Sometimes he spoke from the left side of his mouth.

In the loge on the left stood Unschlicht, a dark agent of the Cheka, surveying the house. Always in the shadow. A man of shadows. In the Kremlin, in the Red Square, in the Bolshoi Theater, wherever Lenin went, the dull, grey, one-day-unshaven face of Unschlicht of the Cheka, was there, somewhat hidden. Little cruel eyes, furtive, quick, dangerous, nervous, forever watching, forever suspicious.

But the mob was always stricken with hero-worship. It cried "Long live the Savior of Russia, long live the protector of the poor," when Lenin arrived. Then he spoke.

"We have come to the doors of Utopia," said Lenin without emphasis, without the theatrical effect of Mussolini who knows a good line when he utters it. Lenin continued simply. "Utopia no longer remains in the dreams of mankind, for we have brought it to earth. Not today nor tomorrow nor in a year shall we enter it, but Utopia is now within sight of the people of our time."

It was his first speech to the common people in many months They sat transfixed. If he were as bombastic as Napoleon or Mussolini you could doubt his sincerity, but he spoke so plainly and with a full heart. Three days earlier he had addressed the delegates to the Third International, a selected gathering of leaders of Communism, orators, debaters, parliamentarians in various lands, a supercilious lot. In neither speech was there any sentimentality, but to these last he could argue world politics.

"We have made stupid mistakes," he said, and a little shudder went through the delegates. Communists never make mistakes. They are Marx's chosen people and can do no wrong. No revolutionary ever admits mistakes. Lenin was the great exception. But even he offered excuses.

"We have made stupid mistakes. No one knows better than I. Because Russia is backward, because we have had no outside help, because we are bureaucracy-ridden.

"Enemies will say Lenin himself admits stupidities and mistakes. I say our mistakes consist of saying two times two are five, while the undoubted stupidity of the Entente and the Second International consists of saying twice two equals a wax candle—or the Versailles Treaty."

The first time I heard and saw Lenin was the day of his first public appearance after his long illness, during which his death had been reported to a satisfied world several times. It was the throne room of the Czars, in the Kremlin, full of tables, chairs and benches. The magnificent windows, the gilt and brocaded walls, and the painted ceiling alone reminded one of ancient splendors. A huge red sounding board had been placed on the stage; behind it, carelessly out of joint, stood the Romanoff throne, no longer an object of curiosity. Krylenko was speaking. This man who had led the illegal Red terror which had claimed thousands of lives, now advocated a change in the code of laws—more laws. The 300 listeners composed the All-Russian Central Executive committee. They came from all parts of Russia and they were all cold. They sat in their fur coats and fur hats on which a greasy sweat had gathered, and they illustrated how terribly human beings can smell. They buzzed and yawned.

All at once there was a stir at the door. Two soldier guards stiffened. They have been told to await someone important and to be careful of passes today. They do not know why but they know their duty.

A little man in a plain black coat, hat in hand, approached them. They did not recognize him and demanded the red card. He fumbled in his pocket and presented it. He looked more the small sleek business man than a communist leader. The soldiers with peasant difficulty made out the name, one read and nudged the other, who read also, and their dumb faces opened in astonishment. The little man passed.

Krylenko was speaking drearily about more laws. The little man came into the room, passed our press table, and I noticed he was walking on his toes. Lenin tip-toeing so as not to interrupt the speaker. Not until he got to the first two steps of the platform, softly, did the congress recognize him, and there was an uproar. Everyone rose. There were a few shouts. By actual count it was an ovation of 35 seconds. While Lenin, who hadn't paused to acknowledge the applause, was still shaking hands with the men on the platform, Krylenko resumed his speech. He had the good sense to cut it short.

Another 20 seconds of applause greeted Lenin as he advanced to the speaker's pulpit. He had discarded his coat. He was dressed in a cheap grey semi-military uniform, a civilian transplanted into ill-fitting army-issue clothes. They were grey-black but the crease in the trousers was already giving because there was too much shoddy in the wool. The tunic, which was high like the American doughboy's, was open at the neck revealing a flannel shirt and a bright blue necktie, loosely tied. His eyes were not half as oriental as the photographs have made him, because he has full eyebrows, not merely stubs at the nose, which the pictures emphasize.

He glanced at the audience in the high arched room, cathedral-like but for the plain windows through which the sun comes in garishly. He looked behind him, at the wall where there is a masonic sign, the Eye of God, which has beheld a dynasty of Czars. Outside the palace are the Kremlin walls; snow-lined, battlements and buttresses, towers with royal pennants in iron, the permanency of the Romanoffs in iron mockery. Beneath, the River Moskva, slow and muddy, drab and lazy, partly frozen, reflecting the gold and azure and red Kremlin in a mighty, tarnished way. Khaki-clad soldiers move in line like centipedes, their coats long to the ground, sweeping the snow along with no sign of individual feet, the effect of mass and machinery, with white human faces in ugly brown helmets, with bright red stars.

"Tavarashi—Comrades," Lenin began.

It was a historic moment for Russia, but no histrionics. He had to tell them of a victory on land and a victory by diplomacy. He reported on foreign and domestic affairs. He never hesitated to acknowledge defeats and failures. But he was always optimistic. My disillusion was profound. I wondered how this man, who has so little magnetism, had come to the fore in a radical environment where spell-binding oratory, silver-tongued climaxes, soap-box repartee, have been the road to success. Only once did he aim to produce a laugh, and even that had his touch of irony. "We have pruned and pruned our bureaucracy," he said, "and after four years we have taken a census of our government staff and we have an increase of 12,000."

He concluded and the congress took a recess. Everyone went to another room, one of the most regal—I shall never forget a delegate trying to pick diamonds out of the cross and crown emblem set in each of the doors. Lenin, Kalinin, Ziovieff, Kamineff and Cheka agents jostled the delegates, the newspaper correspondents, the peasants in their sweaty sheepskin coats and hats, all in good humor, crowding, elbowing, shouting, while the inevitable Soviet photographer tried to organize a historic picture.

Finally it was taken, and we American correspondents crowded around him. "Do you speak Russian?" he asked in Russian. "No, English," we said. "I speak her, ze English language—not zo verry good," replied Lenin and his pronunciation was confirmation. He could reply in German.

"I occupy a large portion of my time with American affairs," he said. "I am interested in everything Senator (William) Borah (an opponent of the League of Nations and at that time chairman of the Senate Foreign Relations Committee) does and says. I watch all events regarding Japanese-American relations. I am interested in the American elections." Then he smiled again and added:

"Your American newspapers frequently report me dead. Let them fool themselves. Don't take away the last hope of a dying bourgeoisie."

We tried to ask all the political questions we could think of, but he was nervous and parried.

"How do you like Moscow? Not quite like New York?" He laughs quietly as if ashamed of his Babbittry.

The artist of a New York newspaper made quick sketches because Lenin was fidgeting to be free. Lenin gave the artist another moment.

"The world says Lenin is a great man," said the artist in his thankfulness.

"I am not a great man, just look at me?" Lenin replied with a gesture deprecating his size and emphasizing his simplicity.

On another occasion he showed the same stubborn prejudices which characterize all the revolutionary leaders.

"When is the war between Japan and America coming?" he asked. He was assured there would be no war because there are no causes for war. "But there must be war," he insisted, "because capitalist countries cannot exist without wars."

But he could return to his broad ironic views. To the Briton of the press corps he said:

"As you know, we in Russia have only one party, and we have to wear ourselves out without a relieving shift."

Is this hypocrisy? There were other parties once, notably the Mensheviks, also radical and communistic, but the Bolsheviks have driven them to Berlin and Paris and Siberia, slaughtered members by the thousand and finally annihilated the movement. But Lenin took the curse of this hypocrisy when he added:

"I think we shall begin a two party system like the British or American—a left and a right party—two Bolshevik parties of course." He laughed.

While Trotsky and all the small orators in Russia were snapping at America, Lenin, who was wise and who had a sense of humor, saw the futility of a radical movement in the prosperous United States.

"You might as well shoot peas at the rock of Gibraltar as to arm the counter-revolutionaries against us," he said, "and in America it is the same: do you think the weak handful of Communists we have there can upset the American form of government by talking much and by making futile little plots?"

Lenin was big enough to see the humor of many little radical episodes. He was fond of telling the story of some labor troubles at the time when he was a refugee in London. He was already known as a Socialist leader then and many times shop committees brought him their troubles. Once, he said, there was a plan for a strike in some works and a delegation came with many complaints, about which they were not definite and could not agree. Finally, in desperation, he asked them for a clear, final statement.

"'All we want,'" he said the chairman told him, "'is world revolution and better toilets!'"

He realized keenly his weakness as an orator, and feeling his lack of power over certain classes of listeners who were bored by fine thinking and quick clear reasoning, he would say twice or three times in his discourse: "I assure you I am not telling you lies."

Frequently he would speak in foreign languages. His many years of exile in Switzerland had made him conversant with French and German, but he was not sure of himself. He would approach the speaker's table nervously, draw papers from his pocket, put his hands to his head as if parting hairs which were not there, and after waiting patiently for noise to subside, would begin in German. Words would fail him. He would then whisper the Russian word to a nearby friend who returned the correct teutonic, quietly, which Lenin would quickly grasp and turn it with force upon his audience. It was an actor being prompted intelligently.

Although militant Communism or the reign of terror was the direct result of attempt on Lenin's life, he tried to stop it. He was never told the truth about the extent or viciousness of the Cheka system. Lenin hated bloodshed.

When Bela Kun was defeated in Hungary and came to Moscow he was received as a hero. Lenin, who knew masses better than individuals, made the mistake of sending Kun to pacify the Crimea after an uprising. In accordance with Lenin's suggestion an amnesty was published among the "White Army" officers and leaders. They were asked three times to register and Lenin's name was pledged for their personal safety. Thirty thousand are said to have registered. Then Bela Kun, in accordance with instructions which the Cheka sent out without Lenin's knowledge, erected forests of scaffolds and hanged all of the 30,000 he could find. Lenin heard of this atrocity. When Kun returned to Moscow Lenin refused to take his hand or listen to explanations of military necessity. He did not want Bela Kun around. The Hungarian ex-dictator, however, was in favor with the Cheka, and could not be cast aside. But he remained in disfavor with Lenin so long as Lenin lived, and most of that time in far away places. (Of course the censor never let us mention the Kun incidents.)

When they addressed him as "Comrade" Ilyitch the word had real meaning: for other leaders it was ridiculous, a word too often profaned. Lenin had the greatness and the human, all-too-human sympathy to be a comrade to all, the group of fellow dictators and the peasants who loved him. In battle with his enemies he was uncompromising and without pity.

He hated power, knowing its corruption.

His political wisdom was great; he understood mob psychology thoroughly but was a little weak in his grasp of individual psychology; he never made a mistake in dealing with the masses but he frequently did in choosing men to share power.

As an orator he was my greatest disappointment. Not understanding a word he said, I waited for his dramatic effects. There were none. Socrates sitting in the house of Cephalus and arguing on the floor was no less theatrical than Lenin addressing the peasant delegates to the Third International. He had no warmth. He was coldly intellectual. He was more effective with his fellow theorists.

His private life was the exact antithesis of Mussolini's. While his enemies blamed his sickness on youthful excesses, not a proof of them was ever produced; on the other hand his family life was exemplary. His moral purity, in another age and condition, could have been a claim to sainthood. He had no mistresses, no secret sex life.

Long before the Soviets changed the name of Petrograd to Leningrad, the peasants of his old home town showed their love for him by substituting his name for the village of Kukushkino. Lenin was so

pleased when the boys he played with sent him this remarkable letter, that
he put it into his diary:

"Dear Comrade Vladmir," they wrote, "do you remember the horses in the
woods we watched together at night? It was 45 years ago. We have now rid
our village of the landlords who for 15 years camped on our necks. Then
came catastrophe—famine. The cattle died. Our property was gone; our
houses were falling to pieces. The famine wiped out everything.

"We cannot send you a present. We have paid the grain levy and two
civil taxes. Two sorrows have befallen us. We have no horses and we have
no school in our village. We know the Soviet government is giving horses
on credit and we ask you as late co-villager to approach the government
for credit horses. Without this we are workers without hands; we have land
and nothing to work it with. We think it also necessary to inform you that
we have asked the Tartar republic to organize a school for professions and
literacy and to be named after your mother Mary Alexandrovno. In conclusion we ask you to save your health because you are the only one for us
in all Russia. When the school is built we ask you to come over to us as a
guest in order that we may reminisce over old days.

"Henceforth village Kukushkino is named after you, Comrade Lenin,
and now, until we meet again, with brotherly greetings,

The community of the Village Lenin.
(late Kukushkino;) "

Now Lenin is dead and worshipped by the peasants. Some never knew
him but as another Czar who supplemented the goodness of that
Alexander who freed the serfs, by apportioning the soil. A myth is growing
throughout Russia and a legend. He was divine, of immaculate birth, and
he did not die but ascended into heaven, where he sits by the side of the
Trinity as special intercessor for poor Russian peasants. This making a Red
god pleases all good atheistic Bolsheviks.

When I think of the Red god's appearance I see always that cheap
shoddy suit he wore. I see the neat crease in the cotton trousers holding
on like wool. In a year I saw Lenin many times and always in the same
clothes. First up from his sick bed the clothes were new. That was in the
Fall. But September's creased trousers became April's baggy rags. They
had held out bravely, as the man within had done. But finally they flapped
hobolike as if acknowledging the surrender of all pretence to bourgeois
respectability. Shortly afterwards Lenin died.

Isadora Duncan Starving, Offers to Sell Love Letters

This is the story of one of the great missed opportunities of 20th Century Literature, a book containing the love letters of Isadora Duncan. A pioneer of modern dance in the early part of this century, her personal life was as flamboyant as her performances. Seldes met Duncan in Berlin, where the excesses of her life had gotten the better of her. He took a gamble and attempted to collaborate with her on a book, What Love Meant to Isadora Duncan. *The book never got beyond the opening chapter, Duncan backed off from the project and returned to the stage. She died a short time later in 1927 in an automobile accident. Seldes wrote about this episode in his 1931 book,* Can These Things Be!

WHEN I first saw Isadora Duncan I was a child; at that time everything in the theater was wonder to me and I saw my adolescent vision of Greece, Diana coursing through the Attic landscape and Aphrodite rising in the best Botticelli manner pink from a cobalt sea, in the dancing of this marvelous girl. Of course I fell in love with her.

The next time I saw Isadora Duncan she was lying, large, bleary and not too sober, in a cheap room of a second-class Berlin hotel which she dared not leave because she had no money to pay her bill. Sic transit. It made me feel very ill.

But the result of that visit was the chapter that follows herewith, the introductory chapter to a book, *What Love Meant to Isadora Duncan,* a book which one of my editors contracted for and which she never finished. What has happened to the trunkful of love letters I do not know. Some of them are worthy of immortality.

When I came to see her in Berlin she said in one breath that she was glad the paper did not send a woman to interview her as she hated women journalists because they did not keep their journalistic faith as men did; they were always trading on their sex, she said, and that wasn't fair either, and they couldn't be relied on to keep confidences confidential, as men did, and wouldn't I buy her just one little drink?

I rang the bell and a waiter came. His manner said plainly he hadn't been tipped for a long time. He was disgusting. I asked Isadora if she wanted Rhine wine, beer, or a cocktail.

"Bring me a quart of gin," she said, suddenly sober enough.

"Will you pay for this?" the waiter said to me in a threatening, much too loud whisper.

I said, "Yes."

She poured a half tumblerful, drank it down, and said:

"There is no great art without perspiration."

She could still be witty, even brilliant.

"I'm at the end of my rope," she replied when I asked her about the reports I had heard in town. "I want to go to France to sell my house there, but the French Consul refuses to give me a visa, says I'm a Bolshevik because I once sang the 'Internationale' in public, and because I organized a school in Moscow for the miserable children there.

"I have nothing left in the world but these love letters—I guess I'll have to sell them." I think she spoke in jest, but it was this remark which caused an entire change in her fortunes, in her life perhaps, and got me this beautiful manuscript.

"I've got about a thousand of them," she continued, hauling out packets and loose sheets from a drawer. "And I haven't got a friend left in this world. Where are all the snows of yesteryear. Cold on the mountains! I used to keep open house. Liberty Hall! Packed with friends and admirers. Or at least so they called themselves.

"Yes, fair weather friends. I had lots of money then—and I don't know anything about money. It all went. I don't care. But now, no one cares to help me. Not only am I poor, but I have been in Moscow—I've worked

there for the miserable poor children—and of course all those sleek hyp-
ocrites are scared of me because the papers call me a Bolshevik.

"What if I publish these letters. Some of the writers, the great ones,
like Gordon Craig, won't mind. The others I don't care about. They are
going to ruin a lot of fat reputations perhaps, but why should I worry—you
can ruin almost any reputation, especially of a man or woman of independent mind, by yelling Bolshevik at them. Do you want to see the letters?"

She moved her puffed body, adjusted a wrap over the loose Grecian
red garment which hung shapelessly billowing from her shoulders, wob-
bled in her sandaled feet and held out a handful of letters. Her hair was
astray and there was only drunken luster in her once marvelous eyes.

"These are from d'Annunzio," she said, handing me some blue papers
written in a large florid way some twenty words to the page. "And these
from Gordon Craig." Pages not written but drawn. Every letter a work of
art—like the words on old Japanese prints. And each page embellished
with drawings in ink and crayon. Some were just drawings with only a few
words of text; some were words and pictures intermingled as one beautiful
work.

"And these from a man I like to call Lohengrin—very plain—a business man's hard handwriting. Here are some from—well, I won't tell you
the name now. He was my lover once, young and beautiful—now he's
married and has three children and writes no more great poetry."

She held her finger clumsily over the name, hiding only half of it.

I looked at the text of a score of letters from old lovers. Artist, poet,
business man, the letters were all aflame with passion. The dates were at
least ten years apart. Yet I remember the thought which occurred in each
and all. It was amazing:

"You are as precious and beautiful to me today as in the first hour of
our passion—you are the only woman in the world for whom my desire
was not cooled by possession!"

Yes, the poet, the artist, the business man, each expressed the same
idea in phrases differing in style and elegance, not passion.

"Yessenin's are in Russian," she said. "You won't understand them—
but they are as beautiful."

"Where is your husband?" I asked.

"Serge has gone into the Caucasus—to become a bandit. He wrote he
wants to get thrills. He will be a robber and write poetry about it."

"And your divorce?"

"Well, it's this way," Isadora replied, "in order to get a divorce in Russia it is necessary to file your application before 12 noon—but neither Serge nor I could ever get to the Divorce Commissariat by noon. We live at night, sleep by day. Now if the Soviets had had sense enough to open their divorce bureau at 12 midnight we would have been divorced—and probably remarried several times nicely."

She helped herself to a quarter-tumblerful of gin and continued:

"I think I'll put them all in the book. I'll call it: 'What Love Means to Different Men'—the poet, the banker, the playwright, the poor man, the idle rich. I'll group the letters under these headings—it'll make an interesting book, I tell you—real human documents."

I promised to help her get a visa to France and sell her book.

The next day, sure enough, I got a reply to my telegram suggesting buying the Duncan material. I was to offer $5,000 for serial rights. Mme. Duncan was to write a book based entirely on her love letters and was to reproduce as many of them as we desired. She could, however, keep the names of many of the writers secret. My cable cautiously concluded with "Unpay money until parts manuscript delivered."

Isadora was very happy to begin work, but she needed money to live on. As my office refused to advance her anything, I took the chance, and paid for her food and drink at the times I called, which was almost daily. I got her to write to Moscow to have her trunks, containing more letters, shipped to Berlin, and I found an English stenographer. Eventually Isadora began to dictate. She insisted that the stenographer come at midnight. "Life begins at midnight," she said, "the day, the healthy day with its sunshine, should be adopted by humanity for healthy sleep. Night is the time to live." She dictated all in jumbles. She would begin with Lenin, mix up her childhood in San Francisco, pass to her troubles with the French police, and suddenly take up Lenin again. My stenographer was wise, and rearranged the paragraphs. The first chapter was done in an hour of enthusiasm. Here it is:

"WHAT LOVE MEANS TO DIFFERENT MEN"
By ISADORA DUNCAN

LOVE AND IDEALS

"I find it difficult to write this book. I find it hard to speak when I know that every word is being taken down. I want this book to be something worth leaving behind. It will be worth doing only if it is a book which will help people to live. I want to tell the truth about my loves and my art because the whole world is absolutely brought up on lies. We are fed on nothing but lies. We begin with lies and half our lives at least we live with lies. Most human beings today waste some twenty-five to thirty years of their lives before they break through the actual and conventional lies which surround them.

"I am not an artist at all. Artists bore me to death. All the singers you meet talking about the A flats they can reach—all the violinists and pianists talking about the size of their audiences and the writers about the size of their royalties. They give me no pleasure at all; these artists are stupid. At a concert the only artist present is the man who wrote the music they produce; at a play the author of the text—theater artists are silly and egotistical persons. All artists as a rule are much overrated.

"Art is not necessary at all. All that is necessary to make this world a better place to live in is to love—to love as Christ loved—as Buddha loved.

"That was the most marvelous thing about Lenin: he really loved mankind. Others loved themselves, money, theories, power: Lenin loved his fellow men. They say to me, 'How can you be so enthusiastic about Lenin—he did not believe in God.' I reply: 'That is simply a phrase, Lenin was God, as Christ was God, because God is Love and Christ and Lenin were all Love.'

"Do you love mankind? Lenin did. That's why he was supreme—because he really loved. When the world once really understands this it will be a tremendous thing because most people really love nothing.

"And that is why I want to publish this book—not for money but because I want to show mankind it does not know how to love.

"What mankind calls love is only hatred in another form. In the flesh there is no love. I have had as much as anyone of that sort of thing which men dare call love—men foaming at the mouth—men crying they would kill themselves if I didn't return their love—love—rot! I had just barely come to the stage when it all began—this declaration of love. From all sides I was besieged by all sorts of men. What did they want? Their feelings, I know now, were the same feelings they have for a bottle of whisky. They say to the bottle, 'I'm thirsty. I want you. I want to drink you up. I want to possess all of you.' To me they said the same things: 'I am hungry. I want you. I want to possess you body and soul.' Oh, they added the soul all right, when they pleaded for the body!

"Was that love? No. It was hysteria.

"Love is the rarest thing in the world. Even a mother's love is largely egotistical. A cat loves her kittens up to a certain age. People talk of a mother's love as the most sacred thing in the world—why, it is just like loving your own arms and legs. It is simply loving a part of yourself. That is not the love I wanted. I wanted a pure unselfish love, the love for humanity, felt by Christ, and Buddha and Lenin.

"When I was in Moscow, I saw little children lying huddled asleep in doorways and on rubbish heaps. Would this be possible if there was love in the world? I took these children into my school and let them sleep there. After Lenin died the Soviet Government would no longer allow this. Was that love? Did you ever go to the East Side of London? What did you see there? If you did not see children actually sleeping in the streets as in Russia you must have seen them under conditions terrible enough. If there is such a thing as love in the world would people allow this sort of thing? Could they go to their comfortable homes knowing that there are children living in such distress? So long as little children are allowed to suffer there is no true love in the world.

"Men have loved me but my only love has been children. All scientific men, all doctors, are amazed at what I have accomplished with children. First of all, I take them very seriously. All children are very serious beings despite the fact that their parents and their teachers treat them as ignorant and inconsequential little animals. They come to me with all sorts of troubles, mental and physical. Many have rickets and bone disease. When I started my first school in Berlin, Geheimrat Professor Doctor Stoffer came to look at my pupils and when he saw them he exclaimed: 'These children are not for you. They are for me—they are in need of surgical care. This is not a school; it is a hospital. You will never make these children dance.'

"And you should have seen the children dance after a year! Simply because I let them do what they liked. I let them dance—I did not ask them to dance. Then I inspired them to better dancing, that is all. They grew and thrived and blossomed.

"Of course it may be egotistical after all. Oh, there is nothing like it. You feel a sort of god, you know. Prometheus! It is marvelous to be able to form human lives! I have taken these children from the lowest proletariat, weak and diseased and destined for misery and early death—the children of men who dig ditches and break stones on the highways—and before I left Moscow they were dancing in the Grand Opera and the people had risen and cheered while they cried.

"Once you are interested in shaping children's lives you will never be interested in anything else again. There is nothing greater. I have never taken a grown-up pupil or a paying one. I worked only when I could work for nothing.

"The world calls me a dancer. It says I have revived the classic art of dancing of the Greek era. But I am not a dancer. I never danced a step in my life. I hate all dancing. All I see in what people call dancing is merely a useless agitation of the arms and legs. I don't like to look at stage dancing. But I can understand ballroom dancing—the tango, for instance, as danced in Buenos Aires. It is quite wonderful there, in the little cafes with the low ceilings; it has a meaning. The man dances with the same girl all the evening and if another man tries to dance with her he runs a dagger through the stranger's back. This is the sort of dancing based on sexual desire and the right of possession. We see all the outward movement. But what of the inward movement, the movement of the mind? I am not a dancer. What I am interested in doing is finding and expressing a new form of life.

"I see only the ideal. But no ideals have ever been fully successful on this earth. Ideals always bring calamities in their wake. People with ideals frequently are driven mad. You follow an ideal, devote your life to it and you may go mad—yet what else is there? Nothing except ideals. Everything else is like having a good meal: it passes the time in a very charming manner and satisfies one of the principal desires of the flesh. That is all.

"Every two thousand years there come certain phases in human conditions and certain forces renew themselves. Ideals incarnate. We have Dionysius and Christ and Buddha—and the force of the present epoch is Lenin. I am certain that in a thousand years from now people from all parts of the world will come to Lenin's tomb, which will be a shrine. He was the person who embodied the new spirit, the renewal of the force of idealism and the new religion.

"I went to Russia because I am interested more in the time hundreds of years from now than the present. A practical person going to Moscow sees only calamity and general catastrophe. This condition followed the crucifixion of Christ and must follow Lenin. In ages from now people will realize this. Now they see only what is taking place—He saw the Ideal."

The next day the English stenographer came to my office, delivered the manuscript, and asked to be paid off.

"I don't like Mme. Duncan's ideas about morality," she said, "and I cannot permit myself to work for a woman who drinks gin."

I paid her, took the manuscript to Isadora, told her it was a fine beginning, and asked her if she would try to write the next chapter. She said she would, provided she could work after midnight and provided she could have a drink now and then to keep her in a creative mood. I promised the frequent drinks.

At that moment one of the many German political crises arose and for a few days I had other things to worry about. But one afternoon I found time to call on Mme. Duncan. She was extremely reticent. She tried to dodge the subject of a book of love letters. I pressed her, and she became angry.

"Look here," she said, "you've already published something about my selling my love letters. Well, I received some telegrams about that. Certain persons are much worried about the publication of these letters. I am sending a friend to France to see about it. I'll phone you about the book."

Days went by. No phone call. I called and got no satisfactory answer— usually a nasty remark from the operator in the hotel where the Duncan bill was growing daily larger.

A week later I called. Everything was in commotion. Smiling maids were packing a new trunk, and Mme. Duncan was happily superintending.

"I'm going to Spa," she said before I could speak. "To take the cure. I've quit drinking. I'm too fat, but I'll reduce in no time. I'm going to have a theater again. I'm going to Nice for the winter. Oh, you must come and see me at my first performance—"

"And your book—and the letters—?"

"Oh, that's all fixed up! Publish my memoirs now? What do you think I am? An old woman? Am I dead? Only the living dead publish their memoirs. Oh, I'll have time enough when I'm dead to begin to write them. Everything is changed now. Life begins again. Life begins again!"

That winter and another winter passed and a summer came. At Juan-les-Pins—where I was having a short vacation—I heard that Isadora Duncan had returned to her studio-theater in Nice. I asked one of her friends about it.

"It's a funny story," she replied. "It seems Isadora was down and out in Berlin once and told some reporter she was preparing to publish her memoirs including her love letters. Then she was very angry because that had got into the papers, but it certainly was lucky for her it did because some gentleman saw the paper and telegraphed her she was foolish, because it would ruin her career, and she had better return to her art— and they would get her a studio if she wished. And so everything has been fine for her ever since."

The theater was hung with deep purple velvet. The stage, which was piled with cushions, was prepared for seating the audience; a piano stood in the otherwise empty parquet. Isadora arrived in the same loose robe she had worn to lunch, a Greek robe lovely on a slim goddess, but revealing rather than concealing the enormous breasts, the distended stomach and the wide hips of a woman prematurely distorted by drink and carelessness. Her once expressive arms were thick and blotched, the flesh of her face hung in folds and her hair was badly streaked with purple and henna.

She pulled the narrow velvet covering from the piano and with ancient deftness threw one end over her shoulder and began encircling her body with the rest. At the same time her Russian accompanist began playing. And then a strange thing happened—I think it happened to all who were there because afterwards each admitted in a different way something of the surprise and thrill of the next few minutes. Because we had seen a miracle. There before us what had been a middle-aged woman, much the worse for hard wear in a hard world, had transformed herself suddenly into something fantastic and super-human. No, she did not dance—as she had danced 20 years earlier when I remember her Spring Song with a vividness of today. She moved, slightly, slowly. Her face became beatific, and kept changing with the music. Her arms, her legs, her body swayed, her head rose and fell, and out of her eyes a light seemed to shine, a light which so affected one as to blind one to the ugliness of aging flesh and weakened human features. It was not a dance; it was an interpretation of music as some Greek artist might have done before Sophocles, to prove to him that irony and pity could be expressed by the dance as deeply as by his tragedies and so achieve the same catharsis.

Then the music stopped, Isadora stopped, the miracle stopped. The mystic circle was broken. There was silence. We were too much moved to applaud or praise. We merely got up and walked with her into the house.

"Oh, I have just begun to live again," she said to her admirers.

I mentioned the book. "But I am not dead broke nor spiritually dead," she replied. "When I'm both I'll write anything for any publisher who gives me the money for a theater, for a school for children—yes, I must start all over again. I must have another school. But now I am happy. When I am unhappy, I'll write. Now I will dance."

Another year went by. All the money was gone. She was writing a book. But she never finished. One day as she went to ride in an automobile, the long red shawl she always affected, trailing behind her, caught in a wheel, so she met her death in just the same tragic, irresponsible fashion in which she had always lived.

Ave Caesar!

In this, the concluding chapter to Seldes' most famous book, Sawdust
Caesar (1935), *he examines the megalomania of Il Duce, Benito
Mussolini. For someone who was almost murdered by Mussolini's fol-
lowers, you might expect a vindictive discussion of his character by Seldes.
Instead, Seldes lets Mussolini expose himself as a foolish egotist through
his own actions and words.*

WHAT EVER the final outcome may be for Italy, for Mussolini the one
thing he confesses has worried him most has now been won: he has made
his mark in history.

There is, of course, nothing strange nor abnormal in the concern
which a leader of men feels about posterity; it is merely part of the
problem of immortality which has confused and inspired mankind from
its first intelligent beginnings. "I am obsessed with this wild desire—it con-
sumes my whole being," said Mussolini to his Egeria; "I want to make a
mark on my era with my Will, like a lion with its claw." It has been made.
The dictator may fall gloriously on an African battlefield or pass away
peacefully in bed half a century from now, but Clio has already provided
ample pages for the Duce's record.

For almost a quarter of a century he has wooed this muse, acting the
Hero, posing before men and moviemen, and time and history, eagerly
watching for the signs of his immortality. Even in his youthful soap-box
speeches he was already conscious of what press and public would say, and
as he grew to manhood he worked on his clipping-books with more enthu-

siasm than a Hollywood star, but always he kept looking ahead, to a place in the future where his name would shine on deathless bronze, when statues would be erected of his likeness side by side with the Napoleons, and better still, the Roman Caesars, and the gods and demi-gods of all recorded time.

At the Lausanne conference a group of diplomats on an upper floor, looking down an elevator shaft, beheld their newest colleague with his back to the operator, making faces and gestures before the rear mirror. The Napoleonic attitudes were unmistakable.

In the history of the world no man has been more photographed. The paintings, sketches, and busts of the Duce surpass in number those of any being to whom deity has not been seriously attributed. A great part of the leader's day is spent reading the press of the whole world, where every item dealing with him and his activities has been marked by subordinates. He reads them with the air of a man seeking something.

Although he never tires of fatalistic remarks about his destiny in the stars, he has retained the peasant superstitions of his childhood. Twenty centuries earlier analogous rulers, dictators, leaders, tyrants, conquerors, strong kings and frightened kings, were sending to the Delphic oracle or looking at blood and entrails, watching the flights of birds and reading signs in thunder and lightning. Mussolini seeks sybilline warnings in the newspapers and the history-books of other revolutions With the same eagerness with which Lenin, Trotsky, and Stalin watched the Bolshevik revolution take the course of the traditional French Revolution, each acting in his own way to defeat the Brumaires and Thermidores and circumvent the Little Corporals, so Mussolini, warned that history takes an inexorable course, strives to impress his superior will upon it.

Curious, but not surprising to psychologists, is this mingling of the belief in free will, predestination, fatalism, and the commonest Forli superstitions. According to Mussolini biographer Margherita Sarfatti, the village "witch," old Giovanna, taught Mussolini her "magic lore"; he became "an adept in interpreting dreams and omens and telling fortune by cards." He is quoted often saying, "My blood tells me" and "I must listen to my blood," and he once declared proudly, "*Que voulez-vous? Je ressemble aux animaux, je renie le temps qui vient, je suis mon instinct, et je ne me trompe jamais*" ("What would you? I resemble the animals, I scent the times, I follow my instinct, and I never make a mistake").

The Duce and the age of dictators have already been explained by the scientists. Freud has expressed his belief that nations, like human beings, can suffer a neurosis; Adler believes that people like individuals suffer from inferiority, struggle hard to shake it off and to become superior, and in the case of Italy and Mussolini the world has its best example. More recently Stekel has presented his authority complex to explain the weakness of the masses and the power of the Mussolinis, the "father-substitutes." The millions of inferiorities of the people mass together to become a superiority; the people identify themselves with the leader, partaking of his authority, and the leaders are usually neurotic, suffering from a "compulsion complex."

"Dictators in general," continues my colleague, John Gunther, in expounding the Stekel theory, "are a sort of regression to childhood. Love of a leader is a reversion to infantilism." Stekel concludes that: "For many generations men fought for democracy, liberty, the right of free assembly and free speech. Thousands of good men have died for these causes. But now one country after another gives up its free institutions, people even vote away their freedom. New dictatorial revolutions . . . are welcomed with relief, not opposed by force. There is a world scramble for authority, for the security of leadership. People everywhere, because their parental sense of authority has disappeared, are looking for a father-substitute, for a strong and beloved parental hand."

Germany in 1933 and Italy in 1922 are the most excellent proofs of the contentions of all three psychologists. Although Italy was known as one of the victor nations in 1918, it was greatly humbled in the peace treaty of 1919 which divided the war spoils among the stronger powers and left little more than a dispute over Fiume in the lap of their colleague. The Italian people, who had for a while come through the shroud of inferiority when Garibaldi and his Red Shirts appeared, were therefore in the psychologically ripe stage to accept the man of promises, the man of violence, the demagogue who defied the oppressors, gratified the national yearning for superiority, and wore a black shirt.

One of the seeming paradoxes of the Italian situation which Italy has not yet discovered, although it could do so easily by reading the officially printed works of the Duce, is that the embodiment of their wish-fulfillment neither loves nor respects the masses who follow him. Time and again Mussolini has quoted Machiavelli's opinion of the common people as "mud" and sneered at public opinion. But the more the Duce shows that he despises his followers, the more they shout their love and loyalty. Unlike the bourgeois gentleman, Lenin, who really loved the world-filling proletariat, the oligarch of Italy, in origin plebeian, almost hates them. "I do not adore this new divinity—the masses," writes the Duce, thereby confirming Stalin's view that even revolutionary leaders at times despise their following and that "an aristocratic attitude of the leaders towards the masses" frequently arises, an attitude which Lenin escaped because his faith in the nobility of the workingman was never shaken.

The greatness of Mussolini can only be measured by the lowness of his worshipers.

He stalks through the world like the one man who wears the mantle of Zarathustra, possesses the mind of Machiavelli, is the inheritor of the power of Caesar, while all the little minds, all the hundreds of millions of unimportant, unthinking, weak, and ineffectual human beings (whom Sinclair Lewis has both immortalized and crucified with a new word) grovel at his feet, proclaiming him the conqueror. Emperor or Galilean? The same hundreds of millions go to their churches on Sundays and proclaim an unarmed Man who was weak and humble, who preached humility and kindness and love and non-resistance. The other six days they arm for war and praise violence. The mob mind can worship both.

In all seriousness Mussolini has been compared by his idolators with everyone from Jesus Christ to Theodore Roosevelt.

After Farinacci's solemn declaration that Mussolini's only logical successor as Duce could be Jesus, the official Fascist press proclaimed the infallibility of its leader, a political dogma meant also for the eyes of the Pope.

No less a person than an American ambassador, Richard Washburn Child, wrote that "the Duce is now the greatest figure of his sphere and time. One closes the door when one leaves feeling, as when Roosevelt was left, that one could squeeze something of him out of one's clothes."

Inasmuch as the Duce himself permits painters to draw a lock of hair over the forehead in the Napoleonic manner, busts made very Caesarian, and a large proportion of the millions of photographs show him a la Bonaparte on horseback or assuming other heroic poses, it is obvious he invites comparison with the world-conquerors.

Mussolini would like to uphold the tradition of the "strong, silent man," but his passion for oratory prevents him from complete achievement. But that he should assume, consciously or unconsciously, the traditions of the world-conquerors, Caesar, Alexander, and Napoleon, is quite natural. All men arriving at similar heights, even the catchpenny Central American dictators, have been known to succumb to the role; Mussolini steps into it as an actor into his make-up.

The Caesar pose was most obvious to those who in April 1926, accompanied the Duce to Tripoli—to that very same colony the annexation of which caused the same Mussolini to attempt an armed uprising two decades earlier. Now he had mobilized more warships for himself than Giolitti had used for the war on Turkey; on the prow of the *Cavour* he strutted and took attitudes which every motion-picture operator worth his pay recorded deathlessly, or he sat with folded arms looking dreamily across the Mediterranean.

He disembarked, he stepped into Africa like a conqueror. The Tripolitans—at least those who were not at the time in rebellion—the native troops, the Italian army, the civilians and officialdom, made a grand uproar.

An American journalist, overcome with the sense of historic emotion, raised his hand and cried, "Ave Caesar!" To the Duce he said, "It is like the old days when a Roman emperor landed."

Mussolini, delighted, said, "Yes."

Others took up the cry. The sun-baked streets of a small African port in an unimportant African colony echoed with the shout of "Caesar," and that very evening numerous red, white, and green posters with the words "Ave Caesar," followed by Mussolini's speech, published by the Fascist officials, were placarded throughout the colony as the expression of its greeting.

Julius, the divider of Gaul, shines over Mussolini; the Duce looks into those cold pupil-less eyes every day while his press reminds him that he is the pure Roman emperor type in face and will, the true successor to the thrice-crown-refusing political ancestor. Even the textbooks of Italy have been changed so that today all the Caesars are unblemished heroes and the tyranny, corruption, and weaknesses of that ruler "who fell an easy victim to the cheap devices of the lewd Cleopatra" have been eliminated by the censor. To make their own hero greater, the idol of comparison has been cleaned and polished.

In the year of the Tripoli voyage Mussolini ordered that "within five years Rome must be restored to the grandeur of the Caesars"; and within a few months he told an interviewer that "we are in the process of renewing the glory of the Caesars. I have a bust of Julius Caesar always before me." And, although neither glory nor grandeur was completely renewed by 1931, in September of the next year Mussolini ordered the prefect of his native district to change the name of the Fiumicino River to "Rubicon." "Foreign visitors ask me where the Rubicon is, and we cannot show them," explained Caesar's successor; "Let us find our river." But he had already ordered the event. Thus it was shown to the world that a problem which harried historians and geographers had disputed violently from medieval times could be settled only through an act of dictatorship.

A year later, at ancient Arminium, where Julius Caesar supposedly harangued the legions for his—or, as it is now called, the first march on Rome, a statue donated by the successor was unveiled to "the great patron of Fascism, the first Black Shirt," whose "mighty conception which he gave to Rome and the world exists again in the blood of the race," and in Mussolini "the heir to the legacy which he bequeathed to Italy."

So the orators. To the podesta of Rimini Mussolini telegraphed: "The statue of Julius Caesar which I have decided to give to your city is similar to the statue in bronze which adorns the Route of Empire [Via dell'Impero, in Rome]. If possible, you will place high on the column the words which Julius Caesar spoke to the militia men of the Thirteenth Legion when, the die having been cast and the Rubicon having been crossed, he decided upon his march on Rome. Every year, on the ides of March, you will take care to beflower the statue of the founder of the Roman Empire."

Four times in his talks with Ludwig the Duce mentioned the man whose bust broods over him: once he confessed that "Jesus was greater"; another time that Shakespeare's play about the hero was "a great school for rulers"; again, "in thrilling tones," "Julius Caesar. The greatest man that ever lived.... Yes, I have a tremendous admiration for Caesar. Still . . . I myself belong rather to the class of the Bismarcks"; and finally, "The assassination of Caesar was a misfortune for mankind. I love Caesar. He was unique in that he combined the will of the warrior with the genius of the sage. At bottom he was a philosopher who saw everything *sub specie aeternitatis.* It is true he had a passion for fame, but his ambition did not cut him off from humankind."

Finally, in the summer of 1935, addressing several thousand former grenadiers, at the time of the mobilization for the Italo-Ethiopian conflict, he reminded them that "Julius Caesar once dominated the world and that every stone surrounding them should recall the fact." (They were crowded into the ruins of the Temple of Venus.) "Nothing forbids us from believing that what was our destiny yesterday may again become our destiny tomorrow."

From Alexander the Great, who sighed for new lands to conquer, and from the time of every prophet and messiah, men have wanted to rule the whole world or to make the whole world bow to their one idea. The men of power and egotism want to be king of kings and many modern rulers use that title. The Ethiopian is not bashful. Caesar, Kaiser, and Tsar are variations on the theme. The idea of world conquest will probably remain forever, even if it is to be eventually democratized into a sort of figure-head, a man of straw and sawdust, a super-secretary of a future super League of Nations, and appear to this individual only in his serenest day-dream of desire.

The last man to seize a large part of the world, Napoleon, called by H.G. Wells, an adventurer, a wrecker, a man of egotism and vanity, a per-sonality archaic, hard, capable, unscrupulous, imitative, and neatly vulgar, is still the hero of the mob. Mussolini has at least this much in common with the Corsican: they were both well-whipped children, therefore des-tined to a rebellious manhood. Bonaparte was whipped by his mother, Mussolini by his father; the one used a birch rod, the other a leather belt.

The mediocrity of the two minds is amazing. The Code Napoleon, which he claimed was a greater monument than his 40 victories, was written by other men. The plan of the Corporate State is not Mussolini's. The "totally uncreative imagination" of Napoleon was influenced by Plutarch towards a revival of the Roman Empire; Mussolini in all his words and deeds has shown the influence of the latest book he has been reading, the last strong-minded politician who has been advising him.

Napoleon was not above issuing contradictory and lying statements, as, for example, proclaiming to Italy that he was coming to free it from tyranny while he told his soldiers to loot the country and wrote to Paris he was going to make the newly conquered State pay an indemnity of $20 million.

When Napoleon faced the Council of Five Hundred he was as fright-ened as Mussolini the day he stammered about Matteotti and promised to "return to legality." Yet both men prided themselves on physical courage.

The Napoleonic plan by which the First Consul had under him an appointed Council of State, which had under it a legislative body and Tribunate, a Senate, etc., is very much the Mussolinian idea of a "hier-archy ending in a pinhead."

When Napoleon became First Consul the whole world was at his feet, there was peace, and any ruler with a first-rate mind would have done something creative to astound the centuries. (When Mussolini took office, he had the support of all parties, there was peace, and a man whose mind was not warped by egotism and lust for personal power could have given

Europe a lead in governing well.) Napoleon, says Wells, could do no more than "strut upon the crest of this great mountain of opportunity like a cockerel on a dunghill. The figure he makes in history is one of almost incredible self-conceit, of vanity, greed, and a grandiose aping of Caesar, Alexander, and Charlemagne which would be purely comic if it were not caked over with human blood." If Bonaparte's aping of Caesar was so ludicrous and so tragic, what can one say of Mussolini's aping of Bonaparte? Perhaps that while he had not a thousandth of Napoleon's success, he has shed but comparatively few drops of human blood.

Both men denounced religion as "opium for the people," Mussolini, actually quoting Marx's phrase, Napoleon in making the famous Concordat saying it was necessary to give the people religion to keep them quiet: "how can you have order in a State without religion?"

Whether either dictator ever felt remorse is debated by historians and chroniclers. It is said that Napoleon, during his fits in St. Helena, regretted his order to murder the Duc d'Enghien and sometimes wept for the dead. Only one person records a sign of regret in Mussolini. "The dead weigh heavily," he once said. On the occasion of the banquet which Italy tendered Ras Taffari, king of Ethiopia, the King and Mussolini found two beautiful envelopes in their napkins. Mussolini opened his and read:

"You are Matteotti's murderer; prepare for the handcuffs."

The King opened his and read:

"Majesty, Matteotti's murderer sits next to you. Give him up to justice."

The King turned pale, but it is reported that Mussolini hid whatever emotions this dramatic reminder provoked under a small laugh.

It is also said that Mussolini sometimes has fits of terror and plans to escape from Italy in an airplane or a yacht. But there is no actual evidence that the conqueror regrets anything.

Napoleon betrayed the French Revolution. Future historians may well say that Mussolini betrayed, or at least delayed, the Italian revolution.

Much more appropriate is a comparison between the Duce and Louis Napoleon, who, like his uncle, also betrayed his republic. For the *decret-loi* of Louis there are the royal decrees which Mussolini forces the King to sign and issues at leisure; there is the same perversion of justice, the liberal magistrates suffering the same fate as the French republicans, expulsion; university professors in the Third Napoleon's time were made to obey the political wind, too, and the press was censored and corrupted. Louis placed government largely in the hands of the omnipotent prefects, and Mussolini appoints sub-dictators called podestas. Hierarchy is similarly established. The pageants, exhibitions, and sports in France preceding Sedan are duplicated in Rome.

Louis Napoleon was vain, empty, trivial. His writings show small culture. He was, like Mussolini, mixed up in liberalism, socialism, and Napoleonism and likewise preached nationalist superpatriotism.

The similarity between the Italian Dux and the last German Rex especially in egotistic oratory, has already been noted.

Of the men who make history today, especially of dictators, one expects great, rich personalities. But Stalin is known for his metallic colorless voice, the absence of flourish, for the tendency to remain inconspicuous, and his inability to sweep an audience with enthusiasm. Like Lenin, he has "a sense of compressed energy, of reserved will power. He is not magnetic." Lenin and Trotsky I saw at the height of their fame; both surprised me because they had nothing of the Communist-Socialist-Radical speaker so well known throughout the world. Lenin reasoned as Socrates once reasoned in the house of Cephalus. The only dictator who answers conventional anticipations is Mussolini, who is magnetic and dynamic, wild, histrionic, who raises and lowers his voice as taught by the best professors of drama, becomes cold, waxes hot, erupts like his own Vesuvius and uses his hands, eyes, shoulders, and breath for the purpose of hypnotizing the mob.

Lenin was the only revolutionary who had a deep sense of humor; his successor, Stalin, makes jokes and laughs over them; frequently they are coarse jokes, and in this Stalin and Mussolini are similar, except that at times Stalin has been able to show a trace of objective humor, while Mussolini has never betrayed it. Intolerance is one of the secrets of Mussolini's success.

In almost every sentence of his speeches, in almost every page of his writings, Mussolini curses his opponents. He is always shouting "scoundrel," "traitor," or "egotist" at some one; his enemies are "soft-brained cowards," "swelled frogs," and "a base and pernicious crew"; he never hesitates to call the man who differs from his opinions a liar; with the utmost contempt he speaks of political enemies and those who have fought duels with him as weaklings, cowards; referring to foreign statesmen and journalists who have said he threatens the peace of the world he replies these are the "accusations of fools"; when he can find nothing evil to say of those whom the world honors he calls them "egocentric," he speaks of their "unbridled egotism"; he is always attacking those who "sell themselves for money, for power," whom he despises—and frequently the word "turncoat" comes up and the six four-letter words in Joyce's *Ulysses*. All of these beautiful phrases are culled from Mussolini's autobiography.

The words of attack most frequently heard are "traitor" and "physical coward" and "egotist"; with them he disposes of all who have met him on the field of honor or who write works on philosophy which fail to include the newest and greatest of all theories, Fascism; everyone who has ideas not in conformity is an egotist and anyone who acts non-conformingly is a traitor, while those who oppose him are cowards.

Need one go to a psychologist for the explanation of such behavior, or is ordinary intelligence sufficient guide? Marcel Proust speaks of "that habit of denouncing in other people defects precisely analogous to one's own." "For," he says, "it is always of those defects that people speak, as though it were a way of speaking about oneself, indirectly, which added to the pleasure of absolution that of confession. Besides, it seems that our attention, always attracted by what is characteristic of ourself, notices that more than anything else in other people . . . an unwashed man speaks only of the baths that other people do not take . . . a cuckold sees cuckolds everywhere, a light woman light women, a snob snobs." There can be no better explanation.

Again, when Mussolini declares: "I have annihilated in myself all self-interest; I, like the most devoted of citizens, place upon myself and on every beat of my heart, service for the Italian people. I proclaim myself their servant. I feel that all Italians understand and love me; I know that only he is loved who leads without weakness, without deviation, and with disinterestedness and full faith," a student of his character can find it the great self-confession of what he lacks most.

One thing he has is a blazing hatred. "Not," as one of his compatriots says, "the hatred of a social rebel which is but another facet of love, like the hatred of Brutus for Caesar, of Bruno for the Papacy, of Mazzini for the tyrants," or the hatred which inspired Milton and Byron and Shelley sublimely and which has made heroes and martyrs. Mussolini's dominating hatred, which was important to his success, was the drop of poison on the swift arrow of his Will.

Of this man's amazing egotism much has been said. It is the most natural trait in human beings who are failures to shout down the successful man, no matter who he is or what he does. Napoleon and Pericles are equally condemned. No distinction is made between the ego which drives a man to lead the world by developing all that is great and powerful within him, and the ego which leads another man to rise high by destroying others. Mussolini's ego is a compound. Sometimes it exhibits itself in all its naive crudity.

Three days after he had seized the government his old friend, Paolo Orano, a comrade who could call him by his first name, came into Benito's office, saying, jestingly, "I want to see how you are preparing to rule Italy."

"Preparing? I?" replied Mussolini, as Orano afterwards recounted. "Why, I'm already in the middle of it. I am ruling. I'll show you how I rule."

Mussolini pressed a button, summoned a secretary, asked that a telephone call be put through to one of the leaders of the march and of Fascism.

"Hello. I am talking. Mussolini. Be—ni—to Mus—so—lini. Listen. You are expecting to receive the field-marshal's baton. Fine. But you are not going to get it just yet. You—are—not—going—to—get—it—just—yet. Get yourself a small cane. Good-bye."

"There," he said to Orano. "I'm not here as a tourist, but to give Italy a government and to govern it. That never was before, but is now: a government. I am it. And all, mind you, all Italians shall and will obey. Italians have never obeyed. The Italians must be ruled and shall be ruled."

Mussolini threw his head high, as if to snap it from his neck and shoulders—a movement that Orano saw for the first time in this man, but which was to be immortalized later in a million photographs and many films.

When *Piemonte*, a newspaper of Turin, printed a questionnaire regarding Mussolini's greatness in history, the dictator telegraphed to the prefect of police: "Call the editor of *Piemonte* and ask him to stop the referendum. Tell him that Mussolini himself does not know exactly what he is and therefore it is difficult for others to judge him. The referendum can be resumed 50 years hence."

At another time he declared that "I am convinced that I am destined to rule Italy some 10 to 15 years more. My successor is not yet born."

The egotism of the ruler is transmitted to the youth of Italy. The Fascist publication for the universities thus informs the coming generation: "The Italian of tomorrow, and that means the Balilla and the Avanguardisti of today, will be the natural heir of the Fascist mentality, and will not need to discuss these four points:

"1. That Italy deserves to be the biggest and strongest nation in the world.

"2. That Italy will become the biggest and strongest nation in the world.

"3. That the Italian laws are the finest in the world.

"4. That the men who now rule are the best and that we owe them honor and obedience."

Of the noble traits in Mussolini's character none stand out more than his emancipation from the degenerate desire for money, exceedingly rare in persons who are born poor and who, on acquiring riches, frequently remain miserly through the fear of ever being poor again. Mussolini insists six separate times in his autobiography that "money has no lure for me." "I ask nothing for myself, nor for mine; no material goods, no honors, no testimonials." "I have annihilated in myself all self-interest." "In politics I never gained a penny. I detest those who live like parasites, sucking away at the edges of social struggles. I hate men who grow rich in politics." "To me money is detestable; what it may do is sometimes beautiful and some-times noble."

His enemies say that if all this is true, why did the Fascist official press, boasting of the new income-tax law, congratulate the Duce on paying his the first day—the sum of 200,000 lire, which would indicate an income of 500,000 lire and a capital of 10 million. And why, ask enemies, does Mussolini insist so much on his contempt for the lure of money, why does he mention it at least six times in his autobiography?

The truth is that Mussolini does not care for money—for himself. But he does not hesitate to use it as a means to power. The 1914 episode of the French funds for founding a newspaper, and the 1919 episode of the "diversion" of Fiume funds, and the 1920 episode of subventions from the employers, while exposing the ruthlessness of the man, are not, even in the charges of enemies, instances of personal greed. Money means power; more so in Europe than in America. In Europe a man is born in a class, and imprisoned in that class as in a fortress. The peasant begets peasants, the proletarian proletarians, and rare is the case of the youth who breaks the caste lines. The workman's son does not go to college and graduate into the professions, and the rich man's daughter never marries the foreman—a fact that causes a wrong laugh over many an American movie. Brains and talent and even genius are wasted in continental Europe because of class distinction and lack of money. And Socialism flourishes for the same reasons. Mussolini, hating money philosophically, has never hesitated to get it and use it to break himself out of his class prison.

Strangely enough, there is a mental parallel. He suffers from claustrophobia. All his life he has felt himself tied down, hemmed in, suppressed by invisible forces. He hated the confines of the schoolroom. He fled. One of the reasons he escaped military service was the dreadful appearance of the prison-like military barracks of his province, and although he tried to forget the iron bars of frequent visits by reading philosophy and politics, prison cells have left their lines on his character.

He cannot stand locked rooms. In the Chigi Palace every interviewer has remarked the enormous chamber some 50 or 60 feet long, which served him as an office. His spirit requires vast spaces.

He loves to fly in an airplane, enjoying the power, the superiority, and the freedom of an unpeopled infinity. He has refused to enter the Blue Grotto of Capri.

In exhibitionism he surpasses all the notable men of our age. Chicherin, the timid intellectual, once appeared in a uniform of the Red Army and did not cut a brave figure. The Kaiser was magnificent in shining breastplates, but Mussolini goes in for Central American splendor. The first time he addressed the Chamber he rigged himself in an operatic gold and spangles which gave the foreign ambassadors their first good laugh under Fascism. Short, stocky, bulgy, myopic, and fairly bald, he poses so well the world believes him heroically tall, with the most magnificent flashing eyes.

His literary judgments are sententious and weak. He is the author of such philosophical gems as "smoking is a distraction" and "the Will to Power is a cardinal point in the philosophy of Nietzsche" and "The hills and the sea give one the feeling of infinity." He has a college freshman's enthusiasm for Nietzsche's "blond beasts" and "the egotism which in men of power does not admit of restrictions"; he is impressed with Nietzsche's quotation from the Arabian sect of Assassins: "To see men suffer is good, to make them suffer is better."

Few of Mussolini's admirers have anything to say about his 20-year record of changing parties and ideals. Sarfatti, for instance, describes her hero as "impulsive and meditative, a realist and an idealist perfervid yet wise, a romantic in his aspirations, but a classic in his handling of public affairs, Mussolini has a groundwork of consistency in him underlying all these seeming incompatibilities." But a more worldly, less fascinated person, Mussolini's Cheka agent, Rossi, goes deeper into his employer's character. "How," asks Rossi, "can certain noble sentiments which Signor Mussolini expresses in his speeches, be reconciled with facts which put such grave moral, political, and penal responsibility upon his shoulders?

"His temperament, unstable by nature, as I am certainly not the only one to know full well, has, together with his mania for Machiavellianism, led him in the last few years into numberless acts of duplicity and change-ableness.

"By turns he is cynical and sentimental, impulsive and cautious, irri-table and calm, generous and cruel, quick to decide and slow to move, uncompromising and conciliatory.

"All the qualities of heart and mind have in him contradictory aspects, but in his activities as head of the government and of the Fascist Party, the tendencies which predominate are duplicity, superficiality, and improvisa-tion."

An explanation of the seeming incompatibilities in Mussolini's char-acter is offered by Adolf Saager: "This is the deeper reason for Mussolini's betrayals: His Unconscious always decides in favor of his hunger for power and his ruler instinct serves the political reaction in the nation; against which his Conscious is always still striving to some union with the Radicals. From that moment when his Unconscious (which is the unfalsified natural power of the man), becomes dominant, his actions gain certainty and con-tinuity, such as would delight an aesthetic observer in the actions of a preying animal.

"This explains Mussolini's periods of trembling and anxiety, because his Conscious and Unconscious are at war.

"Nothing is more ignorant than to understand Mussolini's coat-turn-ings and contradictions, his 'hypocrisy' and his 'betrayals' as signs of char-acter weakness; these things compose his very character, they are his destiny. This is his organic development."

There remains the question of greatness.

He is, for instance, a great journalist but a tenth-rate litterateur. His eloquence is marvelous—emotionally, not logically. He is a great politi-cian, a great leader of the mob, but he is a demagogue and not a statesman.

He is a genius at assimilating the ideas of other persons and making them his own.

He is totally unscrupulous.

He has never done anything original.

He has a tremendous will but an inferior mind.

If achievement is to be measured by such qualifications as strong, well-conceived ambition; difficult struggle to reach the goal, complete accomplishment of ambition; and of most importance, human value of the success gained by the man, Mussolini easily passes the first three tests. His ambition has been superhuman, his struggle one of the most noteworthy in our time, and he has accomplished everything his heart desired. But whether there is any great significance to his work, or any human value whatever, cannot so soon be judged.

Mussolini may found an African empire. He may in a small way emulate Julius Caesar. Or he himself may be destroyed by the monstrous State he has created, but he no longer need worry about his place in history. He has made his lion's mark. Even Mr. Wells, who somehow prefers Jesus and Buddha and King Asoka to the Caesars and Napoleons and Wilhelm Seconds, will some day have to give more space to the Fascist phenomenon.

History will say that Mussolini shows the triumph of the superiority complex, the triumph of Nietzschean catch-phrases, the triumph of the adapter of other people's ideas, the triumph of the book-made egotist.

Reactionary dictators are men of no element of greatness, men with no philosophy, no burning humanitarian ideal, nor even an economic program of any value to their nation or to the world. Grand and imposing as they look in their flaming uniforms and shirts in nationalist colors on marching days, they are almost forgotten the hour a change is made. Who now remembers Waldemiras? What country did he rule? What became of Pangalos? How many Bratianus were there and what happened to them? And how ignoble became that same Primo de Rivera who one day before had stood arm in arm with Mussolini, his treaty-friend, his proud disciple? But it is not too fantastic to imagine a time after Mussolini's disappearance, when the commentators will say that after all he was only a renegade Socialist who could never be trusted, a puny, sententious imitator of Lenin, a rather foolish repeater of Kaiser Wilhelm's foolish phrases, a man mentally and physically ill, a megalomaniac who thought he could change the course of economic forces by the use of magnificent phrases taken from Karl Marx, Nietzsche, Hegel, Vilfredo Pareto, and his former colleagues in the Socialist movement—and nevertheless a person worthy of statues. After all, he is the original Duce of Fascismo, and all the others are merely imitators.

All of Mussolini's monuments will be monuments to the strength of a weakling, monuments to the weakness of his opposition, to the cowardice of the masses, but, above all, monuments to an Ego and a Will.

Mussolini has made his mark in history, but history records the marks of warriors, suppressors, and vandals as well as saviors and liberators.

History and monuments will recall Benito Mussolini as a Caesar—not a Julius but perhaps a Caesar Borgia or perhaps a Kaiser Wilhelm. If not a Napoleon Bonaparte, then at least a Louis Napoleon.

Everywhere new statues appear of Benito Mussolini today and more will be erected in his lifetime. The statues of Julius Caesar will probably remain forever in Eternal Rome—but the day will surely come when in all the noble cities of Italy there will arise the statue of Giacomo Matteotti. A free people will then decide if there will be room also for those of our Sawdust Caesar.

"What Are You Going To Do About It?"

> *This selection from Seldes' 1934 exposé of the munitions industry,* Iron, Blood and Profits, *examines the first unsuccessful efforts after World War I to take the profits out of war and to halt the worldwide arms race. The failure to do both was a contributing factor to the start of World War II and the creation of the permanent war economy in America.*

EVERY FAIR-MINDED person who by accident or design has faced the armament problem feels that something must be done about it.

In the immediate years following the World War, little was done. Woodrow Wilson was among the first to realize his mistakes. He insisted on disarmament and was convinced the Allies would follow Germany. In 1919, speaking in St. Louis, the man who said the war had some connection or other with democracy said, "We all know this was a commercial war." Wilson believed the League of Nations would disarm the world and make war impossible.

Armaments, it is true, have become the crux of the peace problem. In 15 years, the League of Nations has evolved into a disarmament conference. But every man and woman who in political Washington, Geneva, London or Paris works for peace by disarmament has found the road obstructed. Opposition, from newspapers, from patriotic societies, from public servants, which is "secret and powerful...which does not spring from popular apathy toward disarmament, but which is organized by those who have a financial interest in the upkeep of arms," as the Union of

Democratic Control charges, has up to now maintained its stone wall successfully.

"There hasn't been a conference since the beginning of the war that hasn't stirred up more hate and done more harm than it has good," says the wise Will Rogers. The equally wise Salvador de Madariaga, the philosophical Spanish representative in Geneva, believes that disarmament conferences turn into armament conferences. It was war, not peace, talk that echoed through the halls of the League of Nations meeting in 1933, when the delegates from the United States, Britain, France and Italy discussed Germany's demand that the Allies disarm in accordance with the Versailles Treaty or permit Germany to rearm. Ironically enough, one of the Hitlerite delegation's last actions in Geneva was to ask the secretariat to refuse to accept a petition entitled "War against War," signed by 1,000,000 German members of pacifist societies.

In 1927, Commander Kenworthy noted that "the spectre of war stalked always through the rooms at the Geneva Naval Conference of 1927; its shadow darkened the councils; the fear of it led to the naval rivalry unashamedly disclosed," and at the London conference, three years later, Lord Cecil sorrowfully noted that "the peace current is slackening. Old tendencies which ultimately lead to war are beginning one more to reassert themselves...No one who watched the negotiations can have failed to see how much they were conducted in a war atmosphere, how seldom any reference was made to great international instruments for peace...Important leaders of opinion are again preaching that hoary-headed falsehood, 'If you want peace you must prepare for war.'"

The official documents of the League of Nations give all the necessary proofs that the peace current is slackening. There are two reasons for this: the first is the failure of the United States to cooperate in disarmament programs from 1919 to 1933, the second is the fact that Geneva has become a political battleground of professional politicians, including representatives of the armament industry, instead of a peace conference when statesmen not politicians could decide matters.

The most impressive proposal for control of armaments and for world disarmament was made at St. Germain in 1919 and defeated in Washington in 1922 and 1923. Twenty-three nations had signed the pact when the State Department sent its reply which read in part:

"...while the government of the United States is in cordial sympathy with efforts to restrict traffic in arms and munitions of war, it finds itself unable to approve the provisions of the Convention and to give any assurance of its ratification."

This refusal was supplemented 12 September 1923 with a list of reasons for not signing:

"After a careful examination of the terms of the Convention it has been decided that the objections found thereto render impossible ratification by this government. There is particular objection to the provisions by which the contracting parties would be prohibited from selling arms and ammunition to states not parties to the Convention. By such provisions this government would be required to prevent shipment of military supplies to such Latin American countries as have not signed or adhered to the Convention, however desirable it might be to prevent such shipments, merely because they are not signatory Powers and might not desire to adhere to the Convention."

To the League of Nations, this meant that the United States was not opposed in principle to the arming of revolutionaries, and intended to help those parties in Central and South America who were connected with American banking-houses, who would guarantee loans made, and favor certain American interests, such as the fruit companies, oil companies, and other private corporations.

The 1925 Geneva Convention found the United States and Germany represented and the convention which was signed by 29 states provided for the supervision and publicity of the munitions trade, a special system for control for certain parts of the world. Calvin Coolidge submitted the convention to the U.S. Senate in December. So far only 12 states have signed it and it is inoperative.

In 1930 the Draft Convention produced a document which, instead of making conditions more drastic, actually permitted nations to report the value of armaments sold abroad instead of numbers and weights as well.

A program of programs, six points agreed upon by disarmament committees from all parts of the world and formulated by the International Consultative Group in Geneva, follows:

1. Substantial reduction of existing armaments.

2. No rearmament.

3. Abolition of aggressive weapons within a definite period and with the immediate elimination of all bombing from the air, of the air weapons weapons in general, and of poison gas.

4. Limitation of expenditure of to prevent rivalries in armaments.

5. Effective supervision of existing armaments and of arms manufacture and trade.

6. A permanent organization to carry out the above provisions and to carry on the work begun by the Disarmament Committee.

The League's first subcommittee of the Temporary Mixed Commission's suggestions for the control of the private manufacture on arms included the following:

1. No manufacture without a license.

2. No exports or imports of arms without a license.

3. All licenses to be registered at the League of Nations.

4. All company shares to be registered and no bearer shares to be issued.

5. All accounts to be publically audited and published.

6. Those in control of private manufacture should be prevented from controlling or influencing newspapers, etc.

What have the men and organizations not connected with Geneva and pacifist societies done about armaments? They have proposed many measures. It has always been said that any weapon is good to use against a mad dog, and the unleashed dogs of war are always mad. If the world cannot afford to accept an "idealistic" plan as muzzle because it would involve the loss of a few million dollars, and prefers the realistic plans of the military which involve only a few million lives, it might compromise on one or more of the practical ideas of businessmen, statesmen and politicians.

Bernard M. Baruch is one of the brainiest men in America, and although a big businessman, his hobby is finding a cure for war by taking the profits out of munitions. After serving as chairman of the War Industries Board, Mr. Baruch devised the plan of freezing prices by presidential decree; there would be no profits for anyone in wartime; a "ceiling" is fixed as of a year before the declaration of war, and if anyone succeeds in profiteering in armaments the government would get it back by taxation.

Mr. Baruch told the writer he did not believe in radical schemes, the conscription of wealth would result in panics and in smuggling and other abuses. Taking the profits out of war was no equivalent to conscription of wealth, which is a "theoretical project, prohibited by our Constitution, contrary to the spirit of our social and political institutions and impossible in practice." But he would get the profits out of war munitions. "It would go very far toward keeping the peace of the world."

Owen D. Young, General John J. Pershing and Warren Harding approved. Mr. Young said, "If profit is eliminated from war everywhere and if the mobilization of things and dollars is carried along the same basis with mobilization of men in all countries verging on war, there will be less likelihood of joining battle."

To all suggested plans to end the munitions traffic evils there are many objections, some of them valid, some involving national defense, almost all involving private profits. If there is nationalization, conscription, embargoes, control, licensing, publicity, etc., several persons will lose money. If the government rolls its own steel, it will involve a loss because there will be no manufacture of peacetime goods in the unoccupied time. It is therefore a matter of money. But it also is a matter of money or your life.

The World War has proven inter alia that war is bad business for all countries, all men; it has ended that nonsense about war being part of a human nature that never changes; it has knocked into a cocked hat the theory that armaments are like fire insurance when it proved, as R.G. Hawtrey, economic expert of the British Treasury, put it, "the fire insurance companies are the principle incendiaries"; it has been shown that armaments are an incentive, one of the main causes of war and no guarantee for peace; that preparedness is the best way to get war; that profits and no patriotism is the motive of the armament makers and their subsidized patriotic societies.

The 1929 world economic debacle is the direct result of the World War. Whether the world system will survive it is still open to question. Changes in government and economic methods are being made everywhere, from Moscow to Berlin to Washington. One thing is quite certain; another world war will end the present world "set-up" or "capitalism" or whatever the conventional economic system is called.

And yet in these harrowing years a great advance has been made. We have conquered famine and pestilence and cured disease, just as our forefathers conquered slavery and cannibalism. The Four Horsemen of the Apocalypse do not ride over our huts today with ancient thunder. War alone remains to uphold the Mathusian theory of population, but the machine defies it. The machine age has come and made possible unlimited food and clothing and shelter for all of the people of the earth and for the first time in history plentitude can be created. There is now no need of war for trade routes, for colonies, for land for surplus population, for markets, for rivalry in cotton goods and razor blades.

No reason exists for war except sudden profits for the men who run the munitions racket. To defeat them leadership and intelligence are needed which will create the new deal for the whole world, the new deal internationally conceived, internationally ordering the world's machinery, internationally releasing the people from the ancient economic fear of existence, by supplying the needs of all efficiently without the imposition of hardship on any.

The subject of war has been treated here mainly as it involves munitions manufacture and trade, but the question of armaments is so closely linked to war and peace that it is impossible to discuss it separately.

History since the arrival of Big Business in armaments is largely the story of preparations for war. The League of Nations and unofficial private organizations are an attempt to prepare for peace. The ancient falsehood, *si vis pacem para bellum*, served the Romans and every patriotic society in the world uses that phrase or George Washington's translation of it, but the same George Washington also warned against false patriotism and uttered a thought which all professional patriots overlook. "Overgrown military establishments," said the Father of his country at a time when military establishments were like children's toys compared with what they are relatively today, "are under any form of government inauspicious to liberty, and are to be regarded as particularly hostile to republican liberty."

The time has come for the world to revise the axiom of the Romans and to say *si vis pacem para pacem*; there seem to be only two ways in which peace will come, either through the next war, the aero-chemical war which militarists admit will kill millions of civilians in every city attacked, destroying the present civilization and forcing the exhausted survivors to cease hostilities forever, or a change in the mentality of nations which might today adopt the principle, "if you want peace, prepare for peace."

The first real step toward that end is the destruction of the worldwide munitions racket. It will cost millions of dollars. It will save millions of lives.

The Call from Spain

Seldes frequently said that the only war worth fighting was the war against fascism. After seeing the rise to power of Mussolini in Italy and Hitler in Germany, Seldes was convinced that fascism had to be stopped. The first battleground was Spain. He and his wife, Helen Larkin Wiesman, decided to risk everything to go to Spain and report on the Spanish Civil War. The experience profoundly affected them, and they would devote the next decade to fighting fascism in Europe and America. George told the story in his 1953 book, Tell the Truth and Run.

... not a single journalist is really free.
—GEORGE BERNARD SHAW

WE HAD expected to spend the rest of our married lives on a Vermont hill when at the end of 1936 the war which had started in Spain in July showed its true nature to those who refused to blind themselves to truth— to the little facts, whether or not correctly reported in the press, and to the ominous meaning of the facts.

It was at first rightly and honestly reported, even by those journalists who later embraced the Fascist cause, as a conspiracy by traitors, most of them the high commanding generals of the Spanish Republican Army, to seize the government, establish a Fascist dictatorship a la Primo de Rivera, restore the power of the landlords and the Jesuits, and destroy the great

program of land reform and general welfare announced by the recently
elected Republican regime. That was in early July. By the end of that
month and during the next month or two, there were reports of the participation of Hitler's Anti-Komintern Pakt nations on the side of Franco,
the sending of whole armies by the Nazi and Fascist countries, and the
arrival later of many Frenchmen on the Republican side, followed by a
secret, straggling, yet unending stream of volunteers from 50 countries,
over the snow filled passes of the Pyrenees, and eventually to Madrid.

Those who remembered then said Mussolini's prediction had been
made true by him. It was now obviously Fascism moving to conquer, not
yet the world as it did three years later, but moving with organized divisions, with tanks and guns and airplanes camouflaged behind a vast confusing international curtain of propaganda, accusing a democracy of
being a Communist regime, and making mere assertion the ground for
bloodshed and massacre.

By December the vastness of the Fascist conspiracy was almost as evident to the general public as the new practice of willfully murdering civilians instituted by Hitler and Mussolini and Franco's Moors and Salazar's
troops.

Here on our peaceful hills facing the Green Mountains through grey
Chinese mists in serrated rows as far as we could see to the west, Helen
and I read the news and talked and thought about it. We both felt now
that this was more than a war; we felt that it was a conflict of ideas
involving the world, and that we too, like all other people, were involved
in it, although our country was neutral. At the beginning, remembering
the lessons of the First World War, my devotion then to the cause of the
Allies, my disillusion at the time the Page cable was made public (it asked
Wilson to come into the war to save the Morgan loan), and the exposure
of the vast intrigue of the munitions makers (to which I had devoted a
book), I acted cautiously. But by the end of the year the Spanish war had
become, I thought, an attack not only on people but on culture and on
civilization, and it was made by all the forces of reaction in the world, a
reaction which aimed to go back to feudal times, if not to barbarism.

The least we could do, we felt, was to get into this war through daily
journalism, and fortunately for me the *New York Post* was willing to give me
credentials as a war correspondent. Late in 1936 Helen and I went to
Paris, and from there to Barcelona, Valencia, and Madrid.

There were rumors in Paris, true and false—how could one know? People believed those they wanted to believe. We wanted it to be true when we heard the great secret, that men were coming from all over the world, volunteers, men coming to form the International Brigade, the first volunteer international army going to war since the time of the Crusades.

Men were coming, we were told, in the steerage of ships; they were crossing the border into France at every railroad station and on every road; they were coming with false passports and with false names; some were smuggling themselves in; some were paying French officials bribe money; and they were coming by the scores, by the hundreds, so they could go to war against Fascism in Spain.

All the world outside Mexico and Soviet Russia was against them or officially neutral. The Russians could not send armies by land or sea and the Mexicans had neither ships nor a common frontier; the only way to help save the Republic (and the world) from Fascism was through the Pyrenees, in the night, and through bribery. Men and munitions, the rumors ran through Paris, were crossing the Pyrenees.

But was it true? Was there an international army moving secretly across France?

When our credentials had been signed by Luis Araquistan and places at last arranged on the night train out of the Gare d'Orleans, Helen and I were on our way to Spain with no warning that we would ride headlong into the greatest secret of our time, the International Brigade.

We arrived in Cerbere without incident. We transferred to a little train with every window broken and rattled on flat wheels through the long tunnel into Port Bou. The Republican inspection was severe but just. A long slow journey began, creeping and stopping, endlessly. And then we halted for a long time in the big Gerona station.

A guard came in and told us we would have to quit our compartment and find seats in the dining car. New coaches were to be added; we were to take on some soldiers going south.

After hours there was a confused noise in the station; it grew loud and through all the doors and gates many men in plain clothes appeared in small groups, while individuals in uniform shouted directions or pointed up and down. "We have become a troop train," said the Spanish officer in our dining car.

But none of these men looked like soldiers. Perhaps they were boys being recruited for the new Spanish Republican Army we had heard about. But they didn't look Spanish and some were what is known as the

Nordic type, fair and light despite the grey shadows; their voices were decidedly Teutonic.

All of us looked at one another, suddenly tingling and tense, realizing we were in the very center of a historic moment.

"*Deutsche? Deutsche?*" I shouted at a halted column.

"No. *Danske,*" twenty replied in a broken chorus, "*Danemarks,*" and moved on.

"British?" I asked the next Anglo-Saxon looking group.

"Bulgarian," one in that huddle replied.

Finally: "*Wir sind Deutsche,*" a man down the line called out to me, and some 200, thin and pale and ragged, marched up in the half light. I had been stationed eight years in Berlin. "Are any of you Berliners?" I asked.

"*Wir sind aus Dachau,*" a man replied.

At that time Dachau was already known as a political internment camp. Later it and a few other camps were used by Hitler for the gassing and burning, alive or dead, of millions of men and women and children, Jew and Gentile.

Someone shouted "Halt" in German. I spoke quickly to the man nearest the open window.

"Some of us have escaped," he replied. "Some served their time; others here would have been arrested; we all prefer to die in Spain than live in the *Vaterland.*"

Someone gave an order to march on, and the 200 Germans went to their car up ahead.

Then came the largest contingent. "We are French," they told me.

Then a little group which undoubtedly spoke a Slavic language. "Russky?" I asked.

"Yugoslav," one of the men replied. He had been aided to the frontier by one Josip Broz in Paris, the man who was later to lead the Partisans in the liberation of his country from the Nazis—Josip Broz-Tito, as he signed himself on Helen's photograph in Belgrade a dozen years later.

"Are there any Americans?"

"Yes, 80; the first group has arrived; further up front," someone in another national group answered.

"They come from all the world," the officer in the dining car said.

At this moment Helen could not control herself and the tears smudged her face while she tried to smile.

Clare Sheridan said as if to chide her: "This is the most thrilling moment of my life."

The Spanish officer looked surprised, sad. "Why does your wife weep?" he asked me.

"Because she's sentimental," I replied in French, but that wasn't quite true. It was easy to say these words in French, hard to explain the deep feeling created by this parade of youth from all corners of the world to the battlefields of Spain, and the men from Dachau going to end their broken lives in a last heroic gesture.

Twelve hundred men at rough count got into the train, and by this accidental meeting I saw the beginning of the most noble act of our time. These were the volunteers of the International Brigade. They were on their way to reinforce the few hundred French and other nationals who, happening to be in Spain five months earlier when Franco and the officers betrayed their country, had joined with native workers and other civilians to save Madrid.

There was no laughter, no gaiety, forced or false, none of the usual banter and horse play of soldiers everywhere. There was a grimness about this group, a certain tragic lack of the usual brave sounds of soldiers entraining. And suddenly I knew why. These were not the boys of modern armies; almost all were older men, middle aged men, some of them even grey and old.

At last the loud orders were over, the whistles blew in their various keys, and the train started for Barcelona and Valencia and eventually the training camp of the International Brigade at Albacete. The name was no military secret, although it should have been. Everyone discussed everything; everyone mentioned training bases, troop movements, guns, harbor defenses, the results of bombings and attacks. The Republic could keep no secrets.

The train moved slowly. Spanish boys in uniform came into our car, passed their leather wine flasks, laughed as they taunted each other on how far away from their open mouths they could keep the nozzle and yet not miss a drop of the spurting wine. A guitar began to play. Traditional Iqamencos and other songs made the night gay.

But it was a little different. There was a new song about heroic Madrid, and some old songs with new words about the war, and there was always the Internationale and the Marseillaise, and although no one stood up for them, every man and woman in the train held up a clenched fist which was then the symbol of a world of many nations and groups and views united against Fascism.

At times a few civilians, seeing us in the car and not knowing we were privileged foreigners, tried to push their way in. The conductor pushed them out, but one old woman refused to leave. "No classes now," she said, elbowing the guards and taking a vacant seat next to Helen.

After a while Helen offered her a Spanish newspaper.

"Can't read, illiterate," she said, "but speak to me and I understand everything—but in Spanish." We questioned her about religion and politics.

The man who interpreted was a doctor. I asked him to write out his name. I determined at that moment that I would never again report what an anonymous taxi driver or an anonymous hotel porter had said to me about the political situation in a foreign country; I would from now on give the names and addresses of people if they had something to say. On the page of my Spanish notebook on which this is written I find in his handwriting the name: "Lorenso Barea (Doctor), Barcelona."

"We are three brothers," he said, "middle class, a lawyer, a doctor— that's me—and the youngest, twenty, in college. He was the first to enlist.

"Two of our uncles were killed by the Fascists. Why? They were bourgeois like ourselves and like ourselves Republicans. We never had a thought in all our lives of joining with Socialists, let alone Communists and anarchists.

"But all of us saw it was a war for Spain. For the Republic, for the people; against the Fascists, the big capitalists, the dukes, the monarchy.

"When our brother was killed, we all joined up. But that does not make us Communists or anarchists, does it? We are Spain."

These are the words I still find on pieces of paper, the old envelopes, the edges of newspapers on which I kept notes on the way: "We prefer to die in Spain than live in the *Vaterland.*" and "We are Spain" may sound theatrical to you or at least romantic in the heroic fashion, but I assure you they were not false. It was a time of greatness, and simple people spoke that way.

We sat up most of the night in this dining car, sleeping at times, awakened by the noises of railroad stations and the switching of coaches. When we got to Barcelona I walked the length of the train, but the International Brigade was not there. The men had gone somewhere in the night. I knew I would never see them again. I knew they were going to a quick death. I am sure that many of them knew this too, but there was no show of martyrdom. There was the feeling of dedication but not doom. Nine of every ten with whom Helen and I rode that night are buried on the battlefields of Spain.

For three years I wrote about the Spanish War. But I knew in my first five minutes in the trenches near Madrid that it was lost. This was on 10 February 1937, three months and three days after the siege of the capital had begun.

I found out in this way. There was a small piece of field artillery—it might have been a French 75 or an American 3-inch gun—in the front line trenches, its mouth open point blank to the enemy; and my Spanish colleague Menendez said something about it. I asked immediately where the other guns were.

Menendez interpreted and the commanding officer replied: "There is another one in the next trench."

Then I knew that the war was lost for the Republic.

There were no batteries of artillery anywhere behind the front line trenches, and here there was one 3-inch gun and on the left there was another, and perhaps there was one a quarter mile away on the right also, and that was about all. That was how the Loyalist Army was holding its main defense point, Madrid. There were also machine guns—not many— and the soldiers going on leave or for a day's rest in Madrid came back unarmed because there were not enough rifles for all. There were also times when unarmed soldiers stood behind the lines waiting for a man to be killed or wounded so that he could take his place and his gun. This I had known and it did not depress me. But I knew enough from my year in the Press Section of the American Army in 1918 to realize that without artillery a position could not be held; and the Republic had almost no artillery.

It did not even have military maps. One day at the American sector at Morata the position was explained to me on tourist automobile road maps. There were no others; Franco and his officers, deserting, had taken not only the guns but the maps—and everything they could carry off.

But Madrid held out for three years. It held out for two reasons. One was Hitler's order that the capital should not be taken— this secret was revealed a decade later by Goering and others at the trial at Nuernberg; the documents were read showing that the Nazis wanted experience for their aviators and tanks and soldiers so they would have the only trained army when the Second World War began. The overt reason the capital was not taken was the greatness of common men.

Not a few great common men, not a few heroes, but mass greatness, a nobility of the human spirit among the many which in history is usually accredited to individuals, a few heroic ones, a national hero; and sometimes to a little group, but never to multitudes. Here, once in my life, in a time of greatness, I saw the thousands, tens of thousands of illiterate peasants and factory workers, American trade union organizers from Detroit, British poets, and Jews from Dachau who had been little merchants, doctors, professors, and students, but mostly the common ordinary run of working men with rifles in their hands, the "polloi" against whom my first editor had warned me, many men who might have gone to their graves without thinking, without ever feeling deeply, many lifted out of the useless ruts of their lives, up to the level of the time, the time of greatness. This was mass heroism. It was a rare if not unique experience.

When I returned from my first tragic walk through the trench system outside Madrid, Helen was waiting for me at the Hotel Florida. She had gone with Kaysa, the beautiful Swedish militia-girl volunteer, and Walter, the German political refugee turned official photographer, to the Parque del Oeste front of Madrid and had had many experiences. I insisted that she write. I knew that the *Post* would prefer a woman's account of the defense of the capital to mine. When she began her story with the line: "It is a penny ride from Main street to the trenches," I told her she was a born journalist. She described the battlefield as she had seen it from a trench window and concluded: "Two yellow crocuses and a dead man suddenly catch my eye and tell the story. Spring has come to the Madrid trenches and nothing can stop the crocuses from growing in early spring, not even a dead man."

Helen and I sent three series of mail articles to J. David Stern's *New York Post* and *Philadelphia Record*, most of which were published. Some time later I had a serious dispute with Mr. Stern about all the silent canons of journalism and the atrophied ethics of the press, but I never ceased praising him for his courage in printing our Spanish series in defiance of threats and a boycott.

It came from the Cardinal and the hierarchy in Philadelphia; it was popularized by the official diocesan organ, *Catholic Standard & Times*; and a pastoral letter was read by every priest at every Mass over a certain period of time. The faithful were urged to stop reading the *Record* unless it changed its policy from pro-Loyalist to anti-Loyalist.

Mr. Stern had a confidential poll taken which indicated decisively that the laity had not obeyed the orders of the hierarchy. This was not surprising, inasmuch as many leading Catholic laymen were anti-Fascist, and one of the most powerful lay organizations in America, the CIO, with more than six million members, 65 per cent of them Catholic, were on record as opposing Spanish Fascism.

Unable to persuade its followers to stop reading a liberal newspaper, the Philadelphia hierarchy then quietly went to work among the big advertisers, notably department store owners, Protestant and Jew as well as Catholic, and these men, all frightened by the Church, in turn frightened Mr. Stern. On 10 August 1937, the publisher sent his humble apologies to Cardinal Dougherty and called his attention to a new editorial he was running "denouncing the Spanish Government's action against the Catholic Church," and adding that he hoped "it would offset any unfriendly impression created by a previous editorial." Finally, Mr. Stern said to the Cardinal: "I would very much appreciate your advice as to what I should or should not do in the matter."

When I argued with Mr. Stem about this episode on my return from Spain and on many other questions of pressure, intimidation, and blackmail of the press in general, his response in the form of a question was always the same: "Which would you have me do: compromise or go out of business?" There was no other way of life for a liberal newspaper in America in the face of pressure which hit almost every one of the 1,750 dailies and 10,000 weeklies—which certainly descended with forceful pressure upon every publication which took the side of democratic Spain against the Fascist Internationale.

In Paris on our way back to America, we stopped at the Hotel Liberia in the Rue de la Grande Chaumiere, just off Montparnasse. I had known it from the first day I quit the Tribune and began free lancing. It was overrun by artists, many of them Americans, and it cost then as always about a dollar a day for a large room with a washbowl. I had not found it difficult in 1928 to move out of the Hotel Adlon in Berlin, where my ten-dollar-a-day allowance from my paper just covered my living, into a Latin Quarter existence where two or three dollars a day would be all I could afford. I could never understand why Wall Street men at the time of the setback preferred defenestration.

I am sure that I did not register my address at the Embassy. There was a record in the consulate of my passport being amended for Spain months earlier, but could His Excellency have known of my return? One day the telephone in this unknown hole of a Left Bank hotel rang: "The American Ambassador would like to speak to you."

In 1919 I had had a glimpse of William C. Bullitt when he returned from Russia with Lincoln Steffens and tried to report to Woodrow Wilson and Lloyd George that the Bolsheviks wanted peace, would pay the money they owed, sign an agreement not to use propaganda, do everything the masters of the Versailles Treaty insisted on. But Steffens and Bullitt were at once denounced as "Reds," and that apparently ended their usefulness forever.

I got to know Bullitt slightly the times he was in Paris after his marriage to Louise Bryant, who was the widow of John Reed. I thought then that Louise's heart had long ago been buried outside the Kremlin walls, and Louise confessed it years later when she spent her last year, after her separation from Bullitt, living in the same Left Bank Liberia Hotel whose phone was now calling me. (Louise died in unfortunate circumstances and it was one of the few instances I know in my newspaper years in which the press in both France and America restrained itself from involving her former husband, His Excellency, the Ambassador, in scandalous headlines.)

"This is Bill Bullitt; that you George?" said the voice from the Embassy doubly surprising me in the choice of both names. I did not think I had known him that well—those many years ago. "I'd like to see you," he continued, and set the time at the Embassy building, off the Place de la Concorde.

It was more than a friendly call. What Bullitt wanted was a report on what was really happening politically in Republican Spain.

As much as I opposed the collaboration of journalists with governments, I welcomed opportunities to talk to the men who rule. I had twice been invited by Coolidge to report to him, first about Russia and then about Mexico, and by Secretary of State Kellogg and Secretary of State Hughes, and each time I hoped to counteract the poisons I knew they had been receiving both from their own sources and from reactionary newspaper men. In meeting diplomats I always counted on getting more than I gave. I never said a word which I would not have printed or did not print in my papers. If I did otherwise, I would have considered it, not espionage, but surely the act of an "agent," and I never would be the "agent" for anyone, a foreign land or even my own country, within or without the code of ethics of the profession of journalism.

I did not tell Ambassador Bullitt everything I knew about Spain. For example, I did not tell him that there was only one 3-inch gun in the main front line trench at Madrid, and no guns in support, and the next guns far away. This was common knowledge and no doubt our military attaches had reported it. I told Bullitt the contents of the twenty-five articles which up to 24 March I had written for the *Post.*

He interrupted with, "But you say there are no Russians there," and his friendly manner disappeared.

I insisted that there was not one Russian infantryman, not one Russian soldier in Spain, in contrast to 40 or 50 thousand Italians and perhaps half as many thousand Germans, and divisions of Moors and Portuguese and other hired men. I had just come from Brihuega, I had seen the Italians; I had seen the Russian tanks, one or two tank men, one or two airplane mechanics going up in the elevator in the Telefonica building.

"There is a general named Gal who says he is a Hungarian but speaks Russian," I said. "There are perhaps three or four hundred Russians—you know they can't come through via Germany or France except singly and secretly—and no regiments, not even a squad. There are aviators, tankmen, experts, but no soldiers— maybe 400 specialists altogether."

"I know differently," said Ambassador Bullitt.

He gave me a full report on Russian infantry in Spain. I said he was misinformed. I said, "Colonel Fuqua and Captain Griffis, and . . . (I forget the names of our diplomatic representatives in Valencia) could not have possibly informed you that there were Russians there because they informed me there were none."

"We have other sources of information," replied Bullitt angrily.

I became angry too, but in a sort of diplomatic way restraining myself, keeping my temper a degree or two below his. However our voices grew higher and angrier, and it was apparent that I had contradicted all the reports the Ambassador had been sending to President Roosevelt on Russian infantry troops fighting in Spain. I had heard that Bullitt had turned against Russia, but I did not think he would misinform. I insisted on facts.

So, without the usual diplomatic chicanery of hiding his emotion, Ambassador Bullitt touched the supposedly hidden button below the center panel of his desk to summon the diplomatic equivalent of a bouncer in a low saloon—an attache who approached, bowed, informed His Excellency that he had an appointment at the Quai d'Orsay and must leave immediately. I do not remember whether or not we shook hands, but we probably did.

(Some years later I read an original diary kept in Berlin, parts of which appeared in a published book. On 13 December 1936, Ambassador Dodd had written of his report to President Roosevelt that the French Ambassador had informed him that Bullitt was, apparently without instructions, working to prevent the Franco-Russian treaty which was to save Europe from a world war; and also of Bullitt's turning against the Soviets while envoy to Moscow and becoming a friend of the Italian envoy, and finally of Bullitt becoming "attracted to Fascism before leaving Moscow." Ambassador Dodd had protested to Roosevelt against Ambassador Bullitt's policies and his reports, on the ground that his colleague was not furthering peace and goodwill among nations.)

Everything that happened to me from 1936 to now has been conditioned by my experience in Spain. Spain permeated minds, penetrated hearts. Many, many persons who had a part in this war, if only by contributing a sum of money or attending a meeting, have felt it so and tried to express it. Still arguing about Spain in 1950 in letters to *The New Republic*, the writer Kay Boyle, answering a correspondent, said: "Yes, Mr. Esteve, there was something 'so awful' in Spain that it breaks the heart, and breaks it forever, once one has been there."

In mid-1937, full of emotion over the tragedy we had been witnessing, and convinced that it was no longer the Spanish war but our own war, Helen and I returned home determined to give our time (outside of making a living by writing) to helping the Loyalists. We did what we could. We collected material for pamphlets and wrote part of them; we wrote letters of protest to the *Times* and other newspapers; we appeared at public meetings; we joined every organization aiding Spain; and once I got up enough courage to make a public speech.

This was on 6 April 1938, when under the chairmanship of Archibald MacLeish a foreign correspondents' symposium, "The Inside Story of Spain," was held in Mecca Temple, New York City. The money collected was for the Medical Bureau and the North American Committee to Aid Spanish Democracy. The chief speakers were Vincent Sheean, Dorothy Parker, and Ralph Bates; the other participants were Jay Allen, Robert Dell, Leland Stowe, and myself.

At the end of that April one of the planned pro-Loyalist activities was a protest trip to Washington with a visit (if possible) to the White House by a group of writers. I had forgotten all about this activity until years later the Saturday Review of Literature published a request for Tom Wolfe letters. In one of them—dated Hotel Chelsea, 25 April 1938, Wolfe had written me:

> *I would like to know when the committee is going to Washington, but I do not believe I am going to be able to make it. I am working here day after day trying to get as much done as I possibly can, because I am going to Purdue University May 19, and want to accomplish all I can before I go. Therefore, I had not thought of making any more trips at the present time. But let me know about it, and I will see what I can do.*

We had talked it over at my apartment the week before, one of those great nights which should have been recorded for literary eternity, when Tom and Josephine Herbst and one or two others argued about the novel, and art, and life and truth, until the day dawned. There was very little time for politics, but there was no doubt that Tom Wolfe, who hitherto had not been on record on Spain (and most other social-political questions), was on our side, along with almost all the writers in America.

Fascism, international Fascism, the nations of the Anti-Comintern Pact, a union proposed by Foch and Churchill in 1918 and perfected in 1936 by Adolf Hitler, was marching in Spain. It was not attacking Communism (as the Fascist propagandists everywhere and the great Vatican propaganda machine were saying); it was fighting democracy. It was fulfilling the famous Palazzo Venezia speech of 8 October 1931, in which Mussolini predicted a "struggle between two worlds" (Fascism and Democracy)....

It was We or They in Madrid. It was the first battle in a new world war.

The summer of 1937, like all our summers since 1933 when we quit Europe for good was spent in our farmhouse in Vermont, working on a book in the shadow of the Spanish War. We realized somehow on the return home to our panoramic hillside near Woodstock that it was wrong to live in this zone of quiet. We could find no peace while there was a war we knew was our war although it was in Spain. We both felt we had to tell the people of America this was our war. We were compelled, we felt driven, into some decision. We had to quit the peaceful hill and valley, to do what we could. We had to uproot ourselves.

It was only a gesture, Helen and I realized later; but to mark this turning point in our lives, this call to action which came to us in Madrid, we cut the main tie with peace and quiet and returned to the city to devote our years to the fight against Fascism—which threatened us at a distance.

We could work for a popular front against Fascism in America. The new labor movement, the CIO, would be its base, a mass of people, the one necessary condition for success; and we could count on all the intellectuals, including the liberal Catholic writers who were on the side of Loyalist Spain. The Catholic labor leaders, and notably Philip Murray, to their everlasting credit were on the side opposite the Cardinals. Spain united all the people who were against Fascism.

This is what I wrote in 1937. Helen thought so too. We felt we could no longer sit far away in our farmhouse in Vermont and write an article now and then saying we must all unite, we must all work for the people's front, for a world democracy. We felt that now we must engage in action as well as in writing. We sold our house, our beds and our tables; we were free to go to work. Spain had restored our faith in human beings. We could again say, and with passion: The People, Yes.

I Heard the People Singing
Behind the Iron Curtain

In 1948, Seldes embarked on his last major assignment in foreign corre-spondence. He spent several months in Europe, on both sides of the so-called "Iron Curtain," to find out the real story about post-war Europe. His biggest coup during this assignment was an exclusive interview with Marshal Josip Broz Tito, the leader of Yugoslavia. Tito was the only leader of the Soviet satellite nations to pursue his own vision of the socialist state rather than the Comintern's. Tito granted few interviews, but the only place that Seldes' interview was published was in his own paper, In fact, *because the establishment press refused to print it. His account of his visit to Yugoslavia appeared in his 1949 book,* The People Don't Know.

YOU CAN go by airplane from Paris, or you can take the train from Milan (if you have a military pass through Trieste and a Yugoslav visa and intend to disregard the State Department rubber stamp in your passport warning you not to go there) and ride in the dilapidated splendor of the old Orient Express directly into Eastern Europe, the peoples' democracies as they call themselves, the "iron curtain" countries as they are known to the American press.

On a certain night we take our leave of unhappy and corrupt free-enterprise Italy and our train creeps out of Trieste and we pass hours of the black night in customs and visa and money inspections. At 2 o'clock we may be able to fall asleep. But I was awakened at 4 in the morning by the people singing behind the iron curtain.

It is a Sunday morning and there are many people, there are girls and boys in native costume probably going to fairs and celebrations; or perhaps to church; and there are thousands of men in clothes more torn and dirtier than those worn by the hordes of Italian beggars, but they are carrying shovels and picks, they are going to work on Sunday, they are gay and laughing—and they are singing.

This is the first answer to the stories—year after year of stories in the American press—of people enslaved, of misery, unhappiness, of forced labor, of loss of human rights, of the decay and disappearance of human dignity in the "totalitarian" lands, the "satellite" nations, the so-called Iron Curtain countries.

There were only four or five of us foreigners on the whole trip from Italy to Belgrade, and the night before, entraining at Trieste, I had had an earful of hate and poison from the British, American, and Canadian group bidding farewell to some of their number going to Yugoslavia on diplomatic passports. They hated the people, the "natives" whom they—and others in the diplomatic corps and in the journalistic corps also—usually referred to as "damn Jugs"; they hated the government also, and they hated being assigned to Belgrade as one might hate having been condemned to a term on a penal island.

One of my outspoken traveling companions was a colonel. I asked him about the people singing.

"They're trained to do that," he replied.

"But who were all those thousands of boys and girls marching with shovels?" I asked.

"Those are the so-called volunteer brigades," the colonel replied, adding with bitterness: "Slave labor."

It was Sunday morning at Ljubljana. On the next track a train was discharging several thousand persons, some in gay peasant dresses, some in torn work clothes, but all laughing and shouting and a happier crowd than I had seen in England, France, or Italy.

The boys and girls separated themselves from the others on the platform, formed in a line four or five abreast, and started marching away singing merrily, loudly, and passionately.

"They don't look like slave labor," I remarked to the colonel.

"They just don't know any better," he replied.

And that ended that discussion.

It was my introduction to the new world behind the iron curtain.

JOURNEY INTO THE PHRASE "IRON CURTAIN"

Despite an experience of 40 years in newspaper work—and a large number of them spent in criticizing the press—I was not prepared for what I found behind the so-called iron curtain.

On the assumption that where there is a lot of smoke there must be at least a little fire, and after three years of terrible tales of terrorism in the Western newspapers, and most notably in our own, I expected to find at least a little spark of truth behind the flaming press headlines.

Nor would it have been shocking. The country which I was now investigating—and Hungary and Czechoslovakia, which I visited later—had been ruined either by native fascism or by Naziism, and each nation had had a certain number of collaborators and traitors (including priests and monsignori) and many more passive people who certainly could not be relied upon in the formation of any regime, especially a radical one which nationalized industries and generally interfered with the old free enterprise system. If the Eastern lands were indeed police states, if the governments ruled by terrorism, if some people were afraid to speak out, if opponents were slaughtered and political dissidents silenced, it would have been tragic and sad—but not surprising, from the long view of history.

I found nothing of the kind. I did find that there were many people who grumbled and complained—and the fact they did so was in a way a testimonial for the regimes, because they were not terrorized nor were they imprisoned for doing so. Naturally I found that manufacturers and big businessmen and small merchants who had suffered money losses through nationalizations were unhappy about it—and so were the big landowners, and especially the bishops of the Roman Catholic Church whose wealth and subsistence depended greatly on land tenure.

I found waiters, chambermaids, hotel porters—who are, sad to say, among the chief sources of information of many American visiting (but not resident) correspondents, and frequently the persons behind the phrases "well informed sources" and "reliably informed"—were usually angry at the new regimes because it meant less tips and perhaps no tips at all.

I found—when I went out to find—that the peasants of whom millions had been given land and for the first time in their lives owned something, and the workers in the industries—in other words the majority of people in every Eastern country—were not grumbling or fighting the regime;

most of them were better off than at any time in history, and most of them were the backbone of the new system. The majority of citizens—never questioned by the majority of visiting journalists—were in favor.

It was then apparent that the worst iron curtain in the world is not that mentioned by Mr. Churchill but the one imposed by either the newspaper correspondents who cannot or do not report the truth or, most likely, by the editors and publishers of America who do not want to print the truth.

Before we journey further into the fakery and propaganda about the Eastern republics, it might be well to pause for a moment to explain that Churchill's sinister phrase is itself part of the present cold war—and that its use by every American editor and publisher pays a royalty to the Nazi regime.

In March 1949, many great newspapers and radio commentators, including Lowell Thomas, with millions of listeners, joined to honor Winston Churchill for many things, including the coinage of the phrase "iron curtain" in his Fulton, Missouri, speech three years earlier. Thomas, on 30 March, on his CBS network, credited Churchill with the phrase; Bob Considine, Hearst columnist, 3 March wrote, the Fulton speech "will be remembered in history as the unveiling of what has become a part of the language of the earth—the 'Iron Curtain.'"

The British and not the self-styled "free" American press is to be credited for exposing the Nazi origin of the Churchillian phrase which has not only swept the United States but overwhelmed the thinking of a large part of its press.

The liberal *Manchester Guardian*, the cooperative weekly *Reynolds News*, and even The *Times*, the Thunderer itself, have informed Churchill's own nation he was using one of the enemy propaganda tools.

The *Times* provided "chapter and verse" to prove that "iron curtain," a Nazi phrase used to denounce the enemy, the U.S.S.R., was publicly used by Minister of Finance Von Krosigk in wartime, more than a year before Churchill palmed it off on the American public.

Reynolds News commented editorially, "Mr. Churchill has recently found some strange ideological allies, but we are sure he would wish to repudiate any association with the views of so unsavory a person."

The *Manchester Guardian* traced the origin further back—to the master propagandist Paul Josef Goebbels himself. In its 23 February 1945, issue the *Guardian* published an editorial entitled "Goebbels on 'Third World War,'" which was based on a Reuters dispatch quoting a DNB broadcast in which Goebbels predicted a hoped-for World War III in 1948.

At the end of the Second World War, Goebbels shouted into the microphone, "the whole of East and South-eastern Europe, together with the Reich, will come under Russian occupation. Behind an iron screen, mass butcheries of people will begin...." Eventually there would be a third war, he predicted. The translation "iron screen" is merely a variant for "iron curtain."

The phrase was clever, and it was popularized in 1945 by all of Nazi Germany's friends. For example, the pro-Nazi Turkish journalist, Yalcin, wrote (20 August 1945): "Wherever the Bolsheviks have set foot nothing remains of the ideas of 'democratic liberty' and 'democratic rights.' A steel curtain falls and shuts off these unhappy lands from the rest of the world."

Unfortunately most American newspaper editors even today do not know they are using a Nazi propaganda slogan. If they were informed it is likely that a large number of them would desist, leaving the phrase to the Hearsts, Howards, and McCormicks who probably do know its origin and who no doubt would continue to employ it.

The Nazi origin of the phrase is recognized by the American State Department.

Thanks to the reactionaries within that organization a memorandum on the subject has been suppressed. It is a very short document which had been supplied to Secretary James Byrnes, to Assistant Secretary William Benton, to Senators Tom Connally and Arthur Vandenberg, and to notable others. It has been read by at least 200 executives and sub-executives of The State Department. I have been able to obtain a copy and here it is in full.

"THE IRON CURTAIN"

The Iron Curtain: This colorful phrase, a substitute for thought, bids fair to become an essential vocabulary crutch to many people. In the last two days I have heard it used by people in the Department who should know better.

The line from Stettin to Trieste would put behind the Iron Curtain Hungary, Czechoslovakia, Rumania and Bulgaria, where the local press has considerable measure of freedom and where our correspondents have successfully reported what is going on. OIC [State's Office of International Information] operations with films, news, exhibits, lectures have been successfully operated in these countries and should be expected to grow.

I object to the repetition of this phrase (the Iron Curtain) as defeatism. By using the words 'behind the iron curtain' we are psychologically surrendering an enormous area which is intellectually and culturally still bound to the West.

Let us grant there is an iron curtain at the Russian border and that the red fog obscures chunks of Central and Southeastern Europe—but why do we have to make a bad situation seem worse by ringing an iron curtain down ourselves on ourselves?

This is an official United States view, but it remains sabotaged. The Goebbels-Churchill line prevails.

THE IRON-CURTAINED LIFE

To the American press, and that part of the British, French, Italian, and other Western nations' press which in payment for the Marshall Plan follows the American press in falsifying the story of the East, the existence of the Nazi phrase has been a double godsend: it permits both the suppression of the amazing progress which has been made in the East—about which almost no American is informed—as well as the colossal type of fakery.

I would also like to say that the story that is suppressed, the story of a whole nation singing as it goes to work, is also part of the iron-curtain hoax, and I would like to repeat here my first impressions of the daily life of the nation which may open the reader's eyes; they certainly opened mine.

I was awakened before seven the first morning in Belgrade by a repetition of the frontier experience: people singing. But this time it was a company of soldiers marching somewhere without arms. The streets were full of people, they crowded off the sidewalks, and they were on the move. I found the secret later: many, especially government employees, prefer to go to work at seven and continue straight on until two in the afternoon, giving them time for a siesta—which is as necessary in Belgrade as it is in Baghdad, for the heat is tropical and murderous—and free time for pleasure or for volunteer work on the national projects in the late afternoon.

All day long the streets are full of people, more people than in any other city; they are badly dressed, poorly dressed, but proud and smiling people, tall people, full of a great energy, strong-featured men and strong-featured women, walking very erect and smiling.

If I saw one I saw 10,000 women that morning, and not one had rouged lips, or rouged cheeks, or any makeup whatsoever. They were sun-browned and healthy—healthier than any people I had seen in five other countries—and they carried themselves like the proud female figures on the bows of old sailing ships cutting through the waters. But even wooden figures are painted, whereas these tens of thousands of Yugoslav women and girls despite all their summer brownness had a strange look about them which was disconcerting at least for three or four days, until one got used to living in a rougeless world.

The animation of Belgrade is something beyond anything anywhere in Europe, either side of the so-called curtain. It is something like the New York subway rush at the peak hours, morning and afternoon, but here it goes on forever—at least from dawn to bedtime; and in good humor.

People are in a hurry. There is such a jam on the sidewalks that many have to walk in the streets, at least in the center of the city. In every street there are bombarded buildings being reconstructed, or new buildings going up, or buildings being torn down to make room for the vast new public buildings and vast new apartment houses which will be built.

There is no unemployment. There is a shortage of labor. There is above all else a shortage of skilled men and technicians. There is a tremendous demand for everything. And so there is rush and excitement and work going in every direction, and crowds and movement such as cannot be seen anywhere else in the world.

A hardworking people has united to reconstruct a nation ruined by war.

The great tidal wave of patriotism which started in the partisan or liberation movement against the Nazis, the Ustashis, other traitors, and Mikhailovich, has never ebbed. A great part of it has been channelized into hard common labor: into building of roads, clearing up war's destruction, putting up factories and homes, sweating it out under a tropical sun which lights up an unprecedentedly bright future.

The present itself however is tough. Food is scarce, clothing is scarce, housing is scarce, and thousands of comforts which most Americans regard as the marks of civilization are entirely missing. It is therefore quite evident that the Yugoslav people are inspired as no other people in Europe or America by their faith in the future.

I was able to talk to hundreds of persons in German. Workmen who were prisoners of war, lawyers who criticized the government, heads of factories, and even peasants in the fields. Without exception they loved and adored Tito. Tito led them to victory in the war; Tito was reconstructing the country; Tito was creating a nation which in their own lifetime will stand high among the most civilized and most cultured and most progressive nations of the world.

The only persons in all Yugoslavia who spoke against the government and against Tito and against the five-year-plan were many diplomatic officials of many nations and most of the American journalists.

However, when United States Ambassador Cavendish Cannon gave a garden party for diplomats and journalists attending the Danube Conference, I got into a conversation with Political Attache Lenhardt, and the judgment he passed on Yugoslavia was this: "What is happening here is the biggest thing since the end of the war."

I made a date with Lenhardt at the embassy for the next day but the first thing he then said was: "This is for your information; it is off the record," so I cannot quote him any further. But I did agree in his profound conclusion: what is happening in Yugoslavia in many ways is the most important event since the end of the war.

These were my first impressions, set down at random, as impressions always occur. But it seems to me they introduce Yugoslavia better than anything I could write later.

INTERVIEWING TITO

In the late spring of 1948, there occurred an event which was immediately recognized as one of the most significant in world relations since the establishment of the Comintern and the spread of communism throughout a large part of the world.

Tito was excommunicated by the Communist Information Bureau, or the Cominform, as it was better known. This was the first time in history that a rift appeared in the organization which had as its great aim the creation of a universal state.

Tito was, next to Stalin, the biggest name in communism. In August 1948, the time of the Danube Conference in Belgrade, of the hundred foreign journalists who arrived at least ninety admitted they came to get the story of the Tito-Cominform rift and an interview with Tito.

But Tito was not seeing anyone.

We were all disappointed, the *New York Times*, the *Herald Tribune*, the AP and UP and the scores of others, and myself. Tito was at his summer home in Bled. But even the three or four, including myself, who journeyed to that vicinity on the halfway promise of the press office, were doomed to failure.

However, the quest for a Tito interview continued. At this time, the United Nations were meeting in Paris and in the Yugoslav delegation appeared the name of Colonel Vladimir Dedijer, one of the handful of men who had been with Tito since the beginning, in Belgrade where the uprising of the Partisans was planned, and in the field of battle, where he was severely wounded. I had known Dedijer from the time he had been a delegate to the San Francisco Conference in 1945, and now that he was the head of the Direkcija za Informacje, I asked him for some friendly intervention.

It required making the trip from Paris to Belgrade all over again, but it was worth everything if a real interview with the Marshal was assured, and Colonel Dedijer promised me that it was.

The great question of the day was War or Peace? The American press talked war. The people of Europe did not talk war, but every man and woman living in the countries which might be the new battlefield, feared it. East and West were rearming. Tito's answer to this question was of world importance.

The Cominform had excommunicated him. The next pertinent question was Tito's reaction to this event, his position, changed or unchanged, vis-a-vis the Soviets and his former allies.

The Marshal received Mrs. Seldes and myself at his office and spoke to us for an hour-and-a-half. He answered every question with a frankness and sincerity which was impressive. He spoke on peace or war, on the Cominform and on his relations to Russia.

"I would be very glad," he said to me, "to talk about the economic and cultural progress of my country, of the 5-year plan, of our progress..."

But everything, economics, culture, progress, depends today on one and only one thing, I interrupted. Is it war or peace?

Marshal Tito's greenish-blue eyes hardened, and the smile which was almost continually brightens his hard and magnificent face vanished.

"In my opinion, it is not war," he said weighing every word, not saying it was peace. After a second or two of silence, he continued.

"To make war you must have men who want war. Men, not people. People never want war—they are frequently led into war. The people of America I am sure do not want war. Nor do the people of the Soviet Union want war. Nor do we want war. But there must be Americans who do want war. America is making the greatest preparations for war in all history. The danger of war exists, of course. The great danger is a provocation. Some great provocation. Our side is not preparing for war. In my opinion there will be no war now unless it is provoked. We know the reasons for war. We know the reasons for aggression, for expansion, for markets, colonies, for domination. But on our side there can be no reason for a new war." (And with great emphasis, each word clearly:) "WE HAVE NO CAUSE FOR WAR. WE HAVE GOT WHAT WE WANT. WE HAVE FREEDOM."

The calm interview came to this climax with great passion and gesture. Then Marshal Tito was silent.

On returning to Paris immediately I realized that the Tito interview, especially in view of the UN peace and war debates, had a great news value, and that I kept it until I could publish it in my own newsletter, weeks or a month later, it would lose some of its urgency.

I had no intention to sell the interview, as others not engaged in daily journalism have frequently done in like circumstances, but I did offer it to the Associated Press and the *New York Times* on one condition: that its introduction stated it was copyright by myself and my newsletter.

But what followed shocked even an oldtimer like myself who thought he knew what is news and how frequently the press prints what is not news as news, which suppresses what truly is news and in other ways plays tricks with the unwritten law of what is and what is not news.

The *Times* asked to keep the story overnight, after I had warned the Paris editors that the *Times* owners and editors had for years more or less boycotted both my name and that of my publication. The *Times* correspondent ridiculed this thought. Nevertheless the next morning I received the manuscript back with a letter from which I quote:

> *"I cannot tell you how appreciative I am for your kindness in bringing your Tito interview to the* New York Times *and offering us the chance to publish it. However, I regret to say that, after mature consideration, I have decided not to use it. It is not the kind of interview which contained any very newsworthy statements. Printing a few excerpts, therefore, from this piece, would have very little news interest. There is nothing new about Tito's view's stating that Yugoslavia is still on the side of the 'Peoples Democracies' and his thoughts on the chances of war and peace. I am sorry..."*

The Associated Press leaped on this news story. It thought it was the kind of interview which contained many newsworthy statements, that Tito's views on Yugoslavia's position and the chances of war and peace were important news statements. Paris correspondent Preston Glover cabled the main office in New York offering it the news quotation on war and the Cominform, about 800 words.

However, the next day he informed me that the AP had cabled him to send only 200 words—and although I have seen these 200 words printed in some small newspapers, a search of the great metropolitan press has resulted in no trace of them.

The Weapons for Waging Cold War

The Marshall Plan that helped to rebuild Europe after World War II was not done as a purely altruistic gesture by the United States. As Seldes wrote in his 1949 book, The People Don't Know, *it was part of a coordinated strategy to keep Western Europe on the side of the U.S. for the then-expected Third World War with the Soviet Union and its allies. The press of the time, according to Seldes, did not challenge the plans and decisions that created the Cold War that would dominate American foreign policy for nearly a half-century.*

THE MOST powerful weapons with which the West wages the cold war are the Atlantic Pact, the Marshall Plan, of which the former is the logical and collateral offspring, and the Truman Doctrine.

In recent years more words have appeared in the newspaper and magazine press of the world, and more words have been heard over the radio on these subjects than on any other. Nevertheless the Western world at least is less informed about them than even the most "backward" country of Europe.

One significant fact, the authorship of not only the great weapons of the cold war but the whole policy of the United States in world affairs, appeared in the *New York Times's* report of the voting on the Atlantic Pact on 1 May 1949.

Three hundred and thirty-three members of the House of Commons had expressed Britain's desire to accept, and only six persons voted No— the lone Communist, Gallacher, and a few of the independents or Left Socialists in the Labour (Socialist) Party. At the conclusion of the important news item the Times carried this significant paragraph: "In lively mood, Mr. Churchill obviously took delight in the fact that the policy he had advocated at Fulton, Mo., in 1946, had been adopted and even exceeded in the North Atlantic Pact."

In March 1946, at Fulton, Missouri, the rejected former Prime Minister of Great Britain had made the most warlike speech of the post bellum era: he called for a holy alliance, a revival of the *cordon sanitaire* of 1917, of Hitler's Anti-Komintern Pakt of 1936, a new crusade of the Western World against the East. (This was the occasion in which he knowingly had adopted for his own and given worldwide publicity to Goebbels' phrase "the iron curtain.") For America this was something new: it was indeed revolutionary, it was the greatest break with the past in history because it was not merely the forerunner of the Truman Doctrine, the Marshall Plan and the Atlantic Pact, but it was more radical than the Monroe Doctrine, it did not warn Europe away from the Atlantic shores, it meant eventually putting Washington and Jefferson in the discard and entangling the future of the United States with the future of every nation in Europe.

The man who in 1946 started the former British colony on the British path of controlling the destinies of the Continent was very consistently carrying out his great scheme of world control. He had from 1917 to 1920 been the chief instigator of the war of the Allies to destroy the new Russian Soviet state by attacking at Archangel and in Siberia.

When that failed he consistently backed every military, economic and political plan to isolate, boycott, and destroy his chief enemy. In the course of the years he joined with all the Nazis and fascists of the world in aiding this movement. He was Mussolini's greatest apologist in England, a much more significant and successful one than Sir Oswald Mosley who merely donned the black shirt and made anti-Semitic speeches in public squares.

Churchill endorsed fascism while in Rome on 20 January 1927; he admitted it and affirmed his endorsement during the war, in the House of Commons 8 December 1944.

In the early days of Naziism, Churchill wrote that "Adolf Hitler is Fuehrer because he exemplifies and enshrines the will of Germany. In five years he has restored Germany to the most powerful position in Europe."

In that last phrase the student of politics will see immediately the reason Churchill turned against Hitler, and not against Mussolini, or Salazar, or Metaxes of Greece or Franco of Spain: it has always been the tradition of British Foreign Office policy to dominate the Continent through power politics, and every challenge had been defeated by war or diplomacy. Hitler alone among the fascist-Nazi dictators blessed by Churchill menaced his Continental policy.

During the Franco uprising Churchill (on 14 April and again 7 July 1937) endorsed the fascists, and showed his sympathy for the caudillo in a statement on 24 May 1944, and once again in his memoirs as published in *Life* and the *New York Times* in 1948.

Friendship for the Japanese fascist regime for business and other reasons was expressed by Churchill on 23 February 1933, and dredged up by the *London Tribune* in the electoral campaign against the Prime Minister in 1945.

It has been no secret anywhere in Europe that outside of the fascist dictatorships themselves there has been no greater endorser of the ideology and the dictators themselves than this same Winston Churchill, who spent an entire generation in aligning the world for the war against the Soviets and came closest to success when his Fulton, Missouri, speech became the policy first of the United States, and later of the Western coalition.

And yet, not a word of this history appeared in the press of the United States. It did appear, not once, but on many an occasion when Mr. Churchill was in the news, in a large proportion of the press of his own country. Britain, and Europe, are informed about Mr. Churchill, but not the United States. No hero ever has clay feet in American journalism. Or fascist affiliations.

The seed of the Hitlerian Anti-Komintern Pakt which Churchill planted on American soil matured in almost one year to a day. In March 1947 there was announced what became known for only a short time as the Truman Doctrine, the first timid step toward the Atlantic Pact. In the first days of the Spring of 1947 America was still comparatively free from the hysteria, the witch-hunt, the war atmosphere for which the press and radio were largely responsible. Nevertheless, it was a brave and almost unique columnist or commentator or newspaper which could go against the stream of favorable propaganda. In the *New York Herald Tribune* of 6 April William L. Shirer's column was headlined:

TRUMAN DOCTRINE CALLED A STEP TOWARD WAR
Aid to Greece and Turkey Seen Highly Unlikely to Induce Russians
to Quit Europe Without Conflict That Would Destroy Civilization

"Obviously," wrote Mr. Shirer, "our own high command has not got to that point yet—of risking war with Russia. But if the newspaper accounts about the correctness of our decision to exert American military power against Russia in Turkey and Greece have any basis whatsoever, then we have certainly taken a first step. And the American people ought to know why—and what the risk, so far as it can be calculated, is."

The American people ought to know.... Returning to the same subject 25 May, Mr. Shirer added: "The molders of opinion in our press and on the air, for instance, have been almost unanimous in backing the so-called 'Truman Doctrine' as a means of improving our chances for peace. All of the great weight of the White House, of the State Department and of the leaders of both parties in the Senate has been thrown behind their conception. Yet the other day when Town Hall of the Air at the close of a public debate on the issue asked its listeners to express their own opinion as to whether they thought the 'Truman Doctrine' was leading to peace or war, 75 percent of the 13,262 persons who took the trouble to answer said they thought the President's new foreign policy was leading to war."

Obviously the great American official propaganda machine had not yet gone into action or had not been able to achieve what it wanted. Drew Pearson reported (on 16 June 1947) that Secretary of State George Marshall and his aides held secret meetings with private organizations that mold public opinion to sell the Truman Doctrine and offset Henry Wallace's blasts, as the *New York Post* reported. There was opposition in Congress too.

"If, in truth, we have found it necessary to make war upon Russia," exclaimed the conservative Senator Revercomb during the debate (*Congressional Record*, 18 April 1947, p. 3803-4), "why not tell the American people and the world that we are doing just that so they may know where we are going and prepare for it. The talk about this being a step to avert war is to ignore realities.... Why must the American people be fooled.... If we must resort to arms, why not tell them why we must go to war.... This subject is the gravest one which has confronted our Government in many years. Not only is it grave in respect to being a step toward war, but it is also grave in that we shall be undertaking a policy which may mean recurrent and continuous warfare for America...."

Senator Glen Taylor echoed the same protest. "We have therefore embarked upon a course looking eventually to a showdown war with Russia," he told his colleagues (but few others, since the press as a rule omits what Mr. Taylor has to say) on 22 April. At that day's session he also read the following paragraph from a document prepared by the Office of Naval Intelligence:

"Realistically, all wars have been for economic reasons. To make them politically and socially palatable, ideological issues have always been invoked."

And from the *Army-Navy Bulletin* of 18 January, the Senator then quoted the statement that "Today the Army has virtual control of foreign affairs," and charged that "those responsible for the welfare of the country have given up hope . . . that we can get along with Russia peacefully."

He took note of a radio poll showing the public 11 to 2 to turn the matter of aiding Greece and Turkey over to the United Nations, adding: "This is a strange situation. Never before have I seen so many Members of Congress ignore such an overwhelming voice of the people as in this instance."

The secret of the situation—a Senate "not voting as free agents" but as the victims of pressure and hysteria—was then told by Senator Taylor. He quoted an Associated Press news item which referred to the original Truman Doctrine as presented to the joint session of Congress and said:

"Anyone who stood out against Mr. Truman's request would be in danger of appearing to favor communism."

However, this diagnosis of the situation had no result whatever. If anything, it became more intense. In both Senate and House and in the press of the nation the Red label was placed on everyone—except the old reactionary isolationists of the *Chicago Tribune* persuasion—who spoke up for finding other means of peace than arming the whole world as it had never before been armed.

MARSHALL SUCCEEDS TRUMAN

Between the Churchill-Truman Doctrine and the Churchill-Atlantic Pact there was a period in which one of the greatest and most pretentious hoaxes was attempted universally, but with success only against the people of the United States. In no other country did the press fool the people by raising the bright banner of peace and good-will over the workings of the interim instrument of the cold war, the Marshall Plan.

Here again as in actual wartime, the American press fell into war psychology, permitting star spangled patriotism to prejudice its headlines and dictate the suppression or choice of facts which constitute the news. As in wartime, truth was the first casualty. The American press handled the biggest continuing news story of the year just as if it were the press of a nation controlled by a government or a regime in absolute power. No one sent it daily orders, there were no sessions of editors with the spokesmen of government, and the old flag of individualistic liberty still fluttered from the mastheads of the 1,750 dailies. But all conformed.

So it came about that while the Russian press every day was attacking the Marshall Plan, printing everything it could find against it, the American press (with perhaps the usual one or two per cent exceptions) published everything it could find in favor of the Plan. There were no "two sides" to this story, none of the objectivity about which the American press so often boasts, and as a result the American people eventually approved the measure overwhelmingly.

Several volumes have already been written on the Marshall Plan—none of them telling the whole truth—and it would take at least a volume to detail and document the statements made in the foregoing paragraphs. And in doing so the writer would have to challenge public opinion, created by the press, which has pinned the Red label on all criticism of the European Recovery Program and made fair comment almost impossible.

It is true, as the American press has repeated for more than a year now, that Moscow and the Communist press of all nations, including the United States, have opposed the Marshall Plan and done everything in their power to make it a failure. It is true, but only half true.

Millions of Communists in Europe are opposed to the Marshall Plan. But millions of non-communists—and even millions of anti-communists— are opposed to the Marshall Plan. Of these latter, all are agreeable to being aided by it, but there is more in the Marshall Plan than meets the eye.

According to everyone who knows anything in Europe the Marshall Plan is the first instalment payment on the Churchill Plan of uniting the Western nations for the purpose of waging war with the Eastern nations.

No one in political office in Europe, in London, Paris, Rome, Brussels or any other western nation believes that the Marshall Plan was just Santa Claus giving away billions for nothing.

Not only has every leader I have talked with confirmed the view that the Marshall Plan will be succeeded by a more or less public war plan, but this report, whether communist-inspired or not, has gained circulation throughout all of Europe, and scared the life out of millions of people.

These millions, non-communists and anti-communists, do not want war at any price. They do not want to fight anyone. They are indifferent to the ideological conflict between West and East. They do not give a damn about the battle between Capitalism and Communism, between Free Enterprise and Karl Marx, between Truman and Stalin. All they know is that if the battle leads to bloody war it will be fought on European soil; they will be killed, or their loved ones will be killed, and they do not want war at that price.

This is the real story of the Marshall Plan as it is working out in Europe today. It has made friends among government officials, and enemies among the millions. Paul Henri Spaak of Belgium is the leading spokesman for the ERP, but the Belgian people are scared over the next invasion, the next bombing, whether by American or Russian planes. The Labour Party of Britain officially welcomes the Marshall Plan, but the unions which compose the party, and the millions who compose the unions, are almost 100 percent opposed to participation in the next war.

The French people, the Italian people, all the people of the West, regardless of class of society, regardless of party, fascists, semifascists, communists, socialists, reactionaries, and liberals are united on only one point, and that is: the Marshall Plan and the Atlantic Pact are the forerunners of lend-lease, rearmaments, war preparations, and eventually World War III which will destroy most of the European continent and the British Isles, the lives of millions of people, and perhaps civilization itself. The only point of disagreement is whether it is the United States or the USSR which is guilty. It may interest Americans to know that there are about the same number in Europe—non-communists—who accuse the United States and Russians equally. These millions want peace, and being good Europeans they know the historical truth that every armament race leads to war. And no one can deny the armament race.

If all these moves (ERP, lend-lease, the Western Union, Atlantic Pact, etc.) are war moves, the American people should know it, and the American press (and also the radio) should print and broadcast the news. They are the means of mass information. Items of most serious import have appeared, but never in the big press, and never in the big headlines.

For example, the *Financial Times* of London was quoted (in all the newspapers of Brussels on 2 July 1948, when the present writer happened to be there) as follows: "It is possible that we shall discover shortly that our American 'benefactors' have sown dragon's teeth." A mere ironic remark about the Marshall Plan.

But in the Congressional Record of 2 April (pp. A2192-2) there will be found a speech—sensational in more than a journalistic sense—by Representative William Lemke of North Dakota which despite the fact the Congressman once ran on a Coughlinite ticket and has other such marks against his record, was certainly worth news space. Mr. Lemke had said:

"The Marshall Plan will produce only hatred and war. It is as stupid as it is dangerous.... In his armaments race, in his power politics, the President is... entering an undeclared war...."

There can be no doubt about the meaning of Admiral William Halsey's declaration (13 April 1948) that "the Marshall Plan is no longer a charitable gesture but an insurance policy"; or in the 5 June declaration by Congressman George Mahon of Texas that "If ever a war should break out between the East and the West, millions of American lives and billions of dollars would be saved if we had on our side 260,000,000 western Europeans." Since the speech favored the Marshall Plan its warlike content was unmistakable.

There are scores, if not thousands of such items; and eventually in 1949 it is taken for granted—in the small press, but never in the big press—that we are using the Marshall Plan and other political moves for war. The "U.S. wants all Scandinavia lined up on the U.S. side of the fence, tied in to the North Atlantic Pact, ready to fight Russia if and when necessary," states *United States News* (11 February 1949), adding that "peace talk is upsetting," that there is "fear that talk of peace may disturb plans for a military alliance with Western Europe."

Le Monde is the successor to *Le Temps*, which was the most reactionary—and the more influential—newspaper in the France of the Third Republic. Therefore the fact that it also, alone, with the French liberal, socialist and communist press, has not accepted the Marshall Plan at its American face value—the face of Kris Kringle, smiling as he distributes largesse—is of considerable interest. It is of great interest when the basis of *Le Monde's* swing into the opposition is a report from the United Nations meeting in Paris, written by R. H. Shackford and sent out to the whole world (which had the right to suppress it of course) by the United Press.

In France this report in several instances was headlined as "Le 'Mein Kampf' americain." *Le Monde* called it "un plan de guerre" in its leading article by M. Servan-Schreiber (15 October 1948). The UP item stated it represented the plan of Marshall himself, and had already been approved by Mr. Thomas E. Dewey, then a candidate for President of the United States and generally believed as good as elected.

The American plan, as credited to the UP and published in several newspapers in Paris, included the following "ten commandments" which follow, the quotation marks being exactly as they appeared in the French version, and the translation my own:

1. *"Refuse to negotiate on the German question" and attempt to obtain "a moral condemnation of the USSR by an enormous majority at the United Nations";*

2. *"Incite" the nations outside the USSR and the Peoples Democracies, "to march as far as possible along the road to political, military and economic unification";*

3. *"Demand of the American Congress approval of a vast lend-lease military program in time of peace, in favor of West Europe. The initial cost of this program might be five billion dollars."*

4. *"Conclude a 'North Atlantic Alliance' consisting at least of the U.S. and Canada on one side of the ocean, and on the other Norway, Great Britain, the Netherlands, Belgium, Luxembourg, France and Portugal."* [NOTE: The Atlantic Pact mentioned here in October 1948 became a headline news event of February 1949].

5. *"Incite the other European nations attached to the flanks of Western Union—such as the other Scandinavian and the Mediterranean countries—to collaborate as directly as possible with the nations of the Atlantic Alliance, if they are not able or not willing to adhere directly to that alliance."*

6. *"Attempt to persuade all the states of Europe (outside the USSR and the Peoples Democracies) that they will end up in the federation."*

7. *"Continue the diplomatic offensive which began with the Truman Doctrine and which has been followed with the Marshall Plan and with Western Union."*

8. *"Fight against the independence movements of nationalist Asia and sustain Chiang Kai-shek."*

9. "Convince the nations of the British Commonwealth that in allying themselves with Europe they reenforce themselves without weakening the unity of the Commonwealth."

10. "Fight desperately to guard, outside the (democratic) camp, the most menaced zones, such as France and Italy; and prevent the hesitants, and the partisans of 'the middle road' such as India and Argentina, from compromising the solid front."

Naturally enough the anti-Marshall Plan press denounced the foregoing as "un nouveau pact antikomintern," the successor of Hitler's Anti-Komintern Pakt and the Berlin-Rome-Tokyo Axis. *France Nouvelle* (23 October) suggested it should be called the "Frankfort-Hague-Brussels-London-Paris-Rome-Madrid-Canada-Tokyo-Alaska" Axis. The reactionary *Le Monde,* which is generally credited in France with first making public this American news dispatch, wrote of the plan:

"In other sectors, the U.S.... consolidates its position; for example, in South America and Japan, perhaps even in Germany and in Africa, which are also strategic points. But this is not enough: it is necessary that an equilibrium be established wherever there is a dangerous leaning towards Moscow.

"This is an immense enterprise. It requires a worldwide Super Marshall Plan, as large as all the disposable resources of the Americans permit; a plan which must be accompanied, in order to succeed, with exceptional internal pressure in the nations."

It is not surprising therefore to read this headline in *France Nouvelle:* "Plan Marshall: Plan de Guerre." (Marshall Plan: War Plan.)

This is one subject on which communists, non-communists and anti-communists of non-communist Europe agree, that the Marshall Plan is a war plan. The European press discusses the war implications openly.

Not so the American press.

The American press did report that there is a commission with headquarters in London which will eventually change the calibration of all armaments of Britain, America and what the East calls the "satellite nations" of the West. This is an amazing fact. If it means anything at all it means that there will be no difficulty in the supply of fighting material to Europe by America; it means that a big step ahead has been made in preparing for World War III. But although one news item so reported years ago, the American people do not know the fact and its implications.

The Paris edition of the *Herald Tribune* carried, on the morning of 13 October 1948, the headline RUSSIANS SEEN FORCING ERP OUTLAY OF ARMS, and under it, five or six inches of a Washington report which began:

> *Senator Ralph Flanders, Republican of Vermont, told reporters today that the United States had lost a "major and perhaps the decisive battle" in the cold war. He said the Russians were succeeding in diverting the Marshall Plan from the goal of European economic recovery to one of rearmament.*
>
> *Mr. Flanders predicted the Soviets "will not start war for at least three years, because Russia is gaining her ends by forcing an enormous and expensive expansion of the armed forces on this country and West Europe...."*

At this time the *New York Times* was issuing a special airborne edition for the United Nations meeting in Paris, and the next day on its arrival the same news was repeated, with this paragraph emphasized: when Mr. Flanders had remarked on the Marshall Plan being diverted into a rearmament program, he added: "This change in the purpose of the Marshall Plan interferes with European recovery, threatens our own prosperity, and is a victory for Russia."

On 22 November, *Life*, whose editor was born in China and who is No. 1 among America's pro-Chiang propagandists, stated that "The U.S. must drastically shift its official thinking on China . . . the Asiatic problem must cease to be a chore for Paul Hoffman and ECA and become the problem of the Chiefs of Staff.... And what of the Japanese—should they, as some people in the U.S. and in China already are suggesting, be armed for combat on our behalf in Asia? . . ."

And the Methodist Church on 10 December (according to the AP) warned "against the Marshall Plan becoming a 'military lend-lease program for rearming Western Europe.'. . . The church said in a resolution: 'We respectfully urge that the European Recovery Program, known as the Marshall Plan, be kept strictly to its original objectives of relief and rehabilitation.' The church's endorsement of the plan is subject, the board said, to its not becoming a military lend-lease program.'

One can also find a reference by a columnist such as this: "Every Frenchman has at the back of his mind the fear of another war . . .

"The fear of war and the present strategic insecurity of Western Europe are weapons against the Marshall Plan far more useful to the Kremlin than the Western European communists."

But, in a country where headlines are used on very small affairs indeed, and war scares have been a matter of history, there has been almost nothing at all said about "Plan Marshall: Plan de Guerre," the Marshall Plan as a war plan, as the Paris papers not once but frequently, and in some instances approvingly, report.

Outside the communist publications in America it is almost impossible to find anything in print fairly and intelligently analyzing the Marshall Plan and its collateral descendants, Western Union, the Atlantic Pact, or the proposed war commitments of the United States to the West. Ranged alongside the American Communists are some strange individuals and publications. Here is a respective sample of each:

> *Mr. Cox: Mr. Speaker, this is a serious moment in the history of our country and the world and the person who does not see it is blind.... We should strip away the veil of words that conceal the truth and let the people know something of the peril under which they live. Mr. Speaker, there no longer exists any reason why the so-called Marshall Plan should be camouflaged as a purely relief measure. It cannot be justified upon such ground....*
>
> *Mr. Speaker, the saddest thing about the Marshall Plan is that it does not put emphasis upon military assistance rather than upon economic aid. Dollars alone will not stop Russia. Force can only be stopped by greater force....*
>
> *Mr. Speaker, this bill is a war measure . . .*

Thus, in defense of the Marshall Plan as a war plan, Representative Eugene Cox of Georgia, about whom nothing more need be said.

Then there is the Chicago Tribune, which published a secret American war defense plan three days before Pearl Harbor—and was mentioned a day or two after that event by Adolf Hitler in his declaration of war on the United States. Appropriately enough one of the many Tribune editorials denouncing the Marshall Plan as a step toward World War III—the well-known Communist thesis—is introduced into the *Congressional Record* (5 May 1948) by Congressman Clare E. Hoffman of Michigan, about whom also nothing more need be said:

THE NEXT STEP

The Truman administration and the bi-partisan boys in Congress are now talking about a military guaranty for the five-nation western European coalition against the Soviet Union. A revival of lend-lease to rearm these countries and such other allies as can be mustered is also recommended.

Before proceeding to these objectives, the schemers thought it prudent to get the Marshall Plan passed under false pretenses....

Not only will the Marshall Plan fail to save us from these things [defense expenditures] at home, but it is now admitted that the Marshall Plan is not going to save non-communist Europe from communism. . .

As before, the American people are taken a little distance along the road [to war] at a time. . .

Lend-lease will not only hasten the pace of this country toward national insolvency but will put the United States into a position everywhere in the world where it can be taken into war whenever Russia, one of its satellites, or one of the countries to be taken under the American wing chooses to start the firing. . .

If Congress caves in once more, we shall be on the threshold of war just as we were in 1941.

As a peace plan, ERP has been a matter of life or death for a good many Europeans; as a war plan it would be a matter of life or death for the greater part of the civilized world, and its primary importance is certainly worth intelligent reporting and sane discussions. We have had neither in our own country. Every Russian paper without exception has attacked the Marshall Plan, but so have the majority of newspapers of the Eastern countries, and it is equally true that 90 or 98 percent of the American press has endorsed it as fanatically, and only a few warped voices—such as those quoted above—have attacked it. A nation preparing for "defense" with a budget of about 15 billion dollars a year ought to be informed of all the political moves tending toward peace or war.

PRESS, PEOPLE, ATLANTIC PACT

Secretary of State Dean Acheson declared in February 1949 that the North Atlantic Defense Pact was the most important decision in American history. That is how it appeared at the time. History may modify that appraisal but one would be on the safe side in saying it was one of three or four most decisive decisions affecting the lives of the American people.

Nevertheless, it was conceived in the secrecy of a conspiracy.

No attempt was made by the newspapers to inform the public. It was as if a dictatorial State Department had issued instructions for silence in a land where freedom of the press was unknown.

Yet, as early as 24 January 1949, the newsweekly *Time* in one of its rare exhibitions of iconoclasm, betrayed the worst instance of secret diplomacy of the postwar years. "Seldom since the war," it stated, "had a diplomatic document been drafted in greater secrecy. For more than six months in Washington and London, experts of seven nations, like diligent sculptors, have chipped away at it behind closed doors. They were still not ready to unveil their handiwork, the North Atlantic Alliance. But last week, the State Department started a sales campaign to tell the U.S. what its general form would be. To newsmen, the department handed out a 4,000-word brochure, titled 'Building the Peace—Collective Security in the North Atlantic Area'. . ."

Several months later, when secrecy and conspiracy, silence and suppression, were noted in the Senate itself, the press again was among the guilty, and again one of the few exceptions was a conservative columnist with no reputation whatever for disclosures or exposés. Arthur Krock of the *New York Times* noted on 10 March that there had been a protest, and that it had been suppressed. He wrote: "Senator Watkins of Utah voiced the feelings of many when he took the Senate floor to complain of the secrecy in which the State Department has shrouded the process of composing the text of the proposed North Atlantic Defense Pact."

Mr. Krock pointed out that Senator Watkins charged that the State Department planned to issue the document so near to the date fixed for signing that the Senate would not have time for study and debate; that immediately after the parties to the contract signed it a propaganda campaign for ratification by the United States, which Mr. Watkins said is already under way in the press, would be intensified; and that the Senator also said that "if now you turn down the President the whole world will say the communists have won a victory and you . . . are only helping the communists." But from there on Mr. Krock defends the press, saying that the Senator admitted he had depended "on a newspaper columnist for information" upon which to base his indictment of the State Department. Mr. Krock claims the Senator "indicated that in the word 'columnist' he was also covering reporters."

In truth, as *In fact* pointed out (28 March), Arthur Krock was probably the unique exception in this conspiracy of silence.

The Atlantic Pact, as the Truman Doctrine and the Marshall Plan before it, was proclaimed as being in the national interest and directed against certain aggressors not officially named; nevertheless, a patriotic enthusiasm (or hysteria, as the opponents labeled it) was created, the Red flag was hauled out as the alternative choice to the Stars and Stripes, and even the suggestion of "treason" was made against those who opposed the administration policies.

Three days after Senator Watkins' charge of discounting or suppression of this news of opposition, the press confirmed his strictures by its treatment of the Protestant Church Conference in Cleveland. The conference spoke for 35,000,000 Americans in passing a resolution for peace which said in part: "We reaffirm our firm conviction that war with the Soviet Union is not inevitable, and we believe that it is improbable." Burial or suppression was the fate of this news item.

Similarly, the action by the National Farmers Union, a truly liberal organization which speaks the grass roots language of several million men and women, was suppressed almost everywhere. The *Herald Tribune* (23 March) gave it a nine-and-a-half line story, a "shirt tail" to another item, but the rest of the metropolitan press, which boasts it is the best and is usually rated the best in the country, threw this news into the wastebasket. The voice of America's liberal farmers had spoken out against the Atlantic Pact as a war weapon.

The debate in the Senate continued through March, but none of the liberals took the lead. The most conservative members, some of them old-time reactionaries and isolationists, attacked the Atlantic Pact, but while the press was devoting millions of columns to propagandizing it, it could find little or no space for dissenting voices.

Senator Watkins was followed by Senator Malone of Nevada who on 31 March named the Bankers Trust Co., Chase National Bank, National City Bank, Irving Trust, Guaranty Trust, Manufacturers Trust and Central Hanover as the seven Wall Street banks whose directors were the most active propagandists for the Marshall Plan and which were being "paid off" by sharing $316 million worth of business under the program. The press merely reported that Sen. Malone "spoke for six hours and criticized the administration's program."

Isolationist (and frequent Russia-baiter) Senator Jenner of Indiana was Redbaited in the Senate for his opposition to the Pact, but forgotten by the press, when he said on 28 March:

"The field is so large, the misinformation is so great, the whole picture is so obscure, and the American people are so misinformed that I wish to say 'again and again and again' that I believe we cannot do all of these things (Marshall Plan, Atlantic Pact, Truman Doctrine, etc.) all over the world, all at the same time without going bankrupt....

"I have no doubt that the North Atlantic Pact will be ratified and that the Marshall-plan legislation will be passed because men say we have a moral commitment.... But let us tell the American people what we are doing when we sign such a pact. Let us tell them that we are committing ourselves to a European ground war.... If we are committed to a European war, let us tell the American mothers that World War II was a plaything.... Let up quit kidding the American people. We know the next war will not be confined to a European ground war. It will not even be confined to a continent. It will be a global war.... Then let us not kid the people.... If we are to enter into the kind of commitment proposed, the peoples of this nation might as well be told to prepare for universal military training, to get ready to make an armed camp out of the country and, tragically, to turn it over to a military dictatorship. If we do not mean what we say, let us not sign the pact."

Senator Jenner then stressed this point: that it was impossible for the United States to buy the allegiance of the people of Europe through the Marshall Plan aid or other economic measures. "Do not forget," he continued, "that you can bribe a government, but cannot necessarily buy the minds and hearts of its people. If one does not think that American popularity has hit a new low around the world, let him ask any intelligent and informed traveler who has just returned from abroad."

Senator Jenner was followed the next day by Senator Watkins who again charged press suppression of the views of Malone, Jenner, Donnell of Missouri and himself.

"I call attention to the fact," he said, "that the press of the country gave very little notice to any of the questions raised with respect to the pact." (The questions were, first, whether it did not lead to war rather than peace; also its legality; its bypassing the United Nations; its violation of articles 52 and 53 of the U.N. Charter; its break with Jeffersonian tradition.)

"In this country," continued the Senator, "where we pride ourselves on the fact that we have full information, it seems we now have an iron curtain here through which some of us cannot get through to the people with respect to certain phases of this treaty. . .

"I invite attention to the fact that when the Senator from Missouri (Donnell) who is admitted to be a great constitutional lawyer, made a speech on the floor of the Senate, some of the newspapers which claim to publish everything that is fit to print did not even mention what he had said. Yet a day or so before—or perhaps the same day—the distinguished former chairman of the Foreign Relations Committee (Vandenberg) made a speech on the same subject, and the newspapers not only gave the ordinary news story but many of them printed the text of his speech....

"Let anyone raise his voice praising the program and he immediately gets the headlines. But what has been the treatment accorded those who question the treaty? . . .

"The American people must be informed. I hope the American press, of which I have been a part in a very modest way, will at least give some information about the important questions which are being raised in connection with this treaty."

PART TWO

Freedom
Fighter

A Pattern of Behavior

In this, the introduction to his 1953 book, Tell The Truth And Run, *Seldes talks about his childhood and his family. The idealism of his family was a major influence on Seldes and steered him into the life he would lead as an independent and free-thinking seeker of the truth.*

ANYONE WHO was taught from childhood to be a non-conformist, a libertarian, and a free thinker was sure to be in trouble most of his adult days. Even in the freest of lands and the most liberal of professions, where non-conformity was frequently regarded as a virtue and nothing was taken for granted, I see now that my journalistic years, with a few short and minor interludes, have been protest and defense, a sort of forced payment for the behavior pattern which was set for me by others and which probably made my views and actions inevitable.

In the first two decades I had never stopped to consider causes and results. There had been no time. Boyhood years in an American newspaper office were adventurous, exciting beyond anything except war, and then there was the Great War itself, and after that ten years in a revolutionary and changing Europe, with excursions into Asia and Africa, all recorded by me for the entertainment, if not enlightenment, of a million readers of a Middle Western newspaper.

The birth of a new order of society, the march of dictators, the rise of Bolshevism in Russia and Fascism in Italy, the Fabian push of Socialism in one country, the revival of monarchy in another resulted in thousands of news items only a few of which are worth remembering today, but they filled all my days breathlessly and left no time for thought.

Thus the years passed, so full of the moment, so busy with events, that in my encounters with men and history I had no leisure for questioning or reflecting or reasoning—not until certain days in Vienna in 1926 and 1927, in a city where almost every foreign correspondent bumped his head into the new psychology—and many had their minds opened by the blow.

By coincidence and good fortune this did happen to me at the time of my most upsetting experiences, my first American assignment (in 1927) after 11 years of foreign service during which I had been free to write as I pleased. Now, censored and suppressed by the rich and powerful *Chicago Tribune*, as I had been in my boyhood by the poor and hungry and therefore dishonest and venal *Pittsburgh Leader*, I wanted to leave the profession, or trade, of daily journalism, anger and disillusion now forcing a decision.

I was still years away from that third stage of a man's life which, according to Balthazar Gracian, is the chapter of self-examination and meditation. I was now thirty-seven and exactly one half of these years had been given over to the newspaper adventure, and there was more to come. But it was never to be the same, thanks to the change I experienced that year in Vienna.

The catalytic agent in my life was not a metal or a current, but a man. He was Alfred Adler, the founder of the school of individual psychology, onetime disciple of Sigmund Freud (of whom I had heard in the first rare Freudian wave which engulfed only Greenwich Village in 1916) and later his rival (whom I was to introduce to the laity in a *New York World* article in 1926).

He refused the label "father of the inferiority complex," which many tried to stick on him, while insisting that the study of the "feeling" of inferiority was of vital importance.

Dr. Adler changed my attitude and my career just as surely as certain forces shape the lives, the behavior patterns, of all the people in the world in their childhood. He did it in a most remarkable manner because I was not his patient; I was not being treated by anyone. I was in his house one day as a journalist and later, many times, merely as one of his guests, drinking his tea and eating Mrs. Adler's little cakes and listening to a wise man talk in simple words about the forces which shape a life.

He did it with his magic phrases. When he first spoke of "the feeling of inferiority," which, he insisted, every man and woman living and dead had experienced, and the lifelong struggle everyone makes to overcome it, how this feeling expresses itself, the compensations for it, the search for "the equation for one's individual inferiority, the tests for one's behavior pattern through relationship to society, to one's work, and to sex"—speaking without the jargon of the time or the profession—he gave me a true revelation, much more significant for me at least than the experiences of a certain Biblical character on the road to Damascus.

It seemed to me that just as there are now magic bullets being made in laboratories, wonderful drugs which cure certain diseases almost instantly, so there were certain words which men of genius could arrange in a certain order so they became not merely the common tools of everyday communication, but magic shafts of light into the dark and hitherto unpenetrated curtains of the mind. I was as effectively influenced by the Adlerian phrases as one of Tolstoy's characters was by a simple question.

You may remember the story: a man returns home after many years, goes hunting, and that night when his brother begins going through all the crossings and mumblings of the Orthodox Russian rite, he says, "Do you still keep up that thing?" The brother stops mumbling and crossing himself and never again returns to the ritual.

Tolstoy says the words spoken by the brother "were like the light push of a finger against a leaning wall already about to tumble of its own weight. These words but showed him that the place wherein he supposed religion dwelt in him had long been empty, and that the sentences he uttered, the crosses and bows which he made during his prayer, were actions with no inner sense. Having once seized their absurdity he could no longer keep them up."

And so I now tried to explain a long and not uneventful newspaper career in the terms I had heard and had accepted as true. First of all I asked myself why I had gone into this work despite an upbringing which had made me shy, the least forward of all the boys and girls in my schoolrooms, always uneasy, always preferring the background to the "x" which marked the spot of any exciting event.

There was nothing of the true adventurer in me in a time of roaring, brawling, journalism. Was it a coincidence or a compensation that took me for my most exciting years into the camp of the magnificent Floyd Gibbons, whom myths and legends hardly exaggerate. It was Floyd who once addressing a shy and studious lad, inclined obviously toward cultivating the arts and his own personality, gave him the official order to "have personal adventures." And the lad did. He was our colleague Jimmy

Sheean—but the Celtic Gibbons thought that name was too shanty Irish and ordered him to use Vincent.

Floyd also cut the Henry out of my name, and despite my not wanting to scoop the world, or even to push myself forward, or to get on the front page, or to have my signature appear in print, he made an adventurer out of me for a decade as he had of Sheean and other reluctant ones. I hated the first person singular and avoided it always in newspaper work and in the many books preceding this one. Despite Hemingway's writing that "I knew. . . George and he was a damn fine newspaper man," that wasn't so. There were amazing coincidences and the "great scoops" were accidents. Yet it was wholly within the truth when Joseph Brewer put on the dust jacket of my first book a blurb about my beating the world on the rebellion in Syria and the bombardment of Damascus, with the result that the Arabs threatened me with disembowelment and the French in turn accused me of fomenting a revolt in their Foreign Legion; that the Black Shirts had tried to beat me to death with clubs the day after Mussolini had ordered my expulsion from Italy for exposing his personal complicity in the murder of his rival, the Socialist leader Matteotti; that I had previously been expelled from Moscow by Trotsky for smuggling out important, sensational, but nevertheless true stories the Soviets wanted to suppress; that the dictator of Fiume, the purple poet D'Annunzio, had ordered me shot because I had been interviewing secretly his dissident Yugoslavs; that I had fought the censors in 20 countries (a slight exaggeration), participated in three wars and a dozen revolutions, been present always where the hard gem-like flame of journalism burned its brightest over scenes of violence, bloodshed, and death; lived dangerously and magnificently for the benefit of the readers of "the world's greatest newspaper."

Was all this the compensation for my feeling of inferiority? Was all this the fulfillment of the Alderian behavior pattern?

Did the behavior pattern explain youthful actions in Pittsburgh, such as my seeking out and presenting the correspondent of the Socialist *Call* of New York many of the best items the corrupt newspapers were suppressing in 1909, and a mature and spontaneous decision, in which my wife shared, to uproot ourselves in Vermont a quarter of a century later so we could go to the battlefields in Loyalist Spain and counteract in at least one newspaper the daily falsehoods against a true democracy which filled most of the press of the world?

There was an inner compulsion to go to Spain. Was there also compulsion those past decades for speaking and writing, not out of partisanship, but out of a feeling of simple justice for the small, the weak, the minority, the voiceless, the disinherited? Were these compulsions developing out of the old behavior pattern inflexibly set during the years of childhood, shaped by my parents, by those who brought me up and the environment in which I was born and raised? If Adler was right, and in 1927 I accepted him without doubt or questioning, then the life I had lived, the things I had done, the adventures I had gotten myself into and even the self-examination of a later day, had been conditioned by the three pattern-makers: my mother who died when I was six, my father who had to make a living in the city and did not stay long with us on the farm, and an aunt who sacrificed 10 years of her life for my brother and me.

I cannot say surely that I remember my mother, but I do remember the day she died because it was a day of public mourning. All the people of Alliance, the "utopian" town father founded in New Jersey, it seemed to me, were gathered in the rooms of our house and under the big hickory tree which sheltered the kitchen. At least a score of women sat on chairs and on the floor weeping and crying aloud and actually beating their foreheads from time to time, while the men moved about sadly with tears in their eyes. It was the only time in the town's history that death was more than a personal matter. The farmers came from everywhere to tell my grandfather and grandmother that my mother, who was not their daughter, was the best woman they had ever known in their lives. And all the rest of my life on the farm I was to hear from everyone old enough to know her that she was a good woman, the kindest woman they had known.

I remember the day she died: it was in the autumn and I was at my uncle's, that is, my cousin Sidney Bailey who wanted us to call him uncle, helping harvest the sweet potatoes, and as my reward I carried all I could in my sweater which I had turned up a few inches to hold them. It was getting dark when I came home and I could hear the loud weeping from a distance. But in life I remember my mother only vaguely and only in very short flashes, as if the pictures were shown to me only a few seconds. I see her one day going up the stairs and looking back at me, but I do not remember anything that was said. My clearest memory is of the night a friend arrived from the city—his name was Bacall—and the occasion was phenomenal because he brought with him a machine that talked and recited words you could almost understand and sang sad songs—all with a whirling of the flywheel which went so fast you couldn't see the little lead balls, and with an unending accompaniment of a scratching sound which came from each wax cylinder, regardless of subject. I have that glimpse of mother standing in the doorway between the living room and the kitchen that wonderful night, saying that it sounded better in the next room, at a distance.

All the rest, I am afraid, are not memories but the stories told me by my grandmother who had worshipped her daughter-in-law as an angel on earth.

During the next 10 years I was to hear from all the farmers who came to the post office more tributes to their lost friend: she had written their letters, she had advised them on many things she knew of which they were ignorant, she had once gotten up a petition for relief which they sent to an institution, she had been the kindest, the most self-sacrificing, the most unselfish, and the most public-spirited person in the colony. And one day, 55 years later, I got a letter from a man who had read one of my books, and he too recalled my mother in the same way. I asked him if he remembered her at all, and he replied that he remembered only that she had done something good for every member of the community.

My Aunt Bertha, Father's sister, came to Alliance and brought us up through the decade 1896-1906. She had given up her career as a trained nurse in Philadelphia to live on a sandy unfertile farm without the comforts which pass for civilization. There was not one bathroom in the colony, and no one had running water. Electric lines and telephone wires were unknown in this land but thanks to my father the post office he established remained in our house despite rebellious rumblings in favor of rural free delivery. My aunt succeeded my mother as postmistress and continued to receive $50 every quarter from the government when she could show that she had not only sold but canceled that amount in postage stamps. Our $16.66 a month was a larger cash sum than the other farmers ever saw.

Aunt Bertha had nothing to do as a trained nurse except deliver all the babies in a ten-mile radius, and so far as I can remember she never lost a mother or one of the 300 children she brought to light in that decade. She never asked a fee, but it became the custom of the countryside to pay her $10 for the week's attendance, including the birth. The poorer farmers gave her only $5 along with their excuses, and the one exception who gave more than ten was a small clothing manufacturer who could afford $25.

It was a very moral neighborhood without adultery or scandal. But among the newcomers when I was growing up and could understand such things, was a dubious widow and her rather pretty but mentally backward daughter, who had taken over an abandoned house and lived there without any visible means of support. The older boys said that the widow sold beer to the Polish hired hands on Sunday and to strangers from outside the colony, and that there was frequently accordion music in the place and dancing and laughter, and some even hinted of livelier goings on. Then it became obvious to even passers-by that the daughter was pregnant. The farmhouses were full of whispers, "the man" was rumored to be the postmaster of the next village, and incidentally our rival because it was his plan to make his office the headquarters for the rural free delivery which would put us out of business.

My aunt, whose code of ethics was stricter than the Hippocratic oath, worried about it for months, and her fears were justified. One night there was a pounding on the door. It was a sound to which all of us were accustomed, for it happened about once a fortnight for 10 years. But this time it was the widow, the mother of the town moron.

Grandfather opened the door and told her to go get a doctor. We could hear angry voices. Then my aunt came down.

"There are three doctors and other midwives in Vineland," she told the widow. "You can get there in half an hour. I won't have anything to do with you."

The widow cried so loud the lamps went on in the farm across the way.

"No, no, no," she screamed. "You must come. You must come. I won't go away. I'll stay here until you come, and if you don't and my daughter dies, it'll be your fault. I'll give you twenty-five dollars. I'll give you fifty," shouted the widow.

My aunt said, "I don't want your money."

By now my grandmother had also dressed and was downstairs, and she and grandfather were also shouting at the widow to go away, and my aunt was insisting that the Vineland doctors were better, and there was general hysteria. Across the road we could see the neighbor's two grown-up sons in the morning grayness moving in front of their house.

My poor intimidated aunt put an end to the episode by packing her small black leather valise and leaving with the widow for the mile walk to the house of less than good fame. She was gone all morning, and when she came home she was exhausted, not because it had been difficult, but because it was the first illegitimate childbirth in her career. By her own moral code she was implicated in something wrong. She was emotionally upset, she showed a temper for the only time I can remember, she quarreled with her mother and father, she was sharp with us.

But she went through her usual week of daily trips to her patient, looking after mother and child, cleaning up the house, giving instructions on cleanliness, on feeding, on general care. The little bastard was duly registered in the bureau of vital statistics at the state capital, and I, who wrote out the pink slips for my aunt, for the first and only time put the initials "O.W." on one of them and learned the meaning of the words "out of wedlock."

The week over, the widow arrived one afternoon and offered Aunt Bertha a country fortune, three months pay as postmistress, fifty dirty dollars.

My aunt didn't look at the money; she didn't hesitate.

"You will please go away," she said to the widow, "and please never come here again."

The widow did not insist or try to leave the fifty dollars with my grandparents. She went away. And then my Aunt Bertha was herself again, as cheerful as always, as kind to us as she had been from the first days when she won our loyalty and love. This was her great act of renunciation; it was purification, perhaps not through pity and fear, but for her very much like a classical catharsis. It restored her. It cleaned up an evil matter and she could now forget it and live again the normal routine of the farm community, bringing to life about once a fortnight a child born within the honest nine months after the date of the wedding ceremony—a matter on which my grandmother kept unfailing records.

It had been my father's purpose to establish one of the idealistic, Utopian colonies of which there is a long American history. He believed in the fundamental goodness of the human being and the possibility of changing what was commonly called human nature. For that end he preferred, I am quite sure, the modern school rather than political action and revolutionary methods.

Father was a libertarian in the American tradition. I doubt if he had read Karl Marx, but I have no doubt he read and knew Thoreau and Emerson and Wendell Phillips. And just as Thoreau had accepted, without saying where he got it, the motto "The government is best which governs least," so Father, following Thoreau, agreed that "carried out, it finally amounts to this, which also I believe—'That government is best which governs not at all'; and when men are prepared for it, that will be the government which they will have."

To this same end Father sought advice from the two greatest libertarians of his time. For several years he exchanged letters with two persons on this subject: Prince Peter Alexeyevich Kropotkin and Count Leo Nikoleyevich Tolstoy. One of my earliest memories is of Father sorting out the Tolstoy letters which were written on the largest sheets of paper I ever saw, as long as legal paper and somewhat wider, and in obviously foreign purple ink. (Years later, in Pittsburgh, an illiterate washwoman needing paper to start a fire, burned up the contents of a large box containing all the Kropotkin and Tolstoy letters, and the world lost a footnote if not a chapter of its great literature.)

With Kropotkin, Father discussed mutual aid which he hoped to make the guiding principle of the colony; the new American intensive agriculture; Socialism—which Kropotkin had made his political philosophy in Switzerland in 1872—and the philosophical anarchism of the Jura Federation which, in despair over the slowness of Socialism, he had joined a few years later. Kropotkin had proclaimed his faith in "a principle or theory of life and conduct under which society is conceived without government—harmony in such a society being obtained, not by submission to law, or obedience to any authority, but by free agreements, concluded by the various groups, territorial and professional, freely constituted for the sake of production and consumption, as also for the satisfaction of the infinite variety of needs and aspirations of a civilized being" (as he wrote in the old Encyclopaedia Britannica under the initials P.A.K.). This was the noblest concept of the human being in the ideal state ever penned by mortal man, but Father wanted to know how to apply it practically in a colony of three hundred souls, less than a hundred families, most of them poverty-stricken, living on poor land, and badly educated, even in farming. Kropotkin tried to put his philosophy into practice—through the agency of letters to my father—and these are the letters that are lost forever.

The Tolstoy letters, father said, dealt also with the management of a colony of people with an ideal philosophy in which true or pure Christianity was to be practiced as it was in the early days, during the time of the first Christian communities which certain partisan later day writers were to call the first experiments with communism.

With these great correspondents, as with the men and women with whom he argued, there was one purpose, one common goal, the answer to the question; how best to arrive at the perfection of the individual. Prince Kropotkin had actually studied agriculture and its intensification in

America at the time, to prove his theory that the farmer as well as the industrial worker could obtain all he needed for the good life with only half a day's work—giving him the major portion of his time for art, literature, philosophy, and even sport; and thus perfection. Not collectivism, but mutual aid was necessary for this achievement, and he called it "free communism," although he described it as "individualization"—but not the individualism of the times, which brought with it all the evils he would end. From my earliest childhood, therefore, I was indoctrinated with the idea of individualization.

My father argued with his cousin Sidney Bailey, the village philosopher. There was no one else with whom he could talk about anything but farm problems. Occasionally someone with a large beard and flowing hair would come from Philadelphia or New York, and if it was winter the kitchen would be taken over for arguments rather than cooking and eating, and if it was summer the shade of the great hickory tree outside the kitchen would be the scene of such deep and long discussions that food was forgotten by the principals while the famished children were given bread and butter to sustain them through the hours.

It was different in Philadelphia where, after working as a clerk in a drugstore for years while studying law at night, Father finally had to surrender to family pressures. The Commonwealth of Pennsylvania under the Act of 1887 "to regulate the practice of Pharmacy and sale of Poisons, and to prevent Adulterations," issued Father a license under which he opened his own drugstore at Fifth and Carpenter Streets and began wasting a great part of his life in selling patent medicines to ignorant strangers with whom he tried to talk philosophy.

But almost every evening, and late into the night, there were people in the store's back room discussing not only Kropotkin and Tolstoy but Walt Whitman, who lived across the river in Camden, and Thoreau and Emerson, Gorki and Ibsen; and later on, Debs and American Socialism.

To this Philadelphia house I was only a visitor. After my mother's death and during the years Father was making a better living and could have brought the family to the city, he still kept us in the New Jersey farmhouse (dominated now by my aunt instead of my grandfather) in the belief that country air and country food and the care of a trained nurse would bring his boys up in better health than was possible in the city slum in which he ran his drugstore.

It was on one of these occasional visits that I made my first acquaintance with American journalism. It was 1905 now and Father was the secretary of the Friends of Russian Freedom, which had raised money and otherwise aided the attempt that year to upset the Tsar's government. Father had written "A Declaration of Independence for the Russian People," greatly influenced by the American Declaration, the same noble phrases, the same high ideal, but, bowing to the demand of the time, concluding with a ringing appeal for a few dollar contributions for current expenses.

One day when my brother Gilbert and I were in Philadelphia the reporters of all the papers came to get the "local angle" on the Revolution in Russia. Listening to one of them telephone his office, I remember saying to Father in a whisper, "He is quoting you just as you said it," which impressed me very much. And then I learned my first lesson in what is news. The reporter concluded his telephone call in something like these words:

". . . Seldes says that the fight to save the Russian people from the tyranny of the Tsar will go on, and nothing can stop them from establishing a free republic modeled after the United States. He says he is in touch with similar organizations in England and France and elsewhere, and that funds are being raised throughout the world to prepare for future uprisings, if this one fails.

"Next item: There was a spectacular fire this morning at 27 Carpenter street when a string of dry clothes on a line on the flat roof of the building was ignited from an unknown cause. The fire leaped from one clothesline to another and soon the top of the house seemed to be on fire. And wind spread it to clotheslines on other houses. It was a big show for thousands in the street . . ."

The "spectacular" fire was reported on page 1, and my father's prediction that in spite of the tragedy of 1905 the Russian Revolution could not be stopped appeared somewhere on an inside page: it was a follow-up, a shirt-tail to the news, and the news from St. Petersburg was no longer of equal importance with a clothesline fire in Philadelphia.

As one of the leaders of Friends of Russian Freedom, Father became known to all the enemies of the Tsar of Russia everywhere, and his house was their rendezvous. In that same year of 1905 a young actress named Alla Nazimoff—she was unmarried and therefore could not grammatically call herself Nazimova, although the Shuberts later did—and her patron and tutor, the noted Russian actor Paul Orlenoff, came to New York and acted in Russian to small audiences. In Philadelphia, Father and my stepmother Nunya arranged some performances. They were great artistic successes but did not provide even a few months' financial security and Father had to take the two actors into his home for a while.

The following year Father was on the front pages of the nation's press again. The literary world was celebrating the visit of Maxim Gorki, one of the world's great writers who had actually risen from the lower depths, from not only the lowest class but from the outcasts of the working class, the tramps. He had been honored everywhere in Europe, and so had his common-law wife, Madame Andreyeva, with whom he was traveling. But the Russian Embassy in Washington made an announcement to the press that the couple was not legally married, the press spoke of "moral turpitude," and the management of the Bellevue-Stratford, the leading hotel of the City of Brotherly Love, literally threw them out, bag and baggage, into the street, the writer's gold watch disappearing during the excitement. The Gorkis came straight to the drugstore. Moral turpitude became a phrase in all the newspaper-reading nations of the world. The drugstore was overrun with reporters interviewing Gorki; there were foreign "repercussions," there were statements from American preachers, priests, rabbis, and the leading lights of literature. Mark Twain laughed it off by saying that someone should have told the foreigners about American customs and manners: "Why, that man might just as well have appeared in public in his shirttail," he concluded; but Edgar Lee Masters defended the Russian novelist seriously, saying there was "much more at stake than the relations of Gorki and the Russian actress," and he chided his fellow American writer, Clemens, whom he called a "great satirist and cathartic of American pruriency" for missing his chance "in this instance."

Gorki stayed a little while, discussing Kropotkin and the Russian soul, then returned to a civilized old Europe which forgave great men.

The next year was one of economic panic, and a relative persuaded Father to go west—to Pittsburgh, Pennsylvania—where there was more opportunity and where making a living was not so dreary a matter. He bought the drugstore at the corner of Center Avenue and Roberts Street from an old man named Harley who had shown him he could take in $50 a day, which meant a $17 profit, or enough to pay off the mortgages and bank loans and credit advanced for new fixtures and for merchandise. The place was modernized, and over Father's objections a soda fountain was installed.

It was a growing neighborhood crowding into a slum. The first days from morning to night men and women came asking for something mysteriously or merely nodding knowingly or making a motion with their hands or heads in the direction of the cabinet in which Harley had kept narcotics; but when Father, who knew soon enough what they were after, refused to sell them "drugs" his income dropped to almost nothing. Rival druggists near and far continued to sell heroin and cocaine to Negro workmen and white prostitutes, but they were good registered members of the Republican and Democratic Party ward machines, active in politics as all good citizens ought to be, and they paid money to the right people. Later on they made fortunes in whiskey, while Father even had his doubts about the ethics of legal sales of Duffy's Malt, which was advertised as a body builder but never in demand except on Sundays when the saloons were closed. Father had no "protection." He had even ceased to support the Democratic Party now that the great William Jennings Bryan with his cross of gold and crown of thorns was no longer running for President and there was no post office to keep in the family.

The corner policeman, representing law and order and the free enterprise system under which we lived, came to the store the second or third day to ask for a cigar, but he did not attempt to pay for it, which was in the old tradition. But he did not leave. He stayed a long time, then asked if Harley hadn't left word. Harley hadn't. The word was that the policeman expected a sum of money with his cigar every week—hush money, money to hush up the sale of cocaine and heroin and whiskey on Sundays. Father was indignant. He respected the law, he loved the law, he obeyed the law, but the corner representative of the law was our enemy ever afterwards.

We were continually persecuted. One day following the foregoing episode, two United States revenue men stepped off the streetcar, crossed to our drugstore, and arrested Father for keeping the covers of his cigar boxes under them, unattached. Father could prove that each stamp fitted, he had not cheated the government by not paying the tax. But the law said the cover must remain attached, and the plea of saving space was useless. The revenuers confiscated all the cigars before ordering Father to a hearing which cost him a lot of money, and regardless of the suggestion that the people across the street, and the drugstore on the next corner, and everyone around him tore the tops off cigar boxes, the two men boarded the streetcar and never came to this neighborhood again.

But worse than commercial attacks upon Father was unfriendliness and in some instances a boycott by the doctors. He paid no one "kickbacks" nor did he send physicians on whom his living depended expensive reminders of his devotion at Christmas, although such investments would have paid off at more than six percent. He had told them he was going to run an ethical pharmacy, and he meant it, although even then the days of ethics in pharmacy were about over, and merchandizing rather than dispensing of medicines had won out. Nor would Father have more than one or two doctors around socially because their thinking was ordinary and he did not believe in "entertainment" as a way to success. He did not prosper.

He had many sayings by which he guided his life, or repeated as a guide for us. One of them, perhaps not the first in importance to him but surely the one which impressed me most, was: "Never compromise on the great principles." He really never did.

As a libertarian he did not believe one should belong to a party, a group, a sect, an organization—since there never were and never could be organized libertarians—and he believed conformity was a criminal act, a betrayal. "Who would be a man must be a non-conformist," he would say when I was very young. Later, when I began to read books, I knew he was quoting another of his teachers, Emerson.

He urged a questioning mind, no acceptance of the conventional ideas and the conventional lies of our civilization, and from his admonitions I made my motto of those days (and even now): Take nothing for granted.

One of Father's favorite quotations was Proudhon's "Property is theft," and the first words he taught me in French were *la propriete', c'est le vol,* without the accent marks of course.

(Father left no property to speak of; the house in his name was built with my savings and there was little inside it except books. In his last years he spent the weekly allowance Gilbert and I sent him on feeding too many persons and almost starving himself, as we found when we took him to a hospital in New York, where he died in 1931.)

The disappointment of his life had been the failure of the colony he had helped found at Alliance. He had wanted to start it in Oregon where land was good and success possible, but others got a bargain in 3000 cheap dusty acres near Vineland, and there in the 1880's some 300 souls from the slums of the cities tried to make a living. Many died of tuberculosis and typhoid. Many starved. Eventually even the name "Alliance" disappeared because it was not on the railroad and Father's post office gave way to the modern R.F.D.

But Father continued from one experimental colony to an other, constantly disappointed, as who would not be who believed in the perfection of the human being in our own time. The greatest blow he suffered was just before he died. In establishing the Mohegan Colony in New York

State, with the aid of his lifelong friend Harry Kelly, he insisted that it write into its charter a strict warning against any party or group or clique getting totalitarian control; and there were amendments and rules voted at his request to maintain a democratic form of government. Everyone had to have a minimum of ideals—that was the only qualification for admission—and no group was to be boss. But in the course of a few years conflicts which had been philosophical became political, and the vast majority, the liberals and the individualists, were defeated by the town's minority Communists, who alone had organized and planned and intrigued and finally taken over the machinery of the government. The state had not withered, as Marx had predicted; the undisciplined were not happy.

Only once in his life had my father been a member of a social political movement. In 1886 while working as a librarian in New York, he had volunteered his services to a man named Henry George, candidate for mayor of the city (or was it governor of the state?), and accepted the philosophy still known today as Single Tax. In later years he voted for William Jennings Bryan, but he remained a Single Taxer all his life, since this theory did not conflict with individualism. In 1890 he named his first son after his hero, but even in this he was consistent in his iconoclasm, not saddling him with the exact name, to be known and dated always as Henry George Seldes, but giving me the names George and Henry, telling me years later I could place them as I wished. (The Henry was deleted by the almighty Gibbons in 1919.)

My father had a sense of humor and therefore he was not a "character"—an impression the foregoing paragraphs may possibly create. He was in no way fanatical, nor even messianic in his thinking, certainly not in his actions, and he made no effort in the highways to preach and convert the heathen. In those dark days no one expected anything to happen during a lifetime, or in that of his sons and daughters; it was more of a dream than a reality; they had a platonic relationship with "the revolution" in Russia, in Spain, and in other tyrannies.

If a man had ideals, he read great books, he talked, he argued; and if he planned, it was merely for the mental exercise. Father, for instance, did not join the Socialist Party and follow Eugene V. Debs, although he admired him and his practical, optimistic followers who believed in Utopia in our day. Many on the Left in the early part of the twentieth century, Father among them I believe, would have been frightened to death if a practical success for their ideals had suddenly threatened them.

There was no prospect of the Single Tax program or the Debs party coming into power. One ought not to be apathetic about the future; but this future of the great days was as far distant ahead as the Golden Age of Athens was in the past, and equally to be desired, and equally to be considered, philosophically of course. After the failure of 1905 Father never hoped in his lifetime to see the overthrow of the Tsar and the liberation of the Russian people, nor did he ever expect to see anything as radical as the New Deal in America, with government agencies dealing out general welfare and for the first time in the history of the United States giving encouragement to art and science and literature. Certainly he could not even foresee his sons living through a Second World War in which revolutionary forces would overturn not only a large part of Europe but roar across India and China and shake the foundations of the entire Asian continent for the first time in almost 2000 years.

He was content to read and think and talk, and philosophize. He loved to recite Shakespeare and Shelley, rather well too, for he was not a bad actor. My childhood was full of "Men of England, wherefore toil /On the everlasting soil," and I can hear pounding in my ears:

> *The seed ye sow, another reaps;*
> *The wealth ye find, another keeps;*
> *The robe ye weave, another wears;*
> *The arms ye forge, another bears,*

And I knew the legend of Prometheus and was told its meaning before I could understand it. Now I think that although my Father was a tragic and frustrated figure, he was, if only in a minor way, Promethean.

My mother whom I do not remember, my aunt who guided my life for ten years, and my father who came and went—these are the three who according to my mentor Alfred Adler are so greatly responsible for much that I have done and said and the way I have gone through my decades of American and European journalism.

It could not be done without some compromise, but no compromise was the ideal. No compromise. No roundabout, as the boyg suggested to Peer Gynt. Question everything; take nothing for granted. And never commit yourself to a group, a party, a movement; never commit yourself entirely, because that would be bondage.

I have often thought of this during the many years in which book reviewers, opponents in radio debates, and certain members of certain committees of the Congress and others who noted my membership in organizations to fight Naziism and Fascism and the Spanish dictator Franco, have insisted that I was a Communist or, as certain knowing ex-Communists had it, "a Stalinist"—at least until that day in 1948 when I went to Yugoslavia, interviewed Tito, published the first true story of the attempt by the USSR to colonize and exploit his country, and his defiance of the Cominform.

It would have been impossible for me ever to become a member of the Communist Party or any party having iron discipline, forcing one into a fixed and rigid, unbreakable and unbendable program, directing its followers on how to live and breathe and speak. Non-conformity, individualism, were in my behavior pattern, if not my bloodstream. I had attacked the Communist State for its denial of individual expression and for using the policy of the end justifying the means for the plan they alleged furthered the general welfare. I was expelled from Moscow in 1923. But I praised various Communist parties when they joined non-Communists in the Popular Front to save Spain from Fascism in 1936. Again, in 1948 when I saw Russia and its Cominform at work, notably in Yugoslavia, I returned to the attack, and for the same reasons as 1923; I could both damn and praise; I remained, or at least believed I remained, what my father taught me and wanted me to be—a free man.

When Blood Is
Their Argument

It is hard to imagine in the present day the brutal suppression of civil liberties and civil rights that took place in some parts of the United States in the 1920's and 1930's. This brutality was directed at any person suspected of challenging the status quo. Seldes offers some examples of this shameful part of our nation's history in this selection from his 1937 book You Can't Do That.

THE LAWLESSNESS of the police, judicial actions favoring property as opposed to human rights, illegal injunctions, official or unofficial incitement to violence by those in authority frequently cause a state of terrorism. This state of terrorism may exist for only a day or two, as in the 1934 San Francisco vigilante riots, or it may persist for years, as in Harlan County, Kentucky. Very often it produces no visible proofs but sometimes it results in bloodshed and scores of cases of violence.

Though terrorism, violence, bloodshed are usually charged to labor, "the record shows that in 15 years not a single radical has been convicted for an act of violence, but scores have been imprisoned for radical opinions," reports Roger Baldwin, the director of the American Civil Liberties Union, and "the record also shows that those who defend the existing economic system not only advocate but practice violence without fear of punishment."

Baldwin's organization has also published the statement that "in all our experience of the last 15 years in handling free speech cases all over the country, we do not know of a single specific incitement to violence by any radical." Mr. Hearst, the American Legion, the Chambers of Commerce and the majority of the nation's daily newspapers, which have spread falsehoods and propaganda to the contrary, have never presented any evidence or proof.

The fact that all the weapons are on one side is in itself important evidence that almost all the violence is on one side, since it is a military axiom that deadly weapons provoke deadly use.

The yearly analysis of the casualty lists of men killed and wounded in disputes with city police, state militia, national guardsmen and vigilantes, proves that scores of persons lost their lives and the means of livelihood because only one side was armed. That side represented the triumph of property over life and civil liberties. In five months of the New Deal, when labor believed the government had suddenly become its partisan, 22 persons were killed in industrial conflict: an organizer was stabbed by a scab; two men were murdered by vigilantes in California; a Negro union leader was lynched by landlords, two Mexican-Americans were shot to death by sheriff's deputies; one man was killed by national guardsmen who willfully fired 100 shots into a civilian gathering; one man was beaten to death by New York police and one shot for "talking back." . . . In those same five months there was no instance of workingmen or strikers or "mobs" killing a representative of the law.

The press (with perhaps a 10 percent exception) reports neither the issue of property versus lives nor the economic motives of the frequent terrorisms and continual bloodshed. Occasionally, however, there is an instance so flagrant and horrible that the background and motivation must come to light. But even then justice may not triumph.

Twelve men had been kidnapped, of whom one was murdered, another mutilated, all beaten, tarred and feathered by a group of Ku Klux Klansmen and police acting for political grafters and cigar manufacturers of Tampa, Florida. Little was said about these happenings in the press, no one was ever convicted, and when one of the unlucky sadists was arrested he was usually bailed out and defended by many of the best citizens of Florida. But the Committee for the Defense of Civil Rights in Tampa hoped to break this conspiracy by arousing the nation over the murder of Joseph Shoemaker.

Shoemaker was a Vermonter. He was one of the organizers in Tampa of the Modern Democrats. a political organization not affiliated with any radicals and yet devoted to bringing about a system of production for use instead of profit. On the night of 30 November 1935, just six months after Shoemaker had moved to Florida from Vermont, he and his friends were arrested as they were writing the constitution of the Modern Democrats, using the American Legion's constitution as a pattern. On the police docket under "Why Held" appeared the words "Investigate Communists," but since there was no case against them, they were forced, after cross examination, into police cars, taken into the country, and beaten.

Policemen and Klansmen, after flogging Shoemaker with rawhide and chains, poured melted tar into the wounds and burned one foot over a fire. When, the next day, he was found and taken to a hospital the surgeon said, "He is horribly mutilated. I wouldn't beat a hog the way that man was whipped. He was beaten until he is paralyzed. . ." After nine days of agony, Shoemaker died, the victim of the agents of the citrus growers, one of whom told Junius B. Wood, a correspondent for the North American Newspaper Alliance, that "citrus growing is a $100 million industry in Florida, and, as it cannot afford to pay higher wages, labor organizers must be discouraged." The Tampa cigar manufacturers, afraid their workmen also might ask for higher wages put up $9,500 bail for each murderer.

In just the same manner as the steel corporation once fought unionization in the Pittsburgh district, so Tampa, which makes 65 percent of the nation's cigars, is fighting the cigarmakers' unions. In 1910, five labor organizers were lynched; in 1931 manufacturers connived secretly for an anti-union drive, and in 1932 (Anita Brenner revealed in *The Nation*) police and vigilantes of Tampa joined manufacturers in fighting labor. George Googe, Southern representative of the American Federation of Labor, himself a Southerner, told a labor convention that he would "as soon live under the worst foreign dictator as attempt to function as a labor organizer in certain sections of the South."

Under these circumstances the attorneys defending the men, who were eventually found guilty, took the tip from the Hearst press, American Legion, Chamber of Commerce and power company publicity bureaus, and raised the old red flag. "Didn't you know that Communism was so active in Tampa that the business people called on the police and sheriff for protection? . . . " and similar questions, were asked the accused sadists. Unbiased reports from many parts of the state expressed amazement that "aliens" should be so upset by another flogging and tarring, even if one man did die, inasmuch as this practice, and even killing, "are not unusual here as a means of disposing of persons who are disturbing to certain interests, or to what is vaguely called 'social order'." I am not of course implying that the citrus growers and the cigar manufacturers convene and discuss the "disposal" of workmen who want higher wages or leaders who threaten unionization, but it is certain that the businessmen do declare themselves against labor, "foreign agitators" from the North, and native "radicals," and that Klansmen and businessmen resort to the suggested violence. Certainly every sheriff, police captain, and National Guard colonel whose men blackjack pickets or strikers believes he is preserving law and order and will perhaps sincerely swear he is not indulging in violence to protect the interests of the Super-Super Textile Corporation or the Super-Super Orange Growers Association. Nowadays the recourse to bloodshed is indirect but the motivation is the same. Shipping companies, fruit growers, cotton farm owners, the heads of manufacturing concerns are just as responsible for the terrorism that exists today in Alabama and Arkansas, in the Imperial Valley of California, in the coal and steel towns of Pennsylvania and in the manufacturing centers in time of strike as Henry Clay Frick was when he brought up to Homestead in barges the Pinkertons who shot and killed Frick's employees.

Midsummer of 1937 and the Shoemaker case was still being dragged out. In the town of Bartow, six Tampa policemen were on trial charged with the second degree murder when testimony was heard that Bridges (one of the accused) hit Shoemaker on the head with a gun butt. The indictment had stipulated injuries to "the body and limbs," so Judge Dewell ordered the testimony stricken, ruling that the head was not part of the body.

In July 1937, the Florida Supreme Court reversed the lower court's decision which had confirmed the sentence of guilty in the case of the five policemen charged with kidnapping another of the 12 victims, E. F. Poulnot, president of the Florida Workers' Alliance. The Tampa civil liberties committee protested to Governor Frederick P. Cone, citing the following record:

> *(1) Nineteen months after the atrocious crime not one guilty person had been jailed;*
> *(2) Four of the 11 indicted men have never even had to stand trial;*
> *(3) The Florida Supreme Court has held up a decision on the appeal for six months while the convicted men are allowed to roam at will throughout the country;*
> *(4) Judge Dewell has consistently refused to set trial dates on the murder indictments although it is plainly his duty to do so.*

And in Florida in 1937 the Ku Klux Klan again paraded in its night-sheets. Its announced program of hatred was no longer officially directed against Jews, Catholics and foreigners, but was pure Red-baiting.

Who are the present day California vigilantes? In the town of Santa Rosa 300 of them, to give but one illustration of scores of acts of vigilante terrorism, attacked labor leaders with gas bombs "loaned" by county authorities, tarred and feathered, terrorized and deported their victims. In the daily press there were news stories of "a spontaneous outburst of farmers against communist agitators," and it is possible that a few farmers were in the vigilante mob, but none of the county's thousands of bankrupt farmers. The Santa Rosa vigilantes consist of several bankers, a head of the federal reemployment bureau, motorcycle policemen, a member of the state legislature, American Legionnaires, petty politicians, members of the Chamber of Commerce, and, according to a suit filed by a victim in the county court, the mayor himself, who is a banker.

Whereas in Tampa the newspapers attacked the kidnappers, in Santa Rosa the bloodthirsty mob had the support of the press. The *Santa Rosa Press-Democrat* glorified the vigilantes, said mob action would bring "plenty of results that will herald to the world what Sonoma County means to do to Communist agitators," and published a truly remarkable story of mob action written by one of the mobsters. This eyewitness and participating vigilante tells the following story:

"Awaking after a ghastly night of terror that came near reaching the point of bloodshed and lynchings, I am firmly convinced today that Sonoma County will purge itself entirely of all communists—and at any cost.

"Never in my life have I seen such a grim, serious minded band of citizens as determined upon their objective as the vigilantes were in seeking to oust radical agitators.

"It was just at dusk that we assembled after an emergency call from our leaders. Nearly 300 men responded.... We formed in two groups.... It was an awe-inspiring sight ... carrying weapons ranging from rifles to home-made billy clubs and ready to battle against men who ridicule the American flag.... Someone has to teach these communists they are not wanted... "

(*Inasmuch as there was no communist meeting to be raided, the vigilantes in a downtown hall discussed "the impending trouble that is feared in the hop, prune*

*and grape harvests unless Communists are driven out." Then someone shouted
"Let's go drag 'em from their homes." The Vigilante then continues:)*

"Soon six men returned dragging a cringing and pitiful looking spec-
imen of a man to the center of the hall....

"'What'll we do with him?' someone shouted.

"And came a multitude of answers

"'Give him the works.' 'Run him out.' 'Get the tar'...."

(*It was decided to use the man, Jack Green, as a decoy for others. He was taken
to the Sol Nitzberg ranch. When Nitzberg answered the knock, Green "doublecrossed"
his captors, by warning the intended victim and dragging him into the house.*)

"Nitzberg . . . fired one barrel of the gun high as a warning. . . . He
was in plain sight of the vigilante gunmen but they wouldn't shoot
because of fear they might hit the wife or children. It became a strange
siege almost like war days.... Two of the gas shells ripped through the
window into the house but failed to explode. A third struck on the window
sill and burst outside, sending a great wave of painful searing tear gas back
upon all of us. It was awful! After gagging and choking a while our gang,
looking all the wilder with tear-stained faces, finally shot a successful shell
into the house.

"A cry arose as the gas went through every room in the structure. The
woman shouted 'We'll come out, we'll come out.' A cheer went up from
the boys outside.... In a few minutes out walked Nitzberg—sullen, bitter,
refusing to say a word. With him was Green, terror-stricken and gasping at
the thought of going back into the hands of the wild mob. Our boys
surged down onto the pair, seizing them roughly and dragging them
down the road to the cars....

"When we got back to the warehouse, the story of the shooting and
Green's attempt to escape spread like wildfire. The pair was dragged into
the hall—stupefied from fright and beatings. By that time another man, C.
Meyer of Cotati, had also been brought in and a short time later Ed Wolff
of Healdsburg was added to the four victims. It was a sight that few who
saw it will ever forget. Dimmed lights added to the ghastly scene caused by
the milling crowds of vigilantes in varied masks and other disguises.

"It had been an all night task, but at last the climax was near and
everyone was on edge. Our leader addressed us and the radicals caught,
declaring, 'Sonoma County is not large enough for such men as you who
are attempting to overthrow the government under which you live !' . . .

"An American flag was produced and the pair asked to drop to the
floor on bended knees and kiss it. Both refused sullenly, but not for long.

After a count of three, fists swung through the air. Both men dropped to the floor, semi-conscious. They were shaken back to sensibility enough to obey the order and kiss the Stars and Stripes. Wolff pleaded that he was not a Communist . . . . One man pushed his way through the crowd to face Wolff, grasping him around the throat in powerful hands. A hush came over the crowd as the vigilante cursed and berated Wolff with Communist activity and finally ended with a dramatic shout: 'Ed, my hands are on your throat—and the only thing that keeps me from crushing the life out of your cursed body is that I believe in Almighty God!'

"After pleading that he would gladly get out of the country at once and stay out the crowd agreed to release Wolff. Meyer and Ford were given the same warning and also escaped the tar and feathers. But the impatient mob waited no longer with Green and Nitzberg. Clippers were produced and hair hacked from their heads. Shirts were ripped from their backs. Buckets of tar paint were hurled over them. Pillows were broken and feathers hailed down upon the sticky black substance. From two men they had been transformed into fantastic, ghostlike creatures of some other world.

"Communism in Sonoma County was getting its due—and the vigilantes, restrained through most of the night, came near going wild. Kicked, beaten, dragged and shoved the two staggering tar victims—their eyes glazed with torture and terror—were taken out into the street. Then came a procession that Santa Rosa has never seen the like before. Down Fourth Street they walked, clear past the courthouse and on out of the city limits—while behind them followed the wildly shouting and triumphant vigilantes.

"It was a long night, a wild night. But the vigilantes are just as determined that there will be other such nights as long as Communists continue attempts at radical agitation in Sonoma County. The ultimatum has been issued. The vigilantes have proven they are ready and willing to back it up with violence. It's up to the Communists to get out now, or suffer the consequences."

Thus on the night of 21 August 1935, a mob of bankers, business men, Legionnaires, and other "better" citizens, "mobilized by the Chamber of Commerce" according to an ACLU report, with the weapons and moral support of official authorities, overthrew law and order, violated every fundamental right, and boasted about it in their press, while the attorney general refused to look into the business and the governor ignored the violation of state and national constitutions. Six vigilantes were identified and civil suits brought against them when officialdom refused to bring criminal action. Finally the Liberties Union instituted suit against Fred Cairns, charging him with being the leader of the mob. Incidentally, says the ACLU report, Cairns, who is secretary of the Healdsburg Chamber of Commerce, is really an alien—a term always used by certain patriots in attacking Americans from other cities or states who show an interest in local civil liberties.

There are whole districts in the United States ruled by the same terrorism that one finds in Italy or Germany. And as in these countries, it is never seen by tourists—or Tories. But as sure as sunrise, which also is frequently invisible, the terrorists will get you if you enter certain counties in California, certain districts in Alabama, the tenant farm zone in Arizona for the purpose of writing for the liberal press or, worse still, for the purpose of talking unionization. Carleton Beals, the noted writer, informs me that the moment you leave the main highways in Alabama, you are in danger. He himself, arriving in a small town by bus, was immediately visited by vigilantes who questioned him and, although they learned nothing, advised him that for inquisitive "aliens" the next county was much healthier.

This is a typical story of terrorism in the depressed areas in the United States. Howard Kester, organizer for the Southern Tenant Farmers Union, describes what happened to him in February 1936 in Arkansas:

"At night deputy sheriffs and masked men ride the roads, on the lookout for secret meetings of the union.... Beatings are frequent and killings are not uncommon.... Planters even organized a Fascist band wearing green shirts and carrying the swastika as its symbol. . . . Hundreds of our members have been beaten and scores of families have been driven from their homes by terror.... At least 10 of our members have been killed.

"Just a few weeks ago at Earle, Arkansas, armed vigilantes broke up a meeting in a Negro church and shot two men.... The next day while I was addressing 450 white and Negro members of the union in a Methodist church, about 15 armed planters and deputies came into the meeting house. I was dragged from the platform and thrown into my automobile by three men while the others began beating members of the union, men, women, and children. The interior of the church was wrecked."

That terrorism is the weapon of the "better element," the leading citizens, the merchants and Legionnaires and law officials, rather than the method of radicals, is shown in every instance of its use. There is not a single case of vigilanteism in Alabama, Arkansas and California which can be charged to labor. All come from the employer class.

The flogging of Willie Sue Blagden and the Rev. Claude C. Williams in Earle, Arkansas, was fully reported in the national press, as was the arrest of Josephine Johnson, the Pulitzer Prize novelist, Joe Jones, the painter, and Caroline Drew, a labor organizer. Northern papers also reprinted an editorial of the *Earle Enterprize* upholding flogging as a method of preventing "foreigners" from trying to raise sharecroppers' wages from 75 cents a day.

Just five days before the leading citizens of this neighborhood emulated the sadists of a Hitler concentration camp (to the loud cheers of the local editor), Norman Thomas had telegraphed to President Roosevelt, then in the midst of a political campaign in which he held aloft the liberal banner, that "because of the critical development of the cotton strike a word from you is imperatively necessary."

Franklin Delano Roosevelt journeyed to Arkansas and said, "This is the first chance I have had to enjoy the generosity, the kindness and the courtesy of true Arkansas hospitality."

After the president's return to Washington his Socialist rival said: "The president knows all about the situation in Arkansas but because of political expediency he went into Arkansas and did nothing but praise Robinson." From Arkansas he again telegraphed the President "to act in this monstrous perversion of everything decent," adding, "you have just come from Arkansas where you eulogized the state and its leaders without reference to peonage, mob law, and murder."

And that is the important fact. There is not only a denial of civil liberty in Arkansas (Sheriff Campbell ordered Miss Johnson not to talk to anyone about unions and not to talk to colored people on any account), but as Sherwood Eddy, the Christian sociologist reported, "we found peonage, serfdom, poverty, disease—and sometimes terror and violence."

In fact eight million Americans were reported living in conditions approaching peonage. Some were driven to work at the point of a rifle. Mr. Eddy investigated a place near Earle, an hour's ride from Memphis, where a "killer" had built a stockade and kept "slaves"—men arrested for vagrancy—in a concentration camp. City Marshal Paul D. Peacher, a cotton planter, was later arrested on the charge of violating the federal anti-slavery laws and found guilty.

There were of course public trials and public hearings, and a blast by the governor against "foreign meddlers." An armed mob which came to lynch the Civil Liberties attorney, C. T. Carpenter of Marked Tree, was driven off. But since no solution of the economic problem of tenant farming is possible without a radical change which will radically affect the pocketbooks of the landowners, the terroristic situation, which has been called "the training ground for the forces of Fascism in the South" since it is a working agreement between law and private property against labor, must remain. "Leave or be lynched" is still the attitude of the employers of Arkansas.

Carleton Beals found Alabama camouflaged feudalism and serfdom. Negroes who gave him evidence against the planters asked to have their names suppressed because they lived in fear of lynching. Anyone suspected of being a member of the sharecroppers' union is subject to eviction, denial of government relief, persecution, and the threat of physical harm or even death. Eight sharecroppers have been reported murdered in Alabama, many have disappeared, more have been whipped, and about a hundred are in jail.

In August 1935, according to Al Jackson ("the most hunted person in the black belt, writing this in the shadow of the lynch rope"), a strike was called at J. R. Bell's plantation in Calhoun, Lowndes County, Alabama, where Sheriff R. E. Woodruff insisted that the men work. The Negro strike leader, Willie Witcher, was shot eight times. "Under the personal leadership of Sheriff Woodruff of Haynesville a gang of landlords, deputies, and small town rowdies were organized to terrorize the strikers. More than six Negro strikers were carried off at night, beaten almost to death and left in the swamps. On 22 August this same gang raided several homes. Jim Merriwether passed the door of the Calloway shack unarmed. He was seen and shot down. The gang found Jim Merriwether's wife, beat her, hung her from a rafter for 'sport,' and then released her. The local newspapers carried on a rabid lynch-inciting campaign.... On 2 September . . . The vigilante gang went to Hope Hull and attacked the home of Ed Bracy, militant Negro union leader. When Bracy tried to escape he was shot down.... Every vestige of human, civil and constitutional rights has been swept aside by landlords, sheriffs and vigilantes in their murderous campaign to keep the living standards of the farm toilers down to a starvation level. To break the strike, the landlords have murdered five men."

White agricultural workers fare little better than Negroes although fewer are lynched or shot down by deputies and landlords. Industrial workers and labor organizers also experience Alabama terrorism. For example, in June 1936 the offices of the United Rubber Workers Union were destroyed, the labor leaders driven out of Gadsden. In September, Joseph S. Gelders, World War Veteran, former instructor in the University of Alabama, and secretary of the National Committee for the Defense of Political Prisoners, was kidnapped in Birmingham and badly beaten. A year earlier a committee consisting of writers Bruce Crawford, Jack Conroy, Emmett Gowen, Shirley Hopkins and Alfred Hirsch, the majority Southerners, went to Alabama to investigate abuses of civil liberties under the auspices of the aforementioned committee. They first tested the Downs Law, under which 18 persons had been imprisoned. This was a Birmingham city ordinance making possession of a single copy of a radical publication (legal elsewhere in the United States and in the mails) punishable by six months on the chain gang. They distributed the *New Masses, Labor Defender, New Theater, New Republic* and *Nation.* They were seized, pushed into the city jail, and two were photographed for the rogues' gallery and fingerprinted. Hirsch was struck on the head by an officer. Then the writers were told they were not arrested and that the publications were not violations of the law. However, this printed matter was the kind that would offend "a certain element, some anti-radicals" and therefore, said the interrogating detective, "I won't be responsible for what may happen to you.... I can't protect you."

En route to the capital to ask Governor Bibb Graves to veto an anti-sedition law, the two cars carrying the writers were shot at five or six times. "A frame-up for publicity," Governor Graves told the press .

In Harlan County, Kentucky, violence against miners has been common for more than five years. In 1932 the murder of the youthful organizer Harry Sims came to civilized attention, and a group of writers went to investigate. Waldo Frank and Allan Taub were beaten and the press was sent false reports by local correspondents who were as active in Red-baiting and anti-union activities as the owners themselves. Theodore Dreiser headed a second investigation committee and was immediately indicted for criminal syndicalism. A student delegation was deported, its members taken to Tennessee and beaten up. Everyone agrees that civil liberties no longer exist in Harlan, have hardly existed since the economic debacle of 1929 and that a virtual dictatorship does exist, intimidating or controlling the press, the law-enforcement officers and the ministers of the gospel. Dreiser's book *Harlan Miners Speak* is a great human interest document historically important in America's labor struggle.

The terror in the fruit growing valleys of California is also of long duration. Since state and federal officers refuse to intervene, the employers and their hired thugs make the law, which is in the tradition of the old California Vigilantes except that the victims are no longer thieves and murderers but underpaid fruit pickers and other workingmen and women. One of the victims was James Rorty, the writer who came to investigate for the *New York Post* and *The Nation.* Congressman Maury Maverick declared in the House that the California officials responsible for Rorty's deportation are more dangerous than the entire Communist party. General Glassford, the federal conciliator, reported that the "growers have exploited a 'communist' hysteria for the advancement of their own interests."

Behind the terrorism in Gallup, New Mexico, there is the paramount fact that under the New Deal an attempt was made to unionize the American Coal Company, a subsidiary of the Morgan-controlled Kennecott Copper Company. The coal company decided to break the union. You cannot make personal devils out of the Morgans or the owners of Kennecott by charging the murders that followed, or the present injustice, or the state of terror to them; we merely record it as another indictment against the present finance-capital system.

There had been an eviction of a striker. On 4 April 1935, a group of Mexican coal miners legally denied entrance, gathered outside a local court during the trial of a union leader. The prisoner was hustled out of court into a back valley. The crowd followed. The frightened armed deputies threw gas bombs against the unarmed crowd, then opened fire with .45 revolvers. Two miners and Sheriff Carmichael were killed.

Six hundred and one unarmed miners were arrested.

Every conceivable violation of civil rights, revival of every dead-letter law, kidnappings, beatings, deportation of witnesses, terrorization of the populace of five thousand followed, when the new sheriff deputized 200 American Legionnaires and mine employees to round up 15 percent of the entire population on the charge of first degree murder. This charge was made possible by an 1854 law of frontier times which can be applied to every person present at a place a murder is committed.

Witnesses testified Carmichael was killed by mistake by his own men. The statement by deputies that the two dead Mexicans had shot him was disproved; neither had a gun, no weapon was found, the bullet killing the sheriff came from a .45 fired at close quarters, from the left, where his own men were. Of the 10 eventually charged with murder three were sentenced to 45 to 60 years in prison. Those chosen for punishment were those active in unionization. There was no more evidence against them than against the other 598.

Attorney Wirin, for the defense, stated, "I do not say that the attorney general of the state of New Mexico and the district attorney are in the actual pay of the Gallup American Coal Company. I do say that they should be, for they are serving well the interests of the mining corporations of Gallup who will stop at nothing to destroy the workers' organization in order to continue their exploitation."

Attorney David Levinson and Robert Minor, who came to Gallup to investigate the case, were seized in front of the leading hotel, taken by vigilantes into the desert, and beaten. The attorney general of the United States refused to act in this kidnapping despite the fact the crime was committed on an Indian reservation, federal land. The vigilantes donned bed sheets, burned fiery crosses, and threatened all from other states who made inquiries. Judge McGhee jailed persons who distributed leaflets on the case. Mrs. Lorna Stimson, niece of the former Secretary of State, was ordered out of Gallup because she had been seen at the trial.

Years of investigation by the ACLU have resulted in the following indictment of the real advocates of violence, the reactionaries. "Those who call for violence against radicals, strikers and Negroes go scot-free," says the ACLU report. "Not a conviction, not a prosecution in years. Lynching of Negroes in the South is commonly condoned or encouraged in private utterances. Excited employers or professional patriots often urge violence against Reds and strikers. . . . The declarations of various semi-Fascist 'shirt' organizations which have sprung up in recent years advocate far more violence in seizing the government than can be found in communist publications. Yet not a single leader has been prosecuted for such language....

"But the reactionaries not only incite violence; they practice it. Witness the story of almost any strike.... Reflect on the brutal treatment of the Negro, our shameful lynchings. Take the Ku Klux Klan in its heyday.... Over 2000 cases of mob violence were cited in an official investigation of Klan activities in the state of Oklahoma alone. And yet not a single person committing or inciting these violent acts against strikers, Negroes or radicals has ever been punished.

"It is plain, therefore, that those who defend majority prejudice or property rights may not only advocate but practice violence against their enemies without fear of prosecution...."

Libertarians through the ages have agreed that liberty is not a code, a paper, something static, fixed, once one and forever present. Freedom must continue to struggle in its own defense; otherwise it degenerates. Lincoln realized that there was a continual war, a never ending struggle, when he declared that "the cause of civil liberty must not be surrendered at the end of one or even one hundred defeats," and Bertrand Russell believes that "the old battles for freedom of thought and freedom of speech, which it was thought had been definitely won, will have to be fought all over again, since most men are only willing to accord freedom of opinions which happen to be popular." As Leon Whipple, the historian of civil rights, sums up, "Liberty cannot be inherited. It must be won and won fresh for each issue in each generation. Our father's liberties are little help to us. The old spirit may free us but never the old words."

The American tragedy is the mental inability of vast strata of society to distinguish between the real libertarians and the enemies of liberty quoting the founding fathers. The "danger of abridging the liberties of the people" of Abraham Lincoln's time has grown in our time. Not so much the present war on radicals but the intolerance of everything liberal, from culture to statesmanship, which finds extreme expression in murder and lynching, and which in steel mill towns, coal mining regions, in the deep South, on the farms and in California, produces a simulacrum of a Nazi reign of terror, proves our liberties are especially endangered in time of economic danger.

Certainly those who realize human life loses all value when liberty is denied the individual must be willing to unite and work and fight to preserve the old and gain even greater freedom.

In the words of Patrick Henry in 1776, "If we wish to be free we must fight."

A Man on Horseback

Here is a story that seems unbelievable, but is true. In 1934, a group of businessmen and industrialists plotted to overthrow the government of the United States and install a fascist regime. The plotters first approached Marine Corps General Smedley Butler to be the leader of an army of 500,000 men who would march into Washington and seize power. Butler considered the plot an act of treason, and exposed it. The evidence was documented before a Congressional committee, but was eventually supressed by both the press and the committee. Seldes tells what happened in this selection from his 1937 book, You Can't Do That.

THE ULTIMATE and complete destruction of civil liberties is in the program of every reactionary and fascistic group and movement. Liberty and Fascism cannot coexist. Wherever Fascist movements have started, therefore, in order to gain necessary mass support, they have had to supply substitutes for civil liberty—ultra-nationalism, superpatriotism, a popular cause, or the overthrow of a great national injustice, such as the Versailles treaty was for Germany.

In almost all countries where Fascism has stirred, there is a previous record of putsches, coups d'etat, coups de theatre, military fiascoes and violent uprisings. The Beer Hall Putsch in Bavaria 10 years before Hitler's triumph, General Sanjurjo's reactionary-monarchist uprising in Spain in 1932, four years before he started the Spanish civil war, the various Vienna revolutionary days, and the De la Rocque battle of the Place de la

Concorde in February 1934 are certainly the forerunners of more violent climaxes.

If Fascism ever comes to America a certain plot involving several leading Wall Street bankers and several leading American Legionnaires, ridiculed at the time of its exposure by the majority of the press, will gain historical importance as a parallel to the foreign episodes of the pre-ceding paragraph.

The reader, I hope, has long since graduated from that vast mob of millions which enjoys being fooled by the newspapers all the time, and joined that new army of millions which in 1936, with 80 to 90 percent of the press publishing hokum and even lies, went to the polls, elected Mr. Roosevelt and repudiated to a great extent the dishonest journalism of the time.

The present story concerns the testimony of General Smedley Butler and a Wall Street plan to place him, or a high officer of the Legion, on a white horse, march into Washington, and rule the nation, using President Roosevelt in much the same way that Mussolini uses the King of Italy.

It is significant that the newspapers of America did not publish the entire testimony, that many suppressed it, that the majority laughed at it, and that a congressional investigating committee, examining the witnesses months later, came to the conclusion that every allegation in the sensa-tional charge against Legionnaires and bankers was amply proven.

Evidence was obtained, concludes the report of the Congressional Committee on Un-American Activities (74th Congress, first session, House of Representatives, Investigation of Nazi and other propaganda, pages 9 and 10) "showing that certain persons had made an attempt to establish a Fascist organization in this country.... There is no question but that these attempts were discussed, were planned, and might have been placed in execution when and if the financial backers deemed it expedient."

The evidence before the committee, corroborated and accepted, charged Legionnaires, bankers and brokers—the counterpart of the Hitler-Thyssen-Flick-Schutz-Staffel-outfit—with planning to hire General Butler to overthrow the government. The go-between, it was testified, was Gerald G. MacGuire of the brokerage firm of Grayson M.-P. Murphy & Co. Mr. Murphy was a lieutenant colonel in the Rainbow Division, American Expeditionary Force in France, and one of the little group of rich officers who initiated and financed the American Legion in 1919. In the 1936 election campaign he was treasurer of the Du Pont-financed Liberty League. He was also a director of the Guaranty Trust Company, Anaconda

Copper, Chile Copper, Goodyear Tire, Bethlehem Steel and the New York Transportation Company. With other numerous war medals he wore the ribbon of the Crown of Italy awarded him by the Fascist regime.

The other important broker mentioned in the testimony was Robert Sterling Clark, also one of the original financiers of the American Liberty League.

According to General Butler the number of war veterans necessary to establish a Fascist regime was placed at 500,000; the amount necessary for the march, $3 million, was "on the line," according to MacGuire.

In the conference on 22 August 1934, in the Bellevue-Stratford Hotel, Philadelphia, MacGuire proposed the attack within a year, General Butler testified, and after the capture of the capital the soldier organization was to take over the functions of government.

"To be perfectly fair to Mr. MacGuire," continued the general, "he didn't seem bloodthirsty. He felt that such a show of force in Washington would probably result in a peaceful overturn of the government. He suggested that 'we might even go along with Roosevelt and do with him what Mussolini did with the King of Italy.'

"Mr. MacGuire insisted that all of his program was 'constitutional'," continued the General. "He proposed that the Secretary of State and Vice-President would be made to resign, by force, if necessary, and that President Roosevelt would probably allow MacGuire's group to appoint a Secretary of State. Then, if President Roosevelt was willing 'to go along,' he could remain as President. But if he were not in sympathy with the Fascist movement, he would be forced to resign, whereupon, under the Constitution, the Presidential succession would place the Secretary of State in the White House.

"Then he discussed the need for a 'man on the white horse,' and insisted that a show of armed force was the only way to save the capitalistic system. He told me he believed that at least half of the American Legion and Veterans of Foreign Wars would follow me.

"I was amazed at the audacity and bluntness with which the proposition was put to me. I have always believed in democracy, and I felt it my duty to learn all I could of this conspiracy and to see that the information was placed in the hands of the proper governmental authorities."

MacGuire, according to the testimony, then described a trip made to Europe for the purpose of studying the Nazi movement in Germany, Fascism in Italy, and De la Rocque's Fiery Cross in Paris, the part World War veterans played in all, and how these examples could be followed in the United States. He talked of "a man on a white horse," and as alternates for Butler mentioned General Douglas MacArthur, chief of staff of the United States Army, whose term of office was to expire that November, and Hanford MacNider, former commander-in-chief of the American Legion.

At a previous conference, coincident with the reunion of the 29th Division in Newark, MacGuire, according to testimony of General Butler, "came into my hotel room, pulled out a worn wallet, and started to toss thousand-dollar bills on the bed. I asked him what the hell that was for, and he told me it was to pay my expenses to Chicago to make a speech in favor of the gold standard.

"'You know damn well it doesn't cost $18,000 to go to Chicago,' I told him.

"'Don't be a fool, General,' he told me, 'Why don't you do like Harbord and Sims did and make some money out of it? The Government doesn't take care of you, so why don't you act like a business man?'

"I told him to pick up the money before I threw him out. I then suggested that one of the men who were providing all these thousand-dollar bills come and see me, so I would know who was back of it all.

"'Murphy [Grayson M.-P. Murphy] is in Europe,' he told me, 'but I'll have Colonel Clark come to Newton Square on Sunday.'

"Clark called me on Saturday from New York and reminded me that we had served together in China in the Boxer trouble in 1900. He told me that he would like to come and see me and discuss old times.

"Clark came to my home the following day and offered me money to go to Chicago to make the speech on the gold standard which MacGuire had previously given me. MacGuire told me he wrote the speech, but Clark said that John W. Davis, Democratic Presidential candidate in 1924, had written it. After we discussed the proposition for a few minutes, I told Clark he ought to be ashamed to come into a man's home and try to bribe him."

Robert Sterling Clark, Butler testified, said, "I have got $30 million and I don't want to lose it. I am willing to spend half of the $30 million to save the other half." But the General was not tempted. He testified that in his presence Clark telephoned MacGuire to go ahead with a $45,000 fund. The Legion in due time passed a gold standard resolution.

Altogether there were five conferences. At one of them a man named Doyle, a wounded Legionnaire of Boston, was present and a bankbook showing deposits for $64,000 was said by MacGuire to be his expense money for the trip to the American Legion convention where he was to speak for the gold standard:

"At the same time," continued General Butler, "he showed me several checks, drawn for large amounts, signed by Robert Sterling Clark, John Mills and Grayson M.-P. Murphy, which he said were to be placed in his account to cover 'necessary' expenses at the Chicago convention....

"Several months later, when I asked MacGuire who was backing his movement to set up a dictatorship, he said, 'The same people that financed the Chicago propaganda.'

"At all times," said the General, "I refused to accept any money from any of these men....

"The whole affair smacked of treason to me."

He had thought it treason from the beginning. He had called in Paul Comley French of the *Philadelphia Record* on 1 September 1934 and French, who later also testified before the Congressional Committee, helped him obtain the evidence. General Butler arranged for an interview between French and MacGuire. Mr. French tells what happened:

"On 13 September, I met MacGuire in his office, which is part of the suite occupied by Grayson M.-P. Murphy & Co., on the 12th floor of 52 Broadway.

"At first MacGuire seemed unwilling to talk freely and discussed generalities for a time. Later, however, he warmed up to the subject and told me substantially the same story as that related by the General.

"'We need a Fascist Government in this country,' he insisted, 'to save the nation from the Communists who would tear down all that has been built up in America. The only men who have the patriotism to do it are the soldiers, and Smedley Butler is the ideal leader. He could organize a million men overnight.'

"During the conversation he told me he had been in Italy and Germany during the spring and summer of 1934 making a detailed and comprehensive study of Nazi and Fascist organizations, and the part war veterans had played in their success.

"'The whole movement is patriotic,' he continued, 'because the Communists will wreck the nation unless the soldiers save it through Fascism.

"'All General Butler would have to do to get a million men,' he said, 'would be to announce the formation of the organization and tell them it would cost a dollar a year to join.'

"He suggested that necessary arms and equipment could be obtained from the Remington Arms company on credit through the Du Pont family, which has a controlling interest in that company.

"'I am close to the President,' he continued, 'because I served as a naval aide when he was Assistant Secretary of the Navy.'

"'I think the President could be persuaded to name General Butler as head of the CCC camps,' MacGuire continued, 'and that would give him the basis of an organization. However, if that doesn't work, I have no doubt the General could enlist 500,000 men in a very short time.

"'What we really need is a man on the white horse to save the capitalistic system.'

"He shoved a letter across his desk, saying it was from Louis Johnson of West Virginia, former National Commander of the American Legion. MacGuire said Johnson wrote he would be in 'to discuss what we have talked about.'

"'That's just what we're discussing now,' he told me.

"During our conversation he mentioned that Henry Stephens of North Carolina, another former National Commander of the American Legion, was interested in the plan.

"'Roosevelt hasn't got the real solution to the unemployment situation,' MacGuire said, 'but we'll put across a plan that will be really effective. All unemployed men would be put in military barracks, under forced labor, as Hitler does, and that would soon solve that problem. Another thing we would do immediately would be to register all persons in the United States, as they do in Europe. That would stop a lot of Communist agitators wandering around loose.'"

Mr. French concluded with the statement that MacGuire hoped to get General Butler's consent "to head a Fascist movement" within a few weeks.

General Butler had hardly concluded his testimony before the Congressional Committee, confirming the French story, when J. P. Morgan and Thomas W. Lamont arrived from Europe. Mr. Morgan was silent. But Mr. Lamont, believing the testimony "too utterly ridiculous for comment," declared it "perfect moonshine"; Colonel Grayson M.-P. Murphy said it was a "fantasy," adding "it is absolutely false so far as it relates to me and my firm, and I don't believe there is a word of truth in it with respect to Mr. MacGuire." The latter thought it was "a publicity stunt," and denied it "completely."

From Paris came word that Mr. Clark denied he was either a Fascist or Communist, affirmed he was an American, admitted he had asked

General Butler to influence the Legion. The newsweekly *Time* in which there is a Morgan interest (through Harry P. Davison) spoke of a "plot without plotters." The venerable *New York Times* spoke of "Fascist plot" in quotations, devoted half its front page story to denials, and later referred to "the so-called plot of Wall Street interests" and affirmed that it "failed to emerge in any alarming proportions."

The Congressional Committee, headed by Representatives John W. McCormack and Samuel Dickstein, was apparently thoroughly frightened by the dangerous disclosures. It had started out ostensibly to get the evidence on a few German Nazis in Hoboken. It was to conclude by turning the committee into a forum for fine Red-baiting, the wildest rumors and malicious falsehoods. But it certainly had not intended to step on bankers' and brokers' toes, let alone place pistols to their fascist heads. So it ran for cover. "This committee," it announced, "has no evidence that would in the slightest degree warrant calling before it such men as John W. Davis, General Hugh Johnson, General James G. Harbord, Thomas W. Lamont, Admiral William S. Sims or Hanford MacNider." However, the committee heads said they would call Mr. Clark. The committee did not mention the most mentioned name, that of Broker Murphy.

Murphy was never called. Legion Commander Belgrano was never called. None of the men whom General Butler named as the financial backers of the Fascist march on Washington was called by the McCormack-Dickstein committee. The sensation was allowed to die down. The big business press tried to laugh it to death. Then on the fifteenth of February 1935 the committee's findings were published confirming the allegations of General Butler and the fact that Wall Street had plotted to establish Fascism. As for the denials made by Gerald C. MacGuire, the Congressional Committee concluded: "MacGuire denied these allegations under oath, but your committee was able to verify all the pertinent statements made by General Butler, with the exception of the direct statement suggesting the creation of the organization. This, however, was corroborated in the correspondence of MacGuire with his principal, Robert Sterling Clark of New York City, while MacGuire was abroad studying the various forms of veterans organizations of Fascist character."

Whereupon, having proven a Fascist conspiracy against the Republic, the committee devoted almost its entire report to denouncing Communism and made no suggestions about combating the Fascism of Wall Street.

The big business press, caught cheating again, either suppressed the story or gave the part of the report dealing with Butler the least possible space. But the General, on the other hand, sprang another important sensation. Using the radio to make his charges, he accused the McCormack-Dickstein committee itself of suppressing the most incriminating parts of his testimony, of failing to disclose the names he had mentioned, of failure to call the important witnesses, of "slaughtering the little and allowing the big to escape." If the committee cared to get at the whole truth, said General Butler, it should call:

Grayson M. P. Murphy, Wall Street broker.

Louis McHenry Howe, secretary to President Roosevelt.

Alfred E. Smith.

Governor Ely of Massachusetts.

General Douglas MacArthur, Chief of Staff of the United States Army.

Hanford MacNider, former Commander of the American Legion and former Minister to Canada.

Frank N. Belgrano, Commander of the Legion.

William Doyle, former Department Commander of the Legion in Massachusetts.

He repeated Clark's offer—"if necessary, to spend half that $30 million to save the other half"—adding, "this was no piker setup. This was no shoe-string khaki shirt Fascist movement.... If you are interested in your Government, if you are interested in retaining your democracy, if you are opposed to all un-American activities, don't let this thing drop. Don't let this testimony be suppressed forever. Don't let the big shots of this un-American plot go forever unquestioned. Demand that they publish all the testimony taken."

The big business press did let the thing drop. The patriotic organizations made no attempt to get the un-American activities exposed. The men indicted by General Butler were never questioned. So he went to the radio again some time later and talked about the "Wall Street gang," and gave some of the testimony which the committee had suppressed. Was it because Grayson Murphy was a reputed Morgan man, was it the mention of Wall Street, Morgan, Murphy, the American Liberty League, General MacArthur, or some other person or institution, which caused the committee to suppress the testimony? We do not know. But we do know that the press did not publish it. Fortunately, my friend John L. Spivak, was able to obtain one of the six uncensored copies of the committee report. (The suppressed parts of General Butler's testimony are in italics.)

(General Butler) said, "Is there anything stirring about it?"

"Yes," he says; "you watch; in two or three weeks you will see it come out in the papers. There will be big fellows in it. This is to be the background of it. These are to be the villagers in the opera. The papers will come out with it," *and in about two weeks the American Liberty League appeared, which was just about what he described it to be. That is the reason I tied it up with this other thing about Al Smith and some of these other people, because of the name that appeared in connection with this Liberty League.* He did not give me the name of it, but he said that it would all be made public.

General Butler in his testimony quoted a conversation with MacGuire on the formation of a Fascist army. The committee report suppresses all mention of the American Liberty League in this connection.

Again, the committee suppressed mention of the Liberty League in Mr. French's testimony, as for example (with suppressed parts in italics):

"At first he [MacGuire] suggested that the General organize this outfit himself and ask a dollar a year dues from everybody. We discussed that, and then he came around to the point of getting outside financial funds, and he said that it would not be any trouble to raise a million dollars. *He said that he could go to John W. Davis or Perkins of the National City Bank, and any number of persons and get it.*

"Of course, that may or may not mean anything. That is, his reference to John W. Davis and Perkins of the National City Bank.

"During my conversation with him I did not of course, commit the General to anything. I was just feeling him along. Later we discussed the question of arms and equipment, and he suggested that they could be obtained from thc Remington Arms Co., on credit through the Du Ponts. I do not think at that time he mentioned the connections of Du Pont with the American Liberty League, but he skirted all around it. that is, I do not think he mentioned thc Liberty League, but he skirted all around the idea that that was the back door, and that this was the front door; one of the Du Ponts is on the board of directors of the American Liberty League and they own a controlling interest in the Remington Arms Co."

Other important parts of the Butler testimony were suppressed; for example, the General's question whether Colonel Murphy was responsible "for making the Legion a strike-breaking outfit" and his own answer:

"You know very well that it is nothing but a strike-breaking outfit used by capital for that purpose and that is the reason they have all those big clubhouses and that is the reason I pulled out from it. They have been using these dumb soldiers to break strikes."

The committee was bold enough to publish from Butler's testimony the lines credited to MacGuire that "The Morgan interests say you cannot be trusted, that you are too radical, and so forth, that you are too much on the side of the little fellow," but suppressed the lines immediately following: "They (the Morgan interests) are for Douglas MacArthur as the head of it. Douglas MacArthur's term expires in November, and if he is not reappointed it is to be presumed that he will be disappointed and sore and they are for getting him to head it," referring, of course, to the March on Washington.

To Butler's (suppressed) protest that the soldiers would not follow the much bemedalled head of the army, he testified that MacGuire said "then we will get Hanford MacNider."

The committee also naturally suppressed Butler's statement that MacGuire's opinion was that MacArthur "is going to go right" if the president reappointed him, and if not, "he is going to go left....You know as well as I do that MacArthur is Stotesbury's son-in-law in Philadelphia—Morgan's representative in Philadelphia. You see just how it goes...."

Not only the suppressed testimony, but that part of it made public and vouched for by a conservative committee, proves that an organized conspiracy to overthrow the American government—a conspiracy financed by Wall Street and involving the American Legion and the American Liberty League—did exist. The committee admitted that every charge which the Tory press tried to laugh out of court was actually proved. For 18 years the American press had been publishing rumors and forged documents alleging that there was a Red plot to overthrow the American form of government, but no evidence had ever been produced which had not been fraudulent. The evidence of a Fascist plot to overthrow the government, however, was substantiated. Yet all the forces of law and order, the Congressional Committee, the press, the courts, failed to continue the investigation, or take the drastic action the alarming testimony demanded.

Grayson M. P. Murphy was a director of a Morgan bank and his name appeared on the Morgan preferred list. Murphy was one of the men who handed out money to originate the American Legion at a time businessmen feared the returned soldiers would follow their colleagues in Europe in asking for that New Deal which Wilson, Lloyd George and other statesmen had promised them in 1918 and which of necessity meant a redistribution of wealth.

John W. Davis, once candidate for President on the Democratic ticket, now attorney for Morgan, is a director of the Guaranty Trust.

Gerald C. MacGuire, a $100-a-week employee, was proved by Mr. Spivak to have deposited about $140,000 in his bank one day in July 1934, $150,000 a month later, $45,000 two days later.

Frank N. Belgrano, then commander-in-chief of the Legion, was the first banker officially to head the organization, although bankers have pretty well led and controlled it since its conception. Belgrano was called to Washington for questioning, but his name was stricken out and the committee refused to explain why. Belgrano, A. P. Giannini, his boss, and William Randolph Hearst, cooperate in California ventures.

Murphy, Davis, Belgrano, the heads of Remington Arms, Du Ponts, and other notable persons and concerns mentioned, were never called before the committee. But the thanks of all except the subversive elements masquerading as patriots are due to General Butler who took his stand on the side of the public as against those special interests of which he himself later wrote, "I spent 33 years and four months in active service as a member of our country's most agile military force—the Marine Corps— and during that period I spent most of my time being a high-class muscle man for Big Business, for Wall Street and the bankers. In short, I was a racketeer for capitalism. Like all members of the military profession I never had an original thought until I left the service. My mental faculties remained in suspended animation while I obeyed the orders of the higher-ups. The record of racketeering is long. I helped purify Nicaragua for the international banking house of Brown Brothers in 1909-12. I brought light to the Dominican Republic for American sugar interests in 1916. In China in 1927 I helped to see to it that Standard Oil went its way unmolested."

The Fascist plot which General Butler exposed did not get very far, because he recognized treason when he saw it. But that plot had in it the three elements which make successful wars and revolutions: men, guns and money. The next plot will require the same three elements.

The noted Italian historian Guglielmo Ferrero, writing objectively in a time of freedom (i.e., before 1925), summarized the reasons for the success of Fascism in Italy. Of his 12 points several apply specifically to the Italian scene; others are universal, as the upheaval in Germany has illustrated.

First of all, he mentions the outraged feelings of the "patriots" when the masses brutally showed their hatred for war, indiscriminately cursing the defenders of the country and the war profiteers. The second point is more important: "the terror with which the rich perceived the threat to their property." This is the universal fulcrum of the Fascist lever. But the propertied class, powerful as it is politically, is not numerically superior, and Fascism, like all national movements, must have popular support. This support in Italy, as later in Germany, came from the vast middle class which Ferrero said was impoverished by the depreciation of money and which hated the workers and peasants who, it claimed, had become enriched during the war.

"Loss of faith in the old leaders," Ferrero's eighth point, can also be applied internationally. In Italy there was of course also a hunger for conquest, "the fear of the epileptic seizures of universal suffrage," "bourgeois pride offended by the insolence of the lower class revolt," "the rehabilitation of all the German doctrines and ambitions which had been most universally denounced during the war," the stirring of the principle of authority, and finally the new war-wealthy class "rendered ferocious" by fear of losing its profits.

The United States, unlike Italy, Germany and Japan, is not suffering from nationalistic claustrophobia; our imperialistic adventures in a few islands and in Central and South America have not been successful enough to encourage further penetration, and neither the international bankers nor international manufacturers seem to be driving the government forward, as they so obviously do in imperialistic countries, toward conquest by peaceful penetration, armed intimidation, and finally by war. That Fascism means war is soon to be recognized as an axiom. Fascism is a method of preparing a nation for imperialistic adventures which have in the past and will in the future include wholesale slaughter as one of its means.

Fascism, as Italy and Germany have illustrated, can arise only in time of national distress when the masses demand leadership and better times. In these circumstances usually two opposite ideologies arise. In Germany and Italy, the exponents of the Marxian principles were divided into many groups, their preachments were largely philosophical, and the masses were tired of Marxian dialectics. On the other hand, the "philosophy" of the authoritarian state, whatever it may be, was not handed down to the masses in the words of Pareto, but became the purest demagoguery of superpatriotism.

The three important requirements for Fascist success have been, and will be in America: (a) financial subsidization of the movement by the moneyed classes; (b) affiliation with, or creation of, an armed force to impose the dictatorship upon the indifferent masses and the intelligent opponents; and (c) the right demagogue.

Fascism is the imposed dictatorship of the ruling class utilizing armed force to preserve the social-economic system wherever it is collapsing. The destruction of democracy—"that bourgeois illusion"—the suppression of all civil liberties, the destruction of the trade unions and the intellectuals, the glorification of the State—these are the natural results of the coming into power of a regime whose one purpose is the salvation of the profit system and whose hired leaders are superpatriots, demagogues, militarists, political racketeers, and fanatics. Fascism has no place for the intelligent. It claims a planned economy; what it succeeds in enforcing is planned thinking—and that on the lowest plane. Gleichschalung in Germany and Totalitarianism in Italy and their equivalents in other Fascist states demand the mental as well as the social destruction of the individual.

For Americans there arises the question: are our superpatriots, our duces and fuehrers of the financial-industrial empire which has grown within the walls of the Jeffersonian democracy, ready to break all safeguards of our old liberties in order to preserve their private interests? Are they ready for the militarism, the bloodshed, and the warfare which are inherent in Fascism?

They themselves say No. Super-industrialists like Hearst, the Du Ponts, Sloan, Gifford, Swope, Schwab, Raskob, Grace, will probably tell you that they are as opposed to Fascism as to Communism. Moreover, a vote of popular opinion taken by the reliable Gallup service brings out the astonishing fact that the majority of the American people, i.e., the Republican and Democratic Party voters, wholeheartedly believe that they are liberals, not conservatives.

There are, however, men and organizations which frankly endorse Fascism, as well as perhaps even more fascistic men and organizations who openly denounce the movement, who perhaps sincerely believe they are fighting it, but who are really the forerunners and potential leaders of Fascism in America.

In a interview in January 1923, Commander-in-Chief Alvin Owsley of the American Legion not only endorsed Mussolini and Fascism, but announced his readiness to do what the Duce did, that is, upset the democratic form of government, establish a reign of terror, maintain a dictatorship where the masses of people are deprived of all civil rights.

"If ever needed," he said, "the American Legion stands ready to protect our country's institutions and ideals as the Fascisti dealt with the destructionists who menaced Italy."

Asked whether that meant taking over the government, he replied:

"Exactly that. The American Legion is fighting every element that threatens our democratic government—soviets, anarchists, I.W.W., revolutionary socialists and every other 'Red.' . . . Do not forget that the Fascisti are to Italy what the American Legion is to the United States."

This last statement has been borne out hundreds of times when American labor has sought to exercise its constitutional rights.

("I've never known one leader of the American Legion who has never sold them out—and I mean it," said General Butler to the *New York Times* in 1933.)

Succeeding commanders of the Legion have never so openly declared for Fascism, but several have been as reactionary, and the majority have invited Mussolini to attend their annual conventions.

William Randolph Hearst, in his official editorials, has at times linked Fascism with Communism and other Isms which he opposes, but beyond such a statement he has never attacked Fascism. In fact he has spent thousands of dollars buying the views and opinions of Mussolini. He is considered the leading Fascist in America, and the most powerful. He has actually endorsed both Mussolini and Hitler. On arriving from Germany, 28 September 1934, after he made the $400,000 news agency sale to Hitler, he said:

"The fascist party of Italy was organized to quell the disturbances and disorders of communism. The fascist party of Germany was organized for the same purpose. It was intended to and very likely did prevent Germany from going communist and cooperating with Soviet Russia. This is the great policy, the great achievement which makes the Hitler regime popular with the German people, and which enables it to survive very obvious and very serious mistakes."

The House of Morgan has helped Fascism by the national loan of $100 million and many other loans, made at a time (1925) economists were already pointing out the fraud in the officially declared "balanced" Italian budget. The fraud, invented by Mussolini and American propaganda agents four years after Mussolini himself had written that there had been no communism in Italy when he took power, was apparently accepted, hook, line and red herring, by Thomas W. Lamont. In 1927, when the Italian bonds floated by Mr. Lamont's banking house were waterlogged and sinking, he wrote the following:

"Ask any traveller. . . . When the present regime came into power towards the end of 1922 Italy seemed to be tottering on the brink below which lay communism and bolshevism.... municipal administration as well was burdened with incompetence and extravagance. The finances of the central government were unsound; government debt was piling up and the deficits in the government's budget were increasing....

"Considerable currency has been given to stories that the Italian government has distorted its account of revenues and expenditures and by some method of transferring charges to municipal accounts has manufactured the surpluses which it has reported. These stories may be denied absolutely.... That the government's budget is in fact balanced and has been for the past two and half years, there is not the slightest doubt."

Colonel James H. Logan of Dillon, Read & Co., international bankers, was not to be outdone by the Morgan House. He informed Paris newspapermen he was impressed with the economic and financial development in Italy, which should be credited to "Italy's great son and leader Mussolini .... everyone .... must surely receive the same impression." Dillon, Read & Co. loaned the City of Milan $30 million, every cent of which was wasted or stolen by Mussolini's local duce, Belloni.

Otto H. Kahn was even more frank. "I admire Mussolini.... In the case of every people, more essential even than liberty, and therefore taking precedence to it, is order and national self-preservation.... In the case of Italy, in the years immediately following the war, a situation developed which came close to social chaos. Government was impotent, held in contempt and openly defied.

"To anyone who knew Italy then, the change which came over the country with the advent of Mussolini is little short of miraculous."

Among the great American industrialists (and employers of secret spies, illegal police, and gangsters or pre-Fascist militia in American labor disputes) the first to announce for Mussolini was none other than the then head of the United States Steel Corporation. Overcome with the beauties of peaceful Italy where strikes are outlawed, where labor knows its place (which is as near serfdom as anything we know of in this century), and where the standard of living of the people reached the lowest point in modern history, Judge Elbert Henry Gary declared: "I feel like turning to my American friends and asking them whether they don't think we too need a man like Mussolini."

One of his American friends, a senator from Pennsylvania, a state whose senators for decades had been known as the errand boys of the steel corporation, echoed the words. "What this country needs is a Mussolini," said Senator David A. Reed to his colleagues on one occasion; and on another, "Signor Mussolini has given Italy a particularly strong and stable government; he has restored order where once chaos ruled; he has increased the productive capacity of Italy and conferred happiness upon all classes, high and low, the rich and the poor." Senator Reed was not re-elected.

Almost all dictators have cultural pretensions. Mussolini has called for Fascist art, and Hitler has decreed that culture must go Aryan. It is not at all unlikely that an American dictator will feel the necessity of showing the world that there are writers and painters and some men of intelligence among the terrorists, assassins, businessmen, bankers, opportunists and others who will be called upon someday to establish Fascism here. Let the would-be dictator have no fears. There are already men on the highest pinnacle of intelligence (judging from magazine price per word) who have endorsed Mussolini or Fascism and will come forth to prove that culture is on its side.

In the course of years I have culled the following nosegay from the beautiful pro-Fascist gardens: Isaac L. Marcosson, who approved Mussolini's turning "red terror into white fear"; Irvin S. Cobb, who bowed low and linked Mussolini with great Theodore Roosevelt; Kenneth L. Roberts, who wrote that "Mussolini's dictatorship is a good dictatorship"; S. S. McClure, who thought the Italians "feel they are the only free people in the world"; James Michael Curley of Massachusetts, who declared, drinking a toast, that the Duce "in saving Italy made possible the preservation of Christian civilization," George J. Ryan, ex-president of the New York Board of Education, who regretted that "many things that are beneficial in Italy" could not be adopted in New York; Thomas J. Watson, president of the International Business Machine Corporation, who told the American Society of Italian Orders (he himself wears a Fascist decoration) that Mussolini has "improved conditions of the masses."

There is also Charles E. Sorensen, general manager of the Ford Motor company who, returning on a German ship, told the reporters that Germany was "in marvelous shape and looks prosperous everywhere" (at a time when the objective journalists were writing about increased misery). And there is Charles M. Schwab, who was described as "full of praise for conditions in Germany under the Hitler regime."

And, of course, there is Al Capone, who is for Fascism.

The list of individual names is very long. I have given only a few samples of various kinds. What they do show is that the same classes which support Nazism in Germany, Fascism in Italy, and Franco in Spain are represented by the men who endorse these movements in America. Certain commercial writers, the big money bags, big business, the heavy industrialists, the employers, the landowners, the wearers of foreign decorations, here and there a smart crook, now and again a clever opportunist, are joined in favor of systems or ideologies which are the very antithesis of that created by the founders of the American republic.

It is significant that very few of the important powerful men who have declared for Fascism have been willing to let themselves be quoted as favoring that system for the United States. It is not probable that they will ever do so. The astute politician and potential Fascist ruler, Huey Long, settled that question when he said that "Fascism in America will arrive on an anti-Fascist platform."

The men I have quoted are very few. But they represent a considerable Fascist mentality. The real enemies of the nation's democratic institutions today are the Fascist-minded men with the "ability and willingness to turn the concentrated wealth of America against the welfare of America." Secretary of the Interior Harold L. Ickes made this statement at the annual dinner of the American Civil Liberties Union on 8 December 1937; it was without a doubt the frankest statement on Fascism ever made by a member of the American government.

"Our ancestors," continued Mr. Ickes, "fought to prevent a state censorship of news and ideas. Our ancestors did not fight for the right of a few lords of the press to have almost exclusive control of and censorship over the dissemination of news and ideas. Yet under the stress of economic forces our press and news agencies are coming more and more under the domination of a handful of corporate publishers who may print such news as they wish to print and omit such news as they do not wish to print. They may even color the news.

"A sad part of the long record that has been written on the infringement of our civil liberties has to do with the Supreme Court of the United States. It is commonly believed that this court has been far more liberal than legislative bodies in protecting civil liberties. Unfortunately the facts do not bear out this general belief. On the contrary the Court has gone far to convert the Bill of Rights, which was intended as a charter of human freedom, into a charter of corporate privilege....

"Let no one sleepily believe that our democratic form of government is necessarily secure for all time to come. We have seen dictatorships in other lands reach out and destroy constitutional democracies, states combine not for protection but for aggression. We have discovered that

Fascism has not been quarantined, but that it is capable of leaping wide oceans...."

Mr. Ickes concluded that wealthy and influential men with Fascist leanings were using the Red scare as "a wooden horse within the bowels of which Fascism may enter the shrine of liberty."

Unfortunately, these men are both plentiful and powerful.

A Short History of
American Redbaiting

This selection from Seldes' 1940 book, Witch Hunt, *shows that Redbaiting didn't start with Joe McCarthy. In Seldes' view, Redbaiting in America predates Marx and Lenin and the creation of communism. Since the beginning of American history, people who harbored ideas that went against the status quo have gotten into trouble. From the American Revolution to the Industrial Revolution to the Russian Revolution, every wave of change has created violent opposition to the ideas that created the change. Seldes here explains how Redbaiting evolved and became a catch-all method for discrediting any idea for the betterment of humankind.*

THOMAS JEFFERSON, whom President Roosevelt denounced as a radical as recently as the Jackson Day Dinner of 1940 was not only the founder of our democracy but was so strongly under the influence of the French Revolution that his enemies called him an agent for a foreign government, the spreader of an alien "ism." Tom Paine actually was a foreign radical agitator, although he was not deported by the FBI of his time. And the historian will tell you that from 1806 to 1843 strikes were considered criminal conspiracies—a situation we have not entirely outgrown when one considers the present use of the Sherman and Clayton Acts, originally passed to curb monopolistic trusts, against labor unions. On 2 August

1828 the military was first used to smash labor, and at about this time there was a general attack against the Freemasons.

In the early nineteenth century another minority accused of alienism was made a scapegoat: for twenty years the Roman Catholics were not only baited in the press but attacked in riots (a curious fact for Father Coughlin and Christian Fronters to ponder). In 1830 the Know Nothings controlled five states, just as almost a hundred years later the Ku Kluxers controlled five states, and in both instances the Catholics, the Irish, the aliens, were the victims of an intolerant movement.

In 1886 German-Americans in Chicago striving for an eight-hour day were the victims of police brutality equaled only by the police brutality in Chicago in 1937. The Haymarket bomber was never found; the men executed and imprisoned for the bombing were labor leaders, "foreign agitators" preaching a "foreign doctrine" (that is, shorter working hours, more pay, better living standards, and human dignity). Six years later the Governor of Illinois declared the Chicago anarchists innocent. History regards them as martyrs who helped make the eight- hour day possible.

In 1916 Tom Mooney and Warren Billings, two labor leaders, were charged with planting a bomb in a preparedness parade in San Francisco. Accused of being Reds and therefore capable of any kind of murder, these two men were convicted on the perjured testimony of men who later, but in vain, confessed their perjury. President Wilson saved their lives in 1918 but could not free them. The judge who sentenced Mooney said later it was a "dirty job," and nine of the ten surviving members of the jury publicly regretted their verdict. In 1931 the Wickersham report was to clinch the matter by denouncing the judicial process in California as "shocking to one's sense of justice."

Why had Mooney and Billings been arrested, found guilty, kept in jail, when the intelligent world knew they were innocent? The answer, as given by a reporter who had covered the trial in his youth and who 16 years later wrote up the whole story in what happened in the Mooney Case was that in 1916 there was a wave of Red hysteria in San Francisco—Red hysteria and red-white-and-blue hysteria—because the country was being drummed into a war. Ernest Jerome Hopkins of the *San Francisco Bulletin* wrote: "Sixteen years of printed poison have convinced Californians that, evidence or none, it is better to keep two radicals in prison than remove a nationwide stimulus to radicalism." That was Hopkins's conclusion. And it was fear of the press of California that prevented governor after governor—and eventually Franklin Roosevelt, who was expected to do it—

from pardoning two innocent men. The Mooney-Billings case remains one of America's most alarming instances of the accomplishments of Redbaiting.

Similar was the case of the Industrial Workers of the World who had defended themselves in Centralia, Washington, and had been shot, murdered, and lynched by a mob led by American Legionnaires. The National Catholic Welfare Council and the Federal Council of Churches issued a report which showed that the IWW's had not conspired, that they had not fired on the Legion paraders, that the paraders had attacked them, and that therefore the sentence of the court had been "very severe." But Redbaiting by the "best citizens" prevailed.

In 1917 when we went to war, an espionage act was passed by which the American people were denied all their usual liberties, despite the Civil War decision of the Supreme Court (ex parte Milligan) that the Constitution holds good in war as in peace, that nothing may be changed to curtail or diminish, weaken or abolish, a comma of the Bill of Rights.

In March of that same year there was a revolt against the Tsar, and in November the Bolshevik Party of Russia seized power, and for the first time in history an attempt was made—in an agrarian and illiterate country—to put into practice the theories of Karl Marx and Friedrich Engels, the theory of socialism. This philosophy marched under a Red banner, and from that day on, Redbaiting became a world activity.

So long as the war lasted, the hysterical enthusiasm lasted and only a tiny minority had to be sent to prison for being immune to it. But when the soldiers came home and the great disillusionment began, when times grew hard because of the war that had been won, when jobs grew scarcer, wages lower, and the cost of living higher—then the real Redbaiting campaigns began, aided in spirit and action by the national government.

The name-calling grew fiercer. For example, when Senator Robert La Follette Sr. told Congress that the American troops should be withdrawn from Archangel (generals had done the same, leading reactionary statesmen in Europe had realized the expediency of such an action), his opponents saw a God-given opportunity to harm him. He was denounced everywhere as "the Bolshevik spokesman in America." And again, when the workmen on the Stone & Webster lines struck for a decent living wage, Mayor Ole Hanson of Seattle denounced them as Bolsheviki, crushed them, and became nationally notorious. In every strike of the era the first thing done was to bring out the Red label. Sometimes it won the strike for the employers by itself; always it was the fulcrum on which the police, the press, and the men of big business worked their powerful levers. In Butte, Montana, veterans who had formed the Sailors and Soldiers Association, one of the several non-reactionary organizations antedating the American Legion, were met by the 44th Infantry, with Major A. M. Jones calling them IWW's and Bolsheviki and threatening them with machine-gun fire.

In the great hysteria of 1919 the superpatriots shouted that there were a million foreign Reds in America—or at least 600,000—and one of the many anti-alien deportation waves spread through the country. The government promised to take action. It did. It found that instead of a million, or even 600,000, deportable alien reds there were only some 30,000 who answered a Redbaiter's description of "undesirable," and of these only a handful were subject to deportation. The "Soviet Ark," the S.S. Buford, finally sailed on 21 December 1919 carrying a total of 246 men and three women, among them Emma Goldman, and Alexander Berkman, anarchist leaders.

All the liberal-intellectual publications were smeared as radical. Such magazines as *The World Tomorrow, The Nation, The Dial, The New Republic, The Liberator,* and the newspaper *The Call* all were attacked, and one of the leading patriotic crusaders deplored the fact that intellectual leaders, "the different editors connected with these various publications, Norman Thomas, John Haynes Holmes, Oswald Garrison Villard, Henry Raymond Mussey, Lincoln Colcord, Martin Johnson, Herbert Croly, Walter Weyl, Walter Lippmann, Signe Toksvig, and H. W. L. Dana," were Americans and therefore could not be deported to Soviet Russia.

In March 1919 the New York legislature appointed the notorious Lusk Committee to investigate "subversive" activities. The committee collected many volumes of testimony, most of which has been thoroughly discredited by the leading jurists of our time but which still serves succeeding generations of Redbaiters. The Federal Government under Attorney-General A. Mitchell Palmer indulged in illegal raids and mass arrests, deporting many foreign-born residents and violating with impunity the constitutional rights of citizens.

In April 1919 a score of bombs were found in the mails addressed to leading men of the country, including the "Fighting Quaker," Mr. Palmer, and when this plot failed, a man threw a bomb. It blew the porch off Mr. Palmer's house and killed the thrower. Curiously enough a radical publication, *Plain Words,* was found near the dead man. This "radical" publication was one of the many frauds in which the government engaged at the time; it was actually published by the government, through a certain

Andrea Salsedo, who was later to figure in a mysterious way in the Sacco-Vanzetti case.

This was the year of great strikes, as well as of the first great American Red scare. On the West coast the shipyard workers and the seamen went out. In Lawrence, Massachusetts, scene of a bloody labor battle in 1912 and in Paterson, New Jersey, scene of endless struggles of the silk-workers, there were textile strikes. Four hundred thousand coal miners (in John L. Lewis's union) asked for more wages, shorter hours.

Early American Redbaiting ran the gamut from humor to tragedy. The actors went on strike in New York and Marie Dressler organized the chorus girls. The press then called Equity a "soviet" and Broadway laughed. But it was a different story in Pittsburgh, where the great steel strike—a really important event in American labor history—for an eight-hour day and a few cents more an hour was smashed when the owners, who had made billions in the war, succeeded in smearing the labor leaders as "un-American" and "Red."

President Wilson himself used his high office to attack labor. He characterized the coal strike, called for October 1919, as "a fundamental attack, which is wrong both morally and legally, upon the rights of society and upon the welfare of the country." These are the familiar words of exploiters of labor, but when a President uses them, they can be a powerful weapon. Palmer translated them into action under the claim that the Lever Act, passed in wartime to prevent the breakdown of the supply of food and resources to the government, was still in force; and he succeeded in having Federal Judge A. B. Anderson in Indianapolis issue an injunction against the coal miners, forbidding them to strike.

Since this was a violation of the coal miners' rights, there was an outcry of protest, whereupon the Department of Justice, instead of presenting a bill of particulars, raised a Red scare.

In the West, American infantry drove striking miners back to work at the point of bayonets. Leading officers of the United Mine Workers, notably President Lewis and Secretary William Green, were cited for contempt, arrested, and tried. In Pennsylvania the "Black Cossacks" rode down the assemblies of workers, shooting and clubbing. At Breckenridge they killed Fanny Sellins, an organizer for the UMW.

The hysteria became nationwide. In New York City the Rand School was raided, and in one day no less than a thousand persons were arrested as aliens, foreign agents, Reds, enemies of society. That furnished more scare-lines for the press. But when, within a few hours, 953 of these persons had been released because there was not even a suspicion of a real charge against them, there were only little paragraphs on inside pages to announce that fact. In Bogalusa, Louisiana, the forces of law, order, and mob hysteria massacred five union men in the sawmill strike. "Criminal syndicalism" laws were passed in many states.

As the Anti-Saloon League rode from triumph to triumph in several states of the nation, the liquor interests, rather belatedly, realized their danger and united their ranks. The Drys, they heard, had been spending $2 million a year, and were raising the fund to $5 million for 1919 with the slogan, "America bone dry by 1920." The saloon and liquor men pledged a billion dollars, but this sum never materialized; what did materialize was an alarming series of newspaper advertisements which had a triple purpose: (1) to buy the support of the press; (2) to attract readers to their cause; and (3) incidentally to take a crack at the ubiquitous Reds! Booze was linked with personal freedom, with rugged individualism, with the American Dream—and prohibition with the antitheses of these, including Bolshevism. "Will Bolshevism come with National Prohibition?" read one flaming headline in a paid advertisement, and the answer was that it would. To save America from Red socialism all that was necessary was to support good old "redeye"; a vote for John Barleycorn was a vote against Karl Marx.

On 2 January 1920, G-men began raiding the clubs as well as political headquarters of radicals, liberals, and trade unionists; they hacked, burned, tore, and destroyed property and maltreated men and women. If ever an organization merited the terms Cheka and Gestapo as scornfully used by people who believe "it can't happen here," it was the Federal Bureau of Investigation of 1920. Altogether it arrested 10,000 persons.

One explanation of the brutal and lawless actions of the enforcers of the law was the onward march of labor following the World War. It is true that in certain industries wages were high in wartime; but it is also true that the cost of living was high. In 1919 the cost of living continued rising, but wages came down, and 4,160,348 union and non-union men protested their lot in strikes in that year. The most important, and most threatening, event of 1919 was the great steel strike led by William Z. Foster, of the American Federation of Labor.

When the five duly elected Socialist members of the New York State Legislature were thrown out of their seats—because Socialist meant Red, and Red meant Bolshevik, and Bolshevism, the American people had been told by their press, meant everything that was un-American—George

Bernard Shaw cabled: "It is time for the Mayflower to put to sea again. My old label, 'A Nation of Villagers,' still holds. When is the Bartholdi statue to be pulled down?" The press thought Shaw was clowning as usual; and, besides, no damned foreigner had a right to criticize the august New York legislature.

Every crime of violence involving a bomb is usually laid to a radical. Every assassination is laid to an anarchist, a socialist, or a communist the moment after it happens, the press of the world forgetting all about the rules of evidence in the breathless moment. The report has spread until it is generally believed throughout America that foreigners commit more than their proportional quota of crime, whereas just the opposite has been proven by the Wickersham investigation.

For May Day 1920—traditional labor day of workingmen the world over—A. Mitchell Palmer, attorney-general of the United States, promised a fine, first-class Red revolution, during which the American Bolsheviki would attempt to "plant the Red flag on the Capitol in Washington," after incidentally murdering all prominent gentlemen holding high office or large bond portfolios.

Inevitably, May Day came to Washington as it did to London, Paris, and Berlin, and not a shot was fired in all four capitals, nor was a drop of Red blood, or blue blood, shed anywhere; and for the first time in the years of Mr. Palmer's hysterical Redbaiting he was greeted with laughter and a little derision.

On 16 September 1920 a bomb was thrown in Wall Street, and to this day Reds are accused of the deed despite the lack of an iota of evidence.

In the first 10 years after this bombing there were many arrests, 28 publicly announced; many persons were tortured to make a confession; and a dozen announcements were made by the police and the Burns detective agency that they had proof that "the Reds plotted the crime and sent a man with a horse and wagon and much dynamite into the street opposite the offices of J. Pierpont Morgan"—where the dynamite exploded and killed both man and horse. The police refused to open their ears to the explanation that the crime was that of an individual, a maniac, or a terrorist; they insisted that Reds were behind it. In 1922 when one, Wolfe Lindenfeld, "confessed" in Warsaw that he and Moscow were responsible for the crime, the press and police indulged in a three-day orgy of Redbaiting. Later, the United States Government deported Mr. Lindenfeld as a fraud—he had invented the story as a means of getting free transportation to America—but the press did not give the public three-day headlines repairing the damage it had done.

Nineteen twenty was a depression year, a Red-scare year. It was also the year of the great exposure of the fraud of the 1919 World Series baseball games. It had been a secret; Charles Comiskey of the White Sox had kept quiet; but when the indictments came, Eddie Cicotte, the star pitcher, confessed that "eight or ten of us got together before the game . . . talked about throwing the series . . . decided we could get away with it. I was thinking of my wife and kids and how I needed the money. I told them to have the cash ready ... ten thousand dollars.... All the runs scored off me were due to my own deliberate errors...."

The scandal was too horrible for the mind to encompass. And so the press said that what the incident showed was that "the Bolshevik virus had entered the national sport."

Alfred Noyes immediately came to the front page with the statement that the Bolshevik virus had also entered the minds of the intellectuals, even poets. The new free-verse poetry was Bolshevism. (In London, the American sculptor Epstein was called "an artist Lenin, bolshevizing art" in a popular paper, because of his modern, unconventional style.)

Mr. Calvin Coolidge was shocked to find radicalism in the women's colleges. He wrote for *Delineator,* at a great price per word, the story of how a Miss Smith of Vassar, attending the trial of the Soviet representative Martens in Washington, had said out loud that Mr. Martens had more intelligence than the committeemen trying him. In Radcliffe, Mr. Coolidge discovered there was a Socialist Club. And he had also been informed that a lecturer in a college had had as his topic "The United States of the World." What was the world coming to!

When, in 1923, Charles Lindbergh, father of the "Lone Eagle," ran for the governorship of Minnesota on the Farmer-Labor ticket, he was attacked by the press as a "red-hot radical," a "Bolshevik," a "dangerous Red." Had he not opposed our entry into the war, and, worse, had he not publicly said: "I am an enemy of Wall Street," urging Congress to investigate the "Money Trust"?

Governor Al Smith named Colonel Haskell major-general in command of the National Guard of New York. The colonel, as Hoover's agent, had saved 10 million people from starvation in Russia, had spoken to Lenin several times, and had hinted that the Russian leader was a great man. He had also said in 1922 that the Russian regime would not fall in six months, thus flying in the face of the world press. And so in 1925 the

American Defense Society, one of the professional patriotic groups, demanded that the governor cancel the appointment because "it has been alleged that Colonel Haskell's sympathies are for Soviet Russia."

In 1925 however, good times were at hand. The Red hysteria was waning; so it was no wonder that, in coming to the support of Colonel Haskell, the *New York World* called the attack upon him "foolish words from the American Dementia Society, which has the brains of an ostrich, the courage of a rabbit, and the manners of a polecat."

As the world advanced towards the catastrophe of 1929 times looked so good that there was no necessity for Redbaiting, and a liberal glow settled over America. Free speech, free press, free assembly, were little interfered with by the chambers of commerce, the Legion and other military associations, and the professional or dollar patriots. When Eugene Debs died in 1926 this Socialist, labor leader, pacifist, radical, and spreader of "alien doctrine" was called by the press "distinctly American, of the frontier or colonial type, alas now vanishing"; to save themselves from criticism, the same newspapers said editorially that Debs really was not a Communist, but a pure Yankee non-conformist of the Washington and Franklin type, and more like his own hero, John Brown. (In 1921 the New Jersey convention of the American Legion had held a "Keep Debs in Prison" demonstration, and the *New York Times* had said editorially when President Harding commuted Debs's prison sentence: "Certainly the majority will not approve; a shallow howling, whining minority had its way.")

In 1926 the Illinois commander of the American Legion, accused "this person, Jane Addams" of working to abolish all military training and of turning Hull House into "a hotbed of Bolshevism."

In the great boom days of 1927 in America, news came that there were riots and demonstrations throughout the civilized world because a poor fish-peddler and a shoemaker had been electrocuted on 23 August in the death house at Charlestown, Massachusetts. The men were radicals, and that, apparently, was enough to justify their death, at least in the mind of men like Judge Webster Thayer, who, during the time he was sitting as judge in this famous Sacco-Vanzetti case, referred to the accused men as "anarchist bastards" in conversation at his club.

In 1929 the stock market crashed and, though very few knew it then, a world collapsed with it. As, in the early thirties, the extent of the disaster, politically, economically, socially, and morally, became known, and as this led to a search for a better social-economic system, the endangered rulers of society began to exert themselves in every way to hold on.

By May Day, 1930, there were fear and apprehension throughout the world. It was "Red Labor Day." The police of all nations where such celebrations were still permitted predicted revolutionary uprisings and cleaned their guns; but there were only marches and speeches: not a shot was fired, not a bomb thrown.

In American cities, with winter approaching, there were demonstrations (immediately called Red) of the unemployed, and sometimes riots in which hungry men were killed and wounded. Instead of providing work, the politicians pinned the communist label on the jobless.

Professor and Mrs. Einstein landed in New York on 11 December 1930. "Politically," said Mrs. Einstein, "we are Socialists." "The ideals which have always shone before me and filled me with the joy of living," Einstein wrote as his credo, "are goodness, beauty, and truth." But being the combination of Jew, Socialist, and pacifist made one of the greatest scientists of the modern world the subject of Redbaiting. In the American consulate in Berlin, Professor Einstein had been asked such ridiculous questions about his trip to America that he was forced to say to the vice-consul: "Are you doing this on supreme authority or for your own amusement?" But the so-called diplomat continued to hammer away with questions about socialism, anarchism, communism, and pacifism. When Einstein prepared to go to Princeton, the Woman Patriot Corporation protested and called him a Communist. When he was invited to make a visit to California, the organizer of the Los Angeles branch of the American Legion, Dr. A. D. Houghton, called on the ex-soldiers to prevent the scientist's visit.

In 1932 Georg Grosz, one of the great among German artists, was engaged to teach at the Art Students League of New York only to arouse a storm of protest: Jonas Lie, American academician, thought Grosz was not "healthy," and others whispered "Communist."

Congressman Hamilton Fish investigated communism in America and reported that there were 12,000 dues-paying members of the party in 1930 that it had 82,000 votes and half a million sympathizers. Congressman Nelson said that "the best defense against the red shirt of the Communist and the black shirt of the Fascist is the blue shirt of the American workingman"—but millions of workmen had no money for blue shirts, or shirts of any color.

The Pope in 1931 made two declarations against the Reds. "'Religious Socialism,' 'Christian Socialism,' are expressions implying a contradiction in terms," he said, denying what every Christian Socialist in America takes as a fundamental of the teachings of Jesus Christ. "No one can be at the same time a sincere Catholic and a true Socialist."

A whispering campaign against the banks in March 1932 was denounced as a dirty job of the Reds. The newspapers and magazines took up the subject, explaining to their readers how delicate was the matter of confidence in financial institutions and how villainous were those who questioned what went on in the solid temples of gold. When, however, in February 1933 an epidemic of bank holidays swept the United States it was proved that the whisperers—Red or not—had been right. It was the banks who were "in the red," and on 6 March the President of the United States had to close them all.

But the great event of 1933 was the burning of the German Reichstag in February and the first remark that Adolf Hitler made when he was told about it. *"Das ut das Werk der Kommunsten,"* said Hitler.

But it was not the work of the Communists. The Nazis did produce a moron named Van der Lubbe, whom they tried and executed, but he had been expelled from the Communist Party years earlier. The Nazis accused Georgi Dimitroff, a Bulgarian Communist, of being one of the plotters, but Dimitroff made a fool of Goering and the others at the Leipzig hearings, and even the Nazi legal machinery, frankly announcing itself as serving the ends of the party rather than justice, was unable to convict him or to find new victims. Meanwhile the evidence mounted that the inflammable materials found in the Reichstag had been carried there over a period of weeks by several persons who entered the meeting place of the old parliament through the residence of none other than Herr Goering. The whole affair was a fraud and both the fire and the fraud were the work of the Hitler party. Blame on the Reds was, of course, the declaration of the war of extermination against all opposition parties—red, pink, and even royal purple—which far outnumbered the Nazis.

Within a year of taking office President Franklin Delano Roosevelt had succeeded in producing a program which aroused unthinking emotion in friends and enemies alike. The stock market went down, big business men began talking about the menace of Red revolution, and several even went so far as to talk about the benefits of assassination. "Roosevelt is a Red."

"Roosevelt is following the Communist Party line." That was the sort of talk heard in Wall Street and in the citadels of the status quo.

A great strike wave began. Strikes were the natural answer of millions of workers who had been told the government would maintain their inalienable rights, provide minimum-wage and maximum-hour regulations, better working conditions, a nobler life—and who were unmistakably informed by their employers that they had no such rights. Thus was introduced a new era of anti-labor violence and espionage, renewed Redbaiting and heresy hunting, pressure by so-called patriotic organizations for bigger and better repressive legislation and gag laws.

The press, as the slightest study of American labor history will show, has always been on the side of the employers, but not until 1934 did publishers deliberately unite to strangle the labor movement. Instead of remaining as usual in the background, "agitating" public opinion through editorials, flaming headlines, and distorted news, a group of editors and publishers, inspired by William Randolph Hearst, actually met and planned an attack on the general strike in San Francisco.

The strike had been peaceful, and the press should have known better when it said that the city's infants had been deprived of milk and the city's doctors of gasoline. The strike had had the sympathy of the public—until the owners of the press conspired to break it by fair means or foul. The foul means consisted almost entirely in spreading the magnificent lie that Reds, Communists, and foreign agitators were the instigators, leaders, and potential beneficiaries of the strike.

Hearst had telephoned from London telling the editors how the British government had beaten the general strike of 1926, and urging them to wave the Red flag in order to divide labor into two camps, conservative and radical, and to attack the radicals; and most important of all, to enlist public opinion on the side of business by insisting that the strike was a Red revolution.

The falsehoods were spread so thoroughly that General Hugh Johnson, arriving in San Francisco to mediate, said (or was quoted in the press as saying) that "when the means of food supply—milk for children—necessities of life to the whole people are threatened, that is bloody revolution." The *San Francisco Chronicle* said: "The radicals have seized control by intimidation.... What they want is revolution." The *Los Angeles Times* said: "What is actually in progress there is an insurrection, a communist-inspired and led revolt." The *Sacramento Bee* said the strikers sought to overthrow the United States government. The *Oakland Examiner* accused "the small group of communists" of trying to extend their power over the maritime unions, and then over California. The *Portland Times* said the strikers were refusing to give the public the necessities of life, and blamed "rampant radicalism."

It was one of the best-organized campaigns of universal Redbaiting ever witnessed in America. Although it was founded largely on falsehood, it resulted in mass hysteria. The press of the rest of the country naturally reprinted the news and the editorial views of the Pacific coast newspapers. This flood drowned out the few sane voices (as, for instance, Evelyn Seeley's in *The New Republic* accusing San Francisco publishers of "deliberate journalistic malpractice"; and Will Rogers's, remarking that all was quiet in California and "I hope we never live to see the day when a thing is as bad as some of our newspapers make it").

The *New York Times* was proud to say that public opinion broke the strike. A vigilante reign of terror followed in which hundreds of innocent persons accused of being Reds were jailed and beaten, and private homes, offices, and labor union headquarters robbed and destroyed by ax and fire. Violence in the strike, which began with the police killing two innocent men, ended with a newspaper-inflamed mob running wild in the streets.

A congressional committee, chaired by John W. McCormack of Massachusetts, for the purpose of investigating Nazi and other propaganda, issued a report confirming an alleged conspiracy of Wall Street men and agents to establish a fascist dictatorship in Washington under the guise of saving the country from Bolshevism. The report stated:

> *"In the last few weeks of the committee's official life it received evidence showing that certain persons had made an attempt to establish a fascist organization in this country....*
>
> *There is no question but that these attempts were discussed, were planned, and might have been placed in execution when and if the financial backers deemed it expedient."*

Paul Comley French, the newspaperman who broke the story, testified that Gerald C. MacGuire stated: "We need a fascist government in this country to save the nation from the communists who want to tear it down and wreck all that we have built in America." MacGuire had sent reports to another of his superiors, Robert Sterling Clark, the multi-millionaire who was willing to spend half his fortune for fascism to save the other half from the Reds, describing the excellence of the fascists in Europe and how dangerous the reds were in France, Austria, and elsewhere. Thanks to

General Smedley Butler's giving the story to two liberal papers, the *Philadelphia Record* and the *New York Post,* which in turn forced the congressional committee to take testimony, the plot was destroyed before it became a serious menace to the American system of government.

It did one thing. It showed clearly the fascist pattern here as elsewhere: big business and big money getting together to spend millions backing a Hitler or a Mussolini—or an American general, if he would take the job—to seize power, overthrow a government, and safeguard wealth at the expense of the population. And as always in the fascist pattern the Red scare, the threat of bolshevism, was to be used as the banner under which greed and corruption and violence could join and fight.

These elements made of 1935 (as they were later to make of 1940) a year of Red scares and witch hunts. Hearst, owner of gold mines and vast farming enterprises as well as newspapers, reached the apogee of Redbaiting (and the nadir of journalism) at the same time. Scores of repressive bills were introduced into the House and Senate; seven sedition acts were pending, and among the military bills one, H.R. 4845, went far beyond the 1917 wartime espionage act in depriving the American people of their civil liberties and the numerous enjoyments of freedom listed in the Bill of Rights. Hearst, the American Legion, the chambers of commerce, and all those who stood to profit by repression, backed all this proposed legislation.

Of the red scare of 1935 Roger Baldwin, head of the American Civil Liberties Union, wrote:

"Hunting Reds is so ancient a pastime of patriots and scoundrels hiding their own misdeeds that a new drive just seems familiar repetition. But the new pack of hounds on the trail is more blood-thirsty, and the hunt more promising than in years. I have been through them all, since the first big drive just after the war and the Russian Revolution. I have not, in all that time, witnessed so powerful an alliance as today is in full cry for the complete annihilation by federal and state law of the Communist movement, and with it ultimately, the parties of the left and the militants of labor....

"The New Deal aroused hope among the workers, farmers, and the sinking middle class. It promised the forgotten man his 'rights' and a larger share in the national wealth. It has failed to deliver. Disillusionment is a dangerous reaction. The Huey Longs and the Father Coughlins capitalize it. But they can be brought into line, and anyhow, they cannot be suppressed.

"But the Reds are fair game, and easy marks.... They threaten to be a source of opposition to capitalism from which widespread revolt may grow. The San Francisco general strike struck terror into the whole ruling class, slight as was the participation of the Reds, and the response in raids, prosecutions, and general hysteria was unmatched in recent years. It was from that that the Hearst drive got its inspiration. It fanned into flames the sparks of Fascist vigilantism and of that 'patriotism' organized in a score of commercial and military leagues which does the high-minded stuff for the business rulers.

"They now come to the front with a program designed, they say, to outlaw only 'those who advocate the overthrow of the government by force and violence.' Ignoring the Fascist advocacies of violence, they confine their attack largely to the Left. The report of the United States Chamber of Commerce, by an anonymous special committee, and recently widely circulated, wholly ignores any 'subversive activities' except by anti-capitalist parties. That Fascists can be 'subversive' simply does not occur to them. Their concept is precisely in line with the traditional behavior of the authorities and of the big business crowd behind them. Crimes of violence by reactionaries against strikers or Reds go without punishment, while the slightest suggestion of violence by strikers or Reds is met with hysterical publicity and prosecution.

"The Congressional Committee investigating un-American activities has just reported that the Fascist plot to seize the government, exposed by General Smedley Butler, was proved; yet not a single participant will be prosecuted under the perfectly plain language of the federal conspiracy act making this a high crime. Imagine the action if such a plot were discovered among Communists!

"Which is, of course, only to emphasize the nature of our government as representative of the interests of the controllers of property. Violence, even to the seizure of the government, is excusable on the part of those whose lofty motive is to preserve the profit system. But on the part of those who would upset it in the interests of the producers and consumers of wealth, it is a crime."

If a chart could be made showing the rise and fall of Red witch hunting activities, their intensity and their violence, it would undoubtedly prove to be an exact reversal of the stock market or business barometer.

Bad times have always brought persecution of the scapegoats. President Roosevelt arrived at a bad time, but from the day of his inauguration until the end of 1936 times grew better, and 1936 was quite a good year on the market. It is no wonder then that civil liberties also had a good year in 1936, and that for a while it seemed the red scare of 1934-35 would not be repeated for a long time. Hearst almost alone was screaming 'agents of Moscow' as the labor and Liberal movement marched forward.

On 5 August 1936 there occurred a very important event in American history—the expulsion of one million members from the American Federation of Labor because of their affiliation with the Committee for Industrial Organization. The CIO now began a march which in four years gave it parity in membership with the AFL. From this time on, the professional Redbaiters, all of them enemies of labor, could no longer contain themselves. It was now possible to attack militant union labor in the CIO while hypocritically pretending that one was not opposed to "American" trade unionism, as exemplified in the AFL.

The pink glow over the stock-market and over industry faded in 1937. It was the great year of the sit-down strikes, and the CIO went from success to success in unionizing new industries, notably auto and steel. Governor Frank Murphy of Michigan refused to order troops to Flint to fight the Chevrolet No. 4 plant workingmen and enforce Judge Gadola's injunction ordering evacuation. Peace came with victory for labor. In Pittsburgh, 27,000 workers at Jones & Laughlin's chose the CIO. In New York, Mike Quill's transport workers carried the subways. In Chicago, however, the police murdered ten picketing CIO strikers of the Republic Steel Corporation's plant. In Youngstown, Ohio, Governor Davey sent troops to break the steel strike in that district, but in Johnstown, Pennsylvania, Governor Earle stood on the side of labor.

Testifying in Washington on 24 June Tom M. Girdler, chairman of the board of Republic Steel, said he would never sign a contract with an "irresponsible, racketeering, violent, communist body like the CIO" unless forced to by law. The police had killed Girdler's employees. The police, and not the CIO, had initiated violence. The CIO had no reputation for containing racketeers; it was the old and now respectable AFL that had some racketeering in certain trades. Nor was the CIO communist and irresponsible, for its leading unions were among the oldest, biggest, and most disciplined. But Mr. Girdler's words were trumpeted in the press; and when a former radical writer named Stolberg wrote articles in the Scripps-

Howard papers smearing the CIO, Mr. Girdler quoted him, and the press again quoted Mr. Girdler.

In its 1937 report, the Civil Liberties Union noted that the Redbaiting campaign was again a prominent part of the general attack by the defenders of the status quo (and their brass-check spokesmen) against the forces of democracy; the usual Red smear was being applied to everything progressive, the usual offenders being the Legion, the chambers of commerce, the Catholic hierarchy, the DAR, the KKK, the Nazis, and the like.

Everything progressive, the Union report noted, was attacked as communist or communistic (a more cautious word designed to keep its users from being sued for libel). The Civil Liberties Union itself, whose philosophy made it defend Nazis as well as Communists and which finally expelled Communists from its board, again became the victim of the witch hunt.

The only newcomers on the list of suppressive organizations and Red-smearers was the Catholic hierarchy, which throughout the history of the United States had been a victim of majority prejudices, name-calling, and persecution. This group, which now took up the cry that the Reds were following a "line" from Moscow and a foreign philosophy, went into action when a foreign ruler—namely, the Pope—announced his "line" in an official encyclical issued in a foreign tongue and in a foreign country.

"Next to the Legion," concluded the Union report, "our correspondents cite the anti-communist drive of the Catholic Church and its lay organizations as responsible for the atmosphere in which repression of civil rights thrives."

The stock-market charts, Dun and Bradstreet, the *New York Times,* and *Time's* business indexes agree that the economic trend was downward in 1939, and the students of social economics note that the line of hysteria, alien-baiting, Redbaiting, police and FBI witch hunting mounted very high. In 1939 war broke out between Germany and Poland; it was followed within three days by a declaration of war on the former by Great Britain and France; and on 30 November, negotiations for a peaceful settlement having failed, Soviet troops moved into Finland. The American people, who just 20 years earlier had realized they had been betrayed into the First World War, were now being betrayed into taking sides in the second; but whereas Wilson (perhaps hypocritically, perhaps from the noblest motives) had asked us to remain neutral in mind as well as in acts, Roosevelt encouraged an un-neutral attitude in 1939—and in 1940 practically pledged the country to aid Finland against the Soviets and Britain against Germany—all the time protesting he was not war mongering.

The New Republic for 25 October 1939, noted "with a sinking heart" the repetition of the 1917 and 1920 red scares. We could look back to the first wartime witch hunt with humiliation, but "Today, when the United States is not at war and when everyone declares a firm intention of staying out, we see an ominous return to these activities. Witch hunting is again in progress all over the country. Stimulated by an indiscreet public statement of Attorney-General Frank Murphy . . . zealous patriots everywhere have begun to look for spies, a term that is pretty much equivalent to anybody with a foreign accent whom you don't like.... The Dies Committee . . . is advancing its well-known aim, which is to "smear" the Roosevelt adminis-tration in every possible way, with a new burst of anti-Communist activity.... So serious is the situation all over the country that the ACLU and allied organizations felt it necessary to call in New York a few days ago a National Conference on Civil Liberties in the Present Emergency."

In conclusion it was stated that "the Department of Justice under the liberal Frank Murphy is conscious of the dangers of the situation," but by November it became evident that Murphy himself was an instigator of the red hunt. At his press conference on the 29th of that month, Murphy said that in addition to the prosecution of Earl Browder, head of the Communist Party, there would be a round-up. He was asked by one of the correspondents, Adam Lapin, whether the roundup of subversive persons would include Father Coughlin. He replied that it would not.

The war, the presidential campaign, and the deepening depression in the first months of 1940 undoubtedly added to the intensity of the cam-paign against minorities and progressives.

One of the most flagrant of such actions was the raid on homes of per-sons who had helped send American volunteers to Loyalist Spain. In Detroit the agents of FBI Chief J. Edgar Hoover, taking their lesson from the Hitler Gestapo treatment of Jews and non-Nazis, broke into bedrooms between four and five o'clock in the morning and took men and women, chained to each other, to jail.

Franz Boas, honorary chairman, and Alfred K. Stern, chairman of the National Emergency Conference for Democratic Rights, telegraphed to Attorney-General Jackson (successor of Murphy, who had been elevated to the Supreme Court) protesting "violations of the constitutional amendments" and calling the incident a "dangerous parallel to discredited 1919 raids condemned by a nation." In a press release Chairman Stern said:

". . . the Department of Justice must never become an agency for intolerance and hate-spreading.... In 1919-20 the Palmer raids became the national excuse for blackmailing attacks by vigilante groups and prejudice-ridden individuals.... In 1919-20 it was used by the large lumber monopolies in the west to jail, blacklist, and beat up trade union leaders. In the industrial Midwest it was used as the major excuse for violent attempts to destroy the ever swiftly growing trade union movement.

"We not only remember what happened to democracy in America in 1919-20 when Palmer unloosed his deputized hordes on the country to violate almost every article in the Bill of Rights and every canon of human decency.

"We are acutely aware that in the country today major violations of our fundamental laws are committed daily by men and groups who are more subversive than any of those ever caught in a witch hunt have proven to be."

It should be obvious from the foregoing massing of evidence that:

(1) Redbaiting is itself a big business.

(2) Redbaiting is a powerful weapon of business.

(3) Redbaiting is also a political weapon. It is so powerful it helped Hitler take power, obtained $300 million in loans from Morgan, Dillon Read, etc., for Mussolini; became the main excuse for the Hitler-Mussolini-Franco-Mikado Axis.

(4) Redbaiting is conducted chiefly for profit. The profits may be paid in egoistic satisfaction, in the greatest power any man ever held, in psychiatric coin, sometimes; but mainly, it pays in dollars and cents.

(5) The biggest Redbaiters in America are the members of the chambers of commerce, the National Association of Manufacturers, the Associated Farmers, the Liberty League, and other purely commercial organizations, who Redbait to preserve their wealth, the system which makes their holdings secure, the status quo of Big Money.

(6) Redbaiting is almost universally accompanied by, and is a screen for, labor-baiting, anti-Semitism, anti-Catholicism, and sometimes anti-Masonry and lynching hysteria.

(7) Redbaiting is one of the most important forces in present-day America.

One of the best characterizations of the term Redbaiting was issued by the executive council of the American Federation of Teachers in answer to an attack by Major Charles S. Hart, the Grand and Exalted Ruler of the Elks. Said the AFT:

"Redbaiting is the hallmark of all who oppose the attempts of the American people to secure a more equitable distribution of the wealth their hands and brain produce."

All this may be over-simplification, but I prefer it to obscurantism.

Facts and Fascism

Most of the histories of World War II do not discuss what was perhaps the biggest scandal of the conflict: how American companies supported world fascism before and during the war. Seldes hammered away at this shameful secret in the pages of his newsletter, In fact, *but it was ignored by the mainstream media and now is ignored by most historians. In 1943, Seldes wrote and self-published the book* Facts and Fascism, *which is the most detailed and documented history on how big business subsidized fascism. What follows is the opening section of that book which tells who backed the regimes of Hitler, Mussolini, Franco and Hirohito and who worked for fascism in America.*

THE TIME will come when people will not believe it was possible to mobilize 10,800,030 Americans to fight Fascism and not tell them the truth about the enemy. And yet, this is exactly what happened in our country in the Global War.

The Office of War Information published millions of words, thousands of pamphlets, posters and other material, most of it very valuable and all of it intended to inspire the people and raise the morale of the soldiers of production and the soldiers of the field; but it is also a fact that to the date of this writing the OWI did not publish a single pamphlet, poster, broadside or paper telling either the civilian population or the men and women in uniform what Fascism really is, what the forces are behind the political and military movements generally known as Fascism, who puts up the money, who make the tremendous profits which Fascism has paid its backers in Germany, Italy, Japan, Spain and other nations.

Certainly when it comes to relating foreign Fascism with native American Fascism there is a conspiracy of silence in which the OWI, the American press, and all the forces of reaction in America are united. Outside of a few books, a few pamphlets, and a few articles in the very small independent weekly press which reaches only a few thousand readers, not one word on this subject has been printed, and not one word has been heard over any of the big commercial radio stations.

Faraway Fascism has been attacked, exposed, and denounced by the same publications (the *Saturday Evening Post* for example) which for years ran articles lauding Mussolini and his notable backers in all lands; and the Hearst newspapers, which published from 1934 to Pearl Harbor dozens of signed propaganda articles by Dr. Goebbels, Goering and other Nazis, now call them names, but no publication which takes money from certain Big Business elements (all of which will be named here) will dare name the native or nearby Fascists. In many instances the publications themselves are part of our own Fascism.

But we must not be fooled into believing that American Fascism consists of a few persons, some crackpots, some mentally perverted, a few criminals such as George W. Christian and William Pelley, who are in jail at present, or the 33 indicted for sedition. These are the lunatic fringes of Fascism; they are also the small fry, the unimportant figureheads, just as Hitler was before the Big Money in Germany decided to set him up in business.

The real Fascists of America are never named in the commercial press. It will not even hint at the fact that there are many powerful elements working against a greater democracy, against an America without discrimination based on race, color and creed, an America where never again will one third of the people be without sufficient food, clothing and shelter, where never again will there be millions unemployed and many more millions working for semi-starvation wages while the DuPont, Ford, Hearst, Mellon and Rockefeller Empires move into the billions of dollars.

I call these elements Fascist. You may not like names and labels but technically as well as journalistically and morally they are correct. You may substitute Tories, or Economic Royalists, or Vested Interests, or whatever you like for the flag-waving anti-American Americans whose efforts and objectives parallel those of the Liga Industriale which bought out

Mussolini in 1920 and the Thyssen-Krupp-Voegeler-Flick Rhineland industry and banking system which subsidized Hitler when Naziism was about to collapse. Their main object was to end the civil liberties of the nation, destroy the labor unions, end the free press, and make more money at the expense of a slave nation. Both succeeded. And in America one similar organization (the National Association of Manufacturers) has already made the following historical record:

1. Organized big business in a movement against labor.

2. Founded the Liberty League to fight civil liberties.

3. Subsidized antilabor, Fascist and anti-Semitic organizations (Senator Black's Lobby Investigation).

4. Signed a pact with Nazi agents for political and economic (cartel) penetration of U. S. (Exposed in *In fact*.)

5. Founded a $1 million-a-year propaganda outfit to corrupt the press, radio, schools and churches.

6. Stopped the passage of food, drug and other laws aimed to safeguard the consumer.

7. Conspired, with DuPont as leader, in September 1942, to sabotage the war effort in order to maintain profits.

8. Sabotaged the U. S. defense plan in 1940 by refusing to convert the auto plants and by a sit-down of capital against plant expansion; sabotaged the oil, aluminum and rubber expansion programs. (If any of these facts are not known to you it is because 99 percent of our press, in the pay of the same elements, suppressed the Tolan, Truman, Bone Committee reports, Thurman Arnold's reports, the TNEC Monopoly reports and other Government documents.)

9. Delayed the winning of the war through the acts of Dollar-a-year men looking out for present profits and future monopoly rather than for the quick defeat of Fascism. (Documented in the labor press for two years; and again at the 1942 CIO Convention.)

Naturally enough the President of the United States and other high officials cannot name the men, organizations, pressure lobbyists, and national associations which have made this and similar records; they can only refer to "noisy traitors," quislings, defeatists, the "Cliveden Set" or to the Tories and Economic Royalists. And you may be certain that our press will never name the defeatists because the same elements which made the above nine-point record are the main advertisers and biggest subsidizers of the newspapers and magazines. In many instances even the general charges by the President himself have been suppressed. In Germany, in Italy until the seizure of government by the Fascists, the majority of newspapers were brave enough to be anti-Fascist, whereas in America strangely enough a large part of the press (Hearst, Scripps-Howard, McCormick-Patterson) has for years been pro-Fascist and almost all big papers live on the money of the biggest Tory and reactionary corporations and reflect their viewpoint now.

It seems to this writer that the most important thing in the world today next to destroying Fascism on the field of battle, is to fight Fascism which has not yet taken up the gun.

This other Fascism will become more active—and drape itself in the national flag everywhere—when military Fascism has been defeated. So far as America is concerned, its first notable Fascist leader, Huey Long, a very smart demagogue, once said, "Sure we'll have Fascism here, but it will come as an anti-Fascist movement."

To know what Fascism really is and why we must fight it and destroy it here in America, we must first of all know what it is we are fighting, what the Fascist regimes really are and do, who puts up the money and backs Fascism in every country (including the United States at this very moment), and who owns the nations under such regimes, and why the natives of all Fascist countries must be driven into harder work, less money, reduced standard of living, poverty and desperation so that the men and corporations who found, subsidize and own Fascism can grow unbelievably rich.

This is what has happened in Germany, Italy, Japan and other countries; it is true to a great extent in Spain, Finland, Hungary, Romania, the Polish so-called Republic, and although not one standard newspaper or magazine has ever breathed a word about it, the same Fascist movement—the march of the men of wealth and power, not the crackpot doings of the two or three dozen who have been indicted for sedition—is taking place in America.

PROFITS IN FASCISM: GERMANY

The true story of Hitler-Germany is the real clue to the situation everywhere. In 1923, after his monkeyshines in the Munich Beer Hall Putsch, Hitler received his first big money from Fritz Thyssen. On 30 January 1933, Hitler came into power after a deal with Hindenburg and the big

Prussian landlords (Junkers). Since then, and in all of vast occupied Europe, Hitler has been paying off the men who invested in Fascism as a purely money-making enterprise. A personal dispute put Thyssen out, but his brother and the 1,000 biggest industrialists and bankers of Germany have as a result of financing Hitler become millionaires; the I. G. Farbenindustrie and other cartel organizations have become billionaires.

Big money entrenched itself completely after the departure of Fritz Thyssen, with his rather quaint ideas of placing limits on corruption in business, with his repugnance to the murder of Jews as a national policy, and other rather old-fashioned ethical concepts of monopoly and exploitation which he inherited from his father and which did not encompass robbery and bloodshed as means of commercial aggression. The cartels moved forward with the troops.

There were, of course, exposés of Hitler as a tool of Germany's Big Money, written before he became dictator, but inasmuch as publication occurred in small non-commercial weeklies which few people read, or in the radical press, which is always accused of misrepresentation (by the commercial press which is always lying) the fact remains that few people knew what really was going on. This conspiracy of silence became even more intense when the big American and other banking houses floated their great loans for Hitler—and other fascist dictators in many lands.

As early as 1931 Gerhard Hirschfeld published in a Catholic literary weekly a tiny part of the evidence that Hitler was the political arm of the biggest branch of German capitalism. Recalling that Hitler vowed that the Krupps, the Thyssens and the Kirdorfs, the Mannesmanns, the Borsigs and the Siemens (who are the Garys, Schwabs and Mellons of Germany)—would be stripped of wealth and power, Hirschfeld pointed out that "it is from the ranks of heavy industry, however, that Hitler is drawing much of the money which is making German Fascism something to be reckoned with. Hitler received considerable support from the heavy industries of Bavaria where he started the Fascist movement. The Borsig works and the Eisenheuttenleute (Association of iron forgers and founders) are important pillars of the Fascist structure....From the machine industry of Wuerttemberg and from many other branches of the iron and steel industries, marks flow into the bulging coffers. In addition, money comes from abroad. Swiss friends sent him 330,000 francs just before last year's elections. Baron von Bissing, the university professor, collected many thousands of florins in the Netherlands....German-American friends expressed their sympathy in dollar bills . . . even directors of the French-controlled

Skoda-Works (of Czechoslovakia), famous in the manufacture of armaments, may be found among Hitler's supporters."

It requires neither integrity nor courage today to say that Hitler was made the Fuehrer of Germany by the biggest industrialists of his country. (It does require integrity and courage even today to relate the German men and forces to those in America, to point out the equivalents, and that is why no commercial newspaper or magazine has ever done so.) But as early as Summer 1933, in the Week-End Review, a light which shows up Fascism as nothing but a military-political-economic movement to grab all the money and resources of the world was already focused on Germany by the man who wrote under the name of "Ernst Henri."

He denies, first of all, the myth that Naziism is a "rebellion of the middle classes." The middle classes, it is true, were most united and outspoken for Hitler, they did in fact send in their contributions, but when "these sons of butchers and publicans, of post office officials and insurance agents, of doctors and lawyers" imagined they were fighting for their own interests, when "they swarmed out of the Storm Troops barracks and struck down defenseless workers, Jews, Socialists and Communists" they would not have been able to do it, had they not been mobilized by other sources. "Hitler, the idol of this mass, and himself only a petty bourgeois— a petty bourgeois posing as a Napoleon—in reality followed the dictates of a higher power."

The secret, continues Henri, "must be sought in the hidden history of Germany's industrial oligarchy, in the post-war politics of coal and steel.... Not Hitler, but Thyssen, the great magnate of the Ruhr, is the prime mover of German Fascism."

Thyssen's main undertaking was the German Steel Trust, the equivalent of U. S. Steel. Vereinigte Stahlwerke Aktien Gesellschaft, incidentally, was heavily financed by American banking houses—Episcopalian, Catholic and Jewish—throughout the pre-Hitler and Hitler regimes. The Steel Trust was the basis of German economy, and when it found itself in a desperate situation, during the Bruening regime which preceded Hitler, the foundations of Germany were threatened. It was then that the state came to the trust's aid by buying nearly half the shares of Gelsenkirchener Bergwerke, holding company, nominally worth 125 million marks, at a fantastic price, estimated at double the market. Immediately thereafter the political parties of the nation began fighting for control of this weapon.

The Bruening regime, Catholic, favored the Otto Wolff-Deutsche Bank group which was affiliated with powerful Catholic groups. The Thyssen-Flick-Voegeler group was opposed, although Thyssen himself was a Catholic. Otto Wolff is a leading Catholic, but one of his partners, Ottmar Strauss, is a Jewish liberal. Another affiliate of Wolff's was General Schleicher. The rivalry in Germany was something like that between the Morgan and Rockefeller interests in America, except that the Wolff group was known as liberal and the Thyssen group included Flick and Voegeler, political heirs of Hugo Stinnes who had been, Henri says, "perhaps the first National Socialist in Germany."

Stinnes, Hugenberg, Thyssen and other multi-millionaire owners of Germany had never hidden their participation in political movements nor their subsidization of all reactionary anti-labor political parties. These men put their money into the parties of the right wing and were powerful enough at all times to prevent the Social-Democratic Party, which took over the nation (with the aid of the victorious Allies) in 1918 from doing anything radical to aid the majority of the people—even if the Social-Democrats had sincerely attempted to do so. The historic facts speak for themselves. Germany under Ebert and all the liberal coalitions which preceded the reactionary regimes, which naturally culminated in the advent of big business Fascism never did more than make gestures towards the working class and permitted joblessness and poverty to increase while the Stinneses and Hugenbergs and Thyssens grew in wealth and power.

Thyssen became interested in Hitler in the year of the Beer Hall Putsch, when Hitler was regarded as a revolver-firing clown who would end up in an insane asylum rather than the chancellor's chair. But Thyssen saw possibilities. In 1927 Thyssen took his partner in the Steel Trust, Voegeler, to Rome; they interviewed Mussolini, and when they returned it was noticeable that the Nazi Party suddenly grew rich and began its march to power.

In 1927 Thyssen joined the Nazi Party officially and began that cooperation with Hitler which led to the latter's overthrow of the Republic in 1933.

"Hitler," writes Henri, "never took an important step without first consulting Thyssen and his friends. Thyssen systematically financed all the election funds of the National Socialist Party."

"For the presidential elections of 1932 alone, Thyssen provided the Nazis within a few days with more than three million marks. Without this help the fantastic measures resorted to by Hitler in the years 1930-1933 would never have been possible. Without Thyssen's money Hitler would never have achieved such a success, and the party would probably have broken up at the time of the Papen elections at the end of 1932 when it lost two million votes and the Strasser group announced its secession. In January 1933 Schleicher was on the point of hitting the Hitler movement on the head and putting it under his own command. But, just as before Thyssen had raised Hitler by his financial machinery, so now he rescued him by his political machinery.

"To bring off this coup Thyssen employed two of his political friends and agents: Hugenberg (who is one of the directors of the Thyssen Steel Trust group) and Von Papen. In the middle of January a secret meeting between Hitler and Papen was held at Cologne in the house of Baron von Schroeder, partner of the banking House of J. H. Stein, which is closely related with Flick and Thyssen. Although, thanks to an indiscretion, the news of this meeting got into the papers, a few days later the conspiracy against Schleicher was ready. The allied group Thyssen-Hitler-Von Papen-Hugenberg, which was backed by the entire German reactionary force, succeeded in drawing to its side the son of President von Hindenburg, Major Oskar von Hindenburg, who had so far stood by his old regimental friend, Schleicher. In this way the sudden fall of Schleicher and the sensational nomination of Hitler came about. Thyssen had won, and Hitler set the scene for his St. Bartholomew's day.

"What followed was a continual triumph of the capitalistic interests of the Thyssen group. The National Socialist Government of Germany today carries out Thyssen's policy on all matters, as though the entire nation were but a part of the Steel Trust. Every step taken by the new Government corresponds exactly to the private interests of this clique; Stinnes's days have returned.

"Thyssen had six main objectives: (1) to secure the Steel Trust for his own group; (2) to save the great coal and steel syndicates, the basis of the entire capitalist system of monopolies in Germany; (3) to eliminate the Catholic and Jewish rival groups and to capture the whole industrial machine for the extreme reactionary wing of heavy industry; (4) to crush the workers and abolish the trade unions, so as to strengthen German competition in the world's markets by means of further wage reductions, etc.; (5) to increase the chances of inflation, in order to devaluate the debts of heavy industry (a repetition of the astute transaction invented by Stinnes in 1923); and finally (6) to initiate a pronouncedly imperialist tendency in foreign politics in order to satisfy the powerful drive for expansion in Ruhr capital. All these items of his programs, without exception, have been, are, or will now be executed by the Hitler government." (The reader must remember that this prediction was written in early 1933 within a few months of Hitler's triumph.)

How did Hitler repay Thyssen? There were general and specific ways. Thyssen was made sub-dictator of Germany (Reichs Minister of Economics), in charge of all industry. The labor problem for Thyssen and all employers of Germany was solved when Hitler abolished the unions, confiscated the union treasuries, reduced labor to a form of serfdom. Specifically, Hitler poured hundreds of millions of dollars into Thyssen's pocketbook by the manipulation of Gelsenkirchener. The new capitalization was 660 million marks instead of 125 million. The state, which had owned more than half of Gelsenkirchener, came out holding less than 20 percent of the new corporation, and Thyssen, who had feared the collapse of his empire, came out king of coal and steel again, and therefore the most powerful industrialist in the land.

Within a few weeks after taking power Hitler used his anti-Semitism for commercial purposes as an aid to his main financial backer, Thyssen. Oscar Wassermann, of the Catholic-Jewish Deutsche Bank, had been chief rival of the Thyssen bankers. Hitler retired him on "grounds of health." Thyssen's one opponent within the Steel Trust, Kloeckner, a Catholic like Thyssen, was forced to resign from the Hitler Reichstag. A charge of corruption was filed against Otto Wolff, who led the financial battle against Thyssen. Goering appointed Thyssen chief representative of private capital in his new Prussian State Council. And, finally, the Fighting League of the Trading Middle Class, the little business men who put up their small money and who went into the streets killing and robbing industrial working men and Jews, was ordered dissolved by Hitler early in 1933 because it might menace the upper class.

It is with especial interest that one reads Henri's conclusion and prediction a full decade after he made it. He said in 1933:

"The trade unions have been destroyed. Thyssen can dictate wages through the new 'corporations' and thus reduce still further the prices of export goods in the face of English and American competition. Armaments are being prepared; Thyssen provides the steel. Thyssen needs the Danube markets, where he owns the Alpine Montan-Gesellschaft, the greatest steel producers in Austria. But the primal objective of this new system in Germany has not yet been attained. Thyssen wants war, and it looks as though Hitler may yet provide him with one."

The historic facts are that armaments were being prepared, although the British and French closed their eyes to this fact and believed the promise that they would be used only against Russia; the Nazi army did march into Austria and did unite the Alpine works with their own, and it is also true that Hitler did provide a war, although it was Thyssen's brother, Baron von Thyssen, and Thyssen's partner and successor as head of the Vereinigte Stahlwerke, Voegeler, who reaped the profit, and not Thyssen himself. Naziism paid all its original backers (except one man) and all its present owners colossal profits.

The relation between money and elections was more clearly illustrated in the German elections in the decade of 1923-1933 than in any American elections—although a volume could be written to prove that the Republican or Democratic Party which wins every four years is the party (with only a very few exceptions) which has the larger number of millions to spend.

"Seven months before he (Hitler) got there (the chancellor's seat) he polled his legitimate maximum of 13,745,781 votes, just over one-third of those recorded. Four months later, in the last constitutional Reichstag election, he lost over two million votes. That was in November 1932. The huge Nazi Party was rapidly declining; it had been overblown with millions of mere malcontents, victims of the slump, lured in by desperation rather than Hitler's glib tongue and splendid showmanship. Yet, after the landslide of the November elections, the Party was broke to the wide and in what looked like hopeless dissolution. Hitler moodily (not for the first time nor for the last) threatened suicide. A few weeks later he was in power."

The foregoing statement is from the Fabian Society of Great Britain. It states the situation truthfully. How then explain what followed?

"How had the miracle happened? Goebbels grandly called it 'The National Socialist Revolution'; it was nothing of the kind. It was just a bargain with Big Business and the Junkers. Strong in money, power and influence, but with hardly any popular backing, these vested interests (with arch-intriguer Von Papen as their political representative) were worried by the Schleicher government's threat to expose the worst of their graft; they were even more worried by the possibility of a swing to the Left through a coalition of Schleicher and the Trade Unions. That's why the Papen group, having cold- shouldered the slipping Nazi Party for some time, were now keen on an alliance capable of adding a mass movement to their own financial and industrial power. That's how Hitler got his much-needed cash for his Party and his own appointment as Chancellor in a new Coalition Government."

Hitler's entire history is one of spending big money to build up a party, big money to get millions of votes, and when his backers' money failed to put him in office, he made the conclusive deal with them, finally selling out the great majority who voted for him in the belief he would keep his 26 promises, most of them directed against Big Business, the Junkers and the other enemies of the people.

Hitler's fascist party was never a majority party. In many countries where several political parties exist—and even in the United States at those times when three major parties are in the field—the chancellor or president elected to office represents only a minority of the electorate. Nevertheless, it is true that Hitler did succeed in fairly honest times before he was able to use bloodshed and terrorism for his "Ja" elections, in making his the largest of a score of parties.

Why was he able to do this?

There are of course many reasons, notably the disillusion of the nation, national egotism, the natural desire to be a great nation, the psychological moment for a dictator of any party, right or left, economic breakdown, the need of a change, and so forth. But important, if not most important, was the platform of the Nazi party which promised the people what they were hungering for.

It must not be forgotten that the word Nazi stands for national socialist German workers party, and that Hitler, while secretly in the pay of the industrialists who wanted the unions disbanded and labor turned into serfdom, was openly boasting that his was a socialist party—socialism without Karl Marx— and a nationalist-socialist party whatever that may mean. But it did mean a great deal to millions. The followers of Marxian socialism in Germany, split into several parties, would if united constitute the greatest force in the nation, and socialism and labor were almost synonymous in Germany. Hitler knew this. He capitalized on it. He stole the word.

Hitler was able to get 13 million followers before 1933 by a pseudo-socialistic reform program and by great promises of aid to the common people. In the 26 points of the Nazi platform, adopted in 1920 and never repudiated, Hitler promised the miserable people of Germany:

1. The abolition of all unearned incomes.

2. The end of interest slavery. This was aimed against all bankers, not only Jewish bankers.

3. Nationalization of all joint-stock companies. This meant the end of all private industry, not only the monopolies but all big business.

4. Participation of the workers in the profits of all corporations—the mill, mine, factory, industrial worker was to become a part owner of industry.

5. Establishment of a sound middle class. Naziism, like Italian Fascism, made a great appeal to the big middle class, the small business man, the millions caught between the millstones of Big Business and labor. The big department stores, for example, were to be smashed. This promise delighted every small shopkeeper in Germany. George Bernard Shaw once said that Britain was a nation of shopkeepers. This was just as true for Germany—and German shopkeepers were more alive politically. They were for Hitler's Naziism to a man—and they supplied a large number of his murderous S.S. and S.A. troops.

6. Death penalty for usurers and profiteers.

7. Distinction between "raffendes" and "schaffendes" capital—between predatory and creative capital. This was the Gregor Strasser thesis: that there were two kinds of money, usury and profiteering money on one hand, and creative money on the other, and that the former had to be eliminated. Naturally all money-owners who invested in the Nazi Party were listed as creative capitalists, whereas the Jews (some of whom incidentally invested in Hitler) and all who opposed Hitler were listed as exploiters.

The vast middle class, always caught between the aspirations of the still more vast working class and the cruel greed of the small but most powerful ruling class, has throughout history made the mistake of allying itself with the latter. In America we have the same thing: all the real fascist movements are subsidized by Big Money, but powerful organizations, such as the National Small Business Men's Association, follow the program of the NAM in the hope they will benefit financially when the Ruling Families benefit.

In all instances, however, history shows us that when the latter take over a country with a fascist army they may give the middle class privileges, benefits, a chance to earn larger profits for a while, but in the end monopoly triumphs, and the Big Money drives the Little Money into bankruptcy.

This is one of the many important facts which Albert Norden presented in his most impressive pamphlet, "The Thugs of Europe," a documentary exposé of the profits in Naziism taken entirely from Nazi sources. My thanks are due to Mr. Norden—a German writer who escaped to America and who went to work in a war plant recently—for permission to quote some of the evidence. Norden takes up the matter of Naziism and its promises to the middle class:

"If the Third Reich were for the common man, the middle class would not have been sacrificed to the Moloch of Big Business. If the Third Reich were for the common man, the banks and industries and resources of the sub-soil would belong to the people and not be the private affair of a few score old and newly rich.... As it is now, it is the rich man's Reich. That is why there is such a widespread underground anti-Nazi movement among the German people.

"This war is being waged by the Third Reich, the heart of the Axis, as a 'struggle of German Socialism against the plutocracies.' Goebbels has duped millions of young Germans with this slogan. Not only that: Nazi propaganda outside Germany and particularly in North and South America has succeeded in recruiting trusted followers with this slogan....

"The Nazi theory of a struggle of the Have-nots against the so-called 'sated' nations is as true as the myth that Goebbels is an Aryan and Goering a Socialist. The following facts, taken from official German statistics, prove that in the Third Reich there is a boundless dictatorship of the plutocrats; that a small group of magnates in the banking, industrial and chemical world have taken hold of the entire economic apparatus at the expense of the broad sections of medium and small manufacturers, artisans, storekeepers and workers, and are making unprecedented profits.

"In his program Hitler promised the middle class preference in all government jobs, abolition of interest on loans, breaking of the power of the trusts and cartels, and dividing up the department stores. Each of these points could only have been carried out at the expense of finance-

capital to which Hitler had made definite commitments which, in turn,
spell ruin for the middle class and workers.... The Kampfbund des
Gwererblichen Mittlestandes, a Nazi organization . . . had been schooled
to destroy Marxism. Everywhere they had killed Socialists and
Communists, demolished workers' headquarters and trade union offices.
Now that Hitler had triumphed they wanted to reap the fruits. But the
Nazi leaders offered them cheap laurels instead—laurels which pleased
neither their senses nor their pocketbooks....

"Never yet in modern history has the middle class, relying solely on
itself and without an alliance with other social strata, successfully played
an independent role or triumphed in the social struggle. . . The Nazi
leaders did not hesitate one moment in their decision when the big industrialists and bankers began to complain. One after another, Hitler,
Goering and Hess in May, June and July 1933—issued sharp warnings
against 'attacks on business'; and Hess ordered all activities against department stores to cease.... Already by August 1933, the high hopes which millions of little people had pinned on Hitler had been rudely shattered....
Leaders of the struggle of the middle class against the trusts . . . were sent
to concentration camps. Before the month had ended the Fighting
League of the Middle Class was no more.... The massacre of the entire
leadership of the Storm Troopers on the pretext of homosexuality closed
the short chapter of independent action by the middle class with a
smashing political victory by Big Capital....The department store of the
Jewish owner Tietz was handed over to a consortium consisting of the
three largest banks, the Deutsche Bank, the Dresdener Bank and the
Commerz-und Privatbank....The large department store Karstadt . . . of its
eight directors four are big bankers, one a large exporter and a sixth an
influential figure in the Deutsche Bank....

"The more Jews were dragged off and murdered in concentration
camps, the richer Germany's magnates became. They let the S.S. and S.A.
mobs riot and trample all human laws under their hobnail boots—meanwhile the Dresdener Bank acquired the Berlin bank of Bleichroeder
(Jewish bank, patronized by the former Kaiser) and Arnhold Bros. (Jewish
bank, one of the best banks in Germany, patronized by U. S. Embassy and
newspapers); the Deutsche Bank seized the Mendelssohn Bank. In the
Berliner Handelsgesellschaft, an important private bank, Herbert
Goering, a relative of Marshal Hermann Goering, replaced the Jewish
partner Fuerstenberg. The Warburg Bank in Hamburg was taken over by
the Deutsche Bank and the Dresdener Bank in conjunction with the

Montan Combine of Haniel and the Siemens Trust. The latter also took out of Jewish hands the Cassierer Cable Works.... The armaments kings of the Ruhr did not shrink from profiting from the pogroms. As a result of Hitler's persecution of the Jews, the Mannesmann concern received the metal company of Wol, Netter & Jacobi, and the Hahnschen Works; while the big industrialist Friedrich Flick (one of the dozen men who put up most of the money to establish Naziism), today one of the 20 richest men in the Third Reich, seized the metal company of Rawak and Gruenfeld. This list could be expanded at will. It illustrates the prosperous business which the solidly established German trusts acquired as a result of the infamous crimes against the Jews. Together with the top Nazi leaders these German financial magnates were the main beneficiaries of the sadistic persecution of the Jews....

"Moreover, the turnover tax on big business was reduced to one-half per cent on all commodities, while for little business it was raised to two percent. The decree establishing price ceilings was eliminated so that Big Business under Hitler was able to raise prices on numerous occasions. Thus in two years immediately preceding the outbreak of the present war, tens of thousands of small businessmen were able to get prices which just barely covered their own costs, and sometimes were even lower. That is why small businesses were liquidated on a mass scale in Germany.... The government of the Third Reich, a long time before the outbreak of the war, had passed the death-sentence on over one million members of the middle class, and carried it out, thus profiting the wealthiest sections of German finance-capital.... The result is inevitably the same: a blood-letting without parallel and impoverishment all along the line. Hitler's regime of a 'people's community' and elimination of the class struggle has hastened, as no previous regime has done the crystallization of classes in German society, dealing terrible blows to the middle class and favoring the upper 10,000 in striking fashion. In 10 years of the Nazi regime the lower middle class in Germany has been more ruined and declassed than in the pre-ceding 50 years."

Another pamphlet which exposes the profits in Naziism is "The Economics of Barbarism" by J. Kuczynski and M. Witt, who, after showing how by violence and by illegal means disguised as legal the Germans have seized the wealth of all occupied Europe, arrive at the conclusion that "The European continent in the hands of German monopoly means the end of the United States as a great economic power. It is the first step towards the enslavement of the Americas."

The Nazi plan, after taking over all of Europe, has been to use monopoly capital to reduce imports permanently and to increase the volume of cheap exports rapidly. German monopoly would exclude American goods from all markets except within the two Americas at first, then enter the South and Central American markets as a formidable competitor and eventually, with the aid of Japan, to exclude the United States and England from both the Asiatic and British Empire markets.

All this of course based on a victory of the Fascist International.

The three principals of fascist economic strategy, according to these authors, are:

1. To achieve the economic subjugation of a conquered nation it is essential to control the heavy industries. The first principle of Nazi economic strategy: keep intact, build up, and above all else, take into their own hands the heavy industries.

2. Fascist economy centers on war production. Since it has no interest in the welfare of the masses of people and prefers to depress wages of workers and farmers and lower their standard. of living, goods for popular consumption are of secondary importance. Since all the big industrialists are linked with Fascism, it is a policy to give the consumer goods manufacturers a monopoly for all of Europe. There is therefore a tendency towards decentralization in the heavy industries, with centralization in Germany of consumer goods industry. The Nazi principle is: kill consumption goods industries outside Germany.

3. The third principle is to increase the numbers of millions dependent upon agriculture with a corresponding increase in the holdings of the great landed proprietors. This pays back the Junkers who financed Hitler, provides materials for the chemical industry and profits the same industry in the sale of artificial fertilizers, and furthers the policy of complete self-independence or autarchy.

These principles of barbarism, conclude the authors, would, if realized, "put back the technical and economic structure of certain parts of Europe a hundred years or more, while over-developing the economy in other parts of the continent."

The pamphlet, written before America was attacked by Japan, warns our country that Fascism is an epidemic disease, and that we cannot escape.

The relationship of the big money system to the Fascist Party itself is more clearly shown in what happened in Italy than any where else. Let us look beyond the Alps.

BIG BUSINESS BOSSED MUSSOLINI

The first modern fascist regime is the Italian. (Fascism itself is as old as history, and although Mussolini is a colossal liar, he told the truth for once when he defined Fascism as Reaction.)

Who put up the money for Mussolini?

Why did they invest in Fascism?

How were they repaid, and who footed the bill?

The original Fascist Party of Italy, likewise the Nazi Party which was formed almost at the same time, was subsidized by a handful of the richest industrialists and landowners who wanted to preserve their wealth and power and prevent the majority of people from living a better life. (The American Legion was organized for the same reason: to preserve the privileges of the few and fool the millions who believed better things would come after victory.)

Here is the complete list of main subsidizers of Mussolini's Fascism— (compiled from fascist, neutral and anti-fascist sources, including Prezzolini, Salvemini, Bolitho and Prof. Robert A. Brady)—and their American equivalents:

1. Lega Industriale of Turin. The American equivalent is the Associated Industries of Cleveland (also A. I. of Florida, Massachusetts, Missouri, New York and Utah). Anti-labor organizations, corrupters of the free press, employers of spies, racketeers and murderers as strikebreakers, users of poison gas, all exposed by the La Follette Committee.

2. Confederazione Generale dell'Industria. Nearest equivalent is the National Association of Manufacturers, which has some 8,000 members but which is run by a small group of men, including the DuPonts, who have subsidized the worst native fascist outfits in America. The NAM works "in secrecy and by deceit," according to the final La Follette report, employs prostitute college professors, prostitute preachers, and prostitute journalists. (Mussolini is the most famous prostitute journalist of our time;

he sold out to the French government for 50,000 francs a month. Documentation in *Sawdust Caesar*.)

3. Associazione fra Industriali Metallurgici Mecannici ed Affini. Similar to the Iron & Steel Institute, operated by our steel barons, including Weir and Girdler, one of whom employed the columnist George E. Sokolsky, the other the idol of Westbrook Pegler.

4. Fiat Automobile Works. Similar to General Motors, largest stockholder of which is DuPonts which is also the largest subsidizer of most native fascist organizations.

5. Societa Ansaldo (shipbuilders); Fiume Oil Corp.; Venezia Giulia steel furnaces; Upper-Italy Hydroelectric Works; and other big outfits. (Equivalents in NAM leadership.)

6. Ente Nazionale per le Industrie Turistiche and Grandi Alberghi associations. No equivalents in the U. S., these being the tourist bureau and the hotelkeepers' association, both more interested in having the trains run on time than the trainmen eating on time—or at all.

7. Landowners Association, chairmanned by Senator Tittoni. U. S. equivalent: Associated Farmers. The Italian outfit consists of feudal landlords, the superwealthy of the nation and is the cause of poverty and starvation among the farming population of Italy. The U. S. outfit includes the packers and canners who control the Farm Bloc in Congress, constitute the Farm Lobby, and are in reality manufacturers of food and the enemies of the homestead farmer.

8. Banca Commerciale of Milan, Banca Italiana di Sconto, and other leading banks, the equivalent of the Chase, National City, Guaranty Trust and other bank which have spread dollar imperialism in Mexico, Cuba, and the rest of Latin America.

Mussolini was subsidized by the Italian equivalent of our NAM and similar Big Money outfits shortly after the seizure of the factories in 1920.

In March 1919, fascist agitators caused the workers to seize the Franchi-Gregorini plant. Mussolini called this a "creative strike," because the workers intended to run the plant for their own benefit. One of Mussolini's colleagues wrote: "At Dalmine he was the Lenin of Italy." At this time Mussolini was trying to get back into the labor movement.

When the factories of Milan and Turin were occupied by the workers Mussolini held a conference with Bruno Buozzi, who then held a place equivalent to that of Sam Gompers in our American Federation of Labor.

He proposed using the factory occupation as the beginning of a military movement to seize Rome and establish a dictatorship of the proletariat. Buozzi indignantly kicked Mussolini out—labor believed in the democratic political processes, and the main proof was that not an act of violence marked the factory seizures, although the press of the world for a month ran daily lies of bloodshed and terrorism.

Within a few days Mussolini had sold the same idea to the owners of the occupied factories—only this time the same Blackshirts were to be used to create a dictatorship of Big Business, rather than of workers. Signor Agnelli, head of Fiat, admitted to Buozzi that Mussolini actually had dealt with Olivetti, of the Confederazione dell'Industria, while dealing with Buozzi. (This document in Chapter VIII of *Sawdust Caesar*.)

Olivetti and company put up the money. Mussolini took Rome. And in payment to the subsidizers his first important act was the abolition of all labor unions—the equivalent of our AFL, CIO and Railroad Brotherhoods.

From the day he became dictator Mussolini began paying back the men who paid him in 1920. He abolished the tax on inheritance, for example, because it was supposed to end big fortunes, and that of course meant loss of money for the rich, who had in a body gone over to Fascism after 1922. But Mussolini did not have the courage to abolish the political democratic system all at once, and he had many opposition parties which criticized and attacked him. His chief opponent was the Socialist deputy Giacomo Matteotti.

The reason Matteotti had to die was because he committed the one unforgivable crime in a Fascist nation: he exposed the profits in Fascism.

There is no program, no policy, no ideology and certainly no philosophy back of Fascism, as there is back of almost every other form of government. It is nothing but a spoils system. We too in America have a spoils system, which is talked about every four years when a President is elected, and sometimes when a governor is elected, but this refers largely to a few jobs, a little graft, a considerable payoff for the boys in the back room of politics. It is also true that we in America have ruling families, men and corporations who put up most of the money for elections, and do not do so because one candidate has baby blue eyes and the other is beetle-browed. It is done for money, and the investors in politics are repaid. But Fascism is a system whereby a handful of ruling families get the entire nation.

It was Matteotti who discovered in 1924 that Mussolini, who had "marched" to Rome in a Pullman sleeper in 1922, was beginning to pay back the secret forces which had paid the money to put Fascism in power.

On 27 May, a few days before he was kidnapped and assassinated by Mussolini's gangsters and family friends, Matteotti denounced in the Italian parliament a law which would have given a monopoly in oil to the Sinclair firm—the same corporation run by Harry Sinclair which was involved in the filthy muck of the Teapot Dome Scandal, and incidentally the same Harry Sinclair who told Dorothy Thompson that he and his associates put up most of the money to buy the Presidency of the United States every four years.

On 10 June 1924, when the entire front pages of the American press were given over to the Loeb-Leopold case in Chicago, Matteotti was killed by Mussolini's own orders, and not a line appeared in most newspapers. On the 16th Arnaldo, brother of the Duce, printed a warning in his Popolo d'Italian against public clamor for an investigation of the murder, saying such a request was in reality a demand that Mussolini abdicate. But the *London Daily Herald* told the truth. Matteotti, having challenged the Sinclair oil deal, had prepared a documentary exposé proving that Balbo, Grandi, Arnaldo, Mussolini himself and the biggest men in the Fascist government had been engaged in a tremendous graft and corruption deal in relation to the oil monopoly.

For all this the Undersecretary of Home Affairs, Finzi, was made the scapegoat; the evidence was plain that he was among the grafters, and as he was also one of the big financial profiteers of a Fascist law legalizing gambling, he resigned in an uproar. In apology the Roman press said that "thousands of jailbirds have joined the Fascist Party since the March on Rome," and that Finzi was not a good party member.

Finzi was a small shot. Matteotti was using the Sinclair oil graft scandal to hit at the big shots, and the Fascists were throwing Finzi to the mob to save the real profiteers of the system. Matteotti had prepared a documentation which showed that the big bankers, the great industrial baronies such as Ansaldo, the great landowners and the war profiteers who had made billions while Italy hungered, were to be given the wealth of Italy. Here is a small part of Matteotti's documentation:

Ansaldo: A decree-law of 14 June 1923 supplied national funds for refloating this private corporation whose owners had been chiefly responsible for the bankruptcy of the Banca di Sconto. The Fascist regime, with

72 million lire (against 78 million lire worth of shares given the creditors), became almost half owner; it also took a mortgage for 41.5 million lire.

Fascism subsidized the Ansaldo shipbuilding company at 900 lire a ton.

It gave Ansaldo 230 locomotives for repair, without accepting competitive bids.

Fiume Mineral Oil Refining Company: On 29 April 1923 the Fascist State purchased 18,000 shares of this corporation for 8,300,443 lire. It made itself party to the success of this private firm. Among the new directors the State put on the governing board were three of the "Fascists of the first hour," Dino Grandi, Massimo Rocca and Iginio Magrini.

Banking Houses: The Banca di Roma was in the same straits as the Sconto. When the latter failed it appealed to Mussolini as a friend and subsidizer of the Fascist movement, and Musso the Duce repaid the directors by by-passing the old law requiring them to make good the bank's losses. One of the men who profited most was a certain Senator Marconi, member of the board of the Sconto, who suddenly joined the Fascist Party in October 1923. In November, Matteotti showed, he was relieved of the financial burden of putting up his fortune to repay the poor devils who had trusted the Sconto and lost all their money. This is, of course, the same Marconi who claimed he had invented the radio—a claim disputed by several. That Marconi made a fortune in wireless is beyond dispute.

War Profiteers: Every nation had a war profiteering scandal after 1918. Mussolini, in his demagogic orations in which he promised everything to everybody, said that he would take back every cent the profiteers made. At the very time he was saying this, Mussolini, as Matteotti later revealed, was accepting big money from the very same profiteers for organizing his Black- shirts and outfitting them with castor oil, clubs and revolvers.

The various regimes before October 1922, had begun the investigation of the war profiteering frauds and several suits resulted in large sums being regained. Mussolini had denounced these suits as slow, the sums returned as small: he promised quick suits and complete confiscation of all the property of the war profiteers. On 19 November 1922, less than a month after he took office, Mussolini with a sweep of his pen wrote Decree No. 1487 which abolished the Committee of Enquiry into War Profiteering, and the crooks who paid for his election were relieved of all worry.

Railroads: The Societa Italiana per le F. S. del Mediterraneo, a private railway line, was granted treasury bonds up to 100 million lire by Decree 1386 of 17 June 1923. A concession for the construction of 80 kilometers of Sicilian railroads was granted two important Fascist industrialists, Nicolini and Romano; the cost of the work was to be about a billion lire, and no government returns, rights, or priviliges were asked. It was purely a big payoff to early subsidizers of Fascism.

Peasant Lands: On this subject an entire book could be written. The whole history of early Fascism centers upon this problem. As early as November 1918 and internationally in the days of the peace conference of Versailles, the promises of "land for the returning soldiers" were being made by leading statesmen of the world, and notably by Giolitti, Orlando, Sonnino and other Italians. But in most lands there was no public domain, and little land available at a small price. There was, on the other hand, a feudal system—it still exists in fascist countries such as Poland, Hungary, Rumania, etc.—where a few land barons were even more powerful nationally than the industrial barons of the mills, mines and factories.

From Armistice Day to the "March" on Rome there had been a slight agrarian reform in Italy and considerable seizure of land by impoverished and dispossessed peasants. Mussolini in his (fake) radical days had urged the returned soldiers and the landless farmers to seize the estates of the wealthy. At this time a new movement arose, the Populari, or Catholic Popular Party, led by the priest Don Luigi Sturzo, which had as its chief aim the restoration of land to the farmers. However, whenever some of his restless and impatient followers seized some land, Don Sturzo would get together some money and make a settlement with the owner, because he was a strict legalitarian.

A study of the history of early Fascism shows that it concentrated its violence and its oratory against the Catholic Party, not against the Left. It was not until Mussolini hired an American press agent in 1925 to help float the Morgan $100 million loan and the Dillon, Read & Co. loans to the municipalities, that the myth of "fighting Bolshevism" was invented to please Wall Street. There was a tiny, ineffective Communist Party in Italy, and a large and powerful Socialist Party with which Mussolini could do (and did) business. But Mussolini could not appease the Populari of Don Sturzo, and he could not do anything to stop the agrarian reform movement. As Bolitho wrote in 1925: "The enemy was not, however, the Communists, but the Catholic peasants of Don Luigi Sturzo's People's Party which was preaching seizure of land."

The landowners (and the industrial owners) were Mussolini's chief backers. No one knew of the subsidies he had received from the great estates. Immediately on becoming dictator Mussolini granted his first important interview to the press of the world. He said:

"I love the working classes. The supremest ambition and the dearest hope of my life has been, and is still, to see them better treated and enjoying conditions of life worthy of the citizens of a great nation.... I do not believe in the class war, but in cooperation between classes. The Fascist government will devote all its efforts to the creation of an agrarian democracy based on the principle of small ownership. The great estates must be handed over to peasant communities; the great capitalists of agriculture must submit to a process of harmonization of their rights with those of the peasants."

This interview was printed in America on 15 November 1922 but on 11 January 1923 less than two months later, Mussolini issued a decree law which dispossessed all the small peasants who since the war had settled on the seized lands of the "latifundia" of the great landowners. Needless to say, there has been no agrarian reform, no division of estates into small holdings, no "harmonization" of "the great capitalists of agriculture." The landowners were paid of with a return of all land which had been given the landless and by the employment of the Blackshirt Militia which prevented any further attempts to divide the land.

Mussolini's one stroke in issuing this decree-law restored more profits to more Fascists than probably any act in the totalitarian history of that land.

Although Mussolini himself had not laid up a cent—or a million dollars—as has Hitler, he has made it possible for all "Fascists of the first hour," be they bankers or burglars, to make all the money possible out of his success.

Dumini, the actual murderer of Matteotti, was given vast sums of money by Mussolini and the Fascist Party. Cesare Rossi, one of the founders of the party, was granted the right to sell concessions to foreigners. It was Rossi whom Matteotti was to expose as dealing with the Sinclair Oil Company for the oil monopoly. The graft was to be shared between him and Filippelli and Marinelli, also implicated in the assassination, and because the others tried to make him the scapegoat Rossi wrote confessions which were later published.

In its July 1934, issue, a song of praise for Fascism, *Fortune* magazine (owned by Henry Luce, a Morgan partner, and other powerful and

wealthy Americans) told of the great corporations and how they pro-
gressed under Mussolini.

"The significant facts to hang on to," concluded *Fortune*, "are these: if
you were an early Fascist, or contributed generously to the March on
Rome, you are likely to enjoy the business benefits that accrue to a high
position within the Fascist Party."

Curiously enough *Fortune* (and Luce's other publications, *Time* and
Life) which had a long record (before Pearl Harbor) of applauding
Fascismo, will not even now print any news which would in any way indi-
cate that there is at least a slight resemblance between the former object
of their affection, and the constant love of their lives, the American Big
Business equivalent of the Fascist industrial system.

THE FIVE WHO OWN JAPAN

Every Japanese gun, bullet, torpedo, ship and airplane that has killed or
wounded an American soldier, sailor, airman or marine has meant actual
cash money in the pocket of Emperor Hirohito.

When the "merchants of death," the armaments manufacturers who
had a financial interest in waging previous wars, and who still do in fascist
dictatorships, were exposed in 1934, it was found that Mitsui and
Mitsubishi were the Japanese members of the cartel, and that the reigning
family was a large stockholder in both.

Hirohito owns 3.8 million acres of land with all the buildings on them,
many being tenements from which he makes a rent. The son of the Sun
Goddess has also invested 300 million yen in the Bank of Japan, the South
Manchuria Railroad, the Yokohama Specie Bank, Nippon Yusen Kaisha
(the shipping line of the Mitsubishi firm), the Imperial Hotel of Tokyo,
and Mitsui and Mitsubishi enterprises.

In the wave of disillusion which swept over the world after the Treaty
of Versailles and proved that the old march of the imperialists would be
resumed and that all international idealism (Woodrow Wilson's for
example) would be destroyed, many secrets were uncovered and one of
the most sensational was that concerning the international of blood—the
cartels of the merchants of death, the armaments makers, who made a
profit on the guns, the shells and the bullets. The manufacturing corporations in many instances were found linked to governments and to have
arranged, even in wartime, for the continuance of their dividends and distribution of their profits.

It should be noted here that just as American Big Business was found at the time of the First World War to be linked to Japanese Big Business through the Harvey cartel, Nobel international trust and other agencies, so just before the outbreak of the Second World War it was discovered that the international of money was even stronger than ever. One of the links was the I.G. Farbenindustrie, which Hitler and Goering controlled and which involved Standard Oil, Standard Drug, General Motors, General Electric and other of our greater corporations.

Just as American Big Business was linked to Japan through the Harvey combine (steel), the Nobel Dynamite Trust (munitions) and the other munitions cartels before the last war, so before the Global War there were the usual international cartels in which both the U. S. and Japan shared with Germany, Italy and other nations.

In addition, according to the San Francisco journalist John Pittman, "among the owners of Japanese business are International General Electric, which operates plants through its subsidiary, Tokyo Shibaura; Westinghouse Electric International, associated with Mitsubishi Electric Manufacturing Co.; Tide Water Associated Oil, handled by Mitsubishi; Libby-Owens-Ford, represented by the Nippon Plate Glass Co.; Standard Oil, with a known direct investment of $5 million exclusive of frozen credits and oil in storage; Ford, and General Motors, with approximately $10 million sunk in Japan proper; Eastman Kodak, and Singer Sewing Machine, with big organizations in the Japanese Empire; United Engineering & Foundry Co., holding a large stake in Shubaura-United Engineering Co.

"Besides these shares in the industry of Japan proper, American capital is heavily invested in Manchukuo and other exploitation companies of a Japanese origin scattered throughout the Far East."

In Japan one of Mitsui's partly owned corporations is the Nippon Steel Works, but this firm was controlled by Vickers. Their French connection was through the Franco-Japanese Bank, founded with the aid of Schneider Creusot, whose 1933 report stated that "our bank has 'acquired' important participation in various activities of the Mitsui group, a group destined to have a fine future."

Baron Hachirumon Mitsui was reported at the time as controlling 65 percent of the industry of Japan, with the Japanese royal family owning a large interest in the Mitsui Consortium. Mitsui, referred to in the Japanese press as King of Armament-makers, Emperor of Steel, Caesar of Petroleum, and Demigod of the Banking System, owned or controlled most of the mines, factories, steamships, newspapers and commercial enterprises of the first order, not only in Japan but in Korea, China, Indochina, Manchuria, the Philippines and Hawaii.

The conquest of Manchuria was popularly said to have been instigated by Mitsui, and there is no doubt that this firm was the largest beneficiary from the coal and steel Japan seized. This firm also gained most from the first Sino-Japanese war. It was also credited with dictating Japan's peace terms at the end of the Russo-Japanese war, using the Tokyo Foreign Office as one of its many handy instruments. It may be remembered that one of the points Japan would not cede was the occupation by its troops of North Sakhalin, and they remained there until the oil deposits were leased to Japan. Russia was forced to agree. The lease was then given by Japan to one of the owners of the government and nation, the Mitsui Consortium.

The so-called "Asia for the Asiatics" doctrine, which means simply "Asia for Japan," found Baron Hachirumon Mitsui its chief exponent. This is a Monroe Doctrine which marches with banners and is followed by an army of salesmen and exploiters. Hachirumon's fascist imperialism burned even more ardently in his successor, Baron Takakimi Mitsui.

"Japan's financial oligarchy," wrote Anthony Jenkinson for the Institute of Pacific Relations, "is composed of great family trusts known as Zaibatsu. Its leading members are the Houses of Mitsui, Mitsubishi, Sumitomo and Yasuda. Between them they own the greater part of industry, trade, banking, and shipping. By 1937 they controlled more than one third of the total deposits in private banks, 70 percent of the deposits in all trust companies, and one third of total foreign trade. By controlling the banks, they controlled the smaller credit institutions throughout the country."

The income tax returns of 1938-39 showed that Japan consists of a vast majority of farm workers and farmers and industrial workers who earn less than the equivalent of $10 a week. There is almost no middle class, only 1.5 million or about one family in 40 which earns less than $2,500 a year, but on the other hand there is a small rich and powerful ruling class consisting of 3,233 persons with incomes of $50,000 or more a year. The top flight consists of 7 persons who paid an income tax on more than $2 million each. (*New York Times*, 2 April 1939)

In all countries where the regime in power prohibits the full development of the nation's industries—or the manufacturers and raw materials producers themselves limit production (the economy of scarcity), as in the

United States—there must be poverty. In Japan, thanks to the fact that four industrial families and the royal family have colossal wealth—Mitsui is said to be richer than Ford—the majority of the people, farmers and workers, are poor. Moreover, the International Labor Office of the League of Nations reported in 1938 that one quarter of the entire population did "not earn enough to maintain health and efficiency." Official Japanese statistics as of May, 1941, show the average wage for men at 82 yen ($19.25 at current rate of exchange) and 31 yen ($7.30) for women.

The trade unions were abolished in 1940 when the royal-military dictatorship began following the Fascist Axis line in action as well as form. "Workers," writes Jenkinson, "were ordered to become members of the League for Service to the State through industry," which approximates the Mussolini labor corporations and the Nazi Hitler's forced labor. The Minister of Welfare in announcing the abolition of the trade unions made this statement: "Our primary aim is to drive communist ideas and dangerous social thoughts from the minds of the people by ordering the dissolution of the established labor unions, which have a tendency to sharpen class consciousness among workers, which hamper the development of industry, and disturb the peace and order of the country." On 23 November 1940 the Japanese Patriotic Industrial Society, or Sampo, absorbed the League, and claimed it had 4.5 million members. 'It was declared to be a wing of the Imperial Rule Assistance Association.

This Imperial Rule Assistance Association (IRAA) is an outright fascist body. Up to 6 July 1940, there had been many parties in Japan, which gave the nation the semblance of a constitutional monarchy in accordance with its Constitution, granted by the Emperor in 1889 and modeled on that of Bismarck's Prussia. Like Prussia it created a Diet consisting of a House of Peers and a House of Representatives actually elected by popular vote. Leading parties were the Seiyukai and Minseito, both controlled by the big industrialists, the Zaibatsu (very much as our Republican and Democratic Parties are frequently, but not always, controlled by the National Association of Manufacturers). In 1936, however, the Minseito Party came out against Fascism and won a victory and the Social Mass and Proletarian Parties elected 23 working men to the Diet.

But on 6 July 1940 the Social Mass Party was ordered dissolved, and within a few weeks all other parties dissolved "voluntarily." An attempt to form a Laboring People's Party was suppressed.

This left the IRAA in control, a one-party system without an official dictator, but Japan is actually a fascist dictatorship ruled by the Emperor, the Army and Navy, and the Zaibatsu.

No one can tell where the political rule and industrial ownership of these three elements (Royal Family, Big Business, Military) begin and end; they intermingle and draw their money profits from the same seizure and exploitation of foreign lands, exploitation of the impoverished majority not only of Japan but Korea, Manchuria and China.

Japan has been described as an ancient feudal, modern capitalistic, fascist dictatorship. Wilfred Fleisher dubbed it a "collective dictatorship."

Fascism, as any study of Hitler-Germany shows, has been built up as a system of super-colossal robber barons, thanks largely to the international cartels, of which I. G. Farbenindustrie was the largest.

Nationally, all forms of Fascism have flourished thanks to the aid the state has given them in maintaining monopolies or trusts. In every instance where business men subsidized a reactionary party—whether it was the Fiat works in Italy paying Mussolini or a landed estate owner bribing a Rumanian premier—the party and the most powerful few of the subsidizers have always engaged in forming national monopolies when they took over the rule of the country.

Professor Robert Brady points out the fact that it was because the old system of feudalism prevailed longer in Japan than elsewhere that "the new Japanese totalitarianism has been easier to achieve than in any other major industrial-capitalistic country." The "feudal and patriarchal-minded hierarchies of business" and the political and military bureaucracies were identified and centralized. Government and business are more intermarried in Japan than anywhere else, much more so than in the ruling family of Goering-Hitler and company. But all in all the fascist pattern is pretty much the same in all countries where wealth and power have taken over the military-economic-political rule. Professor Brady writes that in Japan the elements "are not greatly dissimilar to those noted for other totalitarian systems of the general fascist type." He lists:

"1. The Zaibatsu, the monopolistically-oriented enterprises centered around them, and the extensive network of trade associations, chambers of commerce, cartels, and similar bodies of which they are the acknowledged leaders, constitute an elaborate, semilegal hierarchy of graduated economic power....

"2. The hierarchy works very closely with the civil and administrative bureaucracy of the state.... This constitutes the Japanese version of National Socialism....

"3. The military is becoming increasingly part and parcel of the same control pyramid....

"4. And finally, the psychopathic, ideological, propaganda cement which holds the Kokutai (Corporate State) amalgam together in the fused power of Shinto (the main religion) and Bushido (Precepts of Knighthood)."

WHO PAID FOR FRANCO'S WAR?

Fascism in Spain was bought and paid for by numerous elements who would profit by the destruction of the democratic Republican Loyalist government. There were generals who wanted glory and others who wanted the easy graft money some of their predecessors had made. There was the established Church, and more especially the powerful Society of Jesus, which had suffered loss of property when King Alfonso was thrown out. There was the aristocracy, and there were other elements as there are in all fascist regimes, but more important than all these forces combined was the force of Money.

The Big Money conspired with General Sanjurjo and the Nazi government in early 1936 to establish a fascist regime which would not only protect profits but insure bigger profits at the expense of the majority and end the heavy fear that the masses preferred the benefits which even a weak republic could obtain for them.

Prominent among the owners of Spain and Fascism are:

1. The Duke of Alba. Of him it has been said that he could cross Spain from the French border at Irun to the outskirts of Gibraltar and never take his feet off his own land. True or not, it is a fact that he is one of the holders of vast lands, in a nation where thousands starve to death and millions pray for two or three acres.

2. Juan March. This multi-millionaire crook is typical of one element of all fascist regimes. In Italy Mussolini had his murderers and assorted gangsters whom he gave big graft jobs and made into millionaires as a reward for their aiding him before 1922. Matteoti's assassins are known. March has a penitentiary record as a common smuggler, and also a record as the holder of the state monopoly in tobacco. He is said to have put more millions into the Franco movement than any other man.

3. Rio Tinto. This is one of the biggest mining ventures in the world. Big British and Spanish capital is invested in it, and it is a truism that all

big capital prefers a fascist regime, which it can own completely, to a democracy where elections change things—and the tax rate. The British probably have the controlling interest in Rio Tinto. When Claude Bowers, American Ambassador to Spain, suggested to the British Ambassador that if Franco won, Britain would have Hitler at Gibraltar and perhaps lose the control of the Mediterranean, "the lifeline of empire," the British Ambassador answered that "private interests at home are stronger than national interests." He meant that Rio Tinto and other Spanish mine, electricity, railroad and other stockholders in Britain preferred Fascism and even Hitler in Spain to the safety of Britain itself.

In all agrarian countries—notably Poland, Hungary, Spain, Romania—the big landowners are almost without exception fascists. The Duke of Alba, who put millions into the Franco investment, was joined by all the Spanish holders of estates who, with the Church, had owned the best and largest areas of fertile Spain.

There had been no large seizure of land under the Republic, but all the liberal parties were pledged to agrarian reform. Big pieces of land had been bought from the great landlords and parceled out—in three or four acres and perhaps ten—to several thousand landless. The Republic did accomplish something, but although it was not anything very big, it was enough to scare the multimillionaire estate owners. They therefore joined the conspiracy with Franco so that they could keep the land. It was as simple as all that.

Of course the people of Spain—the vast majority, the farmers and workers—wanted land and a decent living. Franco therefore did the usual fascist thing: he made big promises.

In the Twenty-Six Points of the Phalanx, the ruling Fascist Party of today—all other parties have been abolished and Spain is totalitarian—the nation was to be turned into "one gigantic syndicate of producers," so that there would be plenty for all, instead of superabundance for only the rich, as had been the case under both monarchy and fascist dictatorship; the banks were to be nationalized, land was to be irrigated, and those large estates which were found to be neglected were to be broken up.

What does the balance sheet today show of the Franco "experiment" of 100 parcels of land, the distribution of a glorious total of 17,000 acres in 1938 and the promise that at least neglected estates would be broken up? The writer-journalist Thomas J. Hamilton presents the latest and final report:

"The landed aristocrats of Spain . . . had little real cause for complaint against the Franco regime which addressed itself to the work of undoing any damage to their interests that they had suffered from the Republic. This was not large. The grandees had been frightened by talk of breaking up the great estates, but they had managed to sabotage the Republic's first Agrarian Reform Law and the second was just getting into operation when the Civil War began. Only a few hundred thousand acres had actually been taken over, either in accordance with law or as a result of the movement among the peasants in the spring of 1936 to seize the land without waiting for the slow operations of the government.

"The test of any Spanish regime was its attitude toward this fundamental question, and it may be supposed that some of the grandees had anxious moments when Franco adopted the Phalanx program with its demand for land reform. Carlists and moderate royalists together, however, proved more than strong enough to prevent the regime from harming the interests of the landowners. All land which had been occupied by the peasants, legally or otherwise, was returned to the owners, and soon there was no longer even any mention of breaking up the great estates....

"In general, the old nobility, fighting very much the same type of fight that it had under the Republic, managed to keep the Phalanx from hitting its pocketbook."

Mussolini's prediction, made years before World War II broke out in September 1939, that the entire world was lining up in two camps, Fascism and Democracy, and that it was "Either We or They," showed itself a matter of fact in the so-called civil war in Spain. It was actually a rebellion of the military leadership—which committed wholesale treason by betraying the government to which it had taken an oath of allegiance—armed and paid for by the vested interests. The "We" consisted of Fascists from all parts of the world, hundreds of thousands of soldiers from Germany, Italy and Portugal, all fascist lands, whereas the "They" of Democracy consisted of some 30,000 men of the International Brigade, not one a conscript soldier as were all on Franco's side, but every man a volunteer, a man of intelligence, a first fighter against Fascism. (Of the foreigners on the Loyalist side about 700 were Russians, mostly aviators and technicians, and not one infantry soldier. The press of America,

Britain and other countries as usual lied about Russian aid and perpetu-
ated the myth that the Loyalists were Communists.)

On Franco's march to Madrid he took not only the labor union
leaders but a large percentage of the industrial workers of each town he
captured, lined them up, and shot them down with machine guns. In
Madrid the Fifth Column of Fascism killed as many of the working class as
it could.

From Madrid early in 1937 this journalist wrote to the *New York Post*
that Fascism had made it a class war in Spain; that Fascism was determined
to kill off all leaders of the working class so it could enslave the workers,
whereas the Loyalists had as their objective the redistribution of land and
wealth.

The most enlightening proof of a class war was given in Madrid on the
7th and 8th of November 1936, when the capital was given up as lost,
when the censors in the Telefonica let the newspapermen send out the
most pessimistic reports, and the Loyalist militiamen sat around waiting
for Franco to arrive and murder then.

On the 8th there was considerable shooting in the streets. It was
Franco's Fifth Column—the hidden pro-fascist column which the fascist
international has created in every country, and which still flourishes in the
United States, and has its supporters in Congress. The Loyalists estimated
the snipers at twenty or thirty thousand. Now, when Franco appeared
about to enter the city, they boldly appeared in windows and on roofs and
around street corners, and began their guerrilla warfare.

How did the Spanish Fascists know which Spaniards to murder?

Obviously every man in Loyalist uniform was a possible victim. But the
Loyalists never had enough money to put all of their men in uniform, and
tens of thousands fought the war in the blue overalls of their shops and
factories.

The Fifth Column, hidden Fascists, were the people who had subsidized Franco. To them every working man was an anti-Fascist and therefore marked for death. And since the Loyalists in wartime did not wear
white shirts, or white collars, or fine suits of clothes, or felt hats, or even
neckties, the Fascists of the Fifth Column, fighting their guerrilla war in
the streets of Madrid on 8 November 1936 spared every well-dressed
wealthy-looking man as a possible ally, and murdered the men of the
working class. Men in overalls were always shot by the Fascists.

The final lesson from Spain, however, should not be lost by the thousands of American business men, big and little, who from 1922 on have

been saying kind things about Mussolini and others who made trains run on time and seemed to insure bigger profits by outlawing unions, and the rights of the working people.

In Germany a million business men were ruined by Hitler, and only the upper thousand, the wealthiest and most powerful, profited by Nazi rule. As in Italy, so in Germany, the fascist regime had to rob not only the poor and reimpose serfdom on millions, but it also had to rob its own supporters to maintain a new bureaucracy, and a new army on whose bayonets the bureaucracy tried to build a permanent government. Fascism has to exploit either a foreign people or its own people; it has to have money, and if it must pay off the top subsidizers this means it has to destroy its millions of smaller helpers.

Hitler and Mussolini robbed and impoverished their own party members in order to feed the super-monopolists. In Spain the situation is similar. Hamilton writes:

"Spain was traditionally the land of special privilege. Franco's success in restoring these privileges therefore produced a singularly vicious combination: the rich stayed rich, if they did not get richer, and the poor were even hungrier than they had been in the worst days of the civil war.... Suffering was increased immeasurably by the restoration of the old privileges; despite the steadily increasing misery of the poor, the wealthy managed to obtain virtually everything they needed. And a new class of parvenus, who had made their money by the special 'favours' obtained from the government officials in charge of operating the faltering economic machine, spent their profits with an abandon which was one failing that could not be charged against the old families.

"The Franco regime had, in fact, loaded still more privileged classes upon a suffering country...."

In his speech at Burgos on 19 April 1939 Franco announced a Nationalist Syndicalist state which would restore the status quo ante 1931—the time the Republic was overthrown. The *New York Times* headline was: "Franco Reassures Owners of Capital."

THE NAZI CARTEL PLOT IN AMERICA

Only the little seditionists and traitors have been rounded up by the FBI. The real Nazi Fifth Column in America remains immune. And yet there is

evidence that those in both countries who place profits above patriotism—
and Fascism is based entirely upon profits although all its propaganda
speaks of patriotism—have conspired to make America part of the Nazi
Big Business system.

Thurman Arnold, as assistant district attorney of the United States, his
assistant, Norman Littell, and several Congressional investigations, have
produced incontrovertible evidence that some of our biggest monopolies
entered into secret agreements with the Nazi cartels and divided the world
among them. Most notorious of all was Alcoa, the Mellon-Davis-Duke
monopoly which is largely responsible for the fact America did not have
the aluminum with which to build airplanes before and after Pearl
Harbor, while Germany had an unlimited supply. Of the Aluminum
Corporation sabotage and that of other leading companies the press said
very little, but several books have now been written out of the official
record.

The document which follows, and which was first published by *In fact*
on 13 July 1942 goes much further than the mere cartel conspiracies of
Big Business of both countries, because it has political clauses and points
to a bigger conspiracy of money and politicians such as helped betray
Norway and France and other lands to the Nazi machine. The most powerful fortress in America is the production monopolies, but its betrayal
would involve, as it did in France, the participation of some of the most
powerful figures of the political as well as the industrial world. The real
Fifth Column is built on more than economic penetration, and much
more than a few pro-Nazi preachers, Red network manipulators, publishers of cheap and lying anti-Semitic pamphlets, and crackpots of all
sorts. In Spain, where the term Fifth Column originated, it was not
reported generally that the pro-Franco traitors within Madrid, who hid on
roofs and murdered people in the streets, were—except for hired
gunmen—members of the upper ruling class, the aristocrats, the
landowners, and the members of the big business ruling families, and all
the dead and wounded were working men.

Our press, which had nothing but praise for Mussolini for almost a
generation, and which has always protected Fascism, Naziism and reaction
in general by Redbaiting every person and movement which is anti-Fascist,
anti-Nazi and anti-reactionary later made a grand noise over the traitors,
seditionists and propagandists such as Father Charles Coughlin, Fritz
Kuhn and William Pelley, who were the outstanding loudmouths at the
time of Pearl Harbor. These small-fry fascisti and the Rev. Gerald Winrod

and numerous others spread the same lies which they received from Hitler's World-Service (Welt-Dienst) of Erfurt; all these noisy propagandists and traitors, repeating Hitler's propaganda, did succeed in raising a huge smokescreen over America. Behind this artificial Redbaiting, anti-Semitic, anti-New Deal fog of confusion and falsehood, however, there was a real Fifth Column of greater importance, the great owners and rulers of America who planned world domination through political and military Fascism, just as surely as Hitler did in Germany, and like groups and like leaders did in other countries. There is no reason to believe that the United States was the one exception to the spread of Fascism.

Nine men, two representing Hitler and several leading American industrialists, members of the Congress of the United States, and representatives of large business and political organizations met at a hotel in Boston, on 23 November 1937—at a time Hitler was trying out his Condor Legion, his dive bombers, his new tanks and his Panzerdivisionen and his Blitzkrieg tactics on the poor and practically unarmed people of Spain—to formulate a working agreement by which American forces would join Nazi forces in the monopolistic control of the world's business and the political and military domination of the whole world.

The document which follows is a memorandum written at the conclusion of the meeting. The secretary who collected the notes from five of the persons present, each of whom contributed a part, was not versed in social, economic and political matters, but was impressed somehow with the importance of the event, and although her notes were taken away from her, she did succeed in retaining a carbon copy of the document. It had a long journey, went to Scotland, was copied by persons who realized its value, and brought back to the United States, where I was able to obtain it for the readers of *In fact*. Here it is in its entirety:

TEXT OF THE NAZI-U. S. CARTEL MEMORANDUM

"The purpose of this draft is not to commit anyone who attended our formal conference. On the contrary, the memorandum should only retain and preserve the main topics of our conversation which, if desired, could be reported to proper organizations or individuals having the competence and privilege to draw practical conclusions or take appropriate steps.

"1. One of our German guests emphasized in his statement that he has no authority to give any official viewpoint. Nevertheless, his personal impression is after yearslong service in connection with consular representations here that radical changes took place in America's foreign policy with regard to Germany. 'Our country,' he said, 'was accustomed to regard the United States as a source of friendly influence. Its contributions have alleviated Germany's burden under the peace treaty. President Hoover's step leading up to the complete elimination of the financial debt resulting from the Versailles treaty was considered always as characteristic manifestation of the American attitude towards the German people.

"'The Roosevelt Administration has introduced important changes which tend to alter the German opinion concerning the American attitude. A certain agitation was allowed to interfere with German-American relations. Instead of cooperating in the opening of tremendous potential markets, Germany and America were forced to join hostile diplomatic camps. The potential markets China and Russia cannot be organized with(out) the active collaboration of American capital, however. World recovery is thus delayed.

"'Germany is therefore willing to undertake everything humanly possible, in order to approach directly the financial and industrial leaders of the United States. The creation of a Japanese monopoly in the Far East is not desirable. Nor is for that matter a Chinese victory. The new Presidential elections must bring the United States on the side of the powers fighting for the reorganization of the world markets.

"'To support those trends in the American public opinion which definitely favor such a change, is the paramount task of the German foreign policy. This support does not only include the swinging of the German-American vote to a presidential candidate definitely sympathetic to the aforementioned aims, but also all possible cooperation with truly national forces. This, of course, cannot be construed as interference into American internal affairs, since the concrete form as well as the extent of that support must be determined by the political groups concerned.'

"2. Our second German guest, who was just recently appointed to a diplomatic post in this country, supplemented the above statements with the following points:

"Germany has been grossly misrepresented before the American public by Jewish propaganda. 'In order to clarify the picture,' he said, 'it is necessary to recall that Germany of the Republican period has thrown a remarkable confusion into the minds of the Germans. The state has been identified with some popular welfare institution. Creative capital was over-burdened by the effects of a Utopian "social welfare" legislation. Unemployed insurance, sick, old-age, and death benefits, social security and war pensions meant terrible handicaps already. Trade union wages and hours have lifted productive costs above world standards.'

"What is the paramount achievement of National Socialism? 'The spirit of New Germany was conducive to a kind of national solidarity. Exaggerated demands and "social service" were reduced and production costs realistically brought into harmony with the requirements of competition on the world markets. This is what we have done. Not more and not less. It is true that many objections had to be overcome. The conception featuring the State as a supreme welfare agency had to be eradicated and a policy of increased production pursued instead. We had to silence therefore all centers from where class struggle was being fomented and imprison dangerous Utopians and sentimental philanthropists. It is true that Jewish propaganda was able to capitalize on some stern measures and slander New Germany before the world opinion. This is undoubtedly a detrimental fact. But we have gotten more by the rebirth of national solidarity and the cooperation of all for the same purpose.

"'Without wishing to arouse any semblance of interfering with domestic questions in the United States, I cannot help mentioning that today's America presents a very close picture of Social-Democratic Germany. Unrealistic "welfare legislation" sponsored by the Administration, chaotic class struggles and wage demands absolutely out of any proportion, strong Jewish influence in the political, cultural and public life of the country are disquieting phenomena. We Germans, at any rate, are disquieted. We carry on a good work for world recovery and we know what potential danger an increasing Red influence in the United States would mean for the whole world.

"'Another disquieting characteristic of the situation is the lack of unity and clear-sighted leadership in the scattered national camp. You cannot start a strong concerted drive of all forces and agencies for the revival of American nationalism as long as this situation prevails.

"'It is time to think seriously of the centralization of all forces of American nationalism and traditionalism. We Germans are seeking the cooperation of all American nationalists. Above all we believe in cooperating with the economic leaders of the country, whatever the suitable form of the cooperation may be. There is little comprehension on behalf of the United States Government, but in our belief there must be comprehension for our viewpoint on behalf of business.

"'We would advance the idea of such informal conferences between responsible business and political leaders in order to consider questions of national and international importance affecting economic and, yes, political recovery.'

"The following opinions were expressed by the American participants of the conference:

"(a) The substance of the German suggestion amounts to changing the spirit of our nation as expressed by recent elections. That is possible but by no means easy. The people must become aware of the disastrous economic effects of the policies of the present Administration first. In the wake of the reorientation of the public opinion a vigorous drive must start in the press and radio. Technically it remains a question as to whether this drive may center around the Republican National Committee.

"(b) Farsighted business men will welcome conferences of this kind. A tremendous inspiration might come out of them. There is no reason why we should not learn of emergencies similar to those prevailing in our own country and the methods by which farsighted governments were trying to overcome them. It is also clear that manufacturers, who usually contributed to the campaigns of all candidates, must realize that their support must be reserved to one, in whose selection they must take an active hand.

"We must just as well recognize that the business leaders of this country must get together in the present emergency. By now they must have realized that they cannot expect much from Washington. We will have to resort to concrete planning.

"We can all agree that it is desirable to convince our business leaders that it is a good investment to embark on subsidizing our patriotic citizens' organizations and secure their fusion for the common purpose.

"Unified leadership with one conspicuous leader will be a sound policy. We will be grateful for any service our German friends may give us in this respect.

"(c) American foreign policy must be chiefly guarded against the danger of the sovietization of the Far East. More than ever we must supervise by Congress what the State Department does. Rapprochement with Germany, while unpopular, is a necessity, if we consider the strong pro-Soviet agitation going on and finding patronage in the United States. It is of the greatest importance that leading and influential figures in our business life and the policy-making bodies of both political parties should be appraised of this first conversation and prevailed upon to discuss the possibilities of a non-partisan cooperation on the subject."

The importance of the foregoing memorandum, the first of a proposed series of notes upon which a political-commercial pact between the Nazi regime and pro-fascist Americans could be arranged, was recognized at the time. Shortly afterwards a so called "little Dies" committee, one of several flourishing in many states in imitation of and sincerest flattery to the big native Fascist Martin, was invited to make an investigation into the origins of the plot. But the informant was told by a Boston member of the Massachusetts Redbaiting organization that this was not the stuff it was after, this memorandum, in fact, was "all right." In other words, plots by Nazis and their American friends were passed over or approved in Boston in just the same manner Nazi activities throughout the United States were passed up by Martin Dies, the fair-haired boy of the Goebbels broadcasting stations.

Each of the five parts, listed as 1 and 2, and a, b, and c, was written by a participant in the 1937 meeting. No. 1 is the work of Baron von Tippleskirch, No. 2 that of Baron von Killinger, "a" was written by a member of the U. S. Senate who was at this meeting, "b" by a representative of General Motors, and "c" by the representative of the DuPont interests.

In 1939, shortly before Germany invaded Poland and started the Global War from which the Nazis and their Quislings and Fifth Columns in all lands but Russia hoped to emerge rulers of the world, a diplomatic representative visited the seven Americans each of whom owned a copy of the foregoing memorandum. The importance of the document lies largely in the prominence and importance of the nine men who attended the conference and the forces and corporations they represented. Of these nine, their governments, and their corporations and other interests, I have information on five. These are:

Baron von Tippleskirch, Nazi consul general in Boston.

Manfred Freiherr von Killinger, then newly appointed consul general in San Francisco. Killinger was one of the eight men who participated in the murder of the Catholic statesman Erzberger in Republican Germany. The fact that he was found persona grata by our State Department, where Mr. Hull has a dozen pro-Fascist assistants functioning even today, is interesting. Killinger arrived just before Japan began her invasion of China, and conferred also with Japanese agents.

General Motors Representative. General Motors was completely involved in Nazi affairs. Until Pearl Harbor it was the owner of the Adam Opel A. G., worth more than $100 million. It had paid $30 million for 80 percent of the stock. It had made 30 percent of Germany's peacetime passenger cars. After Hitler came into power, it began manufacturing the trucks and panzer division equipment with which Hitler waged war. In 10 years it had made a profit estimated at $36 million. But, since Hitler banned the export of capital, and American stockholders were thereby denied these dividends, General Motors invested at least $20 million in other industries, all owned or controlled by Goering and other Nazi officials, and thus General Motors was completely affiliated with Nazi success or failure. (Source for statistics: Poor's Manual.)

Alfred P. Sloan, president of General Motors and director of DuPonts, was charged by the U. S. Treasury (29 June 1937), just five months before the date of our memorandum, with cheating the government out of $1,921,587 in three years through establishing personal holding companies to dodge taxes.

DuPont Representative. The four most important facts about the DuPont Empire are:

a. that it controls General Motors, owning $197 million of General Motors stock;

b. that it financed the Liberty League, Sentinels, Crusaders and one dozen native American fascist outfits;

c. that it knowingly and secretly and in violation of the U. S. and other laws, aided Hitler to arm for this war;

d. that the DuPonts betrayed military secrets to Hitler.

One great cartel of the merchants of death is called Dynamit-Aktien-Gesellschaft (DAG). Exhibit 456 in the Nye-Vandenberg munitions investigation shows that DuPonts not only own stock but a voting right and a voice in the management of the cartel. Exhibit 456 also shows DuPont has a financial interest in I. G. Farbenindustrie, the Nazi cartel which ties up with the Aluminum monopoly, Standard Oil, synthetic rubber, Sterling and other drug concerns.

The DuPont contract with DAG, British Imperial Chemicals and Nazi interests, as published by the munitions committee, says in part: "Each party agrees . . . upon making or obtaining any patented invention or discovery or acquiring any secret invention, to disclose in writing to the other party immediately, or in any event within six months thereafter, full particulars." It may be noted that according to Thurman Arnold the Nazified I. G. Farben obtained Standard Oil synthetic rubber patents, that Standard Oil did not receive all German patents, and that Standard Oil refused to make the German patents known to the U. S. Government even after Germany attacked.

The DuPonts knew that according to the Thyssen plan German Fascism was nothing more than a system by which the biggest German industries got control of the nation, smashing small business, seizing political rule. Wendell R. Swint, director of DuPont foreign relations, testified the DuPonts knew of the "scheme whereby industry would contribute to the (Nazi) Party Organization funds, and in fact industry is called upon to pay one-half percent of the annual wage or salary roll to the Nazi organization." (Munitions Hearing, Vol. XII.)

The relationship of the DuPonts to Nazi Germany—the story of how they armed Hitler with the help of Mr. Hoover—as exposed by the munitions investigation, gives valuable support to the foregoing.

On 4 December 1938 the Associated Press, Moscow bureau, sent out a list issued by the official Tass government press bureau of a "fascist clique" in the United States, which list follows with explanatory facts about each person:

"War Industry Magnate" DuPont. The official statement said the DuPonts had "great capital investments in fascist Germany."

William S. Knudsen, president of General Motors. Knudsen told a *New York Times* reporter (6 October 1933) on arriving from Europe that Hitler's Germany was "the miracle of the 20th Century." Nevertheless paragraph "c" in our memorandum was not written by Knudsen, but by another GM official of equal prominence.

Colonel Charles Lindbergh. In addition to collaborating with the British Cliveden Set, Lindbergh had written an article for the reactionary Reader's Digest stating Hitler's Aryan myth and other fascist doctrines.

Former President Herbert Hoover.

Ambassador to Britain Joseph P. Kennedy. Kennedy's secret report to Roosevelt on the war favored Britain going Fascist.

Henry Ford.

Bruce Barton. One of America's leading advertising men, head of an agency controlling $40 million, Barton has a tremendous influence on America's corrupt commercial press. Barton is a native Fascist. He praised "the sense of national obligation which Mussolini has recreated in the soul of Italy." He wrote: "Must we abolish the Senate and have a dictatorship to do it? I sometimes think it would be almost worth the cost." (*American Magazine*, June 1930. Barton objected to ideas he had written being used against him when he ran for the Senate. He said they were years old. But when he wrote an endorsement of Mussolini, the Duce had already murdered thousands of persons, destroyed the labor unions, outlawed civil liberties.)

Senator Arthur H. Vandenberg. As part of the Nye-Vandenberg Munitions inquiry, Senator Vandenberg went after the DuPonts and exposed their relations with Hitler. This was not a hardship for Vandenberg. He has always been Ford's friend, and Ford was the rival of General Motors, which the DuPonts controlled. By Mussolini's definition of Fascism as Reaction, Vandenberg qualifies as one of America's leading Fascists. In his Congressional record are votes against the Wagner Act (the Magna Carta of American labor), the Wages and Hours Act, TVA, AAA. In opposing the Black-Connery Wages and Hours Bill, three months before the date of the foregoing memorandum, Vandenberg said it would make for a "centralized, authoritarian state with its tyranny of oppressive, government-blessed monopolies." In 1936 Vandenberg had urged a coalition of reactionary Republicans and reactionary Democrats to block the New Deal.

On 27 November 1937, Captain Fritz Wiedemann, Hitler's personal adjutant, en route to the U. S., was exposed in Paris as heading a Nazi political mission whose purpose was to seek the support of leading American reactionaries and pro-Fascists to further Hitler's aggressive aim in Europe.

Mme. Genevieve Tabouis, militant editor of *L'Oeuvre*, one of the two percent of the French press which was not bribed, wrote in her paper that day that it was the object of the Nazi mission to make contact with Senator Vandenberg of Michigan.

The United Press cabled a similar statement from Paris that day, adding that it was based on information from a reliable source in Berlin.

Mme. Tabouis stated that Germany was seeking assurances from the United States and Britain in order "to leave her hands free in the East, particularly concerning expansion in Central Europe towards Russia." (Note: Mme. Tabouis, also called "Cassandra," was proved absolutely right when Germany attacked Russia in June, 1941.) Mme. Tabouis continued:

"The aim of the mission is to try to convince the American people that Germany wants peace but desires facilities in Central Europe. It also wants to show that Germany's great aim is opposition to Communism throughout the world. This mission will enter into close relations with Senator Vandenberg...."

NAM: THE MEN WHO FINANCE AMERICAN FASCISM

The two corporations which were part of the Nazi cartel plot in the United States are two of the main vertebrae of the backbone of American Fascism. Lammot DuPont and Alfred P. Sloan, Jr., of the DuPont Empire and General Motors respectively, have been exposed by Congressional committees as subsidizers of fascist organizations and movements. Both corporations and both men are also among the top flight rulers of the National Association of Manufacturers.

Before producing a small fraction of the documentation—it would require volumes to present a real indictment—showing that the NAM is the center of American Fascism, and that its leaders are the Thyssens, Flicks and Voegelers of America, this statement must be made about the organization.

The NAM is something like a nation, like a people—say the Finns, or the Germans. Our country passed through a great emotional phase which favored the Finns, and is naturally emotionally set against the Germans, nevertheless—thanks largely to the press—the American people as a whole refused to accept the fact that Finland has been in fascist hands for a long period of its independent history, and also refuses to accept the view that there are millions of good and innocent Germans. The facts are that both Finland and Germany are in the hands of fascist rulers, that a large proportion of the population in each country accepts Fascism, and that it is necessary in the war against Fascism to destroy not only the leadership but as large a part as possible of its armed might in the field. But it is the leadership which is totally vicious, and it is an unfortunate fact which apparently cannot be changed by the innocent, no matter how many of them there are, that rulers and ruled have a united destiny.

It may therefore be true that the majority of the estimated 15,000 members of the NAM are as innocent as the Finnish man-in-the-street, or the German farmer or industrial worker, of the crimes of Fascism, but it is truer yet that the inner group which rules the NAM is just as vicious a clique as the one Thyssen organized to put Hitler into power.

There are actually three groups in the NAM, as the National Maritime Union's organ, *The Pilot*, once pointed out:

"The large majority of NAM members are reasonably assured that a United Nations victory is in their own and the country's best interests. A smaller group moves along with the feelings strongest at the time and yields one way or the other if pressured. A still smaller but very much more powerful group is in the saddle now and its program is remarkable for a nation at war.

"The group swinging the NAM whip is headed by Frederick C. Crawford, who has no beef with the Axis. He has the perfect background for a model version of a homegrown Fascist. During the middle thirties he was active as a director in Associated Industries, a Cleveland strike-breaking agency which tried to doctor up its records when the La Follette Committee went to work on it. The FBI proved that this fink outfit paid out to a labor spy agency. . . which means he okayed the hiring of goons, spies, thugs, and stoolies, and financed the use of tear gas, sawed-off shot-guns and blackjacks, etc.

"Mussolini got splashed with Crawford's praise after a trip to Europe in 1939. About Hitler he said: 'What difference does it make if the dicta-torship of Germany is consuming one-fourth of production for military grandeur, or whether the bureaucracy of the New Deal is consuming one-fourth of production to maintain itself? ...'

"Crawford's fighting a war . . . but it's a war against President Roosevelt, against the American people, and against the coming defeat of Hitler."

Crawford, DuPont, Sloan and a handful of others boss the NAM. Several years ago, when it had only half its present membership, the La Follette Committee reported that "about 207 companies, or approxi-mately 50 of the NAM, are in a position to formulate the policies." Actually a dozen or so native Fascists control the most powerful private organization in the history of America, but they control it as absolutely as Hitler, Mussolini, Hirohito and other Fascists controlled their own nations (until their downfall); they are just as responsible for its political and social activities, and the entire NAM is just as guilty (or innocent) as the mass of people is in each fascist nation. (In this connection it may be pointed out that whereas a German cannot very well quit Germany in wartime, although there are Germans who have done better than that by becoming guerrilla fighters, it is easy for an American business man or corporation to quit the fascist NAM on the spur of the moment, and General Mills, for one example, did do so when one of its presidents, a Mr. Witherow, said we were not fighting the war to put TVA's on the Danube.)

From the foregoing and following facts the reader may decide for himself whether the NAM, which represents the best part of American industry, and whose annual meetings are said to represent $60 billion, is to be blamed as a whole, or whether a distinction is to be made between its Fuehrer (plural) and its following. But there can be no question about certain things, and the first and most important of all is that the NAM, which had been merely one of many trade associations from 1895 on, became a national force when it became the spearhead of the anti-labor movement at its convention in New Orleans in April, 1903.

The history of this campaign of the biggest industries of America to prevent the majority of the American people from forming any sort of organization which would improve working conditions and raise the standard of living of the nation, is punctuated by three Congressional investigations which show up the NAM for exactly what it is: the counterpart of the fascist organizations of the fascist nations of Europe and Asia.

1. The Garrett Committee disclosed the existence of the NAM lobby in Washington, its "secretive" and "reprehensible" activities, its "questionable and disreputable" means of defeating Congressmen who refused to obey it, and its general criminal character in using money in a corrupt manner to fight the labor unions.

2. The La Follette Investigations into the violations of the rights of free speech and the criminal actions used against labor established the fact that certain corporations—almost without exception leading members of the NAM—employed poison gas and machine guns in their plants, also spies, thugs, stool pigeons and murderers and other racketeers; also that the NAM corrupted public opinion in America by using the largest network of propaganda.

3. The O'Mahoney Monopoly Investigation showed in one of its reports that 200 industrial and 50 financial families own, control and rule America and that of the industrial families 13 are the most powerful. Ford is not a member of the NAM; the others are also its heaviest subsidizers. Another report shows that the NAM uses its money and power for its own profits, and against the general welfare of the people of the United States.

The Garrett Committee's work is better known as the Mulhall investigation, thanks to the fact that "Colonel" Martin M. Mulhall, who was one of the chief secret lobbyists of the NAM, consented to expose that organization and did so in a series of articles which began running in the *New York World* 29 June 1913.

Mulhall's charges dealt chiefly with the NAM's corruption of members of Congress. The reader should note that Mulhall had been employed in 1903, the year the NAM became the chief labor-busting outfit in the country, and the year it decided to become a power in politics in Washington. It is still that power. What Mulhall proved is that it was not content to get anti-labor legislation through Congress as it is today by putting up the money to elect members, but that it passed out cold cash in a criminal manner.

Speaker Champ Clark could not turn deaf ears or blind eyes to the national scandal, although few wanted the *World's* charges aired. A committee headed by Majority Leader Finis J. Garrett of Tennessee finally began a four-month inquiry and published 60 volumes of findings condemning the NAM as a crooked outfit.

In other words, the 10 years during which the NAM employed Mulhall, James A. Emery and other lobbyists, were also the 10 years it devoted its time to fighting labor, and coincidentally the 10 years in which it committed criminal acts for which private individuals would have gone to the penitentiary.

Said William J. McDonald, Michigan Progressive, of the Mulhall exposé of the bribery of Congressmen by the NAM:

"The naive effrontery shown upon the witness stand by officers of the NAM in assuming that the committee would accept at face value the bald denials and ridiculous evasion and perversion of the meaning of actions all too plainly corrupt and sinister . . . cannot be permitted to pass without mention. Their plainly shown attitude was that the American Congress was considered by them as their legislative department and was viewed with the same arrogant manner in which they viewed their other employees, and that those legislators who dare to oppose them would be disciplined in the same manner in which they were accustomed to discipline recalcitrant employees."

Of the NAM lobby Representative McDonald, who was the backbone of the Garrett investigation of Mulhall and Emery, NAM lobbyists, said:

"They did, by the expenditure of exorbitant sums of money, aid and attempt to aid in the election of those who they believed would readily serve their interests, and by the same means sought to and did accomplish the defeat of others whom they opposed. In carrying out these multifarious activities, they did not hesitate as to means, but made use of any method of corruption found to be effectual . . . they instituted a new and complete system of commercialized treachery."

Caught and exposed as bribers and corrupters of the American Congress—and incidentally of the American Way of Life about which it brags—the NAM decided at that time to reorganize and to concentrate on another way in which to corrupt the American people to its way of doing business. It decided to corrupt public opinion. In doing so it planned on using every available method but concentrating chiefly on corrupting the American press. It was highly successful. It is still the greatest force controlling the American press today.

The real picture of American Fascism emerges from the numerous volumes of reports of the Committee on Education and Labor, better known as the La Follette investigation.

There is only one major difference between the Fascism practiced by the NAM and the Fascism practiced by its modern leaders, Hitler and Mussolini: the latter established by force what the former either wholly or partly succeeded in establishing by other means.

Hitler confiscated the treasuries of the labor unions and later established the so-called Labor Front which put the workmen of Germany in a state between serfdom and slavery, while Mussolini organized his so-called corporations in which labor and capital were supposed to have equal rights, whereas in truth capital runs Italy and the living standards of labor have been reduced to their worst point in modern history. The NAM could not destroy labor by official decrees, but it fought labor with its hired gunmen, thugs, racketeers, gangsters and murderers; it did employ poison gas in strikes, and machine guns; it did shoot and kill; and it did poison the minds of the majority of the American people by carrying on a campaign against labor and especially against labor unions, in 1,995 of the 2,000 daily news-papers of the country. The NAM needs no lessons in the way to corrupt a people by propaganda; it was in this business long before Dr. Goebbels came to power.

In the hearings of one day—2 March 1938 to be exact—the following points were made for which documentary evidence was later entered into the record:

1. That the NAM is directed, controlled and financed by only 207 firms, each giving it more than $2,000; that the leading firms are General Motors, DuPont, Chrysler, Weir's National Steel and the Pennsylvania Railroad.

2. That the leading contributors to the NAM and the leading directors are also the leading contributors to a number of purely fascist, anti-Semitic and reactionary organizations such as the American Liberty League, the Crusaders, the Sentinels of the Republic, National Economy League, Farmers' Independence League and Johnstown Citizens' Committee, the last named a vigilante outfit later exposed as secretly started by the Mayor with $50,000 received from Bethlehem Steel.

3. That these 207 firms purchased 60 percent of all the tear gas used in the United States; they also used the majority of spies in industry, the majority of strikebreakers, the majority of criminals. The NAM is associated with the Metal Trades Association, the Associated Industries of Cleveland (and other large cities) and other similar organizations which have taken the leading part in industrial espionage and the use of violence in labor troubles.

4. That the NAM ran the largest propaganda network in America; that it worked this propaganda campaign in secrecy, and that it employed deceit as a method—these are actual quotations from a summary published later. This point is especially important because right now the NAM is engaging in a larger campaign than ever in its history to poison the minds of the American people so that it will accept "free enterprise" rather than any plan for social justice and social security.

The foregoing charges were made by Robert Wohlforth, secretary of the La Follette Committee, which immediately began grilling witnesses it had called, notably W. B. Weisenberger, a vice-president, Noel Sargent, the secretary, J. A. Emery, chief counsel, and John C. Gall, attorney. The day was notable for the fact that these NAM officials made certain statements which were immediately proven absolute falsehoods after Senators La Follette and Thomas produced documentary evidence from the NAM files (which had been seized) proving the mendacity of the defenders of this native-fascist outfit.

In establishing the fact that the NAM was founded primarily to fight labor, and that it was still doing so, Senator La Follette introduced a statement published in 1904 in a NAM magazine called American Industries. In objecting to the only large union of its time—1904—this publication said: "We are not opposed to good unionism if such exists anywhere. The American Federation brand of unionism, however, is un-American, illegal and indecent."

On the same subject, the usual NAM statement that it was not against unions but insisted on unions that were "properly conducted," the leading humorist of the time, Finley Peter Dunne, wrote: "Shure," said Mr. Dooley, "if properly conducted. An' there we are; an' how would they have thim conducted? No strikes, no rules, no contracts, no scales, hardly iny wages an' dam few members."

The O'Mahoney Monopoly Investigation did not disclose anything as sensational regarding the NAM as its bribery of Congressmen or its use of gangsters and poison gas, but its scores of volumes of evidence furnish a complete and unanswerable indictment of the entire American Big Business system.

When the O'Mahoney committee released its Monograph 26 the newspapers of the nation, always happy to suppress anything that is critical of the hand that feeds it—that is, Big Business, through the medium of advertising, obliged by refraining from mentioning the matter at all, or, like the *New York Times*, published a report that lobbying had been condemned but omitted the name of the NAM.

The *Times*, which did publish a column story, and therefore did publish much more than other papers, nevertheless omitted most of the following quotations—which will give the reader a taste of the tremendously important material Monograph 26 contains:

"The American people are confronted with the problem of who shall control the government." The monograph then discusses the big pressure group, notably the American Legion lobby, farmers, peace groups, but concludes that the National Association of Manufacturers, the Chamber of Commerce, and their agents, the lawyers' associations, the newspaper publishers' associations, rule the country.

"From the beginning, business has been intent upon wielding economic power and, where necessary, political control for its own purposes.... Even today, when the purposeful use of government power for the general welfare is more widely accepted than at any time in our history, government does not begin to approach the fusion of power and will characteristic of business." Everyone is fighting for power, for control, in Washington, but "by far the largest and most important of these groups is to be found in 'business' . . . as dominated by the 200 largest non-financial and the 50 largest financial corporations, and the employer and trade associations into which it and its satellites are organized." The 200 non-financial corporations in 1935 controlled $60 billion of physical assets. The march of America toward public betterment "has been hindered, obstructed and at times apparently completely stopped by pressure groups."

"Business . . . has fought . . . government ownership. Through the press, public opinion and pressure groups it is possible to influence the political process.... Both press and radio are, after all, 'big business' and even when they possess the highest integrity, they are the prisoners of their own beliefs."

Business, continues the report, operates on the principle that $60 billion can't be wrong.

"In this connection the business orientation of the newspaper press is a valuable asset. In the nature of things public opinion is usually well disposed toward business.... Newspapers have it in their power materially to influence public opinion on particular issues.... With others, editorializing is practiced as a matter of course. And even where editors and publishers are men of the highest integrity, they are owners and managers of big business enterprises, and their papers inevitably reflect, at least to some extent, their economic interest. When organized business deliberately propagandizes the country, using newspaper advertising as one medium, the press is a direct means of channeling business views into the public mind.... Lawyers have remade constitutional guarantees in the image of business.... The law, the newspaper press, and the advertising professions have all helped business by spreading this changed conception of the Jeffersonian idea."

In other words, Business, using lawyers, the press and advertising, has undermined Jeffersonian democracy.

The report names the business pressure lobbies, notably the National Association of Manufacturers, U.S. Chamber of Commerce, Edison Electric Institute, Association of Life Insurance Presidents, American Iron and Steel Institute, American Petroleum Institute, American Bankers Association, American Investment Bankers Association, American Bar Association, and adds: "Through the American Newspaper Publishers Association [Lords of the Press] the country's daily newspapers join their strength for business and against government." This is a most damning indictment. It did not appear in the *Times*. But the indictment against the corporations and the press goes even further.

"Public policy in the field of industrial relations has been formulated by Congress over the bitter opposition of organized industry, an opposition which is still continuing in a determined effort to change that policy. The economic power of business and the 'educational' persuasiveness of its newspaper, advertising, and legal allies enabled it between the years 1933 and 1937 to frustrate the initial efforts of the Federal Government to regulate labor relations. The NAM and the C. of C. are as one in their opposition to the National Labor Relations Act. The American Bar Association indicated its fundamental community of interest with business. The American Newspaper Publishers Association shares a similar community of interest." This was also suppressed in the *Times*.

"National Association of Manufacturers' President Lund in a press release on 7 September 1933, urged 'the strongest possible employer opposition to union organization.' Business has managed to maintain most of its control of industrial relations despite the efforts of labor and government to lessen it...The staying power of corporate business, its resources and ability to give aid and assistance in the fields of law, of the newspaper press, and of advertising, have proved powerful weapons in this struggle, and the intensity of the battle on the labor relations field since 1933 has indicated their effectiveness."

Pages 171 and 172 of the report show how Big Business betrayed the nation for profits in the European War, and how in 1940 "business displayed much of the same attitude.... Profits, taxes, loans, and so forth appeared more important to business than getting guns, tanks, and airplane motors into production."

"Speaking bluntly the government and the public are 'over a barrel' when it comes to dealing with business in time of war or other crisis. Business refuses to work except on terms which it dictates. . . . In effect this is blackmail."

And what is the final conclusion?

"Democracy in America is on the defensive. In the preceding pages it has been shown that pressure groups as now operating usually fail to promote the general welfare."

Since the NAM has been named as the most powerful of the pressure groups, and the publishers' association one of its two agents, the minor one being the bar association, it is merely putting two and two together to arrive at the statement that Big Business is the main enemy of the general welfare of the American people, and the press the main weapon of this enemy.

The main objective of the NAM today is the corruption of public opinion. Of course, the organization calls it "enlightenment" or the spreading of the doctrine of "free enterprise," but it is nevertheless propaganda, and since it is aimed to insure the private profits of the few, as against the general welfare of the many, it is propaganda that corrupts.

The La Follette investigation showed that, after it was caught bribing Congressmen to pass antilabor laws, the NAM changed its tactic to cooperating with the editors and publishers of all the newspapers of the country, all but one of them being dependent upon advertising and all but three or four of them having a record of journalistic prostitution.

Whereas the National Electric Light Association (NELA, the predecessor of the Edison Electric Institute) sent about $25 million each year (sometimes as high as $29 million) to turn public opinion against municipal and public ownership of light and power plants, the NAM lobby got free ads because it was able to blackmail the newspapers, radio, movies and billboard corporations with threats that its membership would withdraw commercial advertising already placed.

The La Follette report tells in detail how labor was smeared, how everything to the general benefit of the American people was labeled "radical," "Red," "unsound" and how men and organizations opposed to the corrupt Big Business program of the NAM were smeared as "propagandists," "impatient reformers" and "disturbers." The NAM did not hesitate, says the report, to present an "uncritical and false picture." The aim of the NAM was the same as that of the old NELA: to pervert the public mind so that it accepted the big corporation program although that program was and is a program for the benefit of 250 ruling families and the enemy of 52 million wage earners. This is happening today.

The new propaganda agency of the NAM is called the National Industrial Information Committee (NIIC). In 1942, when I discovered its campaign to raise $1 million for a fund to fight labor, it denied that it had any relation with the NAM although it was part of the latter's office, had the same phone, and was operated by the same agents. In 1943, however, it sent a letter to its sustainers saying that it was still affiliated, but was becoming more and more a separate organization. These technicalities are of no importance. What is important is that the worst Fascists of the reactionary clique which bosses the NAM are the very men who are behind this new propaganda movement.

The NIIC claims it has 350 of the leading industrialists in its ranks. It was prompted to begin a big campaign in 1942 because the various Congressional committees, notably the Truman and O'Mahoney, and numerous official reports, notably those of Toland and Thurman Arnold, had exposed American Big Business as linked to Nazi Germany in the cartels, as actually doing business with Hitler and planning to do so in case of war, and to resume doing business should a war involve the two countries. Corporations—Standard Oil for one—had been branded traitors in Senate hearings, and the news could not be suppressed that it was due to the monopoly arrangements with I. G. Farbenindustrie that America had a shortage of aluminum for making airplanes, no synthetic rubber at all, a lack of tungsten, carboloy and other vital materials, no substitute for quinine (atabrine), etc. The very same corporations and men who had been exposed by Monograph 29 as ruling America—notably Mellon—were shown to be the men of the Nazi cartels. And on top of this scandal the labor press was proving that Big Business was refusing to convert to war, that Big Money was on a sit-down strike, and that, in short, the men of wealth and power were the traitors while the men in the fields, factories and workshops were working to win the war.

It is true that the *New York World-Telegram* and the 18 other papers controlled by Roy Howard of the Scripps-Howard press, and the 19 papers controlled by America's No. 1 Nazi, William Randolph Hearst, did their best to whitewash Alcoa, Standard Oil, General Motors and General Electric and all the other members of the Nazi trusts. But it is also true that the scandal was so big that enough of it became generally known to cover (not smear) Big Business with the truthful muck of Fascism. Before and after Pearl Harbor America's foremost enemy in the war against Fascism was the ruling clique of the NAM.

Said the NIIC appeal which asked every business to pay a sum to its propaganda fund in proportion to its income:

"Why war increases your need of the NIIC: Because winning the war must mean also restoring a method of living that is traditionally and characteristically American. This the American people must be told and retold.... Because full public confidence in management's motives is an essential raw material to the fabric of maximum arms production and victory. This confidence must be built and held. Because private enterprise must be built firmly into the people's ideals for the postwar world."

This statement also invites anti-labor, anti-progressive corporations to help keep America ignorant of the great liberal and democratic movement throughout the world which is based on the belief that all democratic peoples after overthrowing the main enemy of democracy, Fascism, can remake the world for the benefit of the millions of men who were at the front, instead of the special interests represented by the NIIC.

On 17 September 1942, the resolutions committee of the National Association of Manufacturers met in a secret session at the Hotel Pennsylvania in New York, to prepare a program for the December NAM convention. What took place in that closed meeting amounts to a conspiracy against the government, against the people, and against winning the war. The objectives of the NAM, overriding all other considerations, are: more profits, now and after the war, the destruction of the labor movement, and the wiping out of all New Deal progress.

The delegates heard its research expert, Dr. Claude Robinson, report that the public, when asked which group was most guilty of war profiteering, was answering: Big business, 49 percent; government officials, 40 percent, labor leaders, 11 percent. To the question as to what was the main concern of the people today, the answers were predominantly: "The winning of the war; next important, unemployment in the postwar period." The NAM delegates, after considerable discussion, then took their stand—directly opposed to that of the people as reported to them: Thirty-five delegates voted for dealing with war and postwar problems on an equal basis, fifteen for emphasizing "winning the war" while dealing with postwar issues, and only three for "winning the war" as the only problem for 1943.

Here are some of the things said at their closed meeting of the NAM resolutions committee:

When James D. Cunningham, president of Republic Flow Meters Co., urged the NAM 1943 program to stick to one issue, winning the war, because "if we don't win the war, there won't be a postwar," Lammot DuPont, chairman of the board of E. I. DuPont de Nemours & Co., Liberty Leaguer, supporter of native fascist organizations replied:

"Deal with the government and the rest of the squawkers the way you deal with a buyer in a seller's market! If the buyer wants to buy, he has to meet your price. Nineteen hundred and twenty-nine to 1942 was the buyer's market—we had to sell on their terms. When the war is over, it will be a buyer's market again. But this is a seller's market. They want what we've got. Good. Make them pay the right price for it. The price isn't unfair or unreasonable. And if they don't like the price, why don't they think it over?"

"The way to view the issue is this: Are there common denominators for winning the war and the peace? If there are, then, we should deal with both in 1943. What are they? We will win the war (a) by reducing taxes on corporations, high income brackets, and increasing taxes on lower incomes; (b) by removing the unions from any power to tell industry how to produce, how to deal with their employers, or anything else; (c) by destroying any and all government agencies that stand in the way of free enterprise."

Other notable utterances by delegates not yet publicly named:

"If we are to come out of this war with a Marxist brand of National Socialism, then I say negotiate peace now and bring Adolf Hitler over here to run the show. He knows how. He's efficient. He can do a better job than any of us can and a damned sight better job than Roosevelt, who is nothing but a left-wing bungling amateur."

"We've got Roosevelt on the run. We licked production and the Axis is licking him. The finger points where it belongs. We'll keep him on the run. Let's spend some real money this year, what the hell!—it'll only cost us 20 percent, the rest would go in taxes anyway."

A lot of other things were said, all heading up to the the conspiracy being engineered now by the NAM, which it intends to carry on to the next election. This includes:

A fight against management-labor committees (credited by government officials with a prominent part in getting war production going); driving women out of industry after the war; freeing Wall Street speculation from all restrictions; a propaganda program in high schools and colleges; wiping out of all social agencies set up under the New Deal. Together with this program goes the clear threat to sabotage war production, and to seize on every development to undermine the President's prestige, unless the NAM's demands for taxes that make the poor pay for the war are met.

The facts of the NAM's secret meeting, of which the foregoing is a partial and necessarily inadequate summary, have not appeared in the commercial press, although they are known to all the news agencies and to every newspaper editor in the country.

As forecast by this secret meeting, the NAM convened and elected Frederick C. Crawford president for 1943. This is the man who keeps a picture of President Roosevelt hanging upside down in his office next to a picture of Mrs. Roosevelt with a pipe in her mouth. He also keeps a loaded shotgun and tells people he'll use it if any legislation is passed which he does not like.

This is the same Crawford who told his colleagues of the NAM:

"We are fighting for our freedom. Freedom from renegotiation of contracts. Freedom from Pansy Perkins. Freedom from Prostituting Attorney Arnold. Freedom from the Alice-in-Wonderland War Labor Board. Freedom from that . . . (unprintable) gentleman on the hill."

As *The Pilot* said, "Crawford's fighting a war, but it's a war against the American people and against the coming defeat of Hitler."

Crawford has violated the Wagner Act and has been forced by several NLRB decisions to stop using spies, stop employing a company union, stop interfering with unionization. But the government did not make him hire union men at eight cents more per hour than non-union men, and therefore there were many machines in his Cleveland plant, which make valves for airplanes, which stood idle.

Workmen pasted stickers on them. These read: "This machine works for Hitler."

So do many of the biggest men in the National Association of Manufacturers.

Ever since Pearl Harbor courage is not required to speak out against faraway Fascism. The Scripps-Howard papers, which are under the reactionary rule of a man who never got over the fact he was permitted to kowtow to the Emperor of Japan; the Hearst papers, which had a deal with the Nazi press and which published signed propaganda articles of Goering, Goebbels and Co., Patterson's *New York Daily News*, which said "Let's Appease Japan" because Japan was a good customer, and which favored betraying China because China did not put as much money into

American pockets as the Hirohito regime, have used flaring headlines against the three brands of Fascism which rule the three chief enemy countries. But there are surely not a half dozen newspapers—perhaps not even three— which have ever had the courage to show the relationship between foreign and domestic Fascism.

You will have to read the free and independent press, which is largely the press of small unbribed weeklies, and a few pamphlets and books to get the truth. The truth is not in the commercial press because the truth is a dagger pointed at its heart, which is its pocketbook. Native American Fascism is largely the policy of the employers of gangsters, stool pigeons, labor spies, poison gas, and antilabor propaganda; it is the fascism of the NAM, the Associated Farmers and Associated Industries, the Christian American Association; thc KKK, thc Committee for Constitutional Government, the Constitutional Educational League, the U. S. Chamber of Commerce, the old Liberty League and its present subsidized outfits, and the Royal Family which unfortunately controls the American Legion.

The following statement made by Professor Gaetano Salvemini of Harvard is noteworthy. Professor Salvemini told reporter Joseph Philip Lyford of the *Harvard Crimson* that "a new brand of Fascism" threatens America, "the Fascism of corporate business enterprise in this country." He believed that "almost 100 percent of American Big Business" is in sympathy with the "philosophy" of government behind the totalitarianism of Hitler and Mussolini; the bond of sympathy between Big Business and the Fascist Axis, said the professor of history, lies in the respect of American industrialists for the Axis methods of coercing labor.

There are two means which the industrialist can employ to crush labor, Professor Salvemini explained; one way is to hire strikebreakers to "crack the workers' skulls," the other way is to pass a law outlawing strikes. "Mussolini has used both methods in Italy," Professor Salvemini asserted; "in America Big Business has only been able to use the first." But business is definitely sympathetic to anti-strike legislation, he added, and compared the organization of the Ford plant at River Rouge to the organization of the Fascist auto industry, and the strikebreaking methods used by Ford there to those which had been used by Italian industry to crush the workers on the eve of Mussolini's rise to power.

Salvemini's statement, based on Italian Fascism, paralleled the statement which Ambassador Dodd made on returning to America from Germany. Both these men noted the relationship between foreign Fascism and American business monopolies and the handful of super-industrialists who rule most countries for their own profit.

PART THREE

Press
Critic

One Man's Newspaper Game

It did not take long for Seldes to realize how corrupt the newspaper business was. His experiences as a cub reporter in Pittsburgh were a profound influence on how he would view his profession in later years. In his first comprehensive look at the American press, his 1935 book Freedom of the Press, *Seldes took a look back upon the early days of his career and the joys and frustrations of his life as a newspaperman.*

MY FIRST morning in a newspaper office, the *Pittsburgh Leader*, 9 February 1909, was spent in shifting from chair to chair. Reporters rushed in, yelled their hot news to the city editor, and motioned me away from their desks. The copy boy, taking me for a rival, also intimidated me. He passed the fresh papers, damp and pungent with ink and gasoline, to everyone in the city room but sneered at me. I was timid and scared, but I was also happy. At nine that morning I had been hired as a reporter.

At noon, with two evening editions gone to press, the city editor rose for lunch. "I want to talk to you," he said and began immediately. "What's your idea of being a reporter? What are you after? Do you want to make money, do you want to play politics, do you want to write novels, or what?"

Before I could stammer, he continued. "Because," he said, "this is the lousiest profession in the world—that is, if you stick in it. It's all right for a couple of years. But you'll never make money. You'll get nine dollars a week now and if you're good you'll be making twenty at the end of three years and if you're an ace it will be twenty-five. Do you know that there isn't a man in town, with the exception of the political reporters, making more than that, but the men in the composing-room, who belong to labor unions, are making double?"

His mind was on money. He was an old-timer. I was 18, it was a noble era, and my thoughts were elsewhere. I abhorred the idea of even discussing money. "My view of journalism," I began with all the enthusiasm of my virginal 18 years, "is that it is the finest profession on earth. On the freedom of the press all our liberties are built." I quoted Carlyle's report on Edmund Burke and the Four Estates, and Thomas Jefferson, Washington and the other founders of the nation, and Dana and the great editors. I spoke of Liberty and Truth. In fact, I said everything except that Journalism to me meant the Greek ideal of the Good, the True and the Beautiful. I didn't quite say that.

"Rats," replied Houston H. Eagle, city editor of the *Pittsburgh Leader.* "Do you know what this [sneering] 'profession' is? It's prostitution. Prostitution! Journalistic harlots, that's what we all are, and that's what you'll be if you stay in this lousy business, so if you've any other ideas, can 'em."

"Now, Mr. Eagle," I began.

"Listen, boy," he replied with a bitter vehemence which distorted his face, "if you want to earn a living go into some other trade. Then you'll make it honestly, that is comparatively honestly, but in this business you'll not make a living, and what you do make you'll make whoring for the crooked politicians, and the crooked bankers, and the crooked street-car company, and the crooked department stores . . ."

"But," I protested, "I came to the *Leader* because the *Leader* is the People's Paper; I didn't ask for a job on the *Gazette-Times* or any of the other papers...."

"Then you're a bigger fool than I thought you were," replied Mr. Eagle, "and you'll find that out for yourself. A newspaper needs a lot of young fools—foolish enthusiasm and foolish ideals. We love ideals. And we love enthusiasm. At nine dollars a week."

That afternoon I wrote my first piece for the papers:

"Stanislas Schmidt, aged 32, of 1811 Center Avenue, driver of a Silver Top Brewing Company delivery wagon, was slightly injured at 10 o'clock this morning at Penn Avenue and Liberty street when his wagon was struck by a street car."

Who can describe the trepidation of the ensuing hours waiting for the first final edition? I had watched Thirlkeld, assistant city editor, read copy on my masterpiece, watched the copy boy take it across the bridge to the composing room, watched the clock minute by minute. At last the boy made his rounds. Again he passed me up. Everyone in the office was reading carefully for typographical errors. Someone threw his copy on the floor. I got it. The item was not on the front page. I was depressed. At last under the heading Local, a collection of a dozen paragraphs, I found my own. It read:

"Stanislas Schmidt, 32 years old, of 1811 Center Ave., driver of a beer delivery wagon . . . "

Silver Top was not mentioned; Silver Top was a large advertiser.

My education had begun. It increased amazingly toward evening when the staff retired to the Hotel Henry bar for a round of beer. How proud I was when permitted to buy drinks for the city editor, the assistant city editor, star and other reporters, and the foreman of the composing room, and ten-cent beer at that, the round costing me my day's pay. Everyone hazed me.

"Here's a kid believes in the Freedom of the Press," announced Houston Eagle, and everyone roared heartily.

"Tell it to Andy Mellon," shouted someone, but that meant nothing to me.

Apparently I was promising. In my cubhood years I was sent to interview William Jennings Bryan, to report a banquet speech of Governor Woodrow Wilson, to accompany Theodore Roosevelt for a day, to cover William Howard Taft's Pittsburgh visit, to write a four-column story of Robert La Follette's declaration in favor of woman suffrage. But perhaps I was not as important as I thought I was. The Bryan stunt, for instance: Eagle said, "Ask him if he is going to run for President again," and I did, and I was promptly thrown out of the hotel room when the massive candidate rose in his underwear and insulted pride and shoved me. I came back to the office, and like the legendary reporter who told his city editor that there was no ascension story because the balloon had blown up and killed everyone, I said there was nothing to write because Bryan had put me out.

Eagle said nothing. But an hour later the Leader appeared with its usual three streamers, the middle one in red, devoted to the main sensation of the day, the other two in black, the bottom one reading:

BRYAN ASSAULTS LEADER REPORTER

In this way I learned empirically that we were a Progressive Republican organ and that Democrats were ungodly poison.

As for the La Follette interview, it was a scoop. Neither the Democratic nor regular Republican papers would touch it. (I did not know, of course, that the conspiracy of silence and defamation by the press against the Wisconsin leader had begun.)

The big moment of my cubhood came when I was assigned to cover the Mellon case. Andrew W. Mellon was to us a banker about whom we knew nothing. There were of course the Mellon bank and the Union Trust Company and a few other enterprises, but generally speaking no one suspected we were harboring in our smoky midst one of America's three richest men and one of its ten real rulers. Mellon, like Zaharoff, always preferred the role of mystery.

In the middle of September 1910, suit for divorce had been filed by Banker Mellon against his wife nee Nora McMullen, whom he had married in 1900. The employees of the prothonotary's office hid the papers. "For seven months," Mellon's unwelcome biographer, Harvey O'Connor, wrote years later, "not a paper appeared in the court record. Not a word leaked out in the well-disciplined Pittsburgh newspapers, on some of which Union Trust held underlying mortgages. News agencies in the city also clamped on a censorship, and even the telegraph agencies were summoned to aid. The publishers, all wary men trained in the Pittsburgh tradition, assigned a crack reporter to the case and were kept informed on every minute detail of the charges, counter-charges and proceedings.... Attorney Ache Paul S. Ache, [representing Mrs. Mellon] finally broke through the ring of silence and interested the *Philadelphia North American* in the Mellon case."

I was not a "crack reporter," neither were several of my colleagues; the crack reporters were the gentlemen who came from Philadelphia and later from New York, but otherwise O'Connor is right. And there is much more to the story.

On 20 April 1911, a bill was introduced, passed by the legislature of Pennsylvania and signed by Governor Tener. "This act," telegraphed the *North American* man, while all of us in Pittsburgh kept our mouths shut, "robs a wife of her constitutional right of a jury trial in a divorce suit. Whose powerful influence obtained this astonishing bit of legislation is not known, but nothing could have been designed that would be more useful to Andrew Mellon, the master money-maker of Pittsburgh, who has some $100 million to wage his fight against his young and handsome English wife. Friends of Mrs. Mellon . . . fear the new law is another demonstration of Mellon's skill in noiseless, effective methods in all his undertakings."

I do not here, nor elsewhere for that matter, intend to discuss the details of the divorce suit, which shocked me at the time—shocked me despite a year in Magistrate Jimmy Kirby's central police station court where all the terror and misery in human nature was spread before his Honor and the police reporters to make a column holiday. An endless procession of pimps and prostitutes, drunks, panhandlers, yeggs, dope peddlers and dope victims, all the inhabitants of the cesspools, the gutters, the poverty-stricken alleys of the metropolis, passed in terrible review before us every morning to the accompanying drone of "Ten dollars or thirty days," "Ten dollars or thirty days" from the pink, sleek and fat Republican interpreter of the city's laws.

I lived in this atmosphere of human filth and degradation for a year. I found it again in the divorce courts. And now in the impressive Superior Court the accusations, spy testimony and servants' gossip produced by the leading lawyers of Pittsburgh in the employ of the leading banker, I found again the same foul atmosphere. The human animal, I thought, is pretty low.

There was one important difference I did not then realize: all the others, men and women, would get into the papers and would be stigmatized, while Mellon was safe. With my many hastily scrawled sheets of copy paper I rushed back to the *Leader* office and began typing. "Hot stuff?" asked Eagle. "Hot stuff," I said. He laughed. In my mind's eye were page headlines, screaming newsboys, thousands running to pay their pennies for my story, half a million citizens discussing it that night. I pounded page after page. The story completed, Eagle glanced at it carelessly, and walked out of the city room, up the corridor, into the office of Alexander Pollock Moore, the Big Boss, our awesome editor-in chief. And that is the last the news department ever saw of the Mellon case.

The next day it was the same, and the day after. I did my work; I wrote thousands of words; not one of them appeared in the *Leader*, and the same was true of my colleagues of the six other papers. The "conspiracy of silence" was complete. A German language paper, perhaps intentionally, perhaps by oversight, carried one discreet report; this report found its way to the *Philadelphia North American,* and the next time the Mellon case was in court the *North American* representative was present. We gladly gave him all our previous notes.

Again we watched anxiously for publication. The *North American* arrived, but there was nothing about Mellon in it. It was our turn to laugh. "Mellon's bought you too," we shouted in the court corridor. "You wait," he replied.

What had happened? Probably for the first time in our fair city's history the telegraph companies had also suppressed the news.

The next day the *North American* appeared on the streets of Pittsburgh appeared and disappeared. The newsboys shouted, the papers were snapped up, the police set about beating the newsboys, and soon all was quiet. The next day the *North American* sent out still larger bundles and the New York papers also arrived with the story. Neither Mellon nor the police could suppress it completely.

"Gold and politics appear to have combined against me," said Nora McMullen Mellon to the reporters. "I hope the voters of Pennsylvania and the sons of Pennsylvania who have mothers whom they love will realize that the law just adopted in this state, abrogating the right of trial by jury in divorce cases, is not only directed against me but is also a blow to every mother in Pennsylvania."

Our most prominent churchman, Bishop Cortlandt Whitehead of the Episcopal diocese, denounced the changes in the divorce law; civic bodies voiced a protest against abolition of trial by jury, but not a word appeared in the newspapers printed in Pittsburgh.

It was at just this time that Will Irwin in *Collier's Weekly* began a series of articles on "The American Newspaper: a Study in Journalism and its Relation to the Public." Irwin had gone from city to city, honoring the honest newspapers and telling the truth about the others. He had undertaken, he said, to answer the following charges laymen generally were making against the press:

That the newspaper has grown venal.
That advertisers and great financial interests control it.
That it has grown sensational.
That it has lost its power in public causes.

No one more than the reporters of Pittsburgh awaited the number devoted to our politically purged city. I cannot begin to describe the fury, the enthusiasm, which pervaded the journalistic corps the day *Collier's* arrived telling our sundry citizenry the fact that Pittsburgh's Prostituted Press was about the worst in the nation. It was a harlots' holiday.

It was also a surprise. Mr. Irwin was telling us facts about ourselves which were news. He told us for instance that the *Gazette-Times* and the *Chronicle-Telegraph*, owned by Senator George T. Oliver, were the errand boys of the steel and coal and munitions interests; that the *Post* and the *Sun* had borrowed money from the Farmers' National Bank, "a city depository involved in the graft cases"; that the Oliver papers were indebted to the Frick-Mellon banks; that the *Press* was bought by Oliver P. Hershman whose friends were Chris Magee and William Flinn, the bosses of the town. "Gang-established, gang-favored, unwilling in any event to take the first step—the *Press* was of no use for the purposes of reform," Irwin wrote. Of the so-called liberal *Despatch* and its editor, Colonel C. A. Rook, he said they played "the gang game of silence," and of my own dear *Leader*, that "William Flinn, the old joint-boss with Chris Magee, a contractor grown rich on city jobs, backed Alexander P. Moore, in its purchase."

Salaries were abominably low; as a result employees were permitted to do press-agent and propaganda jobs and take tips from the outside; political reporters got civil service jobs additionally, and places on the registration commissions, paying fifty dollars a week. The owners knew of these corrupting forces but preferred them to paying wages.

The Pittsburgh graft cases had been front-page stuff for more than a year before I got my first job, and the splendid vehemence with which the press, notably the *Leader*, attacked the malefactors of great wealth had given me the impression the press was a noble defender of the public good and that the *Leader's* name led all the rest. In Will Irwin's story of Pittsburgh I learned that the exposure of municipal corruption had been made despite a conspiracy of silence among the seven newspapers; that, in fact, the Voters' League had been forced to issue pamphlets and bulletins for a long time because the press individually and collectively had refused to publish a line about the city's corruption until the League forced them to do so. "Is this true?" I asked the reporters on all the papers. "Of course it is," they replied. Some of them had secretly helped the League.

The individual reporters whom Irwin named as getting money from political jobs were very angry. They said, "Irwin is also a newspaper man, he is fouling his own nest, he is disloyal, he is just a muckraker," but the majority helped spread *Collier's* through the town, made it town talk, hoping both to clean up the rotten situation and shame the publisher into paying decent wages. But naturally nothing happened. So long as Pittsburgh remained geographically about halfway between Chicago and New York there would always be a stream of good reporters to be exploited. Why pay wages?

The Mellon case and the Irwin story, I believe, educated me out of my naive cubhood; the former also taught me a financial lesson: there was money to be made selling suppressed news to outside papers, and a five-dollar bill shone magnificently beside a $12-a-week salary. In fact, the business of dealing in suppressed news became so good that several reporters opened an office especially for that purpose; they called it the Pittsburgh News Bureau, I believe, and they did better than working for regular wages. But there was also news, mostly labor news, crimes committed by the first Fascist army in America, the coal and iron police, privately organized by the Pennsylvania corporations, the Black Cossacks who rode workingmen down on the sidewalks in strike towns, crushing them because they were strikers and foreigners; scandals involving national advertisers, deaths from patent medicines, financial crimes committed by leading citizens within the law—all these news items were not fit to print in most of the newspapers of America, but they were news for a Socialist organ published in New York. *The Call*, however, was not in a position to pay. To the honor of several Pittsburgh newspaper men it must be said that they frequently supplied the *Call* and other publications with the news their own editors were suppressing.

I was sent one day to copy an indictment for rape against the son of one of the owners of a large department store, and the next day to interview the girl. When I turned in the story I asked Eagle what he was going to do with it. He said: "Turn it over to the business office; they will blackmail that store for the next 20 years; you'll see larger ads from now on."

"May I make a copy to give to the *Call*?" I asked.

"Sure thing," Eagle replied, "I'd like to see it published."

I made the copy and gave it to a man named Merrick who represented the *Call*. But the *Call* arrived and didn't carry the story.

I chased after Merrick. He said, "Do you mind if I use it locally? I'm planning a paper in Pittsburgh."

Saturday was a sensational day. A new weekly called *Justice* appeared; it was devoted entirely to the rape case. In addition to my story, which covered the entire first page, there were socialistic diatribes on justice and injustice, the exploitation of the poor by the rich, and the suppression of news in Pittsburgh, covering the entire second page, except for a coupon asking for subscriptions. The newsboys appeared on the street that morning, shouted the story, and within a half-hour were being clubbed by the police who had been asked to do so by the department store and its allies, the business managers of the daily press. The position of the latter was that the venders of *Justice* were not regularly accredited newsboys and therefore violated the honored and sacred freedom of the press.

Next Saturday Merrick reprinted my story, with the story of the police, the department store owners, the publishers of the seven Pittsburgh dailies, and again newsboys were clubbed. And so it went on week after week while *Justice* established itself with a considerable circulation. Again the journalistic fraternity was secretly pleased.

Another big story that came my way was an investigation of the labor situation in the Pittsburgh zone. Eagle had obtained, he never told me how, a sheaf of 40 or 50 pages with more than 2,000 names. Eagle told me it was the black list of the steel corporations. Its publication would be a nationwide sensation. We had caught the steel companies in a conspiracy.

Ever since the Homestead strike, the iron, coal and steel interests of Pittsburgh had employed an espionage system to prevent the unionizing of their industries. Whenever a workingman was heard talking unions or uttering socialistic phrases he was immediately discharged and his name added to the black list which was circulated from company to company in violation of every moral and legal code. I had a hard time finding the men; they were either out of a job or employed in other trades, and each one expressed amazement when I showed him the black list which explained months or years of wandering from town to town in Pennsylvania, West Virginia and Ohio in search of work.

Then came the Stanley Steel Trust Investigation. One morning while I was still asleep, a United States marshal came into my room and read a summons to appear before the congressional committee. I went to Washington. Congressman A. O. Stanley received me in his office, showed me where he kept an assortment of the finest Kentucky whisky and then asked me, not about the black list, but about an earlier job of work, my investigation of the racial change in Pittsburgh labor.

Some months earlier I had worked on that story. I found that since the time of the Homestead strike the employers of the Pittsburgh area had decided to rid their plants of American labor. They wanted unlimited immigration, cheap labor, ignorant labor which would work for low wages and not talk unionization. I had not only obtained this evidence, but also advertisements reading: "Wanted: Balkan workmen, Romanians, Serbians, Hungarians, etc., for steady jobs in the steel plants."

"Have you got the photographs of these newspaper ads?" asked Mr. Stanley. Paul Reilly had taken them for the *Leader*. I had them.

"And," I continued, "I've got a good story." And I told him about the black list.

That afternoon I signed my name two or three lines below that of Andrew Carnegie, the philanthropist, and went into the committee room. Congressman Stanley presided. Mr. Reed, of Pennsylvania, was the attorney representing the steel interests. I was questioned and cross-questioned. I told all about the steel trust's effort to drive out American labor, replace it with the cheapest European labor, and as I testified I watched the Associated Press man and the other reporters taking notes.

The afternoon wore on. And still no one asked me about the black list. I grew impatient. I was young. I was also suspicious. So, when the committee and Mr. Reed were about to dismiss me, I concluded my statement about labor with a voluntary disclosure about the black list on which I had been working.

Mr. Reed leaped to his feet. The members of Congress gasped. "I protest," shouted Mr. Reed. The press stared at me.

"Let the clerk read the last reply," said Mr. Stanley.

The clerk read. Mr. Reed protested. But I insisted on speaking, and I did so amid shouts and murmurs. Mr. Reed moved that my black list testimony be stricken from the record, and this was done. I was dismissed.

None of the reporters present spoke to me. That was puzzling. If I knew anything at all about newspaper values, I knew that I had supplied them with a sensational front page story, and I had indicated in my testimony that I had a wealth of corroborative detail. I also knew that the official order to strike the testimony from the record did not ruin its news value. or that I had the proof next morning, for the press did in fact mention my statement.

Two tiny items on an inside page: one stating that I had testified that a black list existed, the second, a "follow" from Pittsburgh, a single paragraph under the heading: "Editor admits having black list," the whole written in an incredulous and disparaging manner and "buried" almost universally on the back advertising pages.

Thus ended another chapter in my education. I learned that there is news that can be killed—and there is news that can be buried alive.

But all newspaper work, literally and figuratively, is not running to a fire. There were strange interludes of another sort in the *Leader* office.

Alexander Pollock Moore, as I have said, was our editor-in-chief; he wore a velour hat and we regarded him as a well-dressed Napoleon. The city room was in the rear of the building, Mr. Moore's office up a corridor, some 50 feet away, but his rare visits to our department were thrilling. He might ask, "Who wrote that story?" and you could not tell by the tone whether he was going to say, "That's fine, very fine," or "It's lousy." The first year he never noticed me. In the second year I was chosen, thanks to an interest I had shown in the theater, to visit the boss's office once in a while to write interviews with stage folk.

As a rule there would be some flashy petite chorus-girl sitting on the couch; the boss would mumble her name and say, "Write about two columns." The first time it happened he said: "Give her a big break—say she's undiscovered talent—wants to play Shakespeare, Juliet, of course, or that new man, Isben."

"Nora, in *The Dolls House*, by Ibsen," I said, showing off.

"Yeh, that's the guy," the famous actress interpolated.

Still showing off, I would ask questions about the lady's noble ambitions, bringing in the names of all the playwrights I was then reading, Shaw and Ibsen, Brieux and Wedekind and Strindberg, until the editor-in-chief would say:

"Beat it, kid, you've got enough. Two columns. Two-column cut. Here's the picture."

So I would invent a two-column story about the latest talent and the undiscovered Nora or Juliet or Countess Julie up on the couch of the front office.

When Lillian Russell came to town, not I but the chief editorial writer was chosen to do the interviewing. The result placed on the front page. That front page today is worth a fortune. There occurred an error, the shifting of one letter in a four-letter word—and we had in print a major catastrophe.

Like the great majority of newspapers we had what Maxwell Anderson calls a son-of-a-bitch list and what others call the roll of sacred cows. In fact, we had everything. One we called the S—— hook, the blank being a fine old Anglo-Saxon word common to Joyce and Lawrence but hardly suitable here. On this hook we literally spiked stories which contained the names of personal enemies of the bosses, Flinn, Magee, Moore and Mellon and others. Our sacred cows were persons, advertisers, department stores, theaters about whom favorable notices were to be printed frequently. And in addition to all these we had the universally famous B.O.M. or "Business Office Must," the press-agent stuff sent upstairs from the business office, the unearned increment of the advertisers. Every "must" item appeared.

These were the conditions under which freedom of the press flourished in Pittsburgh.

After working hard for several years I was able to save $676, with which I entrained for Harvard. After listening to Copeland and Baker and Taussig and Wendell and George Herbert Palmer in his final lectures on philosophy, and selling to the *Boston Transcript* two stories, which the *Harvard Illustrated Magazine* thought too critical of the football and tutoring systems, I returned to Pittsburgh and to the morning *Post*.

When the war began I was night editor; there was only one person above me in command, Warren U. Christman, managing editor, who retired at midnight. Usually it was I who wrote the war headlines and put the city edition to bed.

Of the first war years I will say just this: I made a total fool of myself when I accepted as true the news reports from New York and Europe which by their volume and repetition overwhelmed what little objective intelligence I had. In those days I regarded the Associated Press as Caesar's wife and when in doubt favored it by spiking all other copy.

For example, there was the story of the sinking of Britain's greatest warship, the *Audacious*. Britain denied; the AP sent the denial, but the International News Service insisted on this victory for a German submarine. I spiked the Hearst story. Two or three weeks later one of the Hearst organizations supplied a photograph of the *Audacious* actually sinking. (Many years later, in London, I learned the truth: the *Audacious* was torpedoed, but in shallow water, and the British Admiralty denied the episode because it hoped to float the superdreadnought in a few weeks.) Then there was the *Lusitania*. All the reports told of a "dastardly" and "heinous" crime against civilians, but the German news bureau said the ship carried munitions. Today the sworn statement of the former Collector of the Port of New York, Dudley Field Malone, gives the exact character and tonnage of these munitions, but in 1915 I played the Allied side. I used all the stories of German atrocities including the Baltimore preacher's "unimpeachable" account of the crucifixion of Canadian soldiers by the enemy. In short, in common with about 90 percent of the American press, I had become a blind but willing agent of the powerful and finally victorious Allied propaganda machine.

My night off was Wednesday; on Thursday morning the *Post* usually carried news of a German success. Christman and I had argued over the war daily; he rightly judged the news we received as unfair to Germany, and to counteract daily Allied victories and German atrocities, he gave Germany Thursday. (It was not until December 1918, when I came into Coblenz with the American Army that I realized how fooled I had been by all those years of poisonous propaganda, the 10 years I worked in Germany I think I did my honest best to repair the damage—to myself if not to others— by writing news which gave Germany a square deal.)

In October 1916, I went to England on the steamer *Adriatic* also carried some 20,000 tons of munitions for the Allies. My first job in London was expanding a 2,000 word skeletonized cable from America into a resounding story of at least 1,000 words which was sold to the *London Daily News*, the *Cork Examiner*, and the leading papers in Birmingham, Leeds and other important provincial cities, each of which labeled the item "From our own correspondent." Later I skeletonized the United Press cable to *La Nacion* in Buenos Aires.

The propaganda department of the British Government at that time arranged trips to the front for sympathetic journalists. I went to the front. The Ypres salient, Mount Kemal, the hospital base at Etaples, a visit to the trenches, an airplane base, tea with General Plumer and dinner with the Prince of Wales' regiment was our program, and our residence, the Chateau of Trammecourt. Our group was composed of French, Italian and American correspondents. At that time we considered ourselves the most favored and on our return we found ourselves the most envied of mortals, and the journals which printed our stories boasted of the fact their own representatives had been at the fighting front. I now realize that we were told nothing but buncombe, that we were shown nothing of the realities of the war, that we were, in short, merely part of the great Allied propaganda machine whose purpose was to sustain morale at all costs and help drag unwilling America into the slaughter.

In 1917, when the United States answered the call of Democracy, Freedom of Oppressed Nations, and more important than these (although known only to the Embassy in London, the bankers in Wall Street and the President) the necessity of safeguarding the war loans, my brother and I went patriotically to the Embassy and registered for war service. Gilbert went back to America and became a machine-gunner.

In July 1917, Joe Pierson of the *Chicago Tribune* established the Army Edition of that paper and Floyd Gibbons, whom I had met in London, gave me the job of being the entire reportorial staff. One morning the managing editor disappeared and that afternoon Pierson appointed me managing editor.

But meanwhile the press section of the army, G-2-D, GHQ, AEF, was being organized. Edward Marshall, the famous war correspondent who had been with Theodore Roosevelt at San Juan Hill and who had left a leg in Cuba, now asked General Pershing for my appointment as a member of this outfit and within a few weeks after landing in France I was at Neufchateau. Here I found Will Irwin, Irvin S. Cobb, Heywood Broun, Edwin L. James, Wilbur Forrest, Herbert Corey, Cal Lyon, Damon Runyon, Martin Green, Major Frederick Palmer, Major Bozeman Bulger, Lieutenant Grantland Rice and other famous or soon-to-be-famous war correspondents.

We all more or less lied about the war.

On Armistice Day four of us took an oath on the battlefield that we would tell the truth the rest of our lives, that we would begin telling the truth in time of preparation of war, that we would do what was humanly possible to prevent the recurrence of another such vast and useless horror. Then we all went back to prosaic reporting in America.

The war had made our country conscious of Europe and our relations with the rest of the world. Foreign news had up to then been almost a monopoly of the Associated Press with its exchanges, the official or semi-official bureaus, such as Reuters, Havas, Wolff, Stefani, etc. Now the *New York Times*, which had had two or three branch offices, began to cover all of Europe and the *Philadelphia Ledger*, the *New York Herald*, the *New York Tribune*, the *Chicago Daily News* and the *Chicago Tribune* instituted or enlarged their foreign services. In 1919 I was assistant to the London correspondent of the *Chicago Tribune*, then Dublin correspondent, and in 1920 I was in Italy for the Fiume adventure; in 1920 in Germany for the Kapp Putsch, and although nominally head of the Berlin bureau for almost 10 years, I was assigned to Italy for the so-called Red uprising in 1920, to Moscow in 1922 and 1923, to the French Army in Syria in 1925 and 1926, to Vienna for the revolution of 1927 and to the capitals in the Baltic and Balkan States for wars, uprisings, peace conferences, assassinations and coronations of kings, and I reported the dictators on the march to power in many lands.

These 10 European years were a continual struggle with censorship.

The suppression of news in America and its corollary, the dissemination of propaganda, are the pragmatic necessities of our social and economic system. Some of the powers which control the press are known to everyone, others are secret and their work is subtle, and there is, moreover, an atmosphere in every newspaper office which defeats all the high hopes and idealism of the young reporter. It breaks him and brands him as a colt is broken and branded on the prairies. But this much must be said for the American reporter in Europe: whether he is or is not so in fact, he at least feels himself a free man.

He has escaped from the pusillanimity of the ordinary newspaper office. He need never in his foreign lifetime stop to consider the local advertiser, the public utility man and the cheap politician who control his town, the quack-medicine man, the president of the First National Bank, the Steel Corporation, the department store, the host of friends and enemies of the publisher. If, on the other hand, his dispatches regarding American entry into the World Court and the League of Nations, or the progress or failure of Fascism, Communism, Nazism, the European cooperatives and other great and vastly more important subjects are aligned with the editorial policy previously set by his editor and publisher, he generally does not realize this influence and boasts that he is superior to the helot in the home office.

I believe I was the first to report that Mussolini was the military arm of the chambers of commerce and the manufacturers' associations of Italy and that he personally was implicated in the assassination of the leading rival politician. These dispatches were published. I smuggled news out of Italy and out of Russia, where as usual and with the encouragement of my editor, I defied the censorship. Naturally enough I was asked to leave both countries. I did the same in Fiume, Hungary, Romania, Syria and wherever I found censorship and suppression of news. Most foreign correspondents do the same. If one uses "diplomacy" one can usually remain in the country. Its use, however, depends on whether or not the home office prefers your dispatches or the glory of having its representatives deported by a dictator. Scores of correspondents have been deported in the past decade of dictatorship. A few have also been imprisoned. It was not until Hitler took over power that the actual risk of limb or life was taken by a newspaper man, and here and now I pay my respects to a score of Berlin colleagues for taking this risk.

In discussing newspaper truth and untruth the point to make, it seems to me, concerns integrity, and intentions, and human fraility. One man makes an honest mistake but another may repeat the falsehood either because a propagandist pays him or because the propaganda fits the views or prejudices to which he is pledged. Newspaper truth is not a question of how many angels can stand on the head of a needle, or how many dead in a wreck or a battle, but it remains a question of the intentions of all the men and women who have to do with presentation of the news.

The suspicions of laymen have never been answered by the press. Newspapers, upholding the right of criticism as a road to freedom, oppose all criticism of themselves. Almost universally they suppress mention of libel suits, which are of course a sort of layman's criticism. Newspapers, like kings, pretend they can do no wrong. I wish they were right.

Why Can't We Tell the Truth? Reporters Answer

Public distrust of the press is nothing new. Seldes had recently departed from daily journalism when he wrote this chapter in his 1931 book, Can These Things Be! *Here, he discusses some of the pressures that journalists face when it comes to reporting truthfully. The principles outlined in the Hearst memorandum reprinted below on reporting to the lowest common denominator are still in use today. But that is not the only reason for poor journalism. Seldes also blames the scoop mentality of reporters, which forces them to rush stories into print with little regard for their accuracy or validity, a process speeded up in the present day by television. He also faults journalists for reporting what their editors want to hear rather than what really happened. Seldes mostly focuses on foreign correspondence in this piece, but his observations apply to reporters on any beat in any town.*

WHO IS to blame, the reporter, the publisher or the public? Why is there a general disgust with the press, summed up in the ignorant remark "You can't believe what you read!"? Why can't journalists write the truth, why can't newspapers print the truth?

All these Whys are the subject of every newspaperman's gathering. Usually it is pretty well agreed that the public is to blame. In this way: the public is a low moron form of human being, which dotes on blood, battle and sex; the successful editor is a man who knows exactly what will please that public; that explains everything in the newspaper situation.

"We discovered sex long before Freud and Greenwich Village," said a Hearst man, and produced a copy of the memorandum one of the Hearst newspapers issued to its staff. It was in part:

"We must consider that the composite newspaper reader does not care a hang about tax rates, budgets, insurance, disarmament, naval appropriations, public utilities policies, municipal improvements, or scores of other subjects which may appear to be important.

"Newspaper readers are most interested in stories which contain the elements most dominant in the primitive emotions of themselves, namely:

(1) Self-preservation.

(2) Love, or reproduction.

(3) Ambition.

"Stories containing one of these elements are good; those which contain two of the elements are better; those which contain all three elements form first-class newspaper material.

SELF-PRESERVATION—Under this heading come stories of murder, suicide, rescues, accidents, fights, facts as to health, food, liquor, etc.

LOVE, OR REPRODUCTION—This element is contained in stories of marriage, scandal, divorce, human triangles, romances, unusual acts done with love motive, jealousy, sex attraction, etc.

AMBITION—The ambition element is contained in articles tending to stimulate the reader to emulate the activity of a character in the story. Sports come under this classification.

"The ambition element is aroused, also, by the mystery factor in a story. Mystery forms a challenge to the intelligence, and it thus stimulates the reader to buy further editions to note whether his solution, perhaps unconsciously made, is verified.

"For example: The Hall-Mills story (a sensational murder case in Chicago in the mid-1920's) contained all three major-interest elements. The killings provided the self-preservation element. The intimacy of the preacher with Mrs. Mills introduced the love element. The mystery of who did the killings, why and how, challenged the intelligence and fired the reader's ambition to solve the problem.

"Let us write our stories for the composite reader."

"You see," commented Mr. Hearst's representative, "the editor who wrote that was a success—because he was building a newspaper down to the level of the 'composite reader.' Very few editors aim at all above the mass public. Certainly all the million and more circulation newspapers have to be slaves of the public."

Foreign correspondents realize they are not subject to the same conditions as the local staffs. But while foreign correspondents do not have to chase scandal stories, they know that muck fills so many home columns that there is little space left for cables. Lewis Gannett, once a foreign correspondent, has summed it up this way:

"The people are more responsible than the editors. The New York newspaper reading public gets as good foreign news as can be had anywhere in the world—probably better than it deserves. The rest of the country could have better service if it wanted it. Every editor knows—from experience—that his public wants scandal news more than it wants honest international political news. All over Europe the correspondents complain that their editors want sensational news, not steady interpretive reporting. The editors want it because the public they serve wants it. No American paper can afford to maintain a first-class full-time man in far-off Romania or even Mexico City; its hardly worth while to fight Mussolini's censors, and the Soviet foreign office."

Ernest Boyd, a former member of the British Foreign Service, also blames the public. His view is:

"It is a pity that all the facts, disgraceful and otherwise, concerning European political and financial intrigue are not available to the American people. It is, however, a rather disconcerting thought that such papers as do attempt to provide the information suppressed or ignored in the popular newspapers, get very little support from the public they are so anxious to serve. The best guarantee of a small circulation is the determination to tell the whole truth. If the public were restive in the face of this conspiracy to deceive it, then the circulation figures of the world's press would be very different.

"The average man no more desires to be accurately and honestly informed about European affairs than he wishes to be accurately and honestly informed about his own affairs. The person who really issues the ukase: 'you can't print that' is not the wicked censor or the timid newspaper proprietor. In the last analysis, it is the consumer, who gets precisely the amount and the kind of truth which he wants, or can, tolerate."

Blaming the public is the least dangerous thing in any circumstance. But recently an anonymous newspaperman who must have had more than an anonymous reputation, otherwise no magazine editor could have permitted him to write as he did, realizing there is something vitally wrong with the newspaper at present, that public confidence in it needs to be restored, blamed his own profession. He said: "We (reporters) are the most vicious element in the newspaper world today."

He took the one element which I believe is nearest to honesty and rightness, and said it is disgracefully and almost irretrievably wrong. He spoke of "our dirty little profession."

It is rather a good sign of the healthiness of the profession to find a member attacking it. I have never found it dirty. When I saw the editors of my Pittsburgh newspaper, back in 1910, selling out their columns for a two dollar a day advertisement, I found the entire editorial staff in revolt. Even the hard, cynical, degraded reporter of public fancy and city-room melodrama is still sentimental enough to believe that the news writer is honest, and how often you find him fighting to keep the profession clean.

I would not make a white angel, aflame with purity, out of any newspaperman, but any fair city editor will admit that the writers—especially the younger and more enthusiastic ones—are the saving grace of every newspaper. It is almost surprising, this inexplicable and sometimes mad desire on the part of reporters to tell the truth. It is a baffling phenomenon, but it exists everywhere in America.

But the anonymous writer argued that the young reporters are all right, "but they get over their enthusiasm for the truth when they learn more about the business. Most of us are a lot of unconscionable liars. We don't care very much about the truth. All we care about is the 'story'—the special kind of story we believe our paper wants."

Of course every paper wants its story, wants it quick and wants it treated in a particular way. There is nothing more illegitimate in this than the employment of style in writing fiction. Would you rebuke Joseph Conrad for not writing the truth as Ernest Hemingway writes it? By the way, I think that one of the reasons for Hemingway's success in fiction is due to his newspaper training. He is a reporter of emotions. He doesn't describe them. When a good reporter covers a big murder trial, he reports the conversation accurately, of course. If he is an artist, however, he could make you see the character behind the conversation by his handling of the dialogue without in any way destroying its inherent truth. That is style, and even cheap newspapers want some style.

But first of all, the damning truth is that the newspaper, the city editor in particular, wants the facts. This insistence upon facts has been the ruin of thousands of boys and girls with literary gifts and bright young imaginations, who thought they were superior to the facts.

The newspaperman, up to and including the city editor, to whom reporters are chiefly responsible, is a slave to facts, to mere information, statistics, things actually seen and heard. He may go beyond them in treatment, but he must bring them in and tell them to his chief, know them well, and treat them with tender respect, until he is told to do otherwise. Which may happen. But that is another matter. The news writers, cub and star alike, get facts, know the truth without any Pilatian quibble, and are ready to tell the truth when they can.

But how do we account for so much variance in reports, so much distortion of news?

As regards the news writer, distortion is a superstition. I am not speaking about chief editors or owners. When I was a cub my city editor used to lecture me on fake news. "It is no use trying to fake a story," he always said. "The truth is infinitely more interesting and more useful to the paper than any fake you may make up on the way home from an assignment. It takes too long to frame up a really good story. I have never asked any man to fake a story and never expect to. There is material enough in the truth if the reporter is keen enough to see it!"

But a fake may be played up or down, hidden, or suppressed, according to the policy of the paper or the wishes of the owner. And inasmuch as a good newspaper or a plutocratic newspaper or a communist newspaper has each its own standards, its own policies, who shall say what news shall be printed, and how?

Then there is the matter of honest mistakes. A million deadly parallels could be printed; if 20 reporters cover the same story there is a chance that in minor details there will be at least five radically differing statements. But that is human incapacity to see and hear and report exactly.

Here is the prize example of mistakes. The item reads:

ACTRESS HANGS HERSELF IN THEATER DRESSING ROOM

Belgrade, Oct. 27—A few moments before she should have appeared on the stage at the Lioubliana Theater, last night, Mme. Alla Berh, a Slovene actress, was found hanging dead in her dressing room. The reason for the suicide is unknown.

By chance I found a local journalist who made the following six corrections:

1. Not in Lioubliana but in Klagenfurt
2. Not Alla Berh but Ella Beer
3. Not Slovene but Viennese
4. Not in dressing room but in hotel room
5. Not "before she should have appeared on stage" but between first and second acts.
6. The reason known.

A six-line item and six major mistakes! Each one an honest one. No question of distortion or perversion of news. But when there is corruption in news, the fact is the reporter and the city editor are usually blameless in the whole affair. You must consider the two together. The city editor is a graduate reporter in almost every case; he remains blood of their blood when he rises to his position and in him works the same desire to see the truth and to tell it. With the managing editor it may be different. He gets his orders from the powers, and he gets it in the neck when "mistakes" occur. The city editor is usually regarded as among the incorruptibles— the reporters. In too many cases, I am sorry to say, the managing editors, or executive editors, are at one with the owners in making the paper's policy.

News is suppressed by interested persons in authority; the city staff, reporters and city editors, are not interested and have no authority.

What about foreign correspondents? Where do we come in?

We are most of us lucky that our papers are so interested in home politics they have no time for us. They never send us orders to boost Fascism or boost Bolshevism; they hire men they think are honest and rely on getting the truth. We are therefore the luckiest men in journalism. When anyone refers to journalism as prostitution, we at least can stand up and refute. We can live and work honestly.

But unfortunately, with America's deeper and deeper plunge into international politics, interest in Europe grows daily and I am afraid we will be asked soon to do international policy pieces, just as some Washington correspondents frequently have to do Republican or Democratic policy pieces; they become special pleaders instead of free agents.

Of course the foreign correspondent, just like the reporter back home, knows who the boss is and what he likes. In some bureaus the men make an effort to please him by using his name in the paper. Hearst is the best example. When the politics and prejudices of the man are known it is natural for certain journalists to cater to them. On the *New York Times* it seems to go even into book reviewing. When Faustino Nitti's "Escape" made a world sensation the *Times* book supplement, which had at one time permitted an honest reviewer like Hiram Motherwell to write on Italy, came out with a nasty attack signed by Walter Littlefield. This reviewer began with the words "It is only fair to state at the beginning that the reviewer does not sympathize with the political attitude of the young man who has written the book or the uncle who introduces it . . . the uncle (ex-Premier Nitti) who is a voluntary exile in Paris . . . self-proclaimed victim of the loss of personal liberty."

While the first statement seems to admit unfitness to review the book, that is more clearly shown in the remark about Nitti. I was in Italy when the Mussolini agents attacked Nitti with the plan to kill him. They beat up everyone they found on the premises and destroyed the furniture and archives of the liberal leader. But Nitti escaped. In Paris he has to be protected from Fascist violence and not a week goes by without a blackshirt spy trying to intrigue him and his family into a plot aimed to cost him his right to asylum, and to lead to his deportation to Italy, where the Fascists can kill him.

I too have had an experience with the same book department of the *Times*. In *You Can't Print That* there is a criticism of the *Times* because its dispatches from Rome are written by a pro-Fascist. The book was sent to the Paris office for review, and numerous expensive cables exchanged about it. Finally it was decided to suppress all mention of it.

While it cannot be denied there are some men everywhere who might color the news to ingratiate themselves with their boss, the European correspondents as a rule are above such work. Sometimes, if you win the first fight, the road for years is easier. I will detail a case. It was the time when the question of government or private ownership of railroads was agitating everybody. Of course my newspaper owners were for private ownership—they held stocks and bonds and they got railroad advertising. So one day every European correspondent got something like this:

"Everybody send adequate cable report failure government ownership railroads his country."

At that time I was Berlin correspondent. Now I did not know a thing about the railroad system, and I assure you I did not have a single prejudice on the government or private question. In fact I was so little interested I got my assistant, who spoke German perfectly, to dig up the subject.

My assistant soon presented me a mass of material. Of course I knew what the boss wanted and why. But I couldn't possibly please him. So I wrote a very mild piece, giving some statistics: rates, prices, profits, conditions of travel, efficiency and so on.

Well, it seems most all correspondents had sent a "failure" story and mine was the only nonconformist. The next day I got a long cable, something like this:

"Your railroad story inadequate stop We want complete story showing failure government ownership especially noting inefficiency service, excessive freight, excessive passenger rates, lack fidelity government employees, sabotage, graft, waste public money, delays freight delivery, failure efficient passenger schedules."

This riled me a bit, so with my assistant I spent the whole day going through all the government figures and then getting the anti-government claims. The result was astonishing. It seems that the greatest part of the Prussian state budget, for example, was paid by railroad earnings, and yet the efficiency and low prices of the Prussian system were universally acknowledged. I learned a lot that day. So I sat down and wrote the most enthusiastic dispatch about the marvelous success of German Government railroads. I sent 1,200 words, and cables used to cost money in those days.

Eventually the railroad series was opened up in my paper. All the big attacks on government ownership came on page 1. The mild ones followed inside. Mine was never printed.

But that isn't all. And this illustrates the character of some reporters. A few years afterwards I was away on an assignment to Bolshevik Russia. It was just at that time that the German mark, which had been declining slowly, fell with a crash. Of course the government bureaus, post office, telegraphs, railroads, etc., could not alter their rates every day (on a dollar basis) as the shops did. So when money went from say 200,000 to a dollar on the first of the month to 20,000,000 to a dollar, it became possible for an Englishman to buy a ticket from Berlin to London for two shillings and six pence instead of four or six pounds. Naturally the railroads also showed a big loss that year.

Blank was my temporary successor in Berlin and he recalled the scandal my refusing to send a lie about government ownership had made some years before. Now he saw his opportunity to get in right with the boss. So he sent a sensation. He showed the German railroads deficit of quintillions of marks. Quintillions made an impression—although, a few months later you could get four quintillions for a dollar. And of course Blank emphasized the government as being the owner of these deficient railroads. Well, that German story got on the first page too, and Blank was noted around the home office as a dependable man, while I was put down as a Bolshevik. For Emerson's wise-crack has been revised to date and reads, "who so would be a nonconformist, must be a Bolshevik."

And now comes the journalist's friend, H. L. Mencken, of many "Prejudices," saying it is not the business office and the editor who are responsible for the low state of metropolitan journalism, but the writing boys themselves. He says we are most of us a lot of boobs, maudlin, sentimental, uneducated, gullible, cocksure, ill-equipped, devoid of knowledge, devoid of intelligence, stupid, cowardly, ignorant, incapable of recognizing the truth, and quite unable to write anything decently.

But Mencken sees a brighter time ahead, despite the success of the picture tabloids. He says that editors do not object to intelligent work. Of course in the office of the *Baltimore Sun* where I believe Mencken got his training, there was always a premium on decency.

Of course there are boob and bad reporters who bring in boob and bad items which are printed, and which make so many papers what they are. But there are more intelligent men who try to bring in intelligent items, only to see them changed into imbecile items, with the result that they may easily give up trying, and accustom themselves instead to the spirit of the office.

That, I think, is the great fault in our journalism: if I had seen the light, and sent the piece about Germany my boss wanted, I would soon be writing more lies to please my boss. What is the history of thousands of home journalists, and many foreign correspondents?

We scent the air of the office. We realize that certain things are wanted, certain things unwanted. There is an atmosphere favorable to Fascism. We find that out when some little pro-Mussolini item is played up, some big item, not so pleasant to the hero of our era, played down, or left out. In the future we send pro-Mussolini stuff only. We get a cable of congratulations.

One episode lights up the subject. Navarre Atkinson and several others were in Bucharest covering an uprising against the vicious Bratianu dictatorship. The Romanian corrupt foreign office of that time wanted (a) to draw attention elsewhere and (b) to put in a blow against Russia because the Romanians were holding a lot of Russian territory.

So one day they held a "revolution" just across the frontier in Ukraine.

This fake the Romanian officials planted in the Bucharest press. Now all newspapermen know that it is "within the law" to pick up stories of this nature and send them to America without further investigation. All you need say is that "a local paper reports."

But here is where the whole question of honest journalism comes in. One journalist knows that his paper is impartial, so he investigates the story; a second knows that his paper favors the Bolsheviks, so he drops the story, and a third knows that his paper is anti-Bolshevik and just eats up all Soviet uprisings, so he sends the story "as is."

That is what Atkinson did. He cabled the uprising in Ukraine, and he too was congratulated on a scoop. But there was more than he bargained for. The congratulatory telegram ordered him to the front as a war correspondent! Atkinson went. He got near enough to Russia to see that all was quiet there. He had had the Bolsheviks and Whites battling everywhere and a vivid picture of the cut-off heads of the Bolshevik leaders, mounted on pikes, being carried through the streets by the revolutionaries. He found nothing. But, yes, he did find something. It seems that in 1919 or 1920 there had been trouble in that district, and some heads were paraded in the streets. Such things had happened—but almost a decade ago!

Meanwhile the Bolsheviks had got hold of the story and they went to Walter Duranty, who is of the same journal, and said, "what about it?" and Walter, who has all he can do writing neutral yet informative pieces, didn't know what about it, so he had to cable a long denial of his own colleague's big exclusive scoop. But I can't blame Atkinson: he was trying to deliver the kind of goods he thought his employer liked.

On the subject of scoops and truth the following case has become a foreign service classic:

Carl Groat, a very careful and responsible journalist, was one of the crowd which went to the Ruhr when the French occupied it. That of course was the biggest news in the world that time. One day the Germans declared something. It seems the Germans have three degrees of martial law or state of siege or something, and they declared one of them, and

Groat—that was before he acquired a very comprehensive German vocabulary—translated what the Germans declared as martial law.

No colleague did. The United Press got the flash "Germans declare martial law in Ruhr" and Groat got the following: "Your martial law exclusive; congratulations." But two days later Groat got another cable. This one read "Your martial law still exclusive; why?"

The scoop hunt has been blamed for a lot that's wrong in our modern journalism. The Irish journalist James P. O'Reilly delivers this pronunciamento on the problem:

"Why cannot foreign correspondents tell the truth? They are as good and as bad as other men. Like most men, their immediate purpose in life is to earn their living. They are not paid to tell the truth; they are paid to write, and their writings must be published. There are many censorships in Europe, and the first matter a foreign correspondent must consider is to write so that his article will pass out of the country. In some countries there is political terrorism as well.

"Then—most important of all—there is the paper's policy, which always depends on the financial interests behind it. I feel that Sir Henry Wootton's definition of an ambassador fits equally well a foreign correspondent—they are both sent to lie abroad for their masters. There is another force which none but the strongest can fight—corruption, direct or indirect, hospitality, decorations, popularity, all of which are freely given to the foreigner who supports the government in power and by his favorable reports brings American or English capital into the country. All these are forces of anti-truth. But there is still another—a common one it seems to me—the natural desire for notoriety that is in most of us, which journalists have in great degree the means of satisfying for themselves. A 'scoop'—an interview at some crucial moment with a great political figure, anything of this kind, may put a journalist's name in every man's mouth. Nice considerations as to accuracy do not always dominate the journalist's mind on such occasions. On the whole it seems to me easier for a rich man to enter heaven than for a foreign correspondent to tell the truth."

"Ken," the Inside Story

This piece, from the 30 April 1938 issue of The Nation, *tells the story of how pressure by big business and advertising agencies scuttled an attempt to launch a liberal, mass-market magazine. Seldes was brought aboard the staff of* Ken *to write investigative articles and press criticism. He thought he found utopia, but disillusionment came quickly when the publishers sacrificed its proposed "one step left-of-center" editorial policy for one that would not offend advertisers. The magazine attracted some of the best of the Left's writers and had an advance sale of 250,000, but when* Ken *backed away from the Left, the Left backed away from* Ken. *Pleasing no one, the magazine folded within a few months. The experience helped to inspire Seldes to start his own paper,* In fact, *two years later.*

THE REPUDIATION of the press by the American people was clearly demonstrated by the 1936 Presidential election. It may not have been complete, but it showed a vast popular disillusion. That someone would capitalize on the situation followed logically. In March 1937, the idea of publishing a magazine for the masses who had lost faith in the newspapers was discussed by three persons in Chicago.

David A. Smart, young and rich, had made a success clothing-trade paper called *Apparel Arts*; Arnold Gingrich, novelist and art connoisseur, had years ago proposed a magazine "for men only"; the two had produced *Esquire*, now selling 600,000 copies a month, and *Coronet*, which thrived despite the depression and the lack of advertising. The third man was Jay Cooke Allen, one of America's great journalists. Allen was to be editor. The magazine was to be called *Ken—the Insiders' World*. Its function would be to tell the truth behind the news, to explore hitherto unexplored fields of American journalism, to defy the forces and men who are forever saying, "You can't print that."

On a boat Paris-bound in April 1937, Smart gave evidence of a social conscience. "This magazine," he said to Allen, "will be the first big break the underdog in America has had." All the Left and liberal writers were to be employed, and at a $150,000 guest house to be bought or erected facing Central Park the contributors to *Ken* were to taste the Smart largess.

Ken's left-of-center policy was definitely settled when Smart, back in America, received a letter from Allen in Paris explaining the French People's Front. *Ken* was to be a magazine for the coming People's Front in America; it was to take no sides in factional disputes of labor organizations and liberal-labor parties but was to represent a united front of all decent and intelligent liberal and progressive elements. "Thrilled by your letter," Smart cabled, and Allen engaged various liberal journalists to write the "inside story" of Europe.

Then the trouble began. Having accepted Smart's promises at their face value, Allen went to work on a large scale, engaging editors, research workers, and assistants, and ordering big investigations which took time and money. There was nothing picayune about the Allen plans. Since Smart had conceived of *Ken* as a Left-wing *Fortune*, the staff prepared a 20,000-word feature on the fascist wars on democracy, to lead the first issue. Then a conference was held; and the left-wing *Fortune* was scrapped in favor of a left-wing *Time*. Again the staff prepared a dummy, concentrating on short items instead of one big lead story; and again there was a dispute over the essential nature of the magazine.

I have seen the dummies, layouts, stories, illustrations and photographs which Allen prepared, all accurate and interesting pieces, superior to anything which has yet appeared in *Ken*, and yet I have heard Smart sneer about spending forty or fifty thousand dollars on the Allen regime "and not having a damn story to show for it." I am now convinced that a desire to economize, not the style or character of the magazine as worked out by Allen, caused the eventual separation of Smart and Allen.

In October, when the Allen staff was hired, I was shown the supposedly final prospectus which was to bear out the magazine's stated purpose—"*Ken* will be one step left of center . . . anti-war and anti-fascist."

Two solid pages boasted that the magazine would not be objective but biased—nobly biased in favor of the awakening liberal-labor movement in America. Gingrich had written that freedom of the press today existed only for the publishers, "and half of them are busy salaaming sacred cows, while the other half are grinding axes on the emery wheel of their own prejudices. Between them they constitute a barrier separating the general public from the insider's world." I was invited to join the staff with the understanding that it would be my job to break down this barrier.

The press department, which I was to edit, would constitute about a third of the magazine, or 30,000 words, including a "lie detector" to which the 10,000 members of the American Newspaper Guild would contribute. Once each month there would be an investigation of the press of a state metropolis. The emphasis was always to be on suppressed news. Gingrich took Dana's motto, "What the good Lord lets happen I am not ashamed to print," as our slogan and made it even more forceful by replacing "ashamed" with "afraid."

My department having been decided upon, I was introduced to Mr. Smart, who reassured me about the policy of the magazine. He spoke of the old days, when his family had been poor and his aunt a friend of Eugene V. Debs. "Even if I were merely doing *Ken* as a business proposition," he continued, "it would be O.K. Here's this new reservoir—the labor movement, the AFL, the CIO, the American Labor Party, the progressives in the West—ten or twenty million people who can read. We're going to tap this reservoir." Smart asked what my conception of the magazine was. I replied, "The kind Lincoln Steffens would have been glad to edit." Whereupon Smart said, clinching the matter, "We want something like a cross between *The Nation* and *Life*—liberal and lively, something for the millions, not high-brow like *The Nation* and *The New Republic*, but popular, full of illustrations, and just as liberal."

In addition to the press department Smart suggested that I do a series of articles on the American Legion and the money behind it; another series on Falsehood in War and Peace showing how it is possible to fool all the people all the time when government and press cooperate; a piece on how Franco and the fascist journalists fake the news; an article on the publishers' use of gunmen, thugs, machine-guns, and gas, based on quotations from the La Follette hearings; a dozen pieces showing how the press colors or fakes the news about such subjects as picketing, the American Labor Party, Red-baiting, the Supreme Court, social security, the public utilities, the President, various political and social minorities. Smart wanted the Legion series right away because it would cause talk, and "we have got to put this magazine over by causing talk."

It was I who first brought up the subject of big business and advertising pressure. "Suppose they attack *Esquire* ?" I said. "If you are going to tell the unpublished truth about everything you'll get in trouble with the advertisers just as magazines and newspapers always do." Smart opened a copy of *Esquire.* "Seventy percent men's clothes," he said, "20 percent whiskey and soda, what is there to expose? We're invulnerable. They can't attack us. You'll have an absolutely free hand." Overcome by enthusiasm I said, "Well, this is a reporters dream of Utopia; I'd work for nothing -" But Smart was magnanimous. He offered to give me a modest salary compared with with the other editors were getting until we got a million circulation, then he would put me "in the upper-bracket income class."

Enthusiasm blinds one. I realize now the journalistic Utopia in which I seemed to live in November 1937, I paid no attention to the following suspicious items: prospectuses which said that Paul de Kruif and Ernest Hemingway were working editors when they were not editors at all but contributors; the sudden firing of almost the entire Allen staff, with, at Allen's request, two weeks' pay; troubles about payment to authors engaged by Allen; Smart's proposal to employ George Sokolsky (I had the minutes of the Nye munitions investigation naming Sokolsky in an arms deal and an investigator of the La Follette committee informed me that Sokolsky would shortly be named as being in the employ of the National Association of Manufacturers); lack of union organization among the workers and their expressed dissatisfaction over wages.

Against these facts was my strong belief that so long as I kept away from men's clothing and the liquor industry I would have a free hand in publishing a fair journal. Accordingly, I wrote seven articles on the American Legion, four on Falsehood in Peace and War, an exposé of the Paris *Herald Tribune,* dozens of items for the lie detector of the press—a total of at least 80,000 words. Meanwhile the gossip columnists and the trade press spread the story that *Ken* was to represent the liberal-labor movement, tell the truth, shame the devious and and defy the foul fiend of big business.

The joy in the editors' offices was more than balanced by the gloom in *Ken's* advertising department. It was not satisfied with the way things were going. Some publishers took space, including my own. Consumers Union telephoned it would take a page, but the shouts of victory from the advertising solicitors turned to groans when the manager decided that a

Consumers Union announcement would further repel commercial manu-facturers. No advertising agency, no big business house appeared willing to be on either friendly or commercial terms with a publication that admitted it favored the liberal and labor movement in America. "All that the ad agencies are asking," one of the solicitors told me, "is that the policy be changed to anti-labor and anti-liberal."

Then the Chicago business office descended on the New York busi-ness office. There was a banquet and a conference with advertising leaders, and immediately afterward Gingrich, who represented the edito-rial department, called me to his hotel and said, "They not only backed me up against the wall, they backed me through the wall." Subsequently I was told to "lay off commodities." Since I had written about politics, not patent medicines, I could not understand this request.

Shortly afterward Smart burst into my office white with fury. "Who told you to write those Legion articles?" he shouted. "You did," I replied. "Well, damn it, I've been trying to sign up the Prudential Life for three years, they keep saying *Esquire* isn't their type. So I'm about to land them for *Ken* when you write a piece saying a bunch of bankers formed the Legion and control it, and Franklin D'Olier of the Prudential Life is one of this royal family. We haven't a chance to get this ad if we run your Legion series."

The series is now in the wastebasket.

Naturally I told the story around the office. Every advertising man could tie or cap it. The *Esquire* office classic is about a writer who men-tioned an Englishman putting plain water instead of soda into his whiskey, "as most Englishmen do." The story passed the editors and got into proof. At the last minute, however, it was caught. "As most Englishmen do" came out, and the author was summoned. "Cracks like that will ruin us," one of the business heads shouted at him. "Do you realize what that would have cost us? White Rock— $50,000; Canada Dry—$50,000; Hoffmann Beverages, don't you think when you write?"

I got along famously with the advertising, circulation, business depart-ments. I liked the new cynicism which pervaded their offices, as it once did the city room—before the Guild arrived. "If journalists are a lot of prostitutes," one of the advertising solicitors said, "what are we? We're the dung collectors."

If big business and soda water and commodities were out, there was still the press department: newspapers didn't advertise much in maga-zines. I got letters from the Associated Press and United Press proving that the Hearst publications were changing "Loyalists" to "Reds" in AP and UP dispatches, and otherwise distorting the news from Spain. I got out a department on Americans who had declared themselves in favor of Mussolini, Hitler, and Franco. In the La Follette civil-liberties reports I found some great stuff on spies, machine-guns, and Red-baiting which no newspaper had published.

Smart thought I was going on at too great length. "Once you've said the news is colored, that's enough," he said. I asked if the press department was out. He said, "No, but it ought to be something else." I wrote to Gingrich asking for an inside letter on the inside situation, but before I got it I learned from one of my friends in the advertising department that a big agency had threatened to withdraw a fortune in advertising from *Esquire* "if so much as one line pro-labor appeared in *Ken*." The next day I noticed a change in the "inspirational talks" which I often overheard in the office next to mine "Tell them we have changed our policy. Tell them we are anti-communist now as well as anti-fascist. Tell your contacts that we're going after the Reds too." Various circulars and letters containing Red-baiting phrases were sent out.

The advertising men who had previously been so friendly to me now refused to talk. Outside the office one of them told me that they had had an order from Smart in Chicago not to talk to me. "You are a bad influence. He says we lose our sincerity as solicitors when we talk to you. You undermine advertising morale." A day or two later I received a telegram from Smart asking me to do my work at home as my office was needed for a photographer.

My "work" now consisted of a series of articles on foreign dictators and their love life, the only subjects I had left which, according to Smart, were "up to *Ken* standards." And finally Gingrich informed me that "the financial winds seem to be blowing the daylights out of that apparently fair-weather form of liberalism that is one of the major tenets of *Ken* as you and I first planned it." Big business, and advertising, its spearhead in the attack on the liberal-labor movement in America, had won out completely. There remained but one mystery: why the press department, the main feature, had not appeared. It may not be without significance in this connection that Mr. Smart has for years also been operating the Esquire Features Syndicate, which sells comic strips and other items to more than 100 papers.

This was the history of *Ken* up to the return of Hemingway from Spain. Hearing rumors in Key West that there had been a change in policy, he telegraphed me for the prospectus and consulted with his fellow "working editor," Paul de Kruif. Even before *Ken* appeared Hemingway had decided he did not want to be listed as an editor. De Kruif had protested against the Red-baiting cartoons in the first issue and also threatened to withdraw his name. He sent in his resignation on 18 April with the announcement that he would not contribute any articles in the future. John L. Spivak, also listed as an editor but actually the roving staff correspondent, left word in New York when he left for Czechoslovakia that he would resign if Red-baiting continued. De Kruif and others have cabled to Hemingway in Barcelona suggesting that he discontinue writing for *Ken*. At a meeting of almost a score of New York contributors a letter was written to Smart demanding that the original policy of the magazine be restored and the pressure or the advertising agencies defied.

The first issue of *Ken*, although filled with anti-Hitler and anti-Mussolini material, contained almost nothing about the United States of America. Red-baiting, the sop for big business, was represented in some hurriedly gathered cartoons, one of which lumped Loyalist Spain with fascist Spain as part of the black plague of dictatorship. The second issue continued to expose Mussolini and Hitler and spies in Mexico. These foreign contributions, it may be admitted, appear to be well documented and reliable. And there have been two articles on domestic labor problems. But it is apparent that far-away fascism is *Ken's* real foe; there has been no mention of vigilante fascism, or the National Association of Manufacturers' brand of fascism as exposed by the La Follette committee, or all the other fascist movements masquerading under patriotic names in America and drawing money from the big business men who are also the big advertisers.

Considerable speculation is heard in various quarters about *Ken's* future. There are persons who would like to make it an anti-Administration organ for the 1940 campaign, the spokesman of big business. The McClure Syndicate release for 20 April stated that Albert Lasker, head of the powerful Lord and Thomas advertising agency, has a financial interest in *Ken*.

The history of *Ken* teches many important lessons. It proves for our time and generation the sad truth learned by a dozen weeklies and monthlies in the great muckraking era of 1905 to 1917—that big business and advertising will either change a magazine's policy from liberal to reactionary or try to ruin the magazine. Having spent $100,000 or more to promote *Ken*, its publishers perceived that a liberal policy might seriously affect advertising revenue. The impossibility of combining progress with profit, demonstrated before the war, is even clearer today with the advertising agencies becoming the leaders in a class-conscious attack on progressive liberalism. On the other hand we have proof that a large audience exists which would support a popular magazine really free from advertising control. When *Ken* announced a left-of-center policy, 250,000 advance buyers appeared. Many of them still want the press department, the lie detector, the truth behind the newspapers, the liberal and pro-labor policy. There is certainly a field for the very magazine which *Ken* promised to be in its first prospectus, which the first two issues fail to be with any degree of completeness. To publish such a magazine for the millions a considerable sum of money is needed along with a certain amount of courage.

Is the Entire Press Corrupt?

The urgency of the fight against fascism makes this critique of the press from Seldes' 1942 self-published book, The Facts Are..., *all the more intense. What follows is an indictment of the American press that ranks with Upton Sinclair's* The Brass Check, *as one of the powerful and detailed accounts of how the press has worked against the best interests of the people and the factors that made it that way.*

IT IS MORE than likely that in the time intervening between the writing of this and the day it is read the World War now being fought far away will have become a reality, a matter of life and death, to millions of Americans. There may be long casualty lists, there may be bombardments of great coastal cities, and the facts of the greatest struggle for the welfare of humanity against its greatest enemy (Fascism) will be felt as well as known.

The conduct of this war, the making of the unity necessary to win it, or the spreading of disunity which for the first time in the history of the Republic may endanger its existence, will depend considerably on the press, and the kind of peace which will follow will depend even more than did the Versailles peace, on the conduct of the press of all nations. Today we are fighting for our lives. We have been attacked. The enemy is Fascism. There can therefore be no room in the anti-Fascist world at this time for doubt about the justness of the war, or its causes, as there were in the last war, but when peace nears all of us will have to be on the alert to prevent the present movement against world Fascism from being diverted into many strange channels by public opinion created by a press which is still in Fascist or semi-Fascist control even in democratic nations.

I believe that the press will be the instrument for uniting America for war and that it will be still more powerful in making a peace which may benefit all peoples or certain interests. I also believe that most of the world press is controlled by special interests and as a result is corrupt. Therefore it is necessary to explain and expose this corruption of the press and to question its handling of the news of the war, so that we may judge its role in creating a better world—for which this war is being fought.

What is the most powerful force in America today?

Answer: public opinion.

What makes public opinion?

Answer: the main force is the press.

Can you trust the press?

Answer: the baseball scores are always correct (except for a typographical error now and then). The stock market tables are correct (within the same limitation). But when it comes to news which will affect you, your daily life, your job, your relation to other peoples, your thinking on economic and social problems, and, more important today, your going to war and risking your life for a great ideal, then you cannot trust about 98 percent (or perhaps 99 1/2 percent) of the big newspaper and big magazine press of America.

But, why can't you trust the press?

Answer: because it has become Big Business. The big city press and the big magazines have become commercialized, or big business organizations, run with no other motive than profit for owner or stockholder (although hypocritically still maintaining the old American tradition of guiding and enlightening the people). The big press cannot exist a day without advertising. Advertising means money from Big Business. The truth about Big Business is told in the three or four hundred volumes of government reports (the 73 volume record of the investigation of the public utilities by the Federal Trade Commission; the 50 volumes of the two La Follette reports on the violations of the rights of labor; the three-score reports of the O'Mahoney monopoly investigation and many more). Besides naming thousands of newspapers, scores of magazines, many writers and college professors as being corrupted by the special interests, and receiving the price paid, which ranges all the way from a $5 bill and a few drinks at a bar to a million dollar mortgage, the reports come to these documented conclusions:

1. America is in the hands of 200 industrial and 50 financial families.
2. These families run this country.
3. They supply the funds which elect the officials of the United States, from state legislatures to the presidency.
4. They control billions in stocks and bonds, they control the economic life of the nation.
5. They control legislation; they control Congress; they maintain the most powerful lobby in Washington, and usually get what they want.
6. They use the American Newspaper Publishers Association (the big newspaper owners) as an instrument to maintain their control of America.
7. They use advertising (in newspapers and magazines) to make this stranglehold on public opinion possible.

In other words, they control *you*.

Very few people will accept these seven statements as facts, yet they are facts known to everyone in the newspaper business, in big business, in politics; they are known to all who read the small free liberal magazines and to everyone who is part of the ruling group. The facts appear in government documents. But these are also the facts which have been suppressed in the popular newspapers and magazines, and that of course is the reason America is kept in ignorance of the most vital matters affecting the life, happiness and welfare of the majority of its citizens.

I have written several books on the press and I am publishing a weekly newsletter devoted largely to criticizing the big city newspapers (the public opinion-making newspapers) and exposing their corruption, because I still believe that the press is the greatest force in the world and can be used for good or evil. And I believe that the American press by its control of public opinion can either fool all the people into restoring a world in which one-third of the nation will again live in economic slavery without sufficient food, clothing and shelter, or it can, if it wants to, bring out of this united effort against native as well as foreign Fascism a world approaching the Jeffersonian ideal.

In 1787 Jefferson declared that "the basis of our government is the opinion of the people"; given the choice of "a government without newspapers, or newspapers without government," he would prefer the latter.

Think of it! Jefferson was willing to let the press itself rule the country instead of merely creating the public opinion that rules.

But Jefferson did not forsee that the American press which creates opinion and which rules indirectly would become almost exclusively a millionaire's press, or a corporation influenced press, or the medium of big business via its advertising, and therefore the corrupt press which serves private interests rather than the public interest. If America is to be bossed by the public opinion created by its press, if it is to fight and win this war, if it is to make a great peace, then it should know the power of the most powerful force which is abroad in this land.

The press which attacked George Washington, which denounced him as everything from a traitor to a drunkard, was not a corrupt press. It was in fact a free press. But the press which from 1932 (or thereabouts) to the present day attacks New Deal F. D. Roosevelt, the same press which tried to suppress the Old Deal Teapot Dome scandal and the doings of Harding's Ohio gang, while sniping at every governmental action for the general welfare of the American people, is a corrupt press.

To understand the news today it is important that the layman should know what motivates the newspapers; why they are united to keep the people ignorant of vital events and movements; why they are, in short, the enemies of progress and the well-being of the majority of the people. What has happened to this great "palladium of freedom," this "spokesman for liberty," this defender of justice and righter of the wrongs of the millions?

Why has the press become corrupt?

What change has come over the American newspapers between the time of Washington and the days of the New Deal and the great World War of the United Nations against the Axis?

The journalistic history of the United States may be divided into four periods:

1. The Revolutionary or Free Press. Anyone with a few hundred dollars could print what he pleased—until stopped, but only temporarily, by the Alien and Sedition Act of our first native-reactionary leader, John Adams. A hand press, some paper, and a desire to say something were all that was required.

2. The Age of Expansion and Pioneering. It was the time of the great editors who from the days of the western migration and the Gold Rush to

the time of the Spanish-American War put the impress of their personality on journalism. Dana, Greeley, et alii.

3. Commercialization. Dana, Greeley, et alii, were in turn succeeded by Pulitzer, Hearst and Scripps. Hearst and Scripps created newspaper chains. At the turn of the century the press became commercial. Yellow journalism, or sensationalism for the sake of mass circulation, followed. This yellowness was superseded by the golden age of advertising. The press was commercial but it still was free.

4. The Age of Corruption. Although it is true that Will Irwin wrote his great series of exposés of the press (in *Collier's* magazine, then free from the control of the House of Morgan) in 1910, it was not until 1920 when Upton Sinclair wrote "The Brass Check," that the American press could be labeled wholly corrupt. (Throughout this book the reader will remember that there are exceptions to this general indictment, that the indictment itself applies mainly to the big city press, the Big Money press, the 200 or 300 papers of metropoli, the press which makes public opinion, which helps run this country—for the benefit of the National Association of Manufacturers, according to the O'Mahoney Monopoly Committee. For two years readers of *In fact*, including thousands of Newspaper Guild members, have been asked to send in the names of honest big city newspapers, but the list is still short of one percent of the total.)

The free press of the first five or six decades of the Republic was free to the point of irresponsibility. "If we are to take George Washington's own statement at face value," writes our greatest historian, Charles A. Beard, "it was scurrilous abuse by the press which drove him into retirement at the end of his second term." It is a human fact that the great of all times have been misjudged by their little contemporaries, and Washington was no exception, nevertheless the garbage and sewer quality of the campaign against our first president by a large part of the free press has never been surpassed in odor in our history. Like the proverbial dead mackerel, it glittered and stank. No tyrant, felon or pickpocket could have been more cruelly treated than was George Washington, and when he finally retired from the presidency, Bache's *General Advertiser* urged the people to exult, because "the name of Washington ceases to give currency to political iniquity and to legalized corruption." One who protested (shortly before he died) was Benjamin Franklin who wrote of the situation "Now many of our printers make no scruple of gratifying the malice of individuals by false accusations of the fairest characters among themselves, augmenting animosity even to the producing of duels, and are, moreover, so indiscreet as to print scurrilous reflections on the government of neighboring states, and even on the conduct of our best national allies, which may be attended with the most pernicious consequences."

Naturally enough there was no let-up when John Adams became president, although in many instances it was another set of journals which composed the journalistic wolf-pack. He too was vilified and his personal life made the subject of editorial falsehoods. One sheet actually printed this characterization of our second president: "A cold-thinking villain whose black blood runs temperately bad." But Adams could not take it, as Washington had, and he persuaded Congress to pass the Alien and Sedition Act under which he threw editors and publishers into jail.

The first great founding father who rightly estimated the power of the press and who became its greatest champion was Thomas Jefferson. It was he who rallied James Madison and James Monroe and other liberals for the fight against the Sedition laws, and upon taking office freed the newspaper editors and publishers and let the legislation die.

Nevertheless Jefferson also was the victim of a vicious press.

The Federalists let loose their journalistic big guns upon a man they called an atheist, an anarchist, a theorist, a dictator, a lover of foreigners and a "leveler"; they abused him for favoring the French republicans, for welcoming Citizen Genet as minister in 1792; they "Redbaited" him as a Jacobin. Jefferson and his friends were accused of publishing and disseminating all the "seditious, slanderous, demoralizing, atheistical publications" which the "industry and the wickedness of the Jacobins" could collect.

It is interesting to know Jefferson's opinion of the free press before he took office, during his presidency, and in his more objective later years. At the beginning he was the most optimistic believer in a free press. His views were:

"Our liberty depends on the freedom of the press and that cannot be limited without being lost."

"When the press is free, and every man able to read, all is safe."

"The people are the only censors of their government; and even their errors will tend to keep them on the true principles of their institutions. To punish these errors too severely would be to suppress the only safeguard of the public liberty....The basis of our governments being the opinion of the people, the very first object should be to keep that right; and were it left to me to decide whether we should have a government, without newspapers, or newspapers without government, I should not hesitate a moment to prefer the latter. But I should mean that every man should receive these papers, and be capable of reading them." (To Carrington, Paris, 16 January 1787.)

And in 1799 Jefferson wrote: "Our citizens may be deceived for a while and have been deceived; but as long as the press can be protected, we may trust to them for light."

But in 1807 the tone changed. Jefferson wrote (to J. Norvell) against the irresponsibility of the newspapers:

"Nothing can now be believed which is seen in a newspaper. Truth itself becomes suspicious by being put into that polluted vehicle. The real extent of this state of misinformation is known only to those who are in situations to confront facts within their knowledge with the lies of the day. I really look with commiseration over the great body of my fellow citizens, who, reading newspapers, live and die in the belief that they have known something of what has been passing in the world in their time; whereas the accounts they have read in newspapers are just as true a history of any other period of the world as of the present, except that the real names of the day are affixed to their fables. General facts may indeed be collected from them, such as that Europe is now at war, that Bonaparte has been a successful warrior . . .but no details can be relied on. I will add that the man who never looks into a newspaper is better informed than he who reads them; inasmuch as he who knows nothing is nearer to truth than he whose mind is filled with falsehoods and errors....

"Perhaps an editor might begin a reformation in some such way as this. Divide his paper into four chapters, heading the first, Truths; second, Probabilities; third, Possibilities; fourth, Lies. The first chapter would be very short."

And in 1812, to Dr. D. W. Jones:

"I deplore . . . the putrid state into which our newspapers have passed, and the malignity, the vulgarity, the mendacious spirit of those who write them.... These ordures are rapidly depraving the public taste."

Now, while it is true that Washington, Adams and Jefferson denounced the press with equal vigor, there is a great historic difference in the character of the attack upon each of the first three presidents. Washington had been accused by certain newspapers of accepting a bribe from England, whereas Jefferson had been accused of Jacobinism in much the same manner as F. D. Roosevelt had been accused (by crackpots, to be sure, rather than reputable newspapers) of being the agent of Moscow Communism.

The press attacks on Washington, Adams and Jefferson may have had the same decibel rating of loudness, the same vulgarity, the same scurrilousness and viciousness, but in the case of Jefferson a new note was already being sounded—the note which was to become the entire symphony of today's journalistic concert not only against a liberal president but against every regime, person and institution which is truly New Dealist progressive, truly democratic, destined for the general welfare rather than the vested interests; it was the note of alarm of the vested interests, the first faint cries of the Haves in fear of the Havenots, the first shouts of Privilege against any and all who might threaten wealth and power. Jefferson knew this. He knew the press was not attacking him, but Democracy. He foresaw perhaps the present era when the press would be the great weapon of all native Fascist forces working against the extension of democracy.

So long as it was possible for an itinerant printer or any tiny minority possessing a few hundred dollars to set up shop and issue a newspaper, there was no monopoly of public opinion. And there was no corrupt press. In Boston, in New York, in colonial days, and later in Washington, and in every city and town in the wake of the pioneers marching westward, wandering printers kept alive the free press and produced the most picturesque era in the nation's journalism. It was still possible toward the end of the 19th Century to get out a newspaper without being a millionaire in a big city, or a company with a soul mortgaged to the banker in a small town. But, as William Allen White—the man always chosen to prove the publishers' claim the press still has integrity—now confesses, it takes a comparatively large bank roll to start a paper anywhere—his own *Emporia Gazette* is worth $70,000, and if a man with another viewpoint wanted to start an opposition sheet in Emporia it would involve a much greater sum. In Chicago or New York it would mean the risk of a million dollars a year for many years.

Mr. White does not disagree with Frank Munsey, the great newspaper wrecker whom he saved from oblivion with the famous phrase: he turned a great profession into an eight percent investment. The indictment goes even further, and in its proper place Mr. White's final strictures will be given. The fact is now accepted that the newspaper is big business. Whether it is therefore ipso facto corrupt because big business is corrupt is still being debated. The present writer has no doubts on this matter.

One of the epiphenomenal pieces of hypocrisy is the statement made by *Editor & Publisher* and other kept voices of the publishers that the integrity, honesty and freedom of the press (and also of the Associated Press, its main source of news) must exist because it serves "every" viewpoint. By every is meant Republican and Democratic parties. For good measure, the publishers throw in what they call "Independent Republican" and "Independent Democrat," and also just plain "independent." Believe it or not, they still use those terms and still make those claims after two elections in which 85 to 95 percent of the press (outside the Solid South) urged the people to vote against Mr. Roosevelt and the New Deal, and many papers, including the *New York Times*, switched parties because all the big advertising money was on the side of the opposition. And they also make their claim in the face of the reports of the directors of the National Electric Light Association that they corrupted four-fifths of the American press with their $25 million a year blackmail and advertising fund.

There is only one viewpoint which the entire press of the nation expresses, respects, represents and works for: the viewpoint of business, money, wealth, and power represented by what is generally known as the God of Things As They Are, or the Status Quo. The press has been united almost to a paper in defending existing conditions and opposing not only some radical plan for change but even all those mild reforms which friends of big money and the status quo, the latest of whom is Franklin Delano Roosevelt, have initiated for the double purpose of helping the Havenots and saving and preserving the system of the Haves.

We have all heard preachers and orators, and even impassioned senators roaring in favor of higher taxes on the poor, make that trite remark about Jesus being crucified again if he were alive today. The newspapers would have branded Jesus a Red and screamed for his arrest; their headlines, cartoons and editorials would have justified both trial and verdict. But one does not have to go that far back. If Jefferson stood up and read the Declaration of Independence in some public square in America today, writes Boston journalist Harold Putnam, he would forthrightly be jailed; he would be subpoenaed by the Dies committee, catalogued by the FBI, and smeared by the reactionary elements of the American press for giving 20th Century voice to some of the 18th Century quotations.

Lincoln believed that a laborer was entitled to the fruits of his labor. Wendell Philips believed that no man had the right to make a profit on the labor of any other man. Lincoln and Philips and Franklin D. Roosevelt believe in the right of labor to form unions, nevertheless unless you take a chance of being tarred and feathered if you are white, or lynched if you are black, you cannot speak for the labor unions in at least one-fourth of the area of the United States. (If you want proof, ask the Rev. Claude Williams or consult the records of the several civil liberties organizations or the findings of the La Follette committee; or read the labor press.)

The change that has come over America is this: that beneath the uproar the press made in our early history, the motivation was not money, it was not commercial. Today the press is motivated almost entirely by the motive of profit for itself and its backers. (William Allen White confirms this.) This profit motive not only affects the handling of all the news about labor, "defense" strikes, wage increases, the whole problem of taxation, a large part of the legislation of state and nation, but it also affects the news of world events.

Let me give you in perhaps too condensed form a few examples, each deserving a whole volume. They are chosen because in each instance the press fooled all the people; it was impossible for any American unless he was a reader of one of the half-dozen liberal weeklies, each with a circulation of thirty or forty thousand, to know the truth, whereas the falsehood spread by the slander press in two of the three cases led very close to bloodshed, if not open warfare.

From personal experience the case of Mexico was the most revealing. From 1909 to 1916 I had been a Pittsburgh newspaper reporter; from 1916 to 1933 I worked in Europe, but in 1927 the *Chicago Tribune* sent me to Mexico to make an investigation. I knew almost nothing about Mexico. I was able, therefore, to approach it with an unusually open and objective mind.

The first thing a newspaper man does on entering a foreign capital is to find out all he can from resident newspaper men (a procedure dubbed "ear-biting" by *New York World* writer Sam Spewack, now a successful playwright). I bit all possible ears.

The Hearst man in Mexico suggested that I keep quiet about a method I had learned in Syria of repelling bandit attacks on trains. There was a double rebellion on in Mexico, the usual revolt of generals bribed by U. S. and British oil money, plus, for a change, a revolt of the Cristeros, or militant Catholics, and Mr. Hearst's man wanted the Catholics to overthrow the republic.

The United Press man, with a pocketful of forged documents libeling everything Mexican, said: "I'll blow this government to pieces when I get to Texas."

The *New York Times* man said: "There is only one side to this story: we are all anti-Calles." Calles was then the great reformist president; later he got rich and became a reactionary.

An Associated Press man said: "I am hoping for victory (for the oil-company paid generals and the Cristeros) in three months."

There were nine or ten American newspaper correspondents in Mexico. All but one were in town. All were anti-government; all wanted the regime which had separated Church and State and which had given land to the peasants to be destroyed. This is what they told me:

"Calles is not a Mexican; he is an Arab, a Syrian. He is a Bolshevik. He gets his orders from Moscow. He is the American head of the Third International."

"Calles is a fanatic against the Roman Catholic Church. He is a high degree Mason. He is a leading member of the Ku Klux Klan, an agent of that American organization. Calles is stealing the wealth of the Church. He is not aiding the peasants. He is stealing the oil from the American oil companies, not restoring it to the people."

"Calles is a crook. All he is doing is making millions which he is investing in mines and in land in Sonora. He doesn't give a damn for the Mexican people."

These, and much worse, were the statements made to me by the entire press corps in Mexico City.

Colonel McLemore, publisher of a Texas paper, told me that Calles went to Moscow just before he became president and received Bolshevik instructions, was made head of the Third International, American section, and instructed about seizing the oil lands and also silver and copper mines (owned by Yanquis). Peter W. Collins, lecturer for the Knights of Columbus, said the same and worse, adding religious propaganda.

The American ambassador to Mexico told me confidentially and not for publication that the Mexican government was Bolshevik because it was dividing the land (stolen from the Mexicans by Standard Oil and other American corporations, only the ambassador said "bought," not "stolen") among the people of Mexico, under the Constitution of 1917.

A secretary of the U. S. embassy said when I mentioned the names of several Americans who had expressed sympathy for the regime, that these men and women were "skunks, liars and traitors to the U.S."

For about two weeks it was the same story: everyone from the embassy to the newspaper crowd, including the business men, the bankers, and the rich Mexican families to whom I was introduced by newspaper men,

agreed that Mexico was a branch of the Moscow government; that a murderous crime had been committed in dividing the land and restoring the
mines to the nation; that Calles was a crook; that the U.S. should march in
immediately either to restore the old system or take over the country forever.

Every reporter in Mexico was sending out this sort of news. Every line
of news out of Mexico was anti-Mexican. Everyone in America therefore
had his mind poisoned about Mexico. It was certainly possible in this
instance to fool all the people.

I became acquainted with Dr. Ernest Gruening, Charles W. Erwin,
Howard Phillips, Frances Toor and other Americans in Mexico. And this is
what they agreed on:

That everything said at the embassy was a lie.

That everything sent out by the entire American press corps (with the
exception of the news from the one man who was on vacation when I
arrived) was a lie.

That Calles was a great emancipator. He had never been to Moscow,
but had visited (Social-Democratic) Berlin in the early 1920's; that he was
not even a Socialist, but a sincere reformer. He was not fighting
Catholicism, but separating Church and State, taking the hierarchy out of
politics and land ownership....

Etcetera. Etcetera to the extent of millions of words, all the exact
opposite of the millions of words uttered by the embassy and the press
corps.

(It so happened that Calles some years later was deported by the
Cardenas regime because he too had eaten of the root of all evil and had
later devoted himself to making a million dollars rather than the general
welfare of the Mexican peons, but that is another story, and a much later
story. The time I was there Calles was a sort of Lincoln and F. D.
Roosevelt; a freer of peons and a great New Dealer, and he had not yet
deserted the people.)

When I returned to Chicago in the summer of 1927 I wrote a series of
20 articles on Mexico, a pro and con on ten subjects. For example, I wrote
one headed "Why the U. S. Should Seize Mexico" and another "Why the
U. S. Should Not Seize Mexico," giving a summary of the views of both
sides. The first half-dozen appeared in the *Chicago Tribune*, but after that
only those articles giving the anti-Mexican viewpoint were published. I
went back to Europe, glad to escape nearness to the Tribune editorial

rooms—which direct the policy in all things American, but which let European correspondents enjoy considerable liberty.

Years later in Congress the story was told how a few members, the liberals such as La Follette, Norris, Huddleston, Borah, aided by the *New York World* and *St. Louis Post-Dispatch* and the liberal weeklies *The Nation* and *The New Republic,* had exposed a plot of special interest to provoke war with Mexico in 1927. The reason I had been sent there was because the *Tribune's* owner, Col. McCormick, wanted a war correspondent on the spot when hostilities began, and he had fore-knowledge that the attack was ready.

From the day the native-Fascist dictator, Porfirio Diaz, was overthrown in Mexico, a movement began in the United States to destroy each anti-Fascist leader as he rose to power. Carranza, Villa, Madero, Calles and Cardenas have been victims of this war-mongering.

The newspapers never informed their readers of the motives behind these campaigns which advocated every action from temporary intervention to permanent occupation of Mexico. You had to read the independent weeklies or the non-fiction books (which sold a few hundred to a few thousand copies) to get the truth. The truth was that the following elements favored war:

1. The newspapers themselves, notably the Hearst press, the *Los Angeles Times,* some Texas and other border papers, the *New York Herald Tribune* and the *Chicago Tribune.* In every instance but the last, the newspaper owners were also owners of land, ranches, silver mines or oil fields in Mexico, or stocks and bonds which were affected by the existence of an anti-Fascist regime.

2. The Standard Oil, Royal Dutch Shell and other oil interests and also copper and other mining interests which stood to lose money if a Fascist regime were not restored, and which used their great advertising and political pressure in the newspapers and Congress for intervention and war.

3. The Knights of Columbus and other religious groups which opposed the anti-state church movement in Mexico.

The press, however, was the main war-mongering element.

President Wilson recognized this fact in 1916. In 1914 he had sent General Pershing into Mexico with orders to capture Villa, who had raided a border town and killed some Americans. (Later historical research established the fact the Villa raid had been organized by

Americans to provoke a war.) Villa eluded capture. The press campaign for war increased.

On 26 March 1916 President Wilson accused the press of lying about Mexico in order to start a war. He laid the campaign of falsehood to "vested interests," using a phrase coined by the Singletaxer Henry George—and added:

"The object of this traffic in falsehood is obvious.

"It is to create intolerable friction between the government of the United States and the de facto government of Mexico for the purpose of bringing about intervention in the interests of certain American owners of Mexican properties. (Unfortunately Mr. Wilson did not have the courage to name William Randolph Hearst, Harry Chandler, the Rockefellers, Lord Cowdray. If you don't name names you lose most of the effect.)

"The people of the United States should know the sinister and unscrupulous influences that are afoot, and should be on their guard against crediting any story coming from the border, and those who disseminate the news should make it a matter of patriotism and of conscience to test the source and authenticity of every report they receive from that quarter."

For 10 years the war movement simmered. In 1926 the State Department planted a fake story in all the papers via the Associated Press aimed to provoke trouble, if not war.

To summarize:

For the past 30 years American public opinion has been turned against Mexico by the press, pulpit, movies, and other means of inflaming emotions, at times it has aroused hatred and led to intervention, and almost to war.

The most important fact behind all these facts is this: the American newspaper and magazine press (with a handful of liberal publications the exception) united in fooling all America on the Mexican question and did it for commercial reasons. The owners, editors and publishers, were in most cases financially interested in exploiting Mexico or in taking the advertising money of Standard Oil and other exploiters of the poor Mexicans. For thirty years this press lied about Mexico and on three great occasions ran a tremendous war-mongering campaign. There were two invasions of Mexico (the seizure of Vera Cruz and Pershing's march after Pancho Villa) and a steady series of threatening notes from the State Department, which was under the domination of Standard Oil, but the annexation of Mexico, the ultimate objective of Hearst, Chandler,

McCormick, Patterson, Sedgwick and other war-mongers, did not take place, thanks to the protests of liberals.

All the American people were fooled all the time by a press motivated by nothing but personal interest in money.

The money motive was hidden from about 98 percent of the American people; but in this case it was plain to the two percent intelligent enough to doubt the truthfulness of the press and to seek the truth in the half-dozen honest newspapers and the free liberal magazines.

However, in two other great instances where the press fooled all the people, the motive was not as clear. It was a question of philosophy, of opposing a new political, social and economic system which abolished the profit or money motive, and could not be traced as easily as Hearst's million dollar investment in Mexico to Hearst's anti-Mexican policy. Only in the case of Paris newspapers, whose owners also owned six percent bonds of the Russian Tsarist empire, could it be said that forfeiture of dividend payment on these bonds resulted in a campaign of lies in the Paris press against the Soviet Russian system.

In America the two big series of fraudulent stories aimed to poison the minds of all the people were dated 1917-1920 and again 1939, although there never was a year from 1917 to 1941 when the majority of our newspapers and magazines did not falsify the news from Russia.

It is one of life's little ironies that the first great exposure of the lies of the press should have been written by two liberal newspapermen who later became the big money writers of the most reactionary among the most powerful newspapers of the country. Dated 4 August 1920 there appeared a pamphlet entitled "A Test of the News" written by Walter Lippmann (one-time member of the Socialist Party, and now syndicated columnist of the Republican *New York Herald Tribune*) and Charles Merz, now editor of the *New York Times*. Both were editors of *The New Republic*, which issued the pamphlet as a supplement. Ironically enough, the newspaper used to test the news—and show that it was a series of falsehoods—was the *New York Times*, of which Merz is now chief editorial writer. The *Times* was chosen not because it was the worst offender; on the contrary, it was one of the smallest offenders, and yet almost everything that appeared in that paper from March 1917 to March 1920 dealing with Russia was either a half-truth or a whole falsehood. Other papers published mostly whole falsehoods, and only the *New York World*, the *St. Louis Post-Dispatch*, and perhaps one or two others, printed news which could be called truthful.

The investigation showed that the *Times* reported the end of the Soviets, or their "tottering," exactly 91 times in three years; the *Times* surrendered Petrograd to the White Russian generals six times. The Russian capital was also "on the verge of capture" another three times; it was also burned down twice, and in state of panic another two times. Petrograd (according to the *Times* and that means according to the Associated Press and according to all the morning papers in America) revolted against the Bolsheviki six times. From 1919 to 1920 the *Times* (and all newspapers) reported victory after victory of Kolchak, Denikin, Wrangel and other generals, each of whom became the White (Russian) hope of the American press. Between them these hopes captured three or four times as many million Bolshevik soldiers as existed; yet, somehow, each of the generals suddenly disappeared in defeat or death.

Lippmann and Merz concluded that "the news as a whole is dominated by the hopes of the men who composed the news organizations.... In the large, the news about Russia is a case of seeing not what was, but what men wanted to see.... The chief censor and the chief propagandist were hope and fear in the minds of reporters and editors. They wanted to win the war; . . . the reporting of the Russian Revolution is nothing short of disaster. On the essential questions the net effect was almost always misleading, and misleading news is worse than none at all...."

Mr. Adolph Ochs, owner of the *Times,* probably owned no Tsarist bonds, as did Paris, London and other newspaper owners, but Mr. Ochs faked the news from Russia with the same enthusiasm. The Associated Press spread the lies to its more than a thousand clients. The United Press and Hearst International News Service served the same lies. It was indeed an exceptional day when a report from Frazier Hunt or the late Lincoln Eyre in the *World* and *Post-Dispatch* as much as hinted that there were two sides to the biggest story in the world. It is fair to say that the press fooled all the people on Russia.

Between the years 1922 and the present, after the Soviets revised their policy of not permitting foreign correspondents to visit the country, there were times when the news was pretty honest. One of the curiosities of this period is the pro-Bolshevik reporting of such men as William Henry Chamberlin of the *Christian Science Monitor,* Eugene Lyons of the United Press, Louis Fischer of the Jewish Telegraphic Agency and later of *The Nation,* also the magazine writer Max Eastman, each of them redder than the rose, each of them more Bolshevik than the Bolsheviki, and today four of the loudest snipers and lowest smearers of the same Soviet system. Like most brasscheckers they too went over to the side of Redbaiting, money, security, and status quo respectability. And like all renegades they have made the ideals and enthusiasms of their youth the main objective of their aging hatred.

There is no room here even to list the forgeries which accompanied the years of lying about Russia—such stories as the nationalization of women, ten thousand fake atrocities, the Zinovieff letter, for examples. This kind of palpable falsehood falls of its own weight; but the falsehoods of the Associated Press, the *New York Times*, and the rest of the papers which Lippmann and Merz exposed, had wings which carried them around the world.

One would think that in the two decades between the Russo-Polish war and the Russo-Finnish war the American public would have been enough disillusioned in its faith in the press, so that it would protest a repetition of the 1917-1920 situation. But, no. When the Finnish war began the entire American press (and when I say entire I make exceptions for one or two big papers) again succeeded in fooling all the American people.

Of the three greatest international lies of our generation, the 1917 European War lie that we were fighting "to make the world safe for democracy," the 1936 Spanish War lie, that it was a Christian Crusade, and the 1939 Russo-Finnish War lie, that the Russians bombed civilians in Helsinki, the capital of "poor little democratic Finland," the first two have already been exposed by the march of history.

American entry into the European War, the Nye-Vandenberg investigation proved beyond the doubt of anyone but the hired editorial writers of *Time* and the *New York Times*, was brought about by the cracking financial system and war pressure, largely through the efforts of the House of Morgan; the Fascist rebellion in Spain was paid for by the landowners, the Duke of Alba who is the British Duke of Berwick, Juan March and other big industrialists, the Rio Tinto mine owners in Madrid and London, and similar commercial interests. In 1939 there was every reason to believe that the campaign of falsehood against Russia was promoted by the Cliveden Set of Britain, by Chamberlain, by Rudolf Hess and other Nazis who were certain Britain and the United States could be linked with Germany in a "holy crusade against Bolshevism."

Beginning 30 November 1939, and continuing through December, the world press, and notably the American, succeeded in fooling the entire people with a continued story headlined *Bombardment of Civilians by*

Russians. Actually it would have been possible for intelligent readers who were not military experts to detect the fraud in a few words within the stories themselves. For instance, the *New York Times* story dated 1 December from Copenhagen stated that Russian planes were "aiming at the terminus" (page 1, paragraph 6), or in the subhead, "Air field bombed first" or the phrase "the airport at Malm (meaning Malmi) was hit." But so far as I know there is not more than one military expert to a million Americans, and if there are 130 military experts writing for the press, not one of them pointed out the obvious fact that an air raid which is directed at railroad stations, docks, shipping installations, airfields and other military objectives is not an air raid against civilians, it is not an atrocity, and that the headlines in all the American papers for months saying the opposite were falsehoods.

The London Times reported 2 December of four more raids, that "some of the bombs had set fire to the oil and naval docks . . . a few hit military objectives" but the United Press—which is still trying to explain away the greatest fake story in the history of the world, Roy Howard's False Armistice on 7 November 1918—sent a story from Helsinki which Roy Howard's *World-Telegram* (anti-C.I.O., anti-Newspaper Guild, anti-labor and pro-Howard profits) spread over its front page under these headlines

RUSSIANS BOMB HELISINGFORS;
FIRES RAGE; HUNDREDS KILLED

"Red planes," reported Norman B. Duell, "roared out of cloudy skies throughout the day and in mid-afternoon unloaded a hail of thermite bombs on the dazed population of Helsingfors ... inflicting hundreds of casualties.... Unofficial estimates of the dead in the first raids were as high as 200...."

It would be only fair to Mr. Duell to explain to readers that the United Press is the stingiest of news agencies and pays the lousiest salaries in the world; it pinches pennies, maintains an inadequate research and morgue department, spends as little as possible in getting news, and therefore skeletonizes its "cableese" so closely that correspondents abroad cannot recognize their stories when they appear expanded in the papers.

It is just possible that Duell never wrote anything at all about "a hail of thermite bombs on the dazed population." He may very honestly have reported that bombs intended for military objectives fall short or overshot the mark—as they did even when aimed by American aviators against

Germans. Mr. Duell does say that the bombs "were aimed at the railroad station, the harbor and the airport." He nowhere in the body of the story mentions anything in the frenzied UP story "lead," which may have been written in New York—the thermite attack on a dazed population—and it is possible that this falsehood was the work of the rewrite (or expansion) desk in New York.

The *New York Post* on 30 November carried the same story as the *World-Telegram*. On 1 December, its bombing story (from the UP) said "Soviet airplanes raided Helsinki three times today, dropping at least fifteen bombs on the working class district." This bombing of the proletariat is a new trick. When Franco deliberately destroyed the workers' homes in Malaga and the two workers' sections of Madrid, sparing the rich residential district where Fascists lived, there were no such headline stories. The *Post* gave the official death toll of 30 November raids as 72.

On 4 December the ex-liberal *Post* apparently felt it was not getting the circulation increases commensurate with its anti-Russian policy, whereupon it printed as vicious an atrocity story as any war has produced. Under an eight-column streamer

HELSINKI FEARS POISON GAS ATTACKS

it published a story which was not even a story but a rumor which the UP dignified by calling it a "report." "Reports spread that Russian fliers planned to bombard the city with poison gas," says the text on which the headline was written. That was all. There were no facts. But there was pure journalistic fraud. I would leave it to the members of the Newspaper Guild to say whether an anonymous story from Finland saying "reports spread" that the enemy "planned" anything was a story worth printing at all as fact, or using under an eight-column heading. The American reader is a headline reader. He sees the heading "poison gas" and that is usually all. He accuses the Russians of an atrocity, whereas in truth the United Press and its thousand papers committed the atrocity.

The Associated Press was not to be outdone in faking the news. It was the first to spread reports that Russian fliers opened up machine-gun attacks on civilians, and it repeated this story frequently even after official denials were issued and Voroshiloff's and Timoshenko's orders of the day instructing the air force not to bomb or endanger civilians were printed.

However, any honest man would have known that civilians were not machine-gunned or bombed because there were no results to prove it.

When there is bombing or machine-gunning of civilians there are thousands of casualties, as this war has proven. But the proof—which even many newspapers recognized at the time—were furnished much earlier. I know something, for example, of the machine-gunning of civilians by Italian Fascists, German Nazis and Spanish Falangistas on the roads out of Malaga in 1937. Here there were few if any anti-aircraft guns and here there was an intention to commit murder. The results were too horrible to describe. But in Finland you had the war correspondents in one breath proclaiming that the Finnish anti-aircraft guns were marvelous and that the Soviet planes came down low and machine-gunned many civilians. One of these two sorts of stories was false.

The truth? I am not a military expert, nevertheless I do not have to call upon General Hidalgo de Cisneros, commander in chief, who gave the orders to the Republican Spanish air force never to bomb civilians on Franco's side, nor do I need the corroboration of American correspondents on both sides to prove these facts:

1. That the Fascists bombed civilians because that is part of Fascist tactics;

2. That the anti-Fascists, including the Russians in Spain (700 men, including aviators, tank men, experts) never bombed civilians;

3. That when civilians are actually bombed there are heavy casualties, and

4. That the bombing of Barcelona was a dress rehearsal of all the Fascist nations for the present World War, that the raid of 16, 17 and 18 March was intended (as John Langdon-Davies wrote) to solve a technical problem, namely the possibility of creating panic and destroying a set area with all civilians within it, and that for Fascist war strategy it was a success.

"At eight past ten on the evening of 16 March 1938," reported Langdon-Davies, "the sirens of Barcelona sounded an alarm. Between that hour and 3.19 p.m., 18 March, there were 13 air raids which produced destruction in every district of Barcelona and in the surrounding towns. The total casualties were about 3,000 killed, 5,000 hospital cases, and roughly 20,000 minor injuries.... From the point of view of the Art of War the operation was the most satisfactory and potentially important. ... The aim was not casualties but the creation of panic.... The raids were not designed to attack or destroy military objectives; indeed the technique deliberately employed made this impossible except by pure accident...."

The population density of most cities is about the same—outside New York and Chinese cities perhaps. For the square block in Barcelona there are about as many people as in London, Berlin or Helsinki. The Fascist aviators raiding Barcelona did not concentrate on a certain sector; only a few planes came on many of the raids, and only a few bombs were dropped. And yet, although the objective was decidedly the bombing of civilians there was no intention to kill civilians: the main objective was to scare them, and concussion and noise actually achieved that objective, and killing was rather incidental. And yet there were 28,000 casualties: 3,000 dead taken out of the ruined buildings, and another 5,000 severely wounded, many of whom died in the hospitals, and 20,000 others wounded.

The Germans and Italians immediately ceased their attack. They could have continued it and perhaps forced a peace a year earlier for Franco, but they were not interested in that matter: what they were interested in was practice in war for use in the next war. It was a case of "pure research" as Langdon-Davies put it.

And now, look back on the reports from Finland—the reports which the press used to whip up a hysteria throughout America. What do we find: we find that when the war was nearly over President Kallio, appealing to America for aid, said that 470 persons had been killed in air raids in all of Finland, which would make the number of civilians killed in each raid one or two. And these raids were not made by three to twelve planes, as in Barcelona, but usually by squadrons. The dozen small raids on Barcelona, some with three planes, did not approximate one raid on Helsinki and the score stood at 28,000 casualties for Barcelona and five or six in Helsinki.

The entire American press knew that there had never been one raid against Finnish civilians. But the entire press was anti-Russian, and throughout the war it faked the news to fit its emotions.

In the summer of 1940 the Institute for Propaganda Analysis issued its report on the press coverage of the Russo-Finnish War. It confirmed my charge that there had been more faking, more propaganda and lies, than in any period in my 30 years of journalism. It concluded: "The simple fact is that the American press told less truth and retailed more fancy lies about the Finnish war than about any recent conflict."

No reason for the American press fooling the American people is given.

The reason simply is this: the press is anti-Russian.

But why is the press anti-Russian?

Because the Russian social and economic system is the opposite of the American social and economic system.

But: the American press does not admit it lies. It claims it tells both sides—the truth.

This is, of course, hypocrisy added to corruption.

It is my claim that the press, which could be the most powerful force in making this country over into an industrial democracy in which poverty would be unknown, wealth equitably distributed, every man certain of the minimum requirements of decent living (as well as the four freedoms) has, on the contrary, become the most powerful force against the general welfare of the majority of the people.

That the press has been throughout our history unfair to labor is now generally admitted. In the early or halcyon days of the Blue Eagle, the New Deal, the N.R.A. and the Wagner Act even commercial (but liberal) newspapers such as the *New York Post* and the *St. Louis Post-Dispatch* said editorially that one of the results of the great era then dawning would be the new policy of treating labor fairly in the newspapers—something which had not been done before. Reactionary papers by editorially promising better treatment of labor indirectly admitted their failure of the past. But even then most newspapers refused to realize that labor is more than the American Federation of Labor, or the Congress of Industrial Organizations or the Railroad Brotherhoods, although these three groups now include the 11 million more enlightened workers in industry. Labor is everyone who works for a living and does not distil a financial profit from the sweat of another man. Labor, as President Murray of the C.I.O. says, is America, and America is labor.

At an earlier period, when the industrial revolution was gaining great momentum, Abraham Lincoln—to whom the Republican Party, which is financed by such enemies of the people as Girdler, Weir, Grace, and Pew, pays lip service—said to these present-day American Fascisti:

"Thank God we have a country where working men have the right to strike. How else could they raise their standard of living?"—(Hartford, 5 March 1860)

"All that serves labor serves the nation. All that harms labor is treason to America. No line can be drawn between these two.

"If any man tells you he loves America yet hates labor, he is a liar. If any man tells you he trusts America yet fears labor, he is a fool. There is no America without labor.

"Labor is prior to, and independent of, capital. Capital is only the fruit of labor and could never have existed if labor had not existed. Labor is superior to capital and deserves much the higher consideration.

"Inasmuch as most good things are produced by labor, it follows that all such things ought to belong to those whose labor has produced them. But it has happened in all ages of the world that some have labored, and others, without labor, have enjoyed a large proportion of the fruits. This is wrong, and should not continue. To secure to each laborer the whole product of his labor as nearly as possible, is a worthy object of any good government." (Springfield, Illinois, 1 October 1854).

The American newspapers have made it a policy to distinguish between labor and the public, between the majority who work for a living and what the press calls "the people," and to build up in the mind of this identical stratum the idea that there is a distinction. President Heywood Broun, newspaper columnist and head of the Newspaper Guild (CIO) pointed this out. He said:

> *Particularly effective have been the splitting tactics of the conservatives. Much has been said about the rights of "the public" as opposed to the rights of "labor." Although the wedge has a cutting edge, it is essentially a phantom. The toilers and the general public are one and the same group. The small employee who writes to the paper with great pride that he always makes a point of going into a store if he sees a picket line outside, is not only playing the role of the meanest man on earth but actually deluding himself. He is cutting his own throat as well as those of his fellows.*

It is imperative that this be understood. The entire alibi of the press consists of its claim that it has championed the general welfare, the public, against one part of it, or labor. The press will never admit it has been the enemy of the people, yet in fighting labor it has actually been fighting the majority of the people, and therefore the general public it pretends to serve. An honest editor will admit it. William Allen White, president of the American Society of Newspaper Editors, did say in a public speech that "Labor as a class distrusts us. It wouldn't distrust us without reason.... It is so easy to policy the news. Indeed it is hard not to policy the news when the news is affected with a vital bread-and-butter interest to the capitalist who controls a newspaper." But most editors and publishers will not admit this, and the majority suppressed this part of Mr. White's recent address.

I do not know of anyone who has made a parallel study of the rise of labor in America and the rising anger of the press against labor, although considerable references can be found in Yellen's "American Labor Struggles." It is interesting to learn, for instance, that when the depression of 1873 led to the railroad strike of 1877 and when Federal troops were for the first time in history called out in peacetime to suppress a strike, the *New York Times* (issue of 26 July) used the following words as synonyms for working men: "hoodlums, thieves, looters, Communists, agitators, law-breakers, bummers, idiots and terrible fellows." On 24 July this same news-paper had printed a Chicago story under a subheadline: THE CITY IN POSSESSION OF COMMUNISTS, and it was at this time that the *Chicago Tribune*, referring to the thousands of wandering unemployed, made the editorial suggestion that a pinch of arsenic put on sandwiches given them by housewives would solve that problem.

In the Pullman strike, led by Eugene V. Debs, the governor of Illinois, Altgeld, protested that "the newspapers' accounts have in many cases been pure fabrications, and others wild exaggerations. You have been imposed on in this matter." This statement he made to President Cleveland, telling him not to send troops, but the General Managers Association had more influence than the governor. The press of the entire nation waged a cam-paign against Altgeld, calling him a "revolutionary anarchist" for siding with labor.

In the Ludlow massacre of 1913, when militia attacked a tent colony, murdering women and children and burning many to death, the press sided with the Rockefellers, who were advertisers. The *New York Times* attacked the victims of the murderous militia and upheld "the right to work" which Pegler, the National Association of Manufacturers, the Committee to Uphold Constitutional Government, and other native Fascisti maintain today, along with the majority of newspapers.

And to this very day for every hundred Americans who believe the Haymarket bombing in Chicago in 1886 was an anarchist outrage there is only one who knows the right and wrong of that event and the fact it was a culminating point in the fight for an eight-hour day for labor. Long before the bomb was thrown—by a person who was never named or cap-tured, although innocent labor leaders were hanged—the press fought for the ten-hour and twelve-hour workday, and for low wages for labor. The historian refers continually to "the steady barrage kept up by the press" against labor and the eight-hour day idea, to "the relentless abuse by news-papers, periodicals, and pulpit."

In the Lawrence, Massachusetts, mill strike the press accepted as fact the police statement that strikers plotted to use dynamite. The *New York Times* said that "when a striker goes on picket duty with a revolver in his pocket there is murder in his heart. When strikers use or prepare to use dynamite they display a fiendish lack of humanity." The dynamite was planted by an enemy of the strikers and an undertaker! The *Times* and the rest of the press did not retract their murderous editorials. When the strikers won, the press began a tremendous campaign against the Industrial Workers of the World because it saw in this new movement a threat against big business and profits, which the conservative American Federation of Labor did not menace. (In 1936 the same press which had attacked the Knights of Labor a generation ago, then the AFL, then the IWW, turned to praise the AFL when it attacked the CIO as too radical, too dangerous to big business and profits.)

In September 1919, the American press again fooled all the people with its stories of the police strike and the "heroic" actions of Governor Calvin Coolidge. The truth came out later—too late—in the report of the citizens' committee headed by Banker J. J. Storrow. But one of the worst conspiracies by the newspapers to break a strike and fool the entire American people occurred in 1919 when the workmen of Morgan's great U.S. Steel Corporation went out. The entire Pittsburgh press lied in the morning and lied in the evening—and since these papers also supplied the AP, UP and INS, the three main services, the falsehood was spread into every village of the nation. But no reader of the newspapers knew that the Farmers' National Bank, the Mellon banks, and other corporations affiliated with the steel corporations held mortgages or notes of all news-papers and controlled their policies. The press helped break the strike. It did labor little good to have this press corruption exposed years later in books.

One of the significant things about the San Francisco strike of 1934 was the boast made in *Editor & Publisher* and in many newspaper editorials that the press broke this strike. In 1934 upon receipt of a cable from Hearst, who was in London, the newspaper publishers organized and planned a propaganda campaign—in which falsehood was a part—to break the labor movement. Hearst's order to brand all labor "Red" or Communist, was carried out. Similar editorials and "news" stories were car-ried in all papers—by journals which had denounced German and Italian and Russian newspapers as carrying similar editorials and news stories on order of official press bureaus. The publishers ganged up on General Hugh Johnson, who came to California as a mediator; they united with the police in bloody raids which clearly violated the Constitution, and they applauded the violence, bloodshed, lawlessness of their side while charging the same methods to labor, which had refrained from using them. Although the trade unions passed a resolution condemning the participating newspapers as enemies and liars and suggested a boycott, it is unfortunately true that labor did not stop reading the press which had betrayed its interests.

It is clear from a summary of the journalistic history of a few big strikes, that the press has always been anti-labor. It is also true that despite the promises of 1933 to be objective and impartial, if not friendly, in the future, the press has failed the majority of the people again. In 1936 in an attempt to smash the CIO it tried to bolster the AFL but failed in both. I do not believe there has been a month in the past five years without at least one editorial in the *New York Times* demanding the emasculation or repeal of the Wagner Act, which labor considers its Magna Carta.

After June 1940, when a defense program was begun by the government, the press, including isolationist newspapers which did not favor this program, used every strike as a club for beating labor. In 1942 government investigations showed that there had been a sit-down by capital, that the aluminum, rubber, airplane production and other programs had been sabotaged by Mellon's Alcoa, Knudsen's and the DuPonts' General Motors, Grace's Bethlehem and Morgan's U.S. Steel. There had been a loss of a thousand times as many man-days due to corporations refusing to expand plants and convert them to war needs as there had been in strikes, but the press (with the usual exception of a few small city papers and two or three metropolitan journals) blamed labor. Papers used headlines such as these: "DEFENSE STRIKES RESPONSIBLE FOR LOSS OF 100 BOMBERS." Official government reports showing corporation sabotage could have resulted in a truthful head saying: "BIG BUSINESS STRIKES RESPONSIBLE FOR LOSS OF 10,000 BOMBERS." But if you will read all the papers you will find the former type of headline in the commercial press, the latter type in the small, liberal weeklies.

In the Spring of 1941—with the defense program almost a year old and with labor offering numerous plans for conversion of plants and greater production of planes, tanks and guns, which the dollar-a-year men in Washington, most of them members of the National Association of Manufacturers, refused to consider because it would lessen the profits of their companies—the Federated Press, a labor news agency, made a survey of the opinion of labor editors. Press unfairness was taken for granted. Alexander Crosby asked editors: "Have the daily papers in your area shown increased unfairness to labor in recent months?" Almost all of them replied "Yes." In only six cities was the press found not guilty of whipping up public opinion against labor. These were: Cincinnati; Cheyenne; Superior; Elizabeth, N.J.; Springfield and Rockford, Illinois. The *Kansas City Journal* and *Milwaukee Post* were recommended for fairness.

Crosby found there was no perceptible variation either geographically or by size of city. Large and small, east and west, it was the same story of increasing labor-baiting by the daily commercial press. If the survey did nothing else, it showed that America's labor editors today clearly recognize that the press and the employers are united and that both are their enemies. These labor editors are the men who could publish a truly free press if they had the money and if the demand were big enough.

If there is any other cause for falsehood in the press except money—and by money I mean everything from a paid ad to a community of interest with wealth and power—I have not been able to find it. On the other hand, it is a simple matter to point out that fact, which I am sure is unknown to 99 percent of the 40 million people who read Hearst newspapers and magazines, that Hearst is a manufacturer, a mine owner, an exploiter of Mexican peons and American industrial workers, a hard-fisted and hardhearted boss, an enemy of unions in the mines and mills he inherited or purchased. Since this is true, how can one expect fairness to labor in Hearst's 20 newspapers and dozen magazines, his newsreels and his radio stations?

In addition to the Mexican ownings, already mentioned, Hearst controls the Homestake Mining Co. in the Black Hills of South Dakota; he owns vast fruit and vegetable lands in California and a canning company, and has huge investments in Peruvian copper. (Curiously enough Hearst's anti-British and pro-German policy is based not on Irish-Catholic hatred of Britain—Hearst himself is not a Catholic but Mrs. Hearst is—but on a more substantial fact: the British opposition to the Cerro de Pasco Investment Company in a fight to control Peruvian resources.)

At home, and more particularly at Homestake, Hearst (according to findings of George Creel and the Walsh Committee on Industrial Relations) locked out 2,000 miners in 1909 and after breaking their strike made them sign a pledge never to join a union. Hearst maintained a seven-day week, 10-hour day. A Catholic bishop who demanded that workmen be permitted to attend church Sundays was attacked in the Hearst press and driven out of town—although at the same time Hearst was the chief journalistic propagandist for the Catholic religion in America. Paul Peterson of Salt Lake City, Utah Federation of Labor president, did not dare visit North and South Dakota towns except in the disguise of a traveling salesman. He found that since 1877 about $400 million in gold had been taken out of Hearst's Homestake mine. The towns were terrorized. Men with guns drove Peterson out of one after another. The American Federation of Labor tried to call secret meetings of miners; it tried to place announcements for union meetings as advertisements, but the small town publishers told him they would be put out of business if they printed anything about unions. Hearst officials said: "We've run this section for years and we won't tolerate labor organizers."

This is the true picture of Hearst, employer of labor, the picture which the film *Citizen Kane* skipped.

And here is part of a document on file in the New York Supreme Court Building in New York City; it is the last part of the *Amended Answer* which the magazine *Friday* filed when Hearst sued for libel. Of Hearst as anti-labor, the document says:

With respect to the Hearst newspapers, their strikebreaking, "Red scare" and news distortion policies:

73. The policy of the Hearst papers, over a period of many years, has been to take a position against all strikes called by organized labor, without reference to the causes or merits thereof; and has been generally inimical to the advancement of the rights of labor, including the establishment of labor's rights to collective bargaining.

74. In the publicity given by the Hearst papers to strike situations over a period of many years, there has consistently been a bias in favor of the employers' side . . . and against the position of labor, regardless of the merits of any such strike....

75. The policy of the Hearst papers on many occasions has been to inflame public sentiment against strikes and to recommend and incite violent actions by the public and the use of police and armed forces for the purpose of breaking strikes and eliminating picket lines.

76. In connection with their policy of recommending strikebreaking the Hearst papers have on many occasions published false, misleading and distorted accounts . . . for the purpose of turning public opinion against the position of labor in such strikes.

77. Over a period of many years, the Hearst papers, pursuant to the policies and instructions formulated and established for them by the plaintiff William Randolph Hearst, have been regularly engaged in the practice known generally as "Redbaiting"; namely, falsely and maliciously accusing persons or organizations whose activities or policies were not approved by the plaintiff, William Randolph Hearst, of being "Reds" or "Communists."

78. Over a period of many years . . . the Hearst papers . . . have regularly engaged in attempts to discredit and injure newspapers, organizations, public figures, and others having political or other beliefs and policies differing from those of the plaintiff, William Randolph Hearst, and to cause doubt upon the sincerity and the truth of their beliefs, policies and public utterances, by falsely and maliciously accusing such newspapers, organizations, public figures, and others, of being "Reds," or "Communists," "members of the Communist Party," "tools of the Communist government," "fellow travelers," or the equivalent.

This man Hearst who is beyond question anti-labor and uses his newspaper chain against labor, has for rival one Roy Howard, successor to Scripps (a pro-labor publisher who founded the Scripps-Howard chain). The other large chains are the Gannett newspapers and the McCormick-Patterson papers, not exactly a chain, but even more powerful than Gannett's.

In addition to Roy Howard, the men responsible for the perversion of the United Press and Scripps-Howard chain are W. W. Hawkins, chairman of the board, and John Sorrels. In addition to an editorial campaign against the best interests of labor, the chain syndicates the anti-labor writings of Pegler and other columnists. It had two liberal pro-labor columnists once, Heywood Broun and Harry Elmer Barnes, but did not renew contracts with them. It will not publish any liberal or pro-labor columns.

The heirs of Joseph Medill of the *Chicago Tribune* are: Colonel McCormick whose *Chicago Tribune* has 1,000,000 daily circulation and is a power in politics in a dozen Midwestern States; Captain Joseph Medill Patterson whose *New York Daily News* has 2,000,000 daily and 4,000,000 Sunday; Eleanor Patterson of the *Washington Times-Herald* .

Whereas "Lusty" Scripps was an honest liberal, and during his lifetime was fair to labor in all Scripps newspapers, and Hearst never a friend of the people, Patterson during his college years was completely won over to humanitarianism and joined the Socialist Party; he wrote Socialist tracts and preached good will to men. After he established the *Daily News* in 1919 he sometimes showed sparks of the old Socialist past, but after the collapse of the economic system in 1929 he became more and more reactionary, until he was not only appeasing the Fascist dictators but actually preaching Fascist ideology wrapped up in the American flag and surmounted with the slogan "Our Country, Right or Wrong."

Of the whole journalistic lot, Hearst, Howard, McCormick and Patterson, it may be said that there is not a spark of social conscience left in them; it never existed in most, and it soured to Fascism in one. These men who own the great news chains which make public opinion are all socially and economically illiterate; they are all socially irresponsible; they are all motivated by nothing above the pocketbook; they are doing nothing to make America a better nation and nothing to advance the welfare of the American people although they are in a position to do more than anyone except a liberal president when he is supported by a liberal majority in Congress—a situation that has rarely happened in our history.

The People Don't Know

The misinformation presented by the media to the American people in the immediate years after the end of World War II angered Seldes. He believed they were being led into thinking that World War III was not only likely, but inevitable. He believed that they were lied to about the accomplishments of Eastern Europe after the war. He also believed that they were not told the truth about the movements on the Left in Europe and elsewhere around the post-war world. All of this is described in the final chapter of Seldes' 1949 book The People Don't Know.

THIS AUTHOR agrees with Dr. Geroid T. Robinson who said that "Never did so many know so little about so much."

Dr. Robinson, onetime member of the great secret Office Of Strategic Services (OSS), made this remark in his address on "Education for Better Understanding" at the conservative *New York Herald Tribune* 1945 Forum. He was referring at the moment to "all the American misunderstandings of Russia." Curiously enough, two years later when the "preventive war" crowd was riding high and William Christian (sic) Bullitt was screaming madly for the use of the atom bomb to destroy Russian civilians—"atomize the Russians" was the battle cry—and the Churchill policy of "containment" of ideas (as well as nations) had become the paramount policy of the Truman administration, a survey made by Princeton University showed that 38 million Americans of voting age "don't know at all what kind of a government Russia has" (William L. Shirer, *Herald Tribune*, 23 February 1947).

The Robinson strictures can be applied not only to Russia and the Eastern nations—against which the West, and most notably the United States has hung not an iron but a newspaper curtain of suppression and silence—but also to China and all of Asia; in fact to most of the world.

Defenders of the press, the medium which should have prevented this deplorable state of affairs, like to shift the blame on the people themselves. People get the government they deserve; people get the newspaper press they deserve. Or want. The people do not want to be informed, they want to be amused, and that is why they spend fifteen hours listening to the comic programs on the radio for each hour they spend listening to news broadcasts or any sort of educational program. Moreover, the survey of a town by the American Newspaper Publishers Association revealed 82 percent of the men and 70 percent of the women reading the comic strip "Dick Tracy" while only 28 percent of the men and 25 per cent of the women read "even one paragraph of the most important news story that day," according to Dr. Gallup (*National Municipal Review*, December 1947). Among other amazing (and frightening) discoveries by the Gallup Poll (on nonpolitical, noncontroversial questions) was the fact that at least a quarter of the American people were unable to locate any one of the Eastern nations on the map. People of voting age only were asked. Thirteen percent, one in eight, knew where Bulgaria was, 17 per cent could locate Romania, 18 percent Hungary, 22 percent Yugoslavia, and 25 percent Czechoslovakia. This at a time 99 percent of the press, to be conservative, was attacking these nations as "satellites" of Russia.

Of course our educational system is also to blame. It fails in arousing an interest in knowledge, to make education itself something greatly to be desired. It turns out millions of high school and college graduates who prefer Dick Tracy and Blondie to information about the Marshall Plan— whose purpose could be stated by only 25 percent of "a representative group of citizens from coast to coast" interviewed by the Gallup organization 1 November 1947.

The people of many countries do not know what is going on in the world and little, if anything, about social, economic, and political forces, causes, and pressures.

The Western world does not even know that one of its most powerful leaders, Churchill, dipped into the propaganda cesspool of Nazi Journalism and came up with the phrase by which it belittles and attacks the Eastern world, the phrase "iron curtain," which implies secrecy and ignorance.

On the other hand, the Eastern world reads every day about the troubles and disgraces of its rival—the economic recessions, the impending collapse of the economic system, the injustices, witch-hunts, crimes of violence, and the lynchings in Alabama, Mississippi, and Georgia.

The Western world likewise reads about the troubles and disgraces of its rival—the economic failures in the planned economies and impending collapse; religious persecution, the denials of civil liberties.

But one of the great differences between East and West is the functioning of the most powerful agency for information—and misinformation—the controlled press of the East and the free press of the West.

The East does not permit the kind of freedom which the press of the United States advocates: the total freedom of the owner and publisher to make of his newspaper an organ of reaction, to be entirely irresponsible, to use free enterprise for his personal gain—financial, political or otherwise—and to fail in all his social obligations, as the Commission on Freedom of the Press brilliantly pointed out. Leaders of the East look upon the press as a part of its system of government, an organ of the body politic, a means to an end, and say so frankly and honestly. The East claims this is good for the nation—it makes no hypocritical pretense at "freedom of the press" which means unbridled freedom for the private owners of the press (and their interests) and no one else.

TEN IMPORTANT FACTS, TRENDS

There is also the important matter of states of mind, of attitudes. What should be the relationship of the editor and publisher (and other manipulators of public opinion) to the events which make up the history of the cold war? The truth was admitted by C. D. Jackson of *Time* magazine, who in his contribution to the book, "Public Opinion and Foreign Policy," edited by Lester Markel of the *Times*, supplied the chapter, "Assignment for the Press," in which he stated (on page 180):

"In this book it has already been argued—and it is hoped, demonstrated—that in the cold war of words all our deeds abroad, all our writings, all our publications, all our expressions of thought must be weighed according to their propaganda impact."

The vice-president of *Time* does not say that our deeds, our writings, our publications, must consist of propaganda as some persons have interpreted it, but that we must at all times be conscious of the propaganda value of what we do, say, and publish. But who can doubt that with this consciousness of effect the American newspaper and magazine press (and the radio and other means of making public opinion) have already done their part in the cold war not only by an attitude, a prejudgment of cause and effect, but by actually manipulating facts, news documentation, happenings, interviews, speeches, and other actions and expressions, for propaganda purposes. When we weigh our writings and publications "according to their propaganda impact" we are no longer engaged in the business of the free press.

In reviewing the volume to which Messrs. Markel and Jackson contributed, Edwin D. Canham suggested that in his 1949 inaugural address President Truman should have added a fifth point to his four for world economic recovery: "one without which the other four cannot hope to succeed. The fifth point is the adequate informing of public opinion at home and abroad."

Mr. Canham, president of the American Society of Newspaper Editors and editor of the *Christian Science Monitor,* one of the very few newspapers of our country generally placed on an honor roll, admits that "there are large areas of ignorance of policy at home, and great misunderstanding and suspicion abroad."

There is no place in this volume for the misunderstandings and suspicion abroad, although it might be said in passing that the Voice of America, so proudly hailed in Congress and blessed with so many millions, is not regarded in Europe as following the code of ethics laid down by Elmer Davis when he operated the Office of War Information. It is accused not of voicing propaganda daily, which it does, but of frequent falsehoods and distortions, whereas the OWI by Davis's order adhered to strict truth as a weapon in foreign affairs.

As for the "adequate informing of public opinion at home," on matters abroad, the present writer would like to offer a challenge to the experts who contributed to the Markel volume and to all editors and publishers.

The challenge consists of the following ten statements, some of which include the most important facts about the European world today as they affect the life, liberty and pursuit of happiness of the American people, and some of which include the most important trends which are equally worthy of space, perhaps even front page space, in our sky-vaunted free press. Some of these statements were put in the form of questions in the introduction to this volume, and some of them have been answered in the text.

1. The entire world has moved to the Left—part Socialist, part Communist, part just Left. The Right, all the way from conservative to fascist, has been defeated almost everywhere. The status quo and reactionary countries, such as Italy and France, Portugal and Greece, are merely held to the Right by American money and pressure, will go Leftward when these forces diminish or cease. Nothing is more important in history than this Leftward trend of the world (including Asia and Africa) and almost nothing is written about it because it is contrary to the American status quo policy (overwhelmingly approved by the American people in several Gallup polls, and endorsed by almost all our editors and publishers despite their public editorial policy of "progressiveness").

2. There will not be a war, or there will not be a successful war for the West because the West has no allies in Europe. Because no one will fight in Europe. Because the labor unions will oppose war from any side and there will be civil wars, or revolts, or sitdown strikes or general strikes in almost every nation of the European Western bloc if war is declared.

3. Nothing can buy friends or allies. The Marshall Plan has not made friends or allies. It has checked the Left temporarily in such countries as Italy, France, and Greece, subsidizing or "freezing" reaction, the status quo, or even a form of fascism.

4. The Marshall Plan has not been a great success from the American viewpoint either. Where it has insisted on influencing the economy of a foreign country, such as Belgium, it has supplied goods rather than raw materials, thereby making workers idle, causing unrest, promising future trouble. By blockading the East it has done more to slow up European recovery than any other action.

5. The great success of the planned economy bloc, the Eastern nations, which have not had Marshall Plan aid, is one of the great (unwritten and unpublished) news stories of our time. Poland and other nations have surpassed pre-war production, Italy and other Marshall nations have not done so well despite the millions poured into them.

6. Not only the planned economy of European nations, but the mutualizing of national economies, is also beginning to change the face of the world.

7. The standard of living, a great test for civilization, is rising under the socialist system of Great Britain and under the planned systems of all

Eastern nations. The standard of living to Marshal Tito, Matyas Rakosi and other Eastern leaders also means culture, and culture begins with the elimination of illiteracy. More has been done in three or four years of the new regimes than in a century of reactionary regimes. The people of the planned economies buy and read more books per person than Americans.

8. The majority of the people of every Eastern country, that is, the industrial worker and the farmer, has been favored by the new regimes; most of them are better off than under the old regimes and all of them will be far ahead of their fathers' generation and eventually far ahead of the citizens of all other countries of Europe upon the completion of the various second and third plans—most of the first plans have been fulfilled and there is every reason to believe the present ones will succeed.

9. The American press campaign and the demarche made in the United Nations by certain countries including those whose regimes are pseudo-fascist if not purely fascist, charging Eastern nations with religious persecution is based on falsehood. The truth is that all the news stories which make the American front pages indicate a conflict—the separation of Church and State; real, total separation, even more complete than in the American system. If the Churches of Hungary, Yugoslavia, Czechoslovakia, Poland and other countries confined themselves to preaching the Gospels there would be no conflict.

10. The Vatican is engaged in one of the greatest political battles of its existence. Always dedicated to the preservation of the status quo, when not actually reactionary, the Vatican realized years ago that the world has changed and that the crisis it faces today is greater than that of the Reformation— greater than any crisis in ancient or modern history. The Vatican therefore is engaged in the cold war with the Kremlin—at times it leads, at times it tells Britain and the United States and of course all its Catholic satellite nations what to do; but at times it reverts to the old policy of adapting itself and making compromises with the Kremlin. Some journalists in Rome foresee the Vatican itself adopting a new course distinctly to the Left. The July 1949 excommunication of Communists indicates otherwise. But the main fact is the tremendous activity of the Vatican in European and American politics, education, the labor movement, and all important nonreligious matters.

And besides these ten journalistic subjects for reporting and documentation I would like to offer another, an intangible, psychological, and philosophical subject for other hands: it is the release not only of the creative forces of the people of many countries, but, as Tito put it, the release of the genius of the people. This has followed the defeat of fascism and the institution of new types of governments. It may not be a front page news story but it is the greatest thing that has happened in Europe since the war.

EDITORIAL NOTE: "EPPUR SI MUOVE!"

The present writer does not believe in dispensing editorial opinion. Let the facts speak for themselves," the Euripidean admonition, seems good enough today to be the one and only guide for the making of a truly free press. If the facts were left to speak for themselves it is understood that they would be presented honestly, that the facts on both sides would be given, that there would be no attempt, as at present, to choose facts which the editor agrees with and suppress the others, or to engage in any one or more of the thousand ways of manipulating facts.

It is one of the tragic ironies of our time that the one chain press exposed from 1914 on, as given to presenting considerable falsehood, the Hearst newspapers, place the word "TRUTH" in capital letters at the top of their editorial pages, and that the Hearst rivals in yellow journalism, the Scripps-Howard 19, place on their masthead the quotation: "Give light and the people will find their own way."

The one and only function of a newspaper should be to publish the news. This is possible. At times it has been done.

Historically the American press has never been for the general welfare. In the 1850's only one New York newspaper, the *Evening Post* was Abolitionist. The *Tribune* opposed slavery. Other journals either condoned or supported it, and published many and weighty editorial arguments aimed to soothe the conscience of slaveholders and others who lived on human misery. Throughout the hundred-odd years of the industrial revolution the American press was on the side of the small minority, the employers, and opposed to the great majority, the industrial workers. The 12-hour day at $1 a day was upheld before the Civil War, and the 10-hour day afterwards. It was hysteria created by the press which was largely responsible for the Haymarket bombing in Chicago, the newspapers of that city being all engaged in fighting the movement for the 8-hour day.

And more recently the press (with of course the usual exceptions, the small percentage of *pro bono publico* papers like the *St. Louis Post-Dispatch*) fought the TVA more bitterly than they still fight the MVA and CVA and other vast projects which might harm the private power and light corporations. Every American knows that the American press, 85 to 95 percent strong, fought not only FDR but the New Deal and later the Truman Fair Deal, notably those parts of it which the National Association of Manufacturers, the United States Chamber of Commerce and other business interests have marked for destruction. Throughout our history the press lined up 90 to 99 percent against such general welfare measures as government operation of power and light and government attack on the impure food and bad medicine makers. Every bill for the public which involved profits, even when those profits came from fake tuberculosis and cancer cures, was opposed by the majority of American newspapers.

The American press opposes the general welfare of the American people and it opposes those who devote their lives for the same cause in other lands. Thus the vast propaganda machine which our editors and publishers control, is set in motion time and again, frequently with recourse to religious hysteria, against all the rulers of the Eastern nations of Europe who—whether we like their ideology or not—have obeyed the American democratic ideal of the greatest good for the greatest number, the farmers and the industrial workers. Both Marshal Tito in Yugoslavia and Matyas Rakosi in Hungary, to give examples on the opposite sides of the Cominform rift, have given land to the farmers, and through the nationalization of industry, have provided a better living for the industrial workers. It is true that certain people have suffered—certainly the owner of a vast steel plant has reason for anger—but the millions are better off, and the fact (suppressed in our press) that the Eastern nations have surpassed production and the pre-war standard of living in three heartbreaking years of reconstruction is the best proof. Tito, Rakosi, all the other heads of the so-called "satellite" nations have raised the general welfare of the majority of people. None has stolen a billion dollars—as the Kung-Soong-Chen-Chiang Kai-shek clique has done. None has taken a cent for himself as Hitler and Mussolini and Franco and all the fascists have done. But because they have attacked the most sacred of all the golden idols of the American press, the money or profit system, they have been universally attacked, vilified, and of course lied about in morning and night editions, year after year.

The result, as expressed by American experts on public opinion and agreed on by even some editors, is that despite our great educational system and despite our free press we are among the most misinformed people of the world.

The reader who at this late moment expects the writer to conclude with editorial suggestions on how all the wrongs complained of can be righted will have to be disappointed. Everything that can be said on this subject has been said.

In fact, all the answers to every book of this sort—whether it deals with the press or politics, or with any phase of human endeavor and behavior as it affects the lives and affairs of other people—have already been written. A few modern technicalities can always be added, but none as important as the suggestions made on Mt. Sinai or in the Sermon on the Mount. We shall have a free—meaning honest—press in America when we have 1,750 editors and publishers of daily newspapers godlike enough to do what the vast majority of people of all faiths and lands have always acknowledged to be their golden rule of life, but never in all history followed. One would be naive indeed to expect the Hearst or Howard outfit to take the lead.

The only note of optimism derives from the fact that the world does move. *Eppur si muove!* For Galileo it moved in circles; for us the well-known circular world moves in a direction, and that direction is Left, the direction where the greatest good for the greatest number is the political, social, and economic goal, as it was for Jefferson and all who believe in the "general welfare." The world does move in the direction of the general welfare. It moves everywhere except in fascist countries, and fascism cannot last. It moves in Britain under the Labour Party, it moves in Yugoslavia under a system the Cominform attacks and it moves in other Eastern lands under a system the Cominform approves. It moves in China and throughout the entire East. There have been moments when it has moved in the Vatican. It moves in the United States under the Fair Deal, and it moves in certain Latin American countries faster than in others. It moves in all European countries, no matter if the regime is a Catholic Party coalition, a Right coalition, a Left coalition, or even a monarcho-fascist coalition as in Greece. Underneath the Marshall Plan dollars there is a movement which this weight of gold cannot stop from going liberal, democratic, or Left.

Nothing can stop the progress of an informed people. Even the American newspaper publishers proclaim this slogan. But nothing can stop the progress of any people, and although the American press will not inform the American people, the world will continue to progress nevertheless. The era of the New Deal was an era of great progress toward the Constitutional idea of the general welfare. It was achieved despite the press, despite the opposition of almost the entire press. We shall continue to make great progress despite the press. There is reason for impatience; but no cause for despondency.

The Education of
a Newspaper Man

The lies of the world press during the Spanish Civil War helped to inspire Seldes to start up his own newsletter, In fact. *It was Seldes' hope that it would reach a wide readership, its peak circulation was 176,000 in 1947, but that number dwindled to 55,000 three years later and he was forced to suspend publication. Seldes wrote about the lessons he learned in* Tell the Truth and Run.

THE TENSE little time between the Spanish War and the Second World War was devoted by many people, who recognized that the first conflict was obviously the prologue to the second, to an attempt to alarm apathetic nations. In Europe as well as in America thousands of persons, political leaders, journalists, writers, artists, and poets felt compelled to act.

It was quite plain to many that there was a new enemy threatening our world—international Fascism—and that in Spain it was merely tasting blood for the first time. It was already clear to some that the Anti-Comintern Pact nations led by Hitler, Mussolini, and Franco were planning to take over, establish a hegemony of terrorism, liquidate millions of people, and substitute a new dark barbarian age for our democratic civilization. All the beginnings were visible, and yet, because of false propaganda, because of Redbaiting and witch hunting, complicated also by a religious issue, and the failure of the non-Fascist non-Communist world press to see beyond its own interests, the free world could not be aroused to the danger.

When in 1937 I wrote in *Scribner's* a warning that Fascism would declare war in 1939, it was neither a supernatural revelation nor a lucky guess; it was merely reporting what was common knowledge in Madrid and elsewhere. It was so well known that our embassy attaches, Colonel Fuqua and Captain Griffis, in Valencia were able to warn the War Department in Washington.

When in my 1938 book on civil liberties "You Can't Do That," I listed the nations of Europe in the order Hitler would attack and conquer them (Czechoslovakia, then Russia, then France, eventually Britain and America) and got only one wrong, I was not playing the ouija board or risking very much. The situation was urgent and evident. But we had to warn America repeatedly. Several war correspondents in Madrid felt it their duty to arouse the non-Fascist world; almost none was satisfied with just being there, adventuring near a battle. It was not a call to messianic undertaking; it was not a demand to do crusading journalism; it was merely a very human impulse to cry out when one sees a building catch fire—and this building we saw was the vast structure of our Western civilization. We saw clearly, or we thought we did.

But there soon followed two events which for me were as confusing as they were challenging. Both had to do with Soviet Russia. On 21 August 1939, the German Government announced that its trade agreement with the Soviets had been followed by a mutual non-aggression pact, and the non-Communist world was shocked to its deepest stratum. The Nazi attack upon the European democracies in September was followed by the Soviet attack on Finland on 30 November. On both occasions the outside world was almost unanimous in expressing its outraged indignation at Soviet actions.

In this almost universal and at times hysterical exhibition I found that I could not join. In Spain I had seen Soviet Russia alone among the great nations fighting for democracy and, even more, for a better and more enlightened humanity. It is true that the Mexican Republic also declared for Loyalist Spain, but it could do little materially; the French working people supplied half the International Brigade, many airplanes, and more help than others, but the French Government, Blum's Socialists, helped betray their sister republic (putting the blame on British Tory blackmail and intimidation); Roosevelt had surrendered to Vatican pressure; and Russia alone sent not only its moral support but smuggled a few men and airplanes through the European cordon sanitaire of hypocrisy. In the light of the Soviet Russian record in Spain, by which I still judged current history, I could not turn against it now. There was perhaps a good non-Machiavellian reason for the frightening pact with Hitler. I would keep my decision open.

With the signing of the pact many notable persons who had been on the USSR train of history or fellow-travelers in one of its special coaches, threw themselves off, or were jerked off by the suddenness and acuteness of the curve which it had hit at high speed. Many of today's still frustrated renegade Communists have recently written loud confessions saying it was the Molotov-Ribbentrop deal which threw them off the train.

I had never been on it. Almost up to the time of the Spanish War I had been anti-Soviet (for my own libertarian reasons); and, since Madrid, neither a Communist nor a fellow-traveler, but certainly now an admirer of the one powerful nation which (I then thought) had acted uprightly and nobly in a great crisis in civilization. In 1938, cheered by the success of the French and Spanish popular fronts I wrote favoring such a political union in America. The enemy then (as now) I wrote, was Reaction; as Catholic Chancellor Wirth of democratic Germany had said in the 1920's, "*Der Feind steht rechts,*" the enemy was always the reaction of the Right—the Right which the American philosopher John Dewey said was in possession of power and force, the guns, the money, and the press. "They can beat us if we stand in separated groups," I concluded. "Fascism and Reaction inevitably attack. They have won against disunion. They will fail if we unite."

The Popular Front seemed to be the one way to save the democratic world. (It was 14 years later that this idea, which Red-baiters even now say was part of a Moscovite plot, was shown to be anything but Russian.) The next year, 1939, found the USSR and Nazi Germany in a treaty agreement, if not a popular front of their own.

In reporting this news, and the news of the Finnish War, as well as the American elections from 1932 on, the American press showed more and more a totalitarian attitude. It was no longer fairly divided on most controversial subjects. It would never be 100 percent totalitarian so long as the United States remained a democratic state, but the march of percentage figures was alarming. The press had been 80 or 85 percent against Roosevelt in 1932, as Captain Patterson admitted; the percentage increased at every election, and in 1952 Stevenson could alert millions to the danger of a "one-party press." It had always been anti-Russian, 99 percent or more, at a time Russia was not threatening America with war, or engaging in conspiracies, or purging its own people—it was 99 percent anti-Russian at a time its news reports dealt with vast revolutionary Marxian projects, with methods the American press opposed, but with objectives which were for the public welfare. In the Finnish War the Gallup Poll showed public opinion 80 to 1 against Russia, and press editorials so far as I know were 100 percent slanted the same way. To editorials one could not object. But when falsehood, distortion, fake photographs, crooked headlines and all the usual tricks which every paper knows can be used against Russia and for brave little Finland, I was alarmed by the totalitarian phenomenon.

My sympathy in this war was for the people of Finland. Few people in American were aware of the fact that its leading citizen, Baron Mannerheim, was as much a fascist as Franco or Hitler or Mussolini and that Finland, like Spain, had a Fascist party and Fascist movement; and that the banker-premier of the country did not deserve the loyalty of liberals or democrats. But the American press, which went hysterically overboard when Molotov signed with Ribbentrop, repeated this amazing acrobacy when the Soviets invaded Finland.

I wrote in December 1939, a series of articles much in the manner of the 1920 Lippman-Merz "Test of the News" and had my literary agent offer it to all of the magazines to which I had contributed in the past. All refused to look at them. The press had created a vox populi which frightened magazine editors and book editors too. The Finnish cause was so sacred that no one dared mention the truth. The manuscript, give gratis to the *New Masses*, was published in four instalments. It opens with these lines:

"In 31 years of journalism I have never witnessed such a universal, concentrated, and intentional campaign of lying as that conducted by press and radio in the month of December 1939, against the Soviet government, its army, and its people."

I do not know what the verdict of history is, but I do know that months later, when it was able to make an objective study of the war, the Institute for Propaganda Analysis, in presenting both sides and criticizing the Communist *Daily Worker* as much as the anti-Soviet papers for partiality, concluded: "The simple fact is that the American press told less truth and retailed more fancy about the Finnish War than about any recent conflict....

Who was to blame for the deception? Were the newspapers engaged in a 'venal anti-Soviet conspiracy' . . . ? The answer is still far from clear." Scores of newspapers attacked me for this series of articles, but not one denied my facts or questioned their truthfulness. Almost without exception what they said was that "it is nevertheless significant that his most recent article appeared in *New Masses*," a magazine considerably devoted to the Soviet side, as the Flint, Michigan, *Journal* stated the case.

One of my facts, which I repeated in writings throughout the 1940's, came from the Encyclopaedia Britannica (14th Edition, Vol. 9, page 254, col. 1); it exposes the hero of 99.44 percent of the American press, Baron Mannerheim, as a collaborator with the Germans in 1918 (as he was again with Hitler in World War II), and guilty of a "White counter terror" in which "some 15,000 men, women, and children were slaughtered." Mannerheim's prisoners, 73,915 "Red rebels, including 4,600 women" were starved to death or murdered or died of disease in his camps, or were tortured and murdered. But no newspaper mentioned this truth, and anyone who tried to repeat a fact so historically true it had appeared in the Britannica, was disbelieved, suppressed, and Red-baited.

The satisfaction in having my article on falsehood in the Finnish War published anywhere was revised considerably downward, until it disappeared altogether and was replaced by the usual pessimism: it had done no good appearing in a radical weekly whose readers needed no convincing; the majority whose views had been fixed by the press and the minority with still a fair and open mind could not be reached.

The matter seemed hopeless. But that very spring of 1940 Bruce Minton, a neighbor in Connecticut and a colleague, suggested seriously that we start a newsletter devoted to public events. I thought it should be devoted to the press. Ever since 1935 I had been thinking of such a publication. At that time one of the reviewers of my "Freedom of the Press," Prof. F. E. Lumley who wrote "The Propaganda Menace," suggested a weekly supplement to my book, keeping the reader informed to the minute on all the subjects discussed and documented, from "bad medicine" to corrupt politics, distortion, suppression, and general corruption of the daily news, for one or many purposes. I never gave the idea a thought because it required money.

Now Bruce Minton had a plan to offer our newsletter, which Helen named *In fact*, to thousands of labor union locals, asking their support not in donations but in group subscriptions on the basis that a publication devoted to exposing falsehood in the press must of necessity devote considerable space to exposing falsehoods against labor. But to get things started, Minton suggested each of us put up $1,000. I wrote the prospectus, from which the following are the first and middle paragraphs:

> In fact, *a fortnightly news letter that I am launching, has as its purpose to supply news for that part of the American people, estimated at 30*

million, which has in several public-opinion polls expressed its doubt as to the honesty of the American press. Although Lincoln held that all the people cannot be fooled all the time, it is possible that the exception to the rule is the newspaper. It can fool just about all the people. It did so in 1914 to 1919. I believe it is doing so now....

In fact will . . . accept no advertising, which is still the most corrupting force in journalism.... For myself, I must say that I belong to no party, no organization, no group, society, or faction. I believe (with Euripides) in letting the facts speak for themselves . . . I do not care what label is pinned on me. The viewpoint of In fact *is simple, it is for what we carelessly call liberalism, democracy, progress . . .it is pro-labor.... It believes in the "general welfare" as written in the Constitution, and challenges any publication feeding out of the hand of big business to prove by acts its policy is the same.*

The true story of the 10 years of crusades and exposés by my weekly newsletter would require hundreds of pages for a mere summary; the main fact pertinent to this chronicle is its instant success—we had six thousand subscribers before the first issue appeared, 20 May 1940, and despite price increases, it reached a crest of 176,000 in 1947.

It was almost universally attacked from its first days to its last. The newspaper press, with few exceptions, took one of two attitudes: silence, or the omission of a credit line when our news items were so big they could not be ignored; or libelous, malicious, false statements against the weekly and myself. I suggested a suit against a group of more than 100 newspapers whose syndicated columnist had libeled me, but my attorney, Mr. O. John Rogge, pointed out it would take at least $25,000, perhaps twice as much, to fight through each of these actions, so all I could do was to ask editors for a correction. I did not get it 98 percent of the time. Hundreds of big and little papers were having their revenge for my years of criticism. The libels continued.

The first attack of which I have a record was made by a 1940 radio program called "Confidentially Yours," and when I protested, they sent a letter discussing "a straightforward statement to the effect that you deny that you are a Stalinist or that pro-Stalinists or Communists have anything to do with your publication." This charge recurred throughout the years. Among the souvenirs in this file I have several letters which state crudely but forthrightly their desire to see a campaign of attacks against the Soviets abroad and Communism per se as proof that I was not a Communist. "Since you are devoting *In fact* to attacking Naziism, Fascism, and reaction, and there are no attacks on Communism," one subscriber wrote, "your readers must draw the inference that you are either a Communist yourself, or a fellow-traveler." In other words, if you are not a Communist, prove it by Redbaiting.

There was no let up in this campaign in the newspaper and magazine press—*Collier's* and *Reader's Digest* were the most prominent in the latter field—during the war in which Soviet Russia was the ally of the United States in destroying Hitlerism. Almost all the attacks on me and *In fact* were based on the editorial items Minton had written in 1940. No one could very well attack my non-editorial news items—they were either true or false, and I published three or four times a year an offer to correct any items found untrue or unfairly worded.

In the annual official circulation statement which Helen, as managing editor, signed for 1948 we still showed 96,570 genuine, unfrightened subscribers.

In June of that year we thought a real change of fare would halt the declining circulation. It was announced that I would return to Europe after an absence of 11 years and write from as many countries as it was possible to visit in six or nine months the true story of what was happening—the facts that were being suppressed and discolored, the news of the new Europe, both before and behind Churchill's "iron curtain." I was determined to be as truthful as it was humanly possible, and I tried my best to clear my mind of every prejudice or conviction, to retain only my oft-stated ideal of letting the facts speak for themselves.

Only one country refused to give me a visa—Soviet Russia.

I arrived in London on a Sunday, and having nothing to do I walked down Fleet Street, recalling the great days there in 1916. The *New York Times* office was open and Herbert Matthews happened to be in, and after we had talked of Madrid and the Spanish War he mentioned a colleague, Philip Jordan, who had also been there and who was now one of the spokesmen for the British Government. And so within 24 hours after my arrival I was at 10 Downing Street and in the presence of a man who wore a cutaway and striped trousers and combed his hair like Disraeli and spoke to me as if he were Mr. Gladstone himself—telling me the "traditional policies" of the British Empire and the present policies of the British Labour Party, or Socialist regime, which had inherited them.

It was quite an experience. It was a British type revolution, I thought. And I confirmed his views with the International Secretary of the Labour

Party, Denis Healey. Then I went to see John Strachey, at one time a political prisoner on Ellis Island, where under the auspices of the American Civil Liberties Union and accompanied by William Rose Benet, I had visited him with the latest news of our effort to get him into America for a lecture tour. He was now a member of the Cabinet—but he alone among my old English friends risen to political heights still addressed me as George and still spoke plainly.

I talked to Charles Duff, who had been in the Foreign Office, Kingsley Martin, editor of *The New Statesman and Nation*, R. Palme Dutt, editor of the *Labour Monthly*, and Tory leaders and newspapermen, and Tom Driberg of *Reynolds News*, and also of the House of Commons, and Konni Zilliacus and D. N. Pritt and others on the Parliament terrace, and Editors Richardson and Gordon Schaffer of *Reynolds*. I collected more documentation and journalistic material in a few weeks than in perhaps a year in my days on the *Chicago Tribune*. And when I had digested the facts and impressions, I wrote in a series of articles that—

Socialism, as practiced in Britain, had done well; the health program (including free milk for every school child) was a great success; that social security, from the cradle to the grave, which was to begin in July, was the greatest achievement of the Labour Party; even the Communists admitted that the internal policy of the socialist regime was good; the nationalization program to date was not much; that the real test was steel, and that when steel was taken over, the official program would be completed with only 20 percent of the nation socialized.

It was apparent to me, afterwards, that these articles did not fit in very well with the views and convictions of many of my readers.

In France, Belgium, Switzerland, and Italy I asked the same questions I had asked in London. Everywhere I went I did not fail to visit the headquarters of the labor unions—Transport House in London, CGT in Paris, CGIL in Rome. Everywhere the spokesmen for labor told me that American journalists never write fairly about labor; they never come to union headquarters for news; they ignore the largest and most powerful organization in every non-Fascist nation in Europe. I myself had failed in my *Tribune* decade. But you cannot report what the people of a country want and think unless you ask their leaders. I now realized this was one of the major faults of American journalism abroad—we always reported what the working people, the majority of a country, felt and thought and said without ever asking them or their leaders. We usually quoted a taxi driver.

After a month in Yugoslavia, I wrote my interview with Tito—the first he had given anyone since the Cominform break (but the *Times* to which I offered it in exchange for only a credit line to *In fact* refused to touch it on these terms)—and a series of articles on all the important questions, from Yugoslavia's relations to the Roman Catholic Church to its progress (or failure) in land reform. I stated unqualifiedly my conclusion that Tito, who had once liberated the Yugoslav people, now had released the genius of a nation—he had led men on the field of battle, he was hero and ruler, one of the few in history who came from the common people, probably the first labor union member in history to govern a country.

Mr. Rakosi did not agree with me. When, coming from Belgrade, I went to interview the vice-premier of Hungary, he took about half the hour he was giving me to denounce his former colleague in the Cominform. And the heads of state in Czechoslovakia did likewise when I visited Prague and concluded my round of the so-called Iron Curtain countries.

On this trip I put into practice a suggestion first made by Floyd Gibbons: visit a country which has a dictatorship or a censorship or which otherwise interferes with the freedom of the press, collect the big news stories which the resident correspondents can not send out, come back to Paris (or go to a nearby democracy) and file the news from there. In Belgrade, strangely enough, I found there was an old Yugoslav proverb which summed up the idea excellently. It is: "Tell the truth and run."

I wrote the interview with Rakosi for *In fact*, faithfully quoting his anti-American views, his defense of the Soviets, of the Communist system in Hungary. I noted the Hungarian land reforms, the opposition movement, the plans of the monarchist and anti-Semitic Cardinal Mindszenty to destroy the Communist regime, an activity which was applauded in foreign lands but which was treason at home.

I wrote the factual story of the 1948 Czechoslovak "revolution," exposing the great headline fakery of the American press which had reported bloodshed and murder, students shot and killed, and other untrue events. The truth was that the Communists were organized and disciplined, and in time of turmoil they united and marched and intimidated the government, and finally took it over. But it had been bloodless.

I wrote what I believed to be the truth about Yugoslavia, Hungary, Czechoslovakia, France, Belgium, Italy and England. I tried to tell the facts. I had taken with me to several countries hundreds of clippings of 1945 to 1948 news stories; in each capital American correspondents helped me compare the reports with the facts. I planned to tell the truth and run. I wrote my stories when I returned home, but I wrote them neither pro nor anti the new nations or the new (or old) movements in Europe.

Thus it came about that in 1949, when I had concluded my long series of articles from Marshall Plan Europe, the "Marshallized countries," the "American satellites" as the East called them, and from the nations we called Soviet satellites, and from Yugoslavia, I also came upon the greatest disillusion in exactly 40 years in journalism. I found that I had pleased no one. Or, at best, only a few who like myself were not committed to any social system or party or movement, but were pledged only to such general ideas as the general welfare. Many readers who were delighted with my interview with Tito were angry with the fact I had given his enemy equal space, and of course the partisans of Rakosi and the Cominform were not only angry with *In fact*, they canceled their subscriptions, threw my weekly out of their bookshops, and denounced it for following the Yugoslav heresy.

This wasn't true. But I had never denied I had been impressed by all the Yugoslavs I had met: Marshal Tito, his ministers Kardelj and Djilas, the ambassadors to the UN, Vilfan and Bebler and their wives, the brothers Dedijer, Vlado, and Stevo, and many others including Monsignor Rittig, the great democratic Roman Catholic leader who had been a member of the Resistance and who deplored the fact that priests of his own church had been on the Nazi side.

Tito, like Lincoln, was a man of, by, and for the people. He was the first and only ruler of a country for whom, during an hour's interview, I had a feeling of personal friendship. I could not explain it even when I felt it, but it was clarified for me later by the head of a European labor union. Did you ever, he asked, meet a president or premier or other leader who had been an ordinary working man—a labor union man—all his life. There have been many who came from the people, but they had become lawyers or even haberdashers before reaching high office, while Marshal Tito alone came up straight from the ranks of labor into the leadership of a nation.

But everyone I met—all I have mentioned and many others—were more than officials of a new regime; they were dedicated men and women—dedicated to the general welfare of the Yugoslav people. The name of their party therefore did not matter to me. But one thing did matter, and it was the important thing because it was at least part of the answer to the questions I had asked my pro-Bolshevik American journalist colleagues in Moscow in 1923: Tito and the Yugoslavs were planning to build Socialism without violence, without a terror, without Moscow Machiavellism, without the-end-justifies-the-means as a policy. They had broken loose from the totalitarian Cominform in 1948, and in that year when they spoke of democracy and individual freedom and the rights of man and nations, I believed them. In 1951, when I returned to Belgrade, I found my faith in the leaders and people of Yugoslavia justified.

The letters from my readers which had always been a problem, since I could not answer two or three thousand a week, in 1948 included the usual quota accusing me of selling out to the Communists, but others charged me with selling out to the anti-Cominform. For a moment I thought I would pass it off lightly by writing a statement that the only party I belonged to was the Non-Conform. That year also marked the beginning of a new stream of letters saying I was now just another frightened liberal pursuing the middle way (which in the letter-writers' opinion led either to hell or nowhere, which was about the same thing). At first they made me angry; at the end they made me think things over.

The middle road is a crowded place (and many on it are crushed by the cars of Juggernaut, radicalism and reaction, pushing inevitably to the Right and the Left). During all these years of work and talk I had had a fine contempt for the frightened majority which traveled the middle road. I had thought of myself as one of the non-conformists along the less-traveled and rather lonely individual path of my own choosing. Now almost all the labels possible had been attached to me, all except "tired liberal," and that one I awaited hourly.

But it was not true that because I had found the Labour Party or Socialist program of Great Britain a sincere and successful effort to better the lives of the majority and said so in print, that I had become a Socialist; or because I had found Rakosi in Hungary engaged in a vast land reform devoted to the welfare of the peasant majority, that I had embraced Communism; or because I had been impressed by Tito and the whole resurgence of the Yugoslav people under his rule, that I had become a Titoist.

It seemed to me that the Yugoslav experience renewed and confirmed my belief that "who would be a man must be a non-conformist." It proved to me at least that I was, as I had been from my father's time, a libertarian, and now, as always, of the Left, since there is no other way for libertarians.

Then in June 1950, some readers demanded that I take an editorial stand on the Korean War. This was a most depressing situation. For a little more than 10 years now we had been preaching the Euripidean precept of letting facts speak for themselves, and I had hoped that we were practicing what we preached. Why take an editorial stand on Korea? Or on anything? If there was news being suppressed or distorted, we would respectively print it or attempt to straighten it out, but to writing editorials and viewpoints I was then as always fundamentally opposed.

When, finally, I wrote that there had been more than 100 violations of the 38th Parallel by the South as well as by the North, but that this was the first deep invasion, and on a scale which even a layman must realize required six months or more of planning, and that therefore the North Koreans, whether justified by grievances or not, must be termed the aggressors, the anger of the Cominformists exceeded that of their first anti-Titoist days.

However, it was the never-ending Redbaiting attacks from newspapers and magazines whose venality we had exposed, which frightened away the majority of our subscribers. We could afford to lose the relatively few Communist readers we had, but not labor. We had had 1,030 union locals at one time taking bloc subscriptions—AFL, CIO, Railroad Brotherhoods and independents, a good third of our circulation—as well as 10,000 professional people, lawyers, doctors, dentists, professors, teachers, and preachers, also 10,000 or more soldiers and officers (in wartime), post office clerks, minor government officials, at least 2,000 fellow newspapermen and a large number of notable persons—including Sara Delano Roosevelt who once wrote me a note saying I was unfairly hard with her dear son Franklin.

It was these frightened thousands (and not the small minority of Communists and Communist fellow-travelers on our subscription list) whose failure to renew caused our circulation to fall from 176,000 to 55,000.

There it remained. We announced the suspension at a time our circulation still about equalled that of the two liberal weeklies (which America, alas, cannot support), *The Nation* and *The New Republic*, combined. I refused to ask financial help from a group of associates or to accept money from wealthy individuals; but since I could not make up the $500 a week loss, *In fact* suspended in October 1950.

It had been a very painful but enlightening adventure.

I had thought that my education as a newspaper man had been completed in Spain; but apparently there was still a lot to learn at home.

The Great Change

The New York Times, Chicago Tribune and Others

After writing for years about the lies and corruption of the American press, Seldes lived long enough to see changes he never thought he'd see. In his 1976 book, Even The Gods Can't Change History, *Seldes writes about how the American press transformed itself and became more honest, more truthful and more conscious of the public interest than at any other time in the 20th Century.*

HERE IS A paradox: in these times, when the honor roll of good newspapers has increased impressively; when the great press lords, every one a reactionary and at least two of them editorial endorsers of Fascism, have all disappeared; when the number of worshipers in the temples of the sacred idols of American journalism, their altars dedicated to Big Money, Big Business, the GOP, and such like, are for the first time since the Industrial Revolution dwindling instead of increasing—there is a proliferation of criticism of the American press.

Today a score or more of publications, several of national circulation, the majority devoted each to its metropolis, act as watchdogs of the mass media, newspapers in particular. Ever since Irwin's 1910 series in *Collier's* muckraking the press, there have always been magazines in which occasional critical articles appeared, but *In fact* in 1940 was the first publication in the United States—if not in the world—dedicated to reporting the wrongdoings, suppression and falsification, and so on, of the most powerful medium molding public opinion. *In fact* had the field to itself for ten years. After 1950 *I. F. Stone's Weekly* frequently published articles on journalism and Lyle Stuart's *Independent* had a large monthly section. The press pages of *Time* and *Newsweek* were not then critical. But now the news stands in big cities sell anything from newsletters to thick magazines (with advertising) that carry on the work of investigating, if not muckraking.

These new publications obviously never lack for material. The golden age of ideal journalism has not yet arrived—and never will so long journalism depends on advertising money and money has other interests than the general welfare. But a day's study—perhaps only an hour's study—of a dozen of these new critics shows that the journalistic condition of the United States is nothing like it was in the time of Irwin, Sinclair, and *In fact*.

There are still subjects today for muckrakers and investigators—but before naming them I would like to note the great change in American journalism in my many decades and especially the greatest change in the recent past, an almost revolutionary change that has resulted in the nation's having a fairer and more honest press than ever before.

THE NEW YORK TIMES

The most striking illustration of the foregoing declaration is the case of the *New York Times*.

If many of the several millions who read the daily and Sunday *Times* believe it is (a) the most important newspaper in the United States and one of the most important in the world, or (b) one of the most powerful, or (c) one of the very best, or (d) all of the preceding, then they will have to agree that this is so because of a great change in its editorial character and policy in the past two decades and that this is the most important fact in American journalism today.

The broken-down *Times* began to rise immediately after Adolph S. Ochs bought it and published his credo, 19 August 1896: "To give the news impartially, without fear or favor, regardless of any party, sect or interest involved." He may have lived up to his credo in the 1890s; he certainly did not do so in my time, and certainly the paper never did between 1932 and 1951, when it was run by Edwin L. James, successor to the great managing editor Carr Van Anda.

Sometime in the late 1920s or early 1930s I met Ochs in Paris. I was introduced by my closest friend of Harvard days, Boris Ostrov, whose step-father had forced the name Louis Kornfield on him. Louis discussed his future on the *Times* with the owner, and later, on the street, he told me that Ochs had offered him the Vienna offlce, with the possibility of being made Paris chief later and perhaps managing editor. He would be paid the top salary but would never have the title bureau head and would not be listed. Ochs, Louis said, was frightened of growing anti-Semitism in the States as well as in Europe; he was sensitive to attacks on the *Times* as a "Jewish newspaper"—just as the Schiffs and Kuhns and others were sensitive to anti-Semitic campaigns against "international Jewish bankers." Louis refused the job.

My first, friendly encounter with Arthur Hays Sulzberger, Ochs's son-in-law and successor, was late in 1937. On returning from the Spanish War I complained to a friend, H. H. Railey (who had been on Fortune and written one of the best books on the Luce empire), about the shabby treatment of Madrid correspondent Herbert Matthews by the *Times*. Railey and Sulzberger were great friends. We were both invited to dinner at the Lotus Club, and for three hours we discussed in the frankest manner not only Spain, but the *Times* in national politics, its relation to advertising pressures, its fairness, and its independence. Sulzberger said frequently that he was not a journalist and granted "absolute freedom" to his editors. When Railey seconded my point that publishing parallel columns from both sides in Spain, one an absolute falsehood, the other an eyewitness truth, was not honest journalism and blamed managing editor James for this, Sulzberger threw up his hands and said desperately that all he could do was again warn the editors to publish only facts, without bias or censorship.

Sulzberger, whose paper had supported FDR enthusiastically in 1932 and reluctantly in 1936, told us of the pressures against Democratic newspapers from the great interests—money in all forms, big business, the advertising agencies. Now that Roosevelt had saved the capitalistic system the situation was worse and the pro-New Deal press was being threatened, Sulzberger said, and gave us an illustration. The Pews, of Sun Oil and other companies, were one of a small group of families that controlled the National Association of Manufacturers and, along with the Du Ponts and Mellons and few others, paid the most money into the Republican-party coffers. When the Pews withdrew Sun Oil advertising because the *Times* was Democratic, the business manager informed Sulzberger the ads were still running in Republican papers. "I telephoned Sunoco," Sulzberger told us, "and they promised to reinstate tens of thousands of dollars' worth of advertising. But they never did. On the order of the Pew of Pews himself, the *Times* was cut off."

This illustrated the price of integrity. "It costs money to uphold one's principles," was his last remark. (Three years later, for the first time in decades, the *Times* supported the Republican party. It endorsed Wendell Willkie.) If Arthur Hays Sulzberger was innocent of instructions or intimidations of his news staff, as writers of the history of the *Times* agree, then all that was wrong with that newspaper for two decades (of great progress in circulation, money, influence, and power) must be blamed on the managing editorship of Edwin L. James and his five assistant editors.

The perversion of the historic news for three years of the Spanish war is unforgivable. For this corrupt journalism James is entirely to blame. James inherited an Italian Fascist propagandist as his Rome correspondent, kept him on, and defended him when the liberal weeklies exposed how crooked the news from Mussolini's Italy had become.

For 10 of the 19 years of the James editorship, a part of the record of suppression and perversion of the news by him and his assistants appears in the bound volumes of *In fact*, 1940-50. For ten years this newsletter carried on a journalistic war with James's editorial policy. It had begun with charges that he had suppressed the Johns Hopkins Medical School tobacco-and-death report and ended, from James's side, with a letter to me saying, "The only answer is that we do not wish to take any lessons in journalistic honesty from *PM* and *In fact*."

James had suppressed and perverted the news from Italy, from Spain during the war of 1936-39, and from the Soviet Union from the day he became managing editor, but it was difficult to pinpoint and document incidents because his offense was mostly perversion of the news and publication of biased and unfair reports. It was, however, an easy matter to charge him with suppressing the fraud orders of the Federal Trade Commission. Of about 400 issued annually many were against little known products and manufacturers but some were against the greatest corporations—and advertisers—of the country. The few honor roll newspapers printed them, while the one-party press, that is, the pro-big business press, suppressed them.

To all charges of news suppression, from FTC orders to the last two of an announced series of eight articles on the Soviet Union from the noted Moscow correspondent Walter Duranty, James had a form reply:

The charge so often made about "suppression" in newspaper offices can only be made in complete ignorance of how a newspaper is put together. We print about 150,000 words of news a night and we receive about 400,000 words.... To say that we suppress 250,000 words ... would be absurd.... it would be just as absurd as saying that we suppressed Mr. Duranty's articles.

But Duranty was one of my oldest friends, and when I said, "Is the *Times* suppressing you?" he replied pointedly, "Mr. James is suppressing me."

In fact watched the *Times's* news reporting from fascist countries, its political news, its switch from FDR to Willkie, as well as its reporting on smoking, patent medicines, fraud orders. The intention was not to make a whipping boy of this newspaper, but to illustrate the handling—or man-handling—of news by the daily generally regarded as the most important in the nation.

The entire correspondence with James is now in my files at the library of the University of Pennsylvania. The last exchange concerned the FTC order against Pond's New Skin Cream and Danya Lotion. It was the usual order, but Pond's was part of the Lamont Corliss Co., owned by Thomas W. Lamont, the famous J. P. Morgan partner. James couldn't see that this connection made it newsworthy. "It was crowded out of the paper along with about 50 columns of other news," he wrote in his note ending our correspondence.

In the liberal weeklies and labor press the *Times* was called antilabor. Was this the policy of the owners or of James? The chief labor reporter of the paper, Joseph Shaplen, testified that the managing editor was to blame. On one occasion, he said under oath, while reporting a textile strike in the South he was ordered by James to slant the news so it would be antiunion. On another occasion during a strike in New York a well-known writer sent in seven letters, under seven assumed names, six favoring the strikers and one opposed to labor. Only the seventh was published. And so it went.

According to Gay Talese's book "The Kingdom and the Power," the sacred cows James worshiped were Chiang Kai-shek and Cardinal Spellman. Talese accuses the editors of blunting and softening reports in which Spellman figured, "sometimes totally ignoring Cardinal Spellman's less glorious moments—his blessing of bombers, his affection for Joe McCarthy, his involvements in New York politics."

This is only a fragment of the history of the James regime, 1932 to 1951—from the materialistic viewpoint, a great success; from the ethical, a great disaster. I hold with the American who changed a famous line to read, *de mortuis nil nisi bunkum;* I approve the motto of the Biographie Uniterselle of France: "To the living we owe some consideration, but to the dead we owe nothing but the truth."

The change in the *Times* began with the arrival of the first of James's several successors, who include Turner Catledge, Clifton Daniel, Harrison Salisbury, Tom Wicker, James Reston, A. H. Raskin, Seymour Topping, and A. M. Rosenthal. When John B. Oakes became chief editorial writer, Harvard's *Nieman Reports* points out, McCarthy was on the crest, and Oakes was one of the first to attack him.

The imposing change in the *Times* is easily documented. It impressed me especially, as one of the original 1936 sponsors of Consumers Union, to see a five-column headline, second section, November 1969: CONSUMERS UNION, 33-YEAR-OLD WATCHDOG, STILL HAS SHARP TEETH. On 30 June 1970, a feature article eulogized Colston E. Warne, head of CU, as a predecessor of Ralph Nader. Other headlines that year: 16 July, "High Metabolism Is Tied to Smoking"; 23 August, "Vatican Halts Convent Payments for Recruiting Indian Girls."

In June and July 1971 the *Times* published the Pentagon Papers.

In 1972, writing the first draft of this chapter, I found some thing in almost every daily issue to document the view that the *Times* had begun to publish all the news, whether it would have been fit to print or not according to its previous decisions.

We come now to an amazing climax: in the face of all public-opinion polls, including its own, giving President Nixon a 30 point or better advantage, unique in polling history; in the face of endorsement of the Republican ticket by almost the entire press (with the usual exception of a few honor-roll newspapers); and in the certainty that the Democrats would be defeated, on 28 September 1972, before Watergate became the big scandal, the *Times* made a forthright editorial declaration in favor of George McGovern. It addressed itself to all those who want "to restore to American life its traditional values of democratic liberalism and social concern"; it spoke of "the things that are wrong with America—politically, socially, economically, morally—that should be righted; it mentioned "the panoply of wealth and the arrogance of power"; it praised McGovern's "humanitarian philosophy and humane scale of values, his courage and his forthrightness"; and it concluded that "in these respects, it seems to us, the Presidency of Richard M. Nixon has largely failed."

On 22 October the Times repeated, "President Nixon has sadly and spectacularly failed," and on 29 October said, "An Administration which engages in blatant favoritism, which is susceptible to the power of money and private influence, subverts law and social order . . . used violent and corrupt means—intimidation and investigation, sabotage and surveillance, bugging and bullying . . . cannot establish justice or insure domestic tranquillity."

Two days later an editorial accused Nixon of playing "irresponsible political games with the [Supreme] Court" and, after documenting this charge, concluded, "The Supreme Court is truly freedom's last line of defense. President Nixon's repeated assaults on that essential bulwark have undermined the authority of the Court and with it public faith in government under law."

The Sunday before the election the Times editorially urged all voters who felt that the Nixon-Agnew administration was corrupting American democracy to vote for McGovern.

Forthright as the Times's stand was in November, when the president and the White House were calling the Watergate crime a "caper" and a "bizarre" episode and "a third-rate burglary" and something "both parties engage in"—and the majority Nixon press was accepting these falsehoods—the *Times's* investigation was second in depth only to that of the *Washington Post*, and it helped convince perhaps the most important stratum of the American public that the Nixon scandal was the most outrageous in the nation's history.

The *Times's* employment of Seymour M. Hersh as a leading investigator is worth a whole chapter, and since it has already been written by *Rolling Stone* (10 April 1975) I will summarize it. Under the headline "Seymour Hersh, Toughest Reporter in America," Joe Eszterhas gives this impressive record:

1. The My Lai massacre.
2. The army investigation of My Lai cover-up.
3. Kissinger wiretapped his own aides.
4. Nixon secretly bombed Cambodia.
5. The CIA involved in the Allende overthrow, Chile.
6 CIA domestic spying.

According to *Rolling Stone*, Hersh was dissatisfied with the press coverage of Nixon for many years, and Vietnam "was the criminal element we missed.... We missed the major crime, so we're not folk heroes." Eszterhas also reports Hersh deploring the fact that while two police reporters exposed Watergate, no one wrote anything during fourteen months of Cambodia bombings.

(An interesting sidelight on the My Lai-massacre story: The *Minneapolis Tribune* poll showed that 49 percent did not believe it and 54 percent said that even if true, it should not have been published. According to Hersh, Calley became a folk hero. "Middle America fell in love with him." Numerous letters called Hersh "a dirty traitor"; several were anti-Semitic. Hersh concluded: "Calley was a scapegoat, but he also was a great mass murderer.")

On 27 June 1973 the Op-Ed page of the *Times* ran an amazing contribution from Herbert Marcuse, professor of philosophy, suggesting that the significance of Watergate "has been hidden or minimized" by the conventional press as a case of corruption, whereas it is really a part of the American free-enterprise system. Nowhere outside the Socialist-party press has such a statement appeared.

And here are some highlights from 1974: On 1, 2, 3, and 4 May, *Times* editorials and Op-Ed contributions from Anthony Lewis and James Reston destroyed whatever belief may still have existed among people who were not morons, that Nixon had not been the man chiefly responsible for the crimes of burglary and deception. On 11, 13, 16, and 25 September, largely the work of Hersh, the *Times* exposed the criminal activities of the CIA in Chile—the CIA having previously been a more sacred cow than even Hoover's FBI. On 9 September the paper said editorially of President Ford's pardon for Nixon that "he could probably have taken no single act of a noncriminal nature that would have more gravely damaged the credibility of this government." On the 23rd it published a letter from an attorney regarding a pardon for Alger Hiss, quoting Justice Douglas's view that Hiss had been convicted on forged evidence. On the 30th the *Times* reported several of its biggest—and previously most sacred—advertisers, Gimbels, Bergdorf-Goodman, Lord & Taylor, were "charged with bilking charge account customers of more than $2.8 million in credit balances" and bargaining for a consent agreement with the Federal Trade Commission.

Finally: let the *Times*, rather than this commentator, say what kind of a newspaper it has now become: Under an inside-page three-column headline, "The *Times* Wins Award for 'Crusading,'" a news story states that the paper had won "this year's Page One Award for 'the best example of a crusading newspaper.'" It was the fourth time since 1969 in this category.

THE CHICAGO TRIBUNE AND OTHER GOP ORGANS

Not until two years after the Watergate burglary and the almost immediate discovery—by those who wanted to discover—that the criminal trail led to the White House, and not until more than a year after a handful of the nation's great newspapers began investigating and exposing the Nixon administration as the most corrupt in history, did the powerful die-hard Republicans turn upon their hero Nixon.

This was an almost unparalleled episode in the relationship between the GOP and the vast majority of newspapers. It is best illustrated by the cover of the 20 May 1974 issue of *Time*, with these words in large red type: NIXON'S SHATTERED PRESIDENCY, surrounded by photostats of the leading Republican mouth organs, notably the *Chicago Tribune, Cleveland Plain Dealer, Kansas City Times, Omaha World-Herald, and Los Angeles Times* and the reproduction of an editorial, "A facing of Facts," signed by William Randolph Hearst, Jr., editor in chief of the Hearst newspaper chain.

The *Chicago Tribune* is another good illustration of the great change in American journalism—a transformation not as sudden as that of Saul of Tarsus on the road to Damascus, but nevertheless significant. As late as 2 July 1973, *Newsweek* referred to the *Chicago Tribune* as "America's most reactionary big-city newspaper." But something was already happening, because Morris Rubin, editor of *The Progressive*, published in its May issue an article by Erwin Knoll, "The *Chicago Tribune* in Transition," which said, "Talk with almost anyone about the new, new, NEW *Chicago Tribune* and sooner or later you are likely to be told that the Colonel (Robert McCormick) must be revolving in his grave."

According to *Newsweek*, "After the Colonel's death in 1955 the paper continued on a rigidly rightward course, but under McCormick's colorless successors the *Tribune* became decidedly tepid.... But now, after a wrenching bootstrap effort, the Chicago Tribune has finally vaulted into the Twentieth century." (It used to be said in our Paris office that the colonel had one of the finest minds of the Seventeenth century.) The turnabout, *Newsweek* believes, came when Clayton Kirkpatrick took over editorship in 1969. The paper has won two Pulitzer prices; "the slanted writngs of the paper's old-line Tory reporters have disappeared"; and a page entitled "Perspectives" offers even the liberal opinions of Nicholas von Hoffman.

A recent examination of the *Tribune's* reporting on Watergate and the Ellsberg episode shows it has been as fair and unbiased as many others that delayed looking into such Republican activities. Both news columns and headlines were free of the corrupting slants of McCormick's time. The *Tribune's* defense of the free press against the first attacks by Nixon and Agnew were excellent.

For 127 years, from the day Medill bought the paper and became Lincoln's chief journalistic spokesman, the *Tribune* never wavered from the (well-paying) Republican-party line; and then on 9 May 1974 it made its most startling political gesture when it published a three-part editorial calling on Nixon to resign for the good of "the Presidency, the country, and the free world." (No mention of the GOP.)

In devoting its 20 May issue to the Republican press, which at long last had begun to see Nixon as the shabby human being he really was, *Time* revealed that Ronald Ziegler, learning of the impending disaster, telephoned editor Kirpkatrick, asking that he omit the editorial. But the decision had been made. The *Tribune* also said that it was "appalled" by the evidence and that "there can no longer be a charge that [Nixon] was railroaded out of office by vengeful Democrats or a hostile press."

The *Omaha World-Herald*, owned by Peter Kiewit, multimillionaire builder, Nixon campaign contributor, and superconservative, spoke of a "revolting picture of conniving and deception." The *Kansas City Times* wrote on Nixon's "moral bankruptcy." The *Providence Journal, Cleveland Plain Dealer,* and *Topeka Capital Journal* were quoted by *Time* as representative Republican papers that had joined in demanding that the president resign. (From the 1950s on, not one of these GOP newspapers had ever noted Nixon's McCarthyite attacks on his rivals for House and Senate, his formation of a CREEP-like committee fraudulently calling itself Democratic, or any of the other dirty tricks in their hero's quarter century of political life.

To my view the forthright editorial stand of William Randolph Hearst, Jr., is even more significant. The senior Hearst had begun his journalistic career as a liberal and reformer, a friend of muckrakers and crusaders; he had suffered disappointments and been converted to reaction and become, as converts frequently do, a fanatic—to the extent that he went far beyond McCormick of the *Tribune*, Patterson of the *New York Daily*

News, and Hills of the Paris edition of the *New York Herald Tribune* (all endorsers of Fascism and Mussolini), by endorsing Hitler when he took power in Germany. The historian Beard referred to the Hearst chain as the "cesspool of journalism." Hearst, Jr., has been rebuilding the remaining members of the chain. He wrote that his editorial disavowal of Nixon was "the most reluctant statement made here in the last 20 years" and concluded that impeachment was inevitable.

NATIONAL NEWSPAPERS, OTHER CHAINS

In addition to the Times, three other newspapers—the *Washington Post, Wall Street Journal,* and *Christian Science Monitor*— circulate nationally. For reasons of distance no daily can blanket this country as several London and Paris newspapers cover theirs; but each of these four influences opinion throughout the nation. The *Post* is number one in the capital and has been for decades. Under the direction of Katherine Graham it has become a great newspaper. That it is liberal goes without saying. The *Wall Street Journal,* which once stated (20 January 1925) that "a newspaper is a private enterprise owing nothing to the public," has for many years now been paying, not only its Wall Street public, but the general public, the debt every good newspaper owes its readers—all the news, honestly reported. Its coverage of the world is small, and the stories are condensed, but they are all there. Its specialized field includes the most sacred of all cows, money. Nevertheless, when the general press was suppressing FTC orders against giant advertisers, automobiles were being exposed as death traps, and great scandals involved great corporations, the *Journal* published the facts and named names. Although it cannot be referred to as either a liberal or a crusading newspaper, it must be credited with printing the facts—and if all the facts were printed crusading would not be necessary and liberal would lose its distinction.

In 1966 the *Wall Street Journal* began a series of 60 major articles, of which 20 appear in a book, "The Press: A Critical Look from the Inside." It calls attention to a rare, if not a unique, phenomenon—a newspaper criticizing newspapers. The articles analyzed individual newspapers, and there are general criticisms, such as those entitled, "Naming Names: Some Papers Don't" and "Unethical Newspaper Practices." A chapter on *Pravda* shows up the dishonesty of a dictator-controlled national journal, and a chapter on *Reader's Digest* gives facts previously noted only by the muckrakers, that it "plants" its stories, that it is biased, that it is a great labor baiter. In one of the *Journal* series, "Gadfly of the Left" (14 July 1970), page 1, column 1, it pays a tribute to I. F. Stone and notes that Stone was "inspired by the earlier success of crusading journalist George Seldes' newsletter *In fact.*"

This is the first and probably the only mention of this newsletter and its editor in a standard publication. During *In fact's* decade not one of its exposés, no matter how important, was credited to it—even the liberal weeklies did not name it.

Oswald Garrison Villard of *The Nation* called Boston the "poor-house of American journalism." The change in the *Globe* under the editorship of Thomas Winship, with Charles Whipple editing the editorial page, has made this newspaper a noted liberal voice, the most important in New England. (When James Higgins in *The Nation* criticized the Globe for removing columnist David Deitch, Winship replied that it had been done to make room for Ralph Nader and the Black Congressional Caucus.) In 1965 Winship told *Time*, "I am trying to make the paper damn courageous and really not afraid of the sacred cows," and in 1972 *Time* praised the *Globe's* courageous antiwar news, its publication of Pentagon Papers obtained independently, and similar achievements.

The *Los Angeles Times* was one of the first big newspapers, and the first Republican paper, to join the *Washington Post* in reporting Watergate in 1972. This newspaper has broken its ties not only with the Nixon party, but with its past record as one of the fiercest labor-hating, liberal-baiting reactionaries in the country. It has gone so far recently as to publish a series of columns reviewing the Alger Hiss case, referring to the former State Department official as a scape-goat of "the McCarthy counterattack against the New Deal." The *Times* syndicates the work of editorial cartoonist Paul Conrad, whose cartoons vie with the *Washington Post's* Herb Block in their liberal crusading viewpoint.

There are probably many more newspapers with similar histories, papers that were the worst reactionaries of the *In fact* decade, the suppressors and perverters of the news media, but today, if not candidates for the honor roll (usually limited to 10 newspapers), are at least on the side of the public—if not of the angels.

TIME, NEWSWEEK AND OTHER MAGAZINES

In any account of the great changes during this century, which began with muckraking and which is presently enjoying the benefits of investigative reporting, several important features must be considered: (1) the new cru-saders, both individuals and organizations—Ralph Nader has powerful colleagues; (2) the new publications, either devoted to exposés or occa-sionally so engaged; (3) the old publications of mass circulation, several once the objectives themselves of the muckrakers, now serving their readers rather than their owners and special interests.

In this third group the most important and most powerful members are *Time* and *Newsweek*, each with many millions of readers at home and abroad.

As watchdog and gadfly of the American press, *In fact* had to expose also the great and powerful news weeklies, *Time* and *Newsweek*, both more reactionary, more biased, more subservient to special interests, than the majority of national newspapers. *Time* was then under Henry Luce's direc-tion, *Newsweek* under bankers' control. To illustrate: The 16 July 1945 issue of *In fact* consisted of only one item, headlined:

PRESS, COLUMNISTS, NATIVE FASCISTS, NAM,
BANKERS, CONGRESSMEN, FIGHT JOBS-FOR-ALL

The article presented documentary evidence sent us secretly by one of the heads of the White House bureau of the Hearst services. FDR and Vice-President Henry Wallace had promised every man willing to work, 60 mil-lion of them, a job when the war ended, under the Murray-Wagner-Patman Full Employment Bill, then in Congress.

Our (and Hearst's!) Washington correspondent informed me that "the greatest propaganda drive America has ever seen is being directed against jobs-for-all," one attack led by *Newsweek*, another "led by Fascists and reactionaries." One of the drive's first successes was to place an article, "The Road to Serfdom," in *Reader's Digest*, although the *Digest's* theory had already "been dismissed as fascist propaganda by the entire lib-eral-labor press of Britain last year." The drive was now sponsored by the NAM. (Hearst men, who would not dare to say a word unfavorable to Hitler or Fascism, wrote in this manner for *In fact*.)

The story concluded with a footnote saying, "The Brown Brothers banking house, the Astors, and the Harrimans own and control this newsweekly. Among *Newsweek's* columnists was Prof. Ralph Robey, noto-rious for doing a hatchet job on liberal and honest books, who wrote for the NAM on June 18. Raymond Moley, his colleague on *Newsweek*, started the campaign against 'A fool employment bill.'" The press, columnists,

and radio oracles sponsored by business interests opposed full employment because employers wanted a pool of unemployed to provide competition for jobs, so that wages could be held down. All united in branding
full employment "Socialism."

When *The Nation* disclosed that the National Publishers Association,
which controlled the magazine field, had boasted in a membership memo
of leading the fight against the Wagner Act, the Unemployment Insurance
Bill, and the Tugwell Pure Food and Drug Law, three *pro bono publico*
pieces of legislation that were later passed, *In fact* reported that the men
fighting such general-welfare measures were notably Malcolm Muir, publisher of *Newsweek*, and Roy Larsen, president of *Time*. For 10 years *In fact*
noted not only slanted news, but dishonest reporting of New Deal legislation, in three magazines.

Newsweek changed from a biased, unreliable, propagandistic house
organ of the financial interests, into an excellent, fair-minded, liberal
newsweekly almost overnight. This change came about simply because
Newsweek's Wall Street owners sold it to the *Washington Post* group, headed
by the Grahams. How liberal *Newsweek* has become is illustrated by its
devoting the cover and main story of one issue to Nader (in shining
armor) and his numerous crusaders; and during the Watergate scandals it
shared honors with the group that owns it and the *Washington Post*. In
August 1973 it could boast that it was the first to disclose the origins of the
Plumbers operation that burglarized Democratic headquarters, the first to
reveal important actions, or lack of actions, by John Dean, and the first to
detail Nixon's master plan for domestic spying.

There is now a newsmagazine imitating *Time* in many literate countries of the world, and *Time* itself has many foreign editions, circulates
internationally, and is a powerful influence.

It has been a power in the United States for decades. When its co-
founder Luce died, his other mass-circulation weekly, *Life*, said in tribute,
"His enormous worldly success was earned by hard work and conscien-
tiously applied intelligence. Yet it seemed almost to embarrass him, for it
came as the by-product, not the goal, of his chief endeavor, of his passionate need to know, to inform, to educate, to improve the world."

Luce was the Great Misinformer. He is quoted as saying (in "The Sin
of Henry R. Luce," by David Cort, 1974): "I am a Protestant, a Republican,
and a free-enterpriser, which means I am biased in favor of God,
Eisenhower and the stockholders of Time Inc." Biased the man was, as
every issue he published made plain to every intelligent reader and cer-

tainly to every journalist in the world who knew what corrupted news was. That his newsweekly was biased in favor of every Republican, honest or crooked, was also apparent, and his free-enterprise bias went far beyond Time Inc.; it extended to the people and the system that helped get him started and supported him and, throughout his time, represented Capitalism with a big C—the Morgan empire.

Reviewing W.A. Swanberg's "Luce and His Empire," the *Wall Street Journal* said that Luce "was less than charitable, less than understanding, and quite often less than honest." His sacred cows were "Big Business, the Republican Party, Nationalist China and the Vietnam War." He published the news to suit his policy, according to Swanberg, and "made pollution of the news not only respectable but admired.... Luce grabbed American journalism, which was becoming respectable, and flung it right back into the 19th century."

Dwight Macdonald, reviewing the same book in the *New York Times*, concludes that "the real horror of the Luce press has always been more cultural than political, its word-catching circulation building formulae make all truth almost impossible," and he mentions Luce's suppression of a last article Macdonald wrote about United States Steel "despite pressure from friends in J. P. Morgan & Co."

The amount of pro-Nazism-Fascism in the Luce press would make a good subject for a book. The chief of the foreign news section, Laird S. Goldsborough, made no secret of his admiration of both Hitler and Mussolini, as has been noted by Luce historian Swanberg and by Claud Cockburn, a former Luce editorial employee. When *Time* chose its annual Man of the Year, Luce sometimes explained that the person on the cover was not necessarily there because he had done the most good or evil, but because he had made the most news. However, when Luce and Goldsborough announced for Hitler one year, some liberal editors protested, but a number of pro-Nazis objected because the first draft of the news story sounded anti-Nazi. They were mollified with the insertion in the second draft of several paragraphs, beginning with the statement: "What Adolf Hitler & Co. did to Germany in less than six years was applauded wildly and ecstatically by most Germans." The revision went on to say that "Hitler's. . . was no ordinary dictatorship; but rather one of great energy and magnificent planning . . . magnificent highways . . . workers' benefits . . ." and more in this vein.

However, the damning evidence of the Luce-Goldsborough devotion to the cause of Fascism, the undisputed proof, is the July 1934 issue of

Fortune, devoted entirely to the glorification of Mussolini and the Fascist ideology.

In the introduction editor Goldsborough wonders "whether Fascism is achieving in a few years or decades such a conquest of the spirit of man as Christianity achieved in 10 centuries" and concludes that "the good journalist must recognize in Fascism certain ancient virtues of the race, whether or no they happen to be momentarily fashionable in his own country. Among these are Discipline, Duty, Courage, Glory, Sacrifice." (This last phrase is directly out of a Mussolini oration.)

In addition to Hitler and Mussolini *Time's* foreign section under Goldsborough's order praised all dictators of the right, everywhere—particularly, from 1936 on, Franco in Spain. Goldsborough compared Franco to Franklin Roosevelt and described the Spanish Republic as "a government of mobsters" and the Loyalists as "shoemakers, cabdrivers and waiters." When the majority of *Time's* editorial employees, liberals, held a fund-raising party for Loyalist Spain, Luce sent the staff a note banning such "outside activities."

In *Life*, 9 June 1941, Luce published a Hitler interview, signed or attributed to John Cudahy, Chicago meat packer and former ambassador to Belgium, in praise of the Nazi cause. It was the parallel of the hoax the Hitler Ministry of Propaganda had perpetrated with a Hitler interview the ministry had written and planted, with the aid of Hearst, in the entire Hearst press. The theme was "America for the Americans, Europe for the Europeans"—a Hitler Monroe Doctrine for the United States to rule the Americas and let him take over Europe.

On 4 September 1944 Luce published in *Life* an article by former Ambassador William Bullitt proposing the division of the world between the Eastern and Western blocs, letting them fight it out for the control of Europe. This was part of Bullitt's campaign to turn the old cold war into a real war, destroying the Soviet Union.

Luce's publications were in the service of the China lobby and its hero Chaing Kai-shek. Luce supported the American government's policy of bigger and bigger intervention in Vietnam, and according to Richard Pollak (*Harper's*, August 1969), *Time's* own reporters' dispatches were suppressed "when they failed to support the company line."

There was also at least a trace of anti-Semitism in *Time's* reporting. All these evidences of Luce's racism are documented in Swanberg's quotations from interoffice memoranda. On one occasion Luce told his staff that "National Socialism is a socialism which works mightily for the masses however distasteful it may be to them personally in many ways."

For ten years *In fact* noted the relationship of the Luce publications to the House of Morgan, whose Dwight Morrow and H. P. Davison helped finance *Time.* The Nye-Vandenberg investigation of the "merchants of death" disclosed documents mentioning the banking house. Time editorialized the news, deriding the committee. When Secretary of the Interior Harold Ickes mentioned the relation between smoking and death on a radio broadcast, *Time* ridiculed Ickes (and the man who supplied him with the documentation, the present writer.)

Time's character did not change overnight. But it began to change immediately after Henry Luce's departure, and it continued under the direction of Henry Luce III, Ralph P. Davidson, and its present editor, Hedley Donovan. As Time itself said on 9 April 1973, "The times had changed—and so had Time Inc." In exposing corruption in Republican-party organizations during the Watergate affair *Time* was honorably mentioned along with the *Washington Post, the New York Times, Newsweek,* and other liberal members of the media. Each of them not only published the news, but investigated the White House scandal. But none had ever been as 100 percent Republican as Luce's *Time.*

In reviewing more than half a century of journalism and concluding (as can be documented) that journalism has, generally speaking, become more fair and more honest, the change in *Time* must be credited as a factor. Consider the sensationally featured page-and-a-half editorial headline THE PRESIDENT SHOULD RESIGN of 12 November 1973 (*Time* claimed that this was its first editorial in its lifetime; actually Luce had perversely editorialized news all its years.) The editorial begins, "Richard Nixon. . . has irredeemably lost his moral authority," calls his explanations "at least partly false," and concludes that Nixon has destroyed his own "integrity and trustworthiness." His resignation therefore would be a sign of this country's strength and health, not weakness.

How *Time* has changed can also be noted from a letter it published 8 April 1974, attacking what the writer termed "its editorial overinvestment in the destruction of the President . . . its phobic Watergate reporting." This attack on *Time's* editorial policy was made by Clare Boothe Luce, widow of its co-founder.

The importance in the change in *Newsweek* and *Time* cannot be overestimated: So long as they were biased spokesmen for special interests, not one publication in the United States with millions of readers could be called fair in reporting and interpreting the news.

The time will never come, it is safe to predict, when an honest liberal publication in this country will have 44 million monthly readers or 18.7 million weekly (like *TV Guide.*) The belt-line people, Mencken's booboisie, the majority discovered by the United States Army IQ tests to have the mentality of children of thirteen or so, will probably continue to buy the publications aimed to please them, all owned by reactionaries, all serving special interests, all pretending to be the friends of the silent majority while actually encouraging its silence and ignorance.

However, the day has at last arrived when a number of publications are able to inform intelligently half a million, or a million, or even four million readers, by publishing unbiased facts, by a fair and honest presentation of views. There was a dark age in journalism between World War I, when the muckraking magazines were destroyed by business and financial interests, and the late 1960s and 1970s (Watergate). Now there is a great change in the magazine field—it parallels a like change for the better in the daily newspapers since the days of Hearst, McCormick, Patterson, Howard, Luce, and other press lords—lords who in their time betrayed the readers they pretended to serve.

Dissenting View: Press Failure at Watergate

Was Watergate one of the great moments in the history of American journalism? Yes and No, Seldes says. While the general improvement of the quality of journalism made it possible for the story to not be totally suppressed, Seldes believes that almost all of the American media missed the real story, that the Watergate break-in was just the latest dishonest act in the long political career of Richard Nixon. In this chapter from his 1976 book Even The Gods Can't Change History, *Seldes explains how the media could have done a lot better in its coverage of the Watergate scandal.*

A NEW HISTORY of American journalism will probably conclude its chapter on Watergate by saying that this was the press's finest hour. This was not my view. Although, as stated at length in the previous chapter, the press and other media of mass communication are now serving the public more fairly and honestly than in the bad old days, Watergate coverage cannot be used as an illustration.

A small, but better proof was an invitation from the Op-Ed page editor of the *New York Times*, Harrison E. Salisbury, to me to contribute an opinion—naturally a dissenting one—on Watergate. The reader can perhaps share this writer's emotion when he remembers, as previously stated, that in 1940 the *Times* managing editor, Edwin James, had ordered the editorial department never to mention either my name or my newsletter and never to review my books, and ordered the advertising department to refuse advertising for In fact. These orders were obeyed even after James passed away in 1955, and they included the *New York Times* Book Review.

My contribution to the Op-Ed page was published in the *Times* and several other important newspapers, 5 September 1973. This chapter is based on what I wrote.

NO REASONS FOR EUPHORIA

On the first anniversary of Watergate, and for several weeks thereafter, the American public read and heard universal praise, appreciation, and applause for a free press in a free country—confirmation in 1973 of Jefferson's 1787 view that newspapers without government would be preferable to government without newspapers. American democracy again had shown the world that a press free from all outside restraint, even from self-criticism by a council, had proved the best of all possible systems.

In editorials, news columns, and addresses at professional meetings there were references to "the finest hour" in investigative journalism, "the press's greatest triumph in recent years," "a time of vindication" for the "role of the Fourth Estate" of the United States.

The very opposite (it seems to me) is true. Watergate (it seems to me) is the latest and best illustration of the failure of the press to serve the public.

We have exactly 1,764 daily newspapers. If instead of the one word *press* the words *an overwhelming majority of the nation's newspapers* were substituted, the preceding judgment would be more accurate. The majority press failed the public; four or five, perhaps one or two more newspapers, not only reported a burglary story 17 June 1972, but continued to investigate and report facts until they could no longer be covered up. The press failed in 1972; one fistful of daily newspapers achieved historic distinction.

In a review of the Watergate year I find, for example, in *Newsweek* this alarming statement: "Many newspapers buried the item, if they bothered to print it at all." They buried or suppressed news of a burglary, not of a home or even a bank, but of one great political party's headquarters by hired representatives of another great political party.

Again, here are the facts gathered by a noted journalist and critic of journalism in 1972, months before Watergate monopolized the headlines. According to Ben H. Bagdikian these are the four newspapers which kept on digging out and publishing the news: *Washington Post* (two fulltime reporters, eight others), *Washington Star-News* (four fulltime), *New York*

Times (wound up with 12), *Los Angeles Times* (three on Watergate first day, more later; this newspaper had endorsed Nixon) .

The great press chains notoriously failed, or refused, to investigate—and the United States is becoming more and more a nation in journalistic chains: Newhouse (21 Washington correspondents, none on Watergate), Gannett (12 correspondents, none on Watergate), Copley (seven correspondents, none on Watergate).

The survey also shows the networks, ABC with 16 correspondents, CBS and NBC each with 25 and not one on Watergate. According to Bagdikian, "no more than 14 reporters" of the nation's 2,200 in the Capital began investigating Watergate in 1972 and reporting the news adequately.

CONFIRMATIONS AND REVALUATIONS

The New Yorker said editorially that "a few people moved quietly in the direction of the truth and the great bully overthrew himself" and that "any credit to contemporaries goes not to the press as a whole but mostly to the Washington Post; not to Congress but mostly to Senator Sam J. Ervin; not to the judiciary but mostly to Judge John J. Sirica. Only these few, and a handful of others, properly used, and thereby saved, our system. The rest of us still have our medals to earn in the battle of the Constitution."

At the journalistic counterconvention—the second such meeting sponsored by MORE (a journalism review) to coincide with the annual meeting of the American Society of Newspaper Editors—Bob Woodward, who with Carl Bernstein gets the most credit for exposing Watergate, told the dissenters that "people are saying this is the finest hour for investigative journalism"; however, "there's much more the press should have done and much more to do." The two *Washington Post* Pulitzer Prize winners wrote more than 200 stories on Watergate during the year, eventually relating the crime to the Nixon Administration. Ralph Nader told the *New York Times*, "It is doubtful if Richard Nixon could have remained the Republican candidate if the facts known now were as widely known in September." In September the press was 93 percent for Nixon. It remained so during most of 1972 when the few papers were telling the truth about the vastness of the Watergate corruption. In other words, the majority press, the 93 percent press, failed.

This failure is implicit in the Gallup Poll of 20 May 1973. It shows that despite eight months of Watergate reporting by a few great newspapers the silence of the majority, and of radio and television, resulted in the uninformed or misinformed public's placing 15 subjects ahead of Watergate in importance. Only one percent of the public placed it first; 62 percent voted the high cost of living first, crime and lawlessness second, drugs third, corruption fourth, pollution fifth, unemployment sixth, and so on, to world peace tenth.

Up to the day the "smoking pistol" of the Watergate crime—the self-incriminating tapes—was found, the Nixon record was not generally known to the public. The reason it was not known is that the American press had favored him throughout his immoral, unethical, and illegal career, even from the day he lied about his military service when accepting the advertised offer of a hometown group to run for office against Representative Jerry Voorhis. (Jack Anderson looked at Nixon's record as far back as 1936, when three Duke law students broke into the dean's office to see if they had lost their grades. One was Nixon; another later said, "We didn't steal anything.' Alfred Adler would have been interested in Nixon's behavior from age five.)

The political record begins with an egotistic lie: According to the *Whittier News*, 3 October 1945, accepting the candidacy and denouncing the New Deal, Nixon said of the war veterans, "I have talked to many of them in the foxholes." In the campaign he issued a leaflet that, Frank Mankiewicz reveals in his book "Perfectly Clear," not only used falsehoods to Redbait Voorhis but referred to himself as a "clean forthright young American who fought in defense of his country in the stinking mud and jungles of the Solomons" while his opponent "stayed safely behind . . . in Washington." Nixon never fought anywhere. Nixon never saw or spoke to a soldier in a trench or in combat anywhere. His job was to set up supply facilities behind the lines, and the only reputation he earned in the great war was as a poker player. (The *New York Times*, 9 August 1974, put his winnings at $10,000.)

Nixon's first criminal action was committed in his campaign against Governor Edmund (Pat) Brown in 1962—in 1946 and 1950, campaigning and defeating Voorhis and Helen Gahagen Douglas, he merely violated the moral and ethical codes that even politicians generally respect. If the press of California at those times had included a reasonable percentage of fair newspapers, Nixon would have been exposed in both campaigns as a man who used false statements and libels, who vilified opponents, who was a shoddy, dirty, tricky character unfit for any public office whatever. But Nixon then, as throughout his career, had between 80 and 90 percent of the press on his side, and this press chose to suppress the truth and accept the falsifications without question. The small-circulation liberal magazines, such as *The Nation*, published the facts then, and they and books are the reliable sources now.

1 9 5 2 . When Nixon's $18,000 slush fund, collected by big-corporation executives, was exposed, Nixon made his famous "Checkers" speech, winning public sympathy.

Although the amount is nothing compared to the millions later illegally raised and accepted for his presidential campaigns, writers now agree that if Nixon had been a Democrat caught in this scandal, he would not have survived. (Drew Pearson not only reported the facts, but he did so despite a threat of Redbaiting phoned him—according to Anderson—by William Rogers.

The Checkers episode is one of the most damning pieces of documented evidence of the failure of the press. In his 1971 book "Don't Blame the People," Robert Cirino writes that the press had the list of Nixon contributors and refused to investigate the oil men, defense contractors, and real estate operators who paid Nixon and expected him to repay them. Who were the men? What were they after? The press was silent.

Although at the end of 1952 the story was voted one of the 10 most important of the year, Cirino found that of 70 leading dailies in 48 states "only seven chose to place the story of the fund on the front page the first chance they had." Two newspapers published Nixon's reply without ever informing the public what he was replying about. Moreover, the big California press, the five Los Angeles dailies, buried the story on inside pages the first two days, when it was "hot."

If you read the 70 leading newspapers in 48 states you did not get the news; if you read the papers of Nixon's home state you got less than nothing. If you read *The New Republic* of 6 October 1952 you found the story headline NIXON, HOW THE PRESS SUPPRESSED THE NEWS. You would be one of 100,000 Americans informed—150 million were not. (Would it be an exaggeration to say they were "betrayed"?)

1 9 5 3 . Nixon's national reputation was born with the Alger Hiss case. Today there are many reasons to believe in Hiss's plea of not guilty and to blame Nixon and the Redbaiting climate. On 6 June 1975 the *New York Times* reported that Hiss was suing the federal government for documents he believes will clear him; he claims that the "pumpkin papers" were forgeries, the microfilms used in evidence could not have been manufactured at the time claimed, the incriminating typewriter had wrong numbers of date of manufacture, and "it was largely because a young Congressman named Nixon said he believed [ex-Communist Whitaker] Chambers I was convicted."

1962. The most thoroughly documented report on dirty tricks and a criminal action antedating Watergate, was written by Joseph C. Goulden for *The Nation*, 28 May 1973. It deals largely with the campaign against Governor Edmund (Pat) Brown of California and the formation, secretly, by Nixon and aides of a fake Committee for the Preservation of the Democratic Party. The press release of this fraudulent CPDP writes Goulden, "abounded in flagrant, deliberate, lies . . . and was intended to mislead both the press and the public in the two weeks before elections. Second, it resulted from a covert political operation, conceived, directed and approved by Richard Nixon and his campaign manager, H. R. Haldeman. Finally, the 1962 California scheme parallels in many respects the bag of dirty tricks—rigged polls, generated letters and bogus front groups—that the Committee to Re-Elect the President (CREEP) emptied on the American public in 1972."

The Democrats immediately sued, and Nixon and Haldeman were found guilty—but Judge Byron Arnold did not pass sentence on them until two years later. In 1962 the California press had another opportunity to publish the facts—and refused.

1968. In *Newsweek* (4 June 1973) William V. Shannon calls the 1968 election "an act of mass amnesia about Richard Nixon's record and personality." He mentions the Vesco case, the 1952 $18,000 slush fund, and the $205,000 "loan" to brother Donald from Howard Hughes and concludes that "for the people to have elected Nixon as the man to make peace, restore domestic tranquility and clean up the moral debris of the Johnson Administration is one of the cruelest jokes fate has played on any nation." Was it fate—or press failure?

In the British edition of *Vogue* James Cameron summed up Nixon as "this unlovely and charmless con man" with a "slimy record of political dishonesties from the days of his Congressional baptism in California in 1946." He concludes that for the American people "it seemed a little late in the day to be shocked by the discovery that they had nurtured a Chief

Executive who had apparently achieved the near impossible; that of being as big a shyster as he looked.... Nixon," says Cameron, "has brought corruption into disrepute."

The readers of the various annual congressional voting summaries, notably *The New Republic's,* knew the record. So did other small minorities who were not deceived by the 93 percent pro-Nixon newspaper press. Here is a part of that man's record:

Voted against Medicare; against minimum wage laws, against the farm bills; to weaken unemployment-compensation laws; against public housing; against the food-stamp program; against new funds for hospitals; against aid to education several times; against state aid to prevent water pollution; against control of pesticides; against limiting involvement in Vietnam.

Is there anything in the record he was for? He was for the impeachment of Supreme Court Justice William O. Douglas, the most liberal member of that body; he tried to pack the Supreme Court with reactionaries; he was for all the business interests that had paid for his elections and had a stake in compensation laws, pollution laws, pesticide laws, and everything Nixon voted on. It was not after Watergate, but before the 1972 election, that Congressman Morris K. Udall placed the Nixon record in the *Congressional Record* (11 October 1972), with an introduction saying, "The President has consistently opposed programs which would have benefitted the working man, the poor and the elderly.... It amounts to a direct disregard of this Administration, compared to those of earlier Presidents, of the will of the people as expressed by Congress." Two thousand Washington correspondents could have sent out this record and statement had they wanted to.

Everything Nixon did as President, Robert Harris said in *The New Yorker* (1 October 1973), "has reflected the deepest desire of the country's most reactionary elements: to reverse 40 years of government efforts to create a more equitable society, and substitute a more authoritarian regime." From authoritarian to fascist is less than one step. In Mussolini's definition the words are synonymous.

One of our foremost historians, Henry Steele Commager, lists the "real crimes" of the President in five major categories: usurpation of war power by the secret war against Cambodia; "denial to the Congress of those powers that are confined to it by the Constitution"; nullification of the legislative power over the purse, "the most important weapon in the arsenal of Congressional independence and the most important instrument of democracy"; nullification of the Bill of Rights, notably the attempt to destroy a free press by prior censorship; and the corruption of democratic processes by dirty tricks, from character assassination to a plan for a police state (*New York Times* contribution, 28 June 1974). The historian believes each of these five crimes was an impeachable offense. They were committed before Watergate—and the great press kept a great silence.

THE ONE-PARTY PRESS

Should the nation rejoice that 7 percent of the press did support Nixon's rival in 1972 and that every honest, liberal magazine, weekly and monthly, either supported George McGovern or at least gave him a square deal? Should we rejoice that we do not have a 100 percent authoritarian press such as Hitler, Mussolini, and Stalin had—and the Soviet Union still has today?

In the 1972 campaign I was shocked by the failure of many newspapers to give fair display or even to mention the poll taken by *Editor and Publisher* on the press choice for president. The night before the news release, Eric Sevareid, commentator on Walter Cronkite's excellent CBS nightly news program, gave notice that the findings would be sensational—but a search of the next morning's papers, notably the Republican-party organs, indicates that this news was either underplayed or omitted.

Editor and Publisher stated that it had asked every paper which candidate it supported, and of those which replied 548 favored Nixon and 38 McGovern.

More shocking yet was the circulation figures: 17,532,456 for Nixon against 1,468,223 for McGovern.

The *Wall Street Journal*, giving this news item good space in its page-1 summary, states that "support for McGovern is so slight . . .that the *New York Times* alone accounts for 55 percent of all the circulation of those papers favoring him. The Times circulation is 874,000." In other words, outside this New York City paper, the press circulation for the Democratic candidate was 594,000.

Even more shocking, although I did not find it emphasized by any publication in the country, was the total absence of McGovern newspapers in 12 states. And since, as Loren Ghiglione, editor and publisher of the *Southbridge Evening News*, informed me, Massachusetts had five McGovern newspapers, this raises the number of states without one to 16. And since other states probably had two or three papers that endorsed McGovern, the possibility exists that there was not one Democratic newspaper in 25 of the 50 states.

In party support times have not changed. Roosevelt had a fair number in 1932 and fewer in 1936, and although *Editor and Publisher* reported FDR 20 percent, Willkie 66 percent, the circulation (according to *The New Republic, The Progressive,* and *Christian Century*) was 80 percent for Willkie— 90 percent if several dailies calling themselves "independent" but actually partisan were included.

Again, in October 1944 *Editor and Publisher* headlined "57% of Dailies Back Dewey, 20% for Roosevelt," which *In fact* said was the sort of half truth that is worse than a lie. For example Utah was listed one for Dewey, one for Roosevelt, two independent. Our local correspondent wrote us that the *Tribune* of Salt Lake City blanketed the state, and its circulation far exceeded that of all Roosevelt papers. "In Utah," our man reported, "better than 95 percent of the press is anti-FDR and the *Editor and Publisher* poll is as funny as a crutch." *Editor and Publisher's* own circulation report was 21 million for Dewey, 4 million for Roosevelt.

Charles Michelson, Democratic-party publicity director, said that although the press was 95 percent for Dewey, FDR would win; he thought radio had something to do with it. Three days before he was elected, Harry Truman said in St. Louis that 90 percent of the press was against him, adding, "Hearst character assassins, McCormick-Patterson saboteurs, all began firing at me, as did the conservative columnists and radio commentators. Not because they believed everything they said or wrote, but because they were paid to do it."

When Adlai Stevenson made his famous "one-party press in a two-party country" speech in 1952 he added that he was gravely concerned "for our American press and our free society." He objected, not to "honest convictions honestly stated," but to the tendency "of many papers . . . columnists, commentators, analysts, feature writers, and so on, to argue editorially from the personal objective, rather than the whole truth." The danger to a free society, which Stevenson foresaw, is evident from the failure of the 90-some percent of the press to join with the honorable few in telling the whole truth about Watergate in the 1972 election—as it had to do in the 1973 hearings.

Nor has it been pointed out that almost simultaneously with the Watergate beginnings, Vice-President Spiro Agnew was unleashed by President Nixon in one of the worst attacks on the press in history, and the "liberal press" he attacked by name were the very papers that investigated the Republican crimes, notably the *Washington Post* and *New York Times*. Was this a mere coincidence, or were both Nixon and Agnew deeply wounded by the fact, as revealed by the *Editor and Publisher* poll, that in their 17 million circulation support there was not one great newspaper, not one of the many that have appeared on any honor roll during a large part of this century? In influencing votes the refusal of half a dozen or a score of newspapers to endorse the GOP meant very little; in *amour propre* it might have been everything. One could presume at that time that possibly Agnew and Nixon were just two very sensitive souls, hurt by any reflection on their honor. But the Agnew confession of a crime and the Nixon betrayal by his own taped words clearly showed that the campaign against the press had been intended to destroy its credibility. For as long as even a few papers spoke out, and spoke the truth, the crooks were not safe in the White House.

PRESS FAILURE DURING THE CAMPAIGN

The student, researcher, or historian of the 1972 campaign must accept the undisputed facts disclosed a year and two later—too late to influence public opinion—that the press in general failed the public from June to November by refusing to put a true valuation on the news five or six investigating reporters had discovered and refusing to accept the charges McGovern and others were making openly.

After 1973, however, the press let the facts speak for themselves. Had it done so in the several months before the "third-rate burglary" and the day the man most responsible for it was elected, the facts would probably have changed the result. It had taken only a few days to connect Watergate to the White House, and from that day on it should, by all journalistic standards, have been the biggest news story of the time. Not in five, but in all 1,764 daily newspapers. In June and the four following months McGovern "set aside his denunciations of the Vietnam bloodshed and the tax-deductible three-martini businessmen's luncheons and sought from time to time to capitalize on the Watergate disclosures." (UPI, 18 May 1973). On 2 October 1972 he alleged that Nixon's network of 50 agents were spying, forging letters, and committing other crimes. "Not one of these facts has been refuted or explained. The only response has been to attack the reporters who searched out the truth" (Mankiewicz in "Perfectly Clear").

McGovern told his audiences that "history shows us it is but a single step from spying on the political opposition to suppressing that opposition and the imposing of a one-party state in which the people's precious liberties are lost."

McGovern had some damning facts, the fistful of Washington reporters had some damning facts, but the one-party press during the campaign ignored them or belittled them or suppressed them.

Joseph Kraft wrote in *The New Yorker* that a colleague, James Fallows, an editor of *Washington Monthly*, said in July 1972—that it defied logic or evidence to believe that Nixon was not deeply involved. John Osborne wrote in *The New Republic*, 9 September 1972, of the press failure to handle Nixon "as a vulnerable candidate should have been handled." The November 1972 issue of MORE, written in October, after praising Robert Woodward and Carl Bernstein for "old-fashioned police reporting techniques," noted that "for the most part, though, the Washington press corps plodded along in its usual rut, relying on the handouts and the official pronouncements."

MORE also exposes the falsity of the study by the American Institute for Political Communications, reported in *TV Guide*, a Nixon outlet, claiming "a considerable amount of bias" in the networks favoring McGovern. The opposite was true, and this truth is documented. *The Nation*, 23 October 1972, called Nixon's "The Lawless Administration." *Time*, the same day, listing a full page of White House crimes, concluded that "it is difficult to tell just what effect the Watergate affair and other episodes of political sabotage will have upon the presidential election." *Time*—was it judging from the press coverage?—suspected it would be swept aside, noting Representative Patman's failure to get a congressional investigation started.

In November 1972, election month, "an iron curtain descended around Watergate," as Philip Nobile recalls in the May 1975 issue of *Esquire*. It was indeed a curtain, strong as iron, but it was a paper curtain—the great American newspaper curtain, the 93 percent Republican press curtain.

This one-party paper curtain has been hanging around for all the years of my journalistic lifetime. Has it ever been thoroughly investigated? Fair-minded editors know of it. When Spiro Agnew was sent out on a mission to destroy the credibility of the liberal or fair-minded press in July 1972—the guilty White House already feared Watergate might explode into a mighty scandal—he denounced the Democratic "liberal" news media at a Manchester, New Hampshire, $50-a-plate GOP dinner. Wrote Peter Selkows in my hometown's small but excellent *Valley News*: "There was hardly a murmur from anyone from 1912 up to the Goldwater campaign protesting the bias in favor of the Republican candidate whoever it might have been.... Obviously the Agnews of this country want the old days of a biased and dishonest press back again."

The biggest—and best—result of the Watergate scandal (it seems to me) is a vital change in attitude of a large number of newspapers previously committed to one party. If enough of these powerful dailies have changed so that now the term "one-party" no longer fits, then we will at last have what we might term a free press. For this free press there will still be a hundred minor Watergates to investigate and expose. The sacred cows of journalism, the golden idols, are still there—and several of them will be named, as a challenge, in the next chapter.

Post Watergate:
Today's Sacred Cows

The 1970's were an exciting time in journalism as the media came closer to its stated mission of reporting the truth than at any other time since the muckraking era of the first two decades of this century. There has been a lot of backsliding since the 1970's, but on the whole, the news media of today is more honest and accurate than it was in the era of In fact. *At the same time, there are many stories that the media has failed to cover. In the conclusion of Seldes' 1976 book,* Even The Gods Can't Change History, *he issues a challenge to today's journalists to report all of the truth.*

Every newspaper ought to nail to the wall of its newsroom,
in a place where no eye can avoid it, this motto:
"There Is No Sacred Cow in This Room but the Truth."
—Herbert Brucker, "Communication Is Power," 1974.

Journalism itself is the most sacred cow in journalism's barn.
—Murray Kempton, MORE, 1975.

THE PRECEEDING chapters have touched on three subjects each worth a volume: the general betterment of American newspapers; the courageous return of the muckraker as investigating reporter and the entry of great nonmuckraking magazines into the field of factual exposé reporting; and the effect of Watergate on mass communications.

Great expectations have been fulfilled. Great taboos have been broken. For the first time in American history the truth about a war was published while that war was still being fought—and truth helped end it. The sacred CIA joined the sacred FBI as a subject for profane investigation. The China lobby disappeared. The crooked un-American committees were finally sent into limbo. For the first time in history, as far as I know, a large enough segment of the mass media capable of creating public opinion, especially the newspaper press, served the people instead of betraying them. The great result of the Watergate scandal, it may truly be said, is that fact-telling in time, while historic events are in progress, creating a public opinion that creates action, spilled over far and wide beyond the Watergate.

Under these splendid circumstances the suggestion that there are still sacred cows in filthy Augean stables that must be flushed, still golden or gilt idols to be overturned into the dust, and still great taboos to be defied, may seem premature, perhaps presumptuous. However, this observer agrees with two authorities who have publicly declared recently that there is much more work to be done now and in the immediate future—perhaps more important work than done by muckrakers and investigators and reformers in all past American history.

In a Conference on Muckraking held at Penn State in May 1970—years before Watergate and the popularization of the term investigative reporting—the keynote was struck by *The Nation's* editor, Carey McWilliams. His speech was reprinted in the Fall 1970 issue of *Columbia Journalism Review* with the title "Is Muckraking Coming Back?" The answer given was, it is not only coming back, but "there is not nearly enough of it." Although the greatest scandal was years away, *The Nation* then was continuing its long record of great investigations, which had included exposés of the FBI, the CIA, unsafe automobiles, cigarette smoking and similar taboo subjects.

In the same issue of the *Columbia Journalism Review*, Doctor Nathan Blumberg, ex-dean of the University of Montana School of Journalism and visiting professor in journalism at the University of California, Berkeley, concludes that "the 1970's, from the evidence, will be the golden age of muckraking, except that we will call it by another name: news reporting." Actually, with Watergate the name used was investigative reporting. "The Seventies will see the television networks regularly and constantly committed to muckraking." This, however, hasn't happened.

"Muckraking will become an ultimately crucial factor in the second American Revolution because control of the content of the orthodox media will begin to be wrested from the publishers and taken over by trained journalists who have some sense of fairness, justice and—finally—news value." This idea is being promulgated by MORE and other journalism critics today.

Dean Blumberg proposes "An agenda for the Seventies" for the new muckrakers, listing notably:

Ecological decency. "For the first time in the history of the American mass media, serious examination of the structure, politics, and practices of the privately owned electric power utilities."

Relationship of the utilities and pernicious political influences on municipal, state, and federal government. "Unwonted influence of these corporations and their agents on the universities of several states."

". . . muck of the corruption of the legal profession . . . large corporations"; courts, judges, the entire judicial system.

Peonage: Mexican-American in the West and Southwest.

Rape of Alaska by the oil companies.

". . . U.S. foreign policy . . . role of the U.S. Government and its agents in the death of democracy in Greece."

This agenda is excellent because it does include great subjects vital to the general welfare of the nation.

However, a mere riffling of the pages—or a glance at the summary of highlights of the decade of *In fact*—clearly insists that there are other equally fundamental subjects for investigators, subjects requiring perhaps more courage and integrity than Watergate. The evils which existed in the 1940's exist now. The enemies of the general welfare that In fact named then are all of them alive, and some of them in possession. The investigating or muckraking reporter, if he or she has the courage, will find a lifetime of work in any one or more of the following fields—still grazed by the most sacred cows of the mass media. I have tried to classify them under two headings:

SACRED COWS, IDOLS, TABOOS—IN GENERAL

The American status quo. Those in possession want nothing changed. Without change there is stagnation, even death.

Reaction and rightists, sometimes referred to as "native-American Fascism," the kind Huey Long predicted would come under the patriotic guise of "Americanism."

The big-business, big-money system—the oligolopolies, the banking, industrial, multinational corporations, the successors to Theodore Roosevelt's trusts—the Morgan empire, the old robber barons.

The United States government (under Democratic as well as Republican party control) support throughout the world of dictators, always rightists or fascists, such as those in Greek, Portuguese, Spanish, Chilean and other South and Latin American "republics"—and opposition to liberal-democratic regimes that are leftist or socialist but not communist dictatorships.

The isms. In the McCarthy era socialism and liberalism were deliberately confounded with communism. Fascism was never mentioned, never exposed, never attacked. The most sacred ism of all is capitalism. No ism should be sacred.

SACRED COWS, IDOLS, TABOOS—SPECIFICALLY

The National Association of Manufacturers, notably the 207 corporations listed in Senate investigations as controlling it and the 12 biggest corporation members of the Standing Committee that rule it.

The United States Chamber of Commerce, which the NAM sponsored; also the Associated Industries, and corporate farming organizations.

The Grocery Manufacturers Association and other opponents of the Agency for Consumer Advocacy. The Business Roundtable, American Mining Congress, and similar anticonsumer outfits.

The American Legion, notably its ruling body known as "the Kingmakers," mostly bankers, corporation heads, insurance-company presidents, which set and furthered its reactionary, antilabor policy.

The advertising agencies, notably the public-relations departments supporting foreign fascist dictators such as Trujillo in the past and the Arab oil billionaire rulers now.

The multimillionaire supporters of native-fascist, hate-mongering organizations, such as H. L. Hunt, whose activities were disclosed in 1975 after his death; such hate-mongering publications as the Reverend Gerald L. K. Smith's *The Cross and the Flag*, a leading publication devoted to anti-Semitism today; and such activities as the $50-million legacy left by Judge George W. Armstrong to found a college in Mississippi to teach white supremacy, anti-Semitism, anti-Catholicism, and so on.

The cigarette-and-death industry—even now.

The federal regulatory agencies such as the Federal Trade Commission, Food and Drug Administration, Securities and Exchange

Commission, and others organized to protect the public but frequently in the service of the business interests.

The American Medical Association—if it ever engages again in such antipublic activities as opposition to Medicare. The *New York Times*, 31 May 1975, reported the AMA "slowly moving to change its image as a conservative often stodgy champion of the medical establishment."

All the subjects to which the American Civil Liberties Union devotes its annual reports, for example: censorship by government and the CIA, secrecy in government, privacy, political surveillance, free speech, Southern justice, women's rights, abortion, prison rights—these are subjects taken from the ACLU 1974 report. Each is worth an investigation.

A TABOO SUBJECT: FASCISM

Long before Hitler came into power a great German chancellor—and leader of the Centrum (or Catholic) party, Doctor Wirth, warned the Reichstag with the opening or concluding lines of many speeches, "*Der Feind staht Rechts*"—"The enemy is the right." It was not only Hitler, who threw fits, and Ludendorff, the founder of a religion that replaced Jesus with Wotan, but the munitions makers, the iron and coal barons of the Ruhr, the cartels, the big-money men behind Nazism who constituted the right, or reaction.

In the United States the noted educator John Dewey had warned that "the reactionaries are in possession of force, in not only the army and police, but in the press and schools."

In all the four decades of mostly fraudulent sensations given the press by the un-American, subversive-hunting, and national security committees of Congress, from McCormack to McCarthy (and Nixon), one and only one real plot, only one conspiracy to overthrow the United States government, was ever found and proved true. If the American people to this day (with the exception of the few readers of liberal weeklies and three or four books) have never heard of this plot—from the right, from reaction, from followers of Mussolini's ideology—it is because the newspaper press suppressed, denied, buried, or denigrated the news.

I am referring, of course, to General Smedley Butler's 1934 testimony of the conspiracy by Wall Street bankers and brokers and American Legion leaders to march on Washington and take the government away from FDR. If this had been a crackpot operation it might have made the headlines. But the committee produced—and itself suppressed—irrefutable evidence and named journalism's sacred herd—money, big business, Wall Street, the House of Morgan, the American Legion. And in the testimony there was mention and praise of Mussolini and Fascism by the money interests and the Legion leaders. So it was suppressed.

Decades have passed, a new generation rules the world, but so far as the United States is concerned the word Fascism—and more important, the real social and economic meanings of Fascism—remain more or less taboo. A recent example: After 20 years of dictatorial rule in Greece, the American press first used the word fascist to describe the military regime, when it was overthrown and Melina Mercouri arrived in Athens and was greeted with the cry "Fascism is dead." Nor was the 50-year rule of two dictators in Portugal ever referred to in the standard newspapers as fascist— until it was overthrown, again in 1974.

Where, in all the press coverage of Watergate, can one read such an editorial as the Reverend Doctor Stephen H. Fritchman (pastor emeritus of First Unitarian Church, Los Angeles) wrote, entitled "Coalition against Fascism," in the January 1974 issue of *The Churchman*? Frichtman says he is glad "for the Watergate exposure of the debris, filth, and bribes . . . because only by seeing the elected leaders wallow in such disaster to their plans can we all begin as citizens to stop the march towards American Fascism."

For 40 years, he continues, he watched Fascism come to Germany, Italy, Japan, "with U.S. money and power often actively involved." Then, returning to Watergate: "The owners of TV networks and newspapers on the whole preferred to go along with the establishment's power juggernaut and share the loot rather than tell the truth.... The defeat of American Fascism is the first precondition for the victory of American democracy."

The mention of Fascism in the mass media is so rare that it was a surprise (for me) to hear a commentator in the Spectrum section of CBS-TV make a forthright attack on it on 2 April 1973.

"As I look at the news these days," said Tom Braden, "I begin to wonder whether this country is undergoing an unconscious revolution. Are we becoming—I don't mean to use the word loosely as those of liberal persuasion often do when they characterize a Tory or a Conservative 'fascist.' That's an abuse of the word. I mean to use it in its ancient philosophical sense. Fascism, as we all know, has been around for a long time, as students of Plato, Machiavelli, and Hobbes will remember. But what is the Watergate except a symptom of Fascism?"

Braden cited the bombing of Cambodia without the authority of Congress, "the belief that the leader can do anything he pleases," "contempt for man, the belief in the absolute relativity of right and wrong, the worship of the state," and other symptoms. And although the nation does not exhibit all these symptoms, he said, "this country is in deeper trouble than Mr. Nixon—or his Democratic critics—seem to think it is."

Another rare mention of fascism in a mass medium: Paul A. Samuelson, Nobel laureate for economics, wrote in *Newsweek* (13 August 1973) that "the reason why the never-ending disclosures out of Washington have been so disquieting is that we begin to see on the TV tube darkly the face of Fascism." In this same newsweekly Stewart Alsop said, "It was essential to clear the vipers' nests out of the White House. The vipers . . . exuded a genuine fascist smell." And in an interview with Oriana Fallaci, published in *Look*, the leading newscaster of the nation, Walter Cronkite, when asked if he thought the United States might experience fascism, if he felt the danger, replied forthrightly, "Very, very definitely. And it is abominable, it is frightful, it is terrible—not that Agnew would do it, but that many Americans would applaud it in a way." Perhaps the day will come when the Watergate-fascism relationship will get a mention on the nationwide Cronkite program.

Watergate and fascism. Money and power. The same relationship exists or has existed in Franco Spain, Salazar and Caetano Portugal, Mussolini Italy, and Hitler Germany. The big money put Mussolini in power in 1922—the names of all the bankers, auto manufacturers, and other industrialists and corporations and their organizations were known but mentioned only in the antifascist press.

In all fairness to the press, which today observe the canons of journalism better than at any time in the recent past, it must be noted that the NAM, still the most powerful lobby in Washington, is now sometimes mentioned when it engages in one of its usual anti-general welfare operations.

In the Nader Congress Project book, *Who Runs Congress?* written by Mark Green, James Fallows, and David Zwick, it is pointed out that in 1970, six of the many candidates struggling for victory in the congressional primaries of North Carolina, Texas, and Pennsylvania found themselves blessed with contributions from the NAM. All six went on to win. Even when dollars are not decisive, they make goodwill. Frequently both Tweedledum and Tweedledee get money (page 24).

Of the oil lobby's friends the book reports (pages 34-35) that:

"These organizations are in themselves powerful lobbies. The [United States] Chamber of Commerce is one of the nation's leading pressure organizations against laws that would protect the public from fraudulent advertising, defective products, occupational hazards, and related abuses.

The Chamber, the NAM, and the American Farm Bureau Federation (an alliance of business leaders and corporate farmers) form the heart of the anti-consumer axis in the nation's capital. Of the three, the NAM has been the most consistently vocal opponent of policies that would restrict its corporate members. NAM's record in the past was dotted with such events as the bribing of several congressmen, publicly admitted in 1913 by association lobbyist Martin M. Mulhall.... Thirty-five years later when Congress finally passed a law to regulate such lobbying excesses, NAM brought the first suit challenging the law's validity...."

On 19 October 1974 George Meany, president of the AFL-CIO, which had once been one of the biggest voting elements, if not the biggest, favoring the Democratic party until endorsing Nixon in 1972, was quoted in the *New York Times* under the two-column headline, "Meany Assails Nixon in Speech Opening AFL-CIO Session." Meany's closing remarks:

"Let us keep in mind that the Watergate and the cover-up was paid for by the great corporations of America—the members of the National Association of Manufacturers and the Chamber of Commerce, who seem more willing to pay out some of their exorbitant profits in order to place their hirelings in strategic spots in a friendly government."

A real test of the press as friend or foe of the general welfare came on 19 September 1974 when it could report or suppress the facts on who supported and who opposed the bill to set up an Agency for Consumer Advocacy. The *New York Times* called attention to the efforts of a few senators to filibuster the bill to death, in one of the most amazing editorials of our time. It said (19 August 1974),

"The ferocity of minority opposition to a relatively modest and limited proposal is something to behold. Massed lobbies from the Chamber of Commerce of the United States, the National Association of Manufacturers, the National Association of Food Chains, the Business Roundtable, and some 300 firms and trade associations have sounded their alarms across Capitol Hill."

This was the first pejorative mention of the NAM I had ever seen. When my wife read the editorial she said, "The *Times* today reads like *In fact.*"

It would be a good job today for investigative reporters to name the 34 senators—a bare two more than needed to continue the filibuster—and list their campaign contributors. The chances are 10 to 1 that it would show that most of the money came from either NAM members or smaller but similarly devoted anti-public-welfare business interests.

The *Christian Science Monitor* names the enemies of the bill as the United States Chamber of Commerce, the NAM, the Grocery Manufacturers of America, and the National Association of Food Chains. The *Times* reported the bill as favored by the Consumers Federation of America and Ralph Nader's Congress Watch organizations. ABC Radio named the opponents. A United Press International roundup a few days later named the United States Chamber of Commerce, the automotive industry, and other corporate interests but omitted the NAM. *Time* blamed the chamber and the NAM for their five-year opposition. It is my belief that no mention of the NAM or its allies would have appeared in any publication named, except the *Monitor*, during the *In fact* decade.

Most of the most sacred cows mentioned here could be classified under one heading: capitalism. Every one of them, from the American Legion to the tobacco industry, from the NAM to the advertising agencies and the mass media they largely control, is a component of our system. Call it the American way of life, free enterprise, or the status quo, it all adds up to capitalism. It is therefore amazing to find as many as two lines of criticism of this system in the media. Up to only the other day it could be said that not only was capitalism the most sacred cow of the press, and its most powerful modern manifestation, fascism when not favored, was at least respected. As Michael Harrington writes in his 1972 book *Socialism*, the United States is almost "the only country on the face of the globe where the word 'Socialism' is a bad word."

A NEW MENACE: PUBLIC RELATIONS

William Allen White, editor of the *Emporia Gazette*, was the first person notable enough to be heard nationally who foresaw a great new danger to freedom of the press—and, as it turned out in the Nixon debacle, a corruptor of public opinion—in a new activity of the advertising agencies. He foresaw the manipulation of the minds of millions of people, not by dictatorial orders of a Stalin or Hitler or Mussolini, but by a private industry in a free-enterprise democracy. White said:

"The new menace to the freedom of the press, a menace in this country vastly more acute than the menace from government, may come from the pressure not of one group of advertisers but from a wide sector of newspaper advertisers.... Advertising agencies ... have lately become advisers of great industrial corporations, which also advertise. These advertising agencies undertake to protect their clients from what the client and agents may regard as real dangers from the inimical social, political or industrial influences. As advisers the advertising agencies may exercise unbelievably powerful pressure upon newspapers...."

The words public relations were not used at this time. But great accomplishments had already been achieved in that field in the 1920's and 1930's. A public-relations job headed by Lamont, the Morgan partner, sought to whitewash Mussolini and his black-shirt Fascism in order to float the Morgan $100 million loan that saved Italy from bankruptcy in 1925. The Lamont campaign's key slogan was a great falsehood—that Mussolini had saved Italy from Bolshevism, a feat Mussolini himself had denied three years previously.

To illustrate how far public relations has gone recently, consider two reports—the employment by the Chilean dictatorship of J. Walter Thompson, revealed in the November 1974 issue of MORE; and the whole dirty story of the White House misuse of public relations, revealed by Jonathan Schell in the 2 June 1975 issue of *The New Yorker*. (This subject is also discussed, but not as fully, by Dan Rather and Gary Paul Gates in *The Palace Guard*, by William Safire in *Before the Fall*, and by Theodore H. White in *Breach of Faith*.)

Schell begins a six-part history of Nixon's campaigns by describing the strategy of creating "the new Nixon"—which tricked even the most astute journalist of his time, Walter Lippmann. "The Nixon Administration's apparent ability in the summer of 1969 to establish an image of itself... sharply at odds with the facts marked a new stage in a public relations revolution that had been under way in American politics for many years," Schell writes.

H.R. Haldeman, the Nixon chief of staff; Donald Chapin, the appointments secretary; Ron Ziegler, the press secretary; and speechwriter William Safire were only a few of the advertising and public-relations men surrounding Nixon. Schell shows how Nixon organized the campaigns, even to listing subjects for the creation of his image, "hard work, dignity... boldness...world leader restoring respect for the United States"—and not forgetting a little human-interest job on the whole Nixon family.

In addition to the usual public-relations activities, floods of letters and telegrams were sent to the White House, to members of Congress, to newspapers and radio and television stations, all fraudulent, all tending to build the image of a great man and to brainwash the public mind, and all done by the new magic without recourse to dictatorial power.

In his 23 June chapter Schell says that "as early as the latter part of 1969, President Nixon had succeeded in subordinating the full range of policymaking to the requirements of public relations scenarios." In his 30 June chapter he enlarges on this view, showing that instead of dealing with "real problems," Nixon policy was directed "to satisfy the needs of public relations." Schell concludes, "The President's plan took the form of a public-relations assault on the totality of American political life.... 'That's what this is, public relations' he told Dean in September. For that matter, there was almost nothing he had done during his years in office which he had not seen in one way or another as public relations."

William Allen White foresaw only the menace to the press, not the danger to "the totality of American political life." He foresaw the social and industrial, as well as the political, menace of public-relations experts directing powerful clients, but it was probably beyond the imagination of even the most astute editors of three decades ago to foresee the time when the White House would become, as Theodore White says, confirming Schell, "a high stake game of Public Relations."

The practitioners of this art or science can well boast. They took a shoddy product—a congressman, senator, vice-president, and finally a president, but always a cheap shyster—and for a while at least made him one of the rulers of the world. It was not the fault of the public-relations experts that their creation (accidentally or stupidly or because of uncontrollable egotism or fanatic lust for a big place in history) destroyed himself by committing certain crimes totally unnecessary and unrelated to the art or science they were practicing.

A FREE PRESS: FINAL JUDGMENT

As it was in the times of Jefferson and Lincoln, the newspaper press remains the most powerful means for making public opinion, and the view persists that a fully informed public provides the best government for a nation. But Americans must face the unalterable fact that the makers of public opinion exist on earned (sometimes unearned) money; that mass-media money usually comes from advertising (although sometimes from secret sources); and that throughout history money has been interested in promoting its owners rather than the general welfare.

The final judgment on the situation of the press was made, not by a muckraker, a critic, reformer, leftist, Marxist, or enemy of the press, but by the same man who first warned against the danger of the public-relations industry, a capitalist, an owner of a newspaper, an unswerving Republican—a notable man in America's journalistic history. His conclusion:

"Sooner or later the truth about any social abuse is gladly received by the middle class and by those who own and control newspaper investments. But off the bat, the newspapers representing the innate conservatism of property interests which crystalize middle-class psychology are sometimes unfair in their treatment of men or movements.

"In the end newspapers cannot be free, absolutely free in the highest and best sense, until the whole social and economic structure of American life is open to the free interplay of democratic processes."

This is part of an address by William Allen White to the graduates of the Wharton School of the University of Pennsylvania. I knew him slightly, admired him greatly. He never hesitated to denounce the venality of the majority of his fellow editors, publishers, and owners and their failure to follow the first ethical principle, which he said was simply "to print the facts truthfully." At times he said, "Let the facts speak for themselves, but present the facts fairly and honestly." He never doubted that truth was known and could be told. He left to theologians and quibblers the question raised by jesting Pilate.

To update White's view, here is a report of the *American Institute for Political Communications*, October 1973, quoting the late Robert W. Mitchell, editor and publisher of one of the best small-city papers in the country, the Rutland (Vermont) Herald. The report concludes, "Newspaper publishing has become big business . . .chains . . . conglomerates . . . the tendency remains for the great majority of newspapers to support the established order and to avoid editorial positions which threaten the conventional business approach."

HISTORY AND MUCKRAKING—A MODEST PROPOSAL

What occurs and what is reported are both history and news. News, as much as history, has always been "the register of crimes, follies and misfortunes of mankind" (Gibbon) or "a collection of crimes, follies and misfortunes among which we have now and then met with a few virtues, and some happy endings" (Voltaire).

Not only are crimes, follies, and misfortunes—war, pestilence, violence, and death—the subjects of history and the news, but both historians and journalists in these enlightened times are more than ever before concerned with the faithful presentation of everything Charles A. Dana's divine Providence permitted to occur.

The matter of setting history right has become more important from age to age—it is not a new problem. Just as Herodotus may be said to have been the first muckraker—he exposed the corruption of the Delphic oracle—so Tacitus (A.D. 55?-120?) may be called the first revisionist historian. Moreover, he was conscious of what he was doing. He wrote:

> "As to Tiberius, Caligula, Claudius and Nero, whilst they yet reigned the histories of their times were falsified through fear; and after they had fallen, they were written under the influence of recent detestation. Thence my own design of recounting a few incidents respecting Augustus, and those towards the latter part of his life; and, after that, of giving a history of the reign of Tiberius and the rest; uninfluenced by resentment and partiality, as I stand aloof from the causes of them." (John Jackson, translator)

From Tacitus to Charles and Mary Beard and William E. Woodward may be indeed a long step, and the end of the road may never be reached. So we have in France today a group of historians known as *Les Annales-istes*, challenging not only traditional but revisionist historians. Their view of history encompasses not only men and events but the social-economic-cultural forces of the lives and times. However, unlike the Marxist materialistic interpreters, these new historians "refuse to make ideological commitments," as Alden Whitman reported in the *New York Times*; in fact, they oppose an ideological viewpoint of any sort.

I do not know if there are chairs of revisionist history, under that title or something similar, in the colleges and universities of the United States or any other country. (I do know that there are departments for the corruption of history in Moscow.) There should be revisionist history taught everywhere; there can be a no more fascinating subject for young and old.

In addition I would like to propose, modestly, the formation of an American Revisionist Historical Society to rival the score of national and international learned bodies concerned with history now listed in my almanac—I find none that could be so characterized. This society could publish reports by its members and supply not only university presses, but commercial publishers, with probably some of the most interesting books of the year.

As to the problem of a free press in relation to factual history, that is a more complicated matter. Why writers on this subject, qualified or not, are usually expected to offer at least some sort of solution in their concluding chapters, I do not know. It has always seemed to me that little can be added to the views long ago expressed by William Allen White and other authorities. If White's axiom—the news fairly and honestly presented—had been exercised by the majority press in the 1950's and surely in the 1960's, the nation would have been informed ("A fully informed people can be depended upon to meet any national crisis"—Lincoln), and the United States would not have had to face the dirtiest scandal in its history in the 1970's.

In the days of the New Deal, which was a change in the national socioeconomic structure, one significant event was the organization of the Newspaper Guild by an old friend and colleague, Heywood Broun. I then asked him and others for suggestions on better journalism and published the following list in "Freedom of the Press" in 1935:

> The adless newspaper (twice tried, twice failed)
> Endowed newspapers (*PM* was an example)
> Dailies, to be issued by universities
> Dailies, to be issued by cooperatives
> Newspapers sponsored by great labor unions
> Newspapers edited and directed by their staffs
> More editorial and directorial power to the Guildsmen
> Support for gadfly journalism publications (there are a score or more today)
> More rivalry with radio (this was before TV rivalry)

Everyone in the profession, from the owners to the copyboys, agreed in the New Deal days that the Canons of Journalism issued in 1923 by the American Society of Newspaper Editors were a failure. (The seven canons were responsibility, freedom of the press, independence, sincerity, truthfulness, accuracy, impartiality, fair play, and decency.) No owner, editor, or publisher of any of the big chain newspapers ever paid attention to the code or to any later codes, plans, resolutions, findings, or plans for dealing with journalistic manners, morals, and ethics. It can be fairly said of them what G.K. Chesterton said of Christianity: "It has not been tried and found wanting, it has been found difficult and left untried." The handful of honor-roll dailies did not need the code; the majority refused to know that it existed.

This same American Society of Newspaper Editors, after 52 years of Cleveland's famous "innocuous desuetude," appeared in the public print 17 April 1975 with a new code of ethics, the chief feature of which would be dropping decency as a canon no longer required, along with a proposal to change the title to "Statement of Principles." The *Times* report began by asking, "Are American newspapers more decent than they used to be?" and adding that the editors' answer "is a resounding 'yes,' no matter what critics may say." Actually, nearly the only critics today who maintain that the press is not better than in the old days are the die-hard Nixonites, Birchites, and such types. Most critics agree with the editor in chief of the *Christian Science Monitor*, Edwin D. Canham, that "conditions of the press— as of free institutions—have changed remarkably for the better."

The failure of the profession to respect the code from 1923 on prompted Henry R. Luce, himself no respecter of any of the canons, to subsidize in the late 1930's the most thorough investigation of the medium in history. The prestigious Commission on Freedom of the Press was headed by Robert M. Hutchins and Zachariah Chafee, Jr. It included William E. Hocking, Harvard professor of philosophy; Harold D. Laswell, Yale professor of law; and the poet Archibald MacLeish. Philosophers, libertarians, and commercial publishers were consulted.

In voluminous reports and books the commission used harsher and more damning language than the original 1910 muckrakers or Upton Sinclair in 1920—it used words for which other critics, then and now, are usually condemned; it spoke of "lying, venal and scoundrelly public expression," "ignoring the errors and misrepresentations, the lies and scandals of which its members are guilty," also of "meaninglessness, flatness, distortion, and the perpetuation of misunderstanding" and of failure to assume "a new public responsibility." It even employed that old, old cliche "prostitution of the press."

To end "prostitution" and "irresponsibility," to save mankind from "vulgarization" and from "devastating wars," the commission made recommendations and proposed remedies too lengthy to be repeated here—with the exception of the only one ever tried anywhere: "We recommend the establishment of a new and independent agency to appraise and report nationally upon the performance of the press."

The United Nations also faced the problem. After a long study the Subcommission on Freedom of Information and of the Press, 23 May 1950, adopted an international code of ethics that deserves some sort of anti-Nobel Prize for international naivete—the United States and Britain abstaining because they thought it too restrictive (!) and Yugoslavia voting no because it was "a compilation of platitudes" that meant nothing. Consider the United Nation's main points:

1. The press shall not knowingly [sic] publish false information.
2. "Calumny, slander, libel, unfounded accusation and plagiarism are also serious offences."
3. Immediate corrections.
4. Identification of rumors as such.
5. Privacy to be respected.

Like Marshall's two boys—one ran away to sea, and the other was elected Vice-President of the United States—nothing more was ever heard of the U.N. code.

The International Organization of Journalists, meeting in London, suggested a court of honor, under the wings of the United Nations—and it is still being talked about.

John Hohenberg in the *Saturday Review* discussed the "missionary movement" of young journalists today, the "dedicated crusading reporters" who "frankly and openly repudiate the historic position that management alone has the right to determine what goes in the paper." And Herbert Brucker, when the editors of Delaware newspapers resigned rather than take orders from the owners, the Du Ponts, wrote on 21 January 1975 that although it is generally accepted that ownership has the right "to call the editorial tune," there is a growing demand for more democracy in journalism. He notes that *Le Monde*, the leading daily in France, has set up a complex system of ownership in which editors and other workers share and that in this country there have been numerous attempts "to set up various schemes of employee ownership."

The idea is not new. The most successful example of employee direction of a great paper (until Hitler destroyed it) was the *Frankfurter Zeitung.* I remember very well the time the French occupied the unruly Ruhr and sent a detachment into the town. A French staff officer stormed into the *Frankfurter Zeitung* office and handed an editor a warning to the population to maintain order. "Print that on the front page," he said, and stormed out.

An hour later the French general got the warning notice back with the conventional rejection slip that accompanies manuscripts; it concluded with the German equivalent of the typical American: "This, however, is not to be taken as a reflection on the literary merits of the enclosed manuscript."

The French were furious. A general with gold braid now came to the newspaper office and shouted.

The editor replied calmly, "The *Frankfurter Zeitung* is directed by its editors. No one can give it orders. The owners have placed this publication in the hands of the editorial board; the board decides on all news.... You can confiscate the newspaper, you can in fact smash the presses, burn down the house, even execute the editors, but one thing no man can do, and that is tell the editors what goes into this newspaper."

The general was advised that if he apologized and "requested" the notice, it would be reconsidered by the staff. He apologized. The notice ran.

Where in all history is there another such example of freedom of the press?

At the 1972 presentation of the Robert F. Kennedy Journalism Awards, Ralph Nader proposed a "center for journalistic policy," which would use the Freedom of Information Act against governmental secrecy, review press coverage of pertinent events, and "consider how the press can be more diverse, more accessible to the people and more inviting to their contributions."

These are a few of scores, perhaps hundreds, of plans and ideas aimed at perfecting the mass media. During its ten years of press criticism *In fact* in occasional editorials proposed remedies, which can now be summed up· in three paragraphs:

1. A constantly sitting commission consisting of such prestigious persons as Hutchins, Chafee, Hocking, Laswell and MacLeish, aided by professional journalists and having the medium of communicating the facts, or setting the historic record straight, immediately.

2. A TVA-type daily newspaper, doing for journalism what the TVA does for power and light—serve as a yardstick, a standard of excellence.

3. A weekly newspaper or newsletter devoted entirely to publishing the news as factually and truthfully as possible—with the cooperation of the Newspaper Guild and friendly editors.

Today I would combine the three suggestions into one: a publication, daily preferable but weekly if sufficient money is not obtainable, nationally oriented, nationally circulated, devoted to publishing the news factually and as truthfully as possible and correcting errors and pointing out falsehoods and keeping the historic record straight, and doing this immediately.

Immediately is emphasized for an obvious reason. A national and powerful newspaper, even a weekly, publishing the facts of the Nixon trickery in his 1946 campaign against Jerry Voorhis (the "use of slander and innuendo," as Voorhis writes in his 1972 memoirs), followed by the same type of exposé of Nixon's Redbaiting of Mrs. Douglas, followed by the story of the Pat Brown campaign, in which a dozen of the Watergate "dirty tricks" were first introduced and approved by Nixon himself—all these news stories, if published immediately in a daily or weekly with the circulation of *Time* or *Newsweek*, would (in my opinion) have saved the nation Watergate. There would not have been a Nixon presidency.

The noted historian Henry Steele Commager wrote in *The New York Review of Books* that "for the first time in our history we have an Administration that lies systematically and almost automatically; it lies about the origins of the war, lies about casualties, lies about the treatment of POW's, lies about bombings, lies about North Vietnamese aggression, lies about the nature of the blockade . . . lies about the nature of American 'withdrawal,' and—from the famous day when L. B. Johnson called Diem 'the Churchill of Asia' to the latest tribute to Thieu's 'struggle for freedom'—lies about the client state on whose behalf we are presumably fighting the war." These are strong words from an authority, and every charge he made should have been investigated by newsmen in 1964 and every year after that and the documentation published immediately. Then public opinion would have been formed immediately—and not after our casualties were 4,884 dead and 30,475 wounded, South Vietnam had lost 575,084 men and many women and children, and the "enemy"—a term used by presidents and press—had suffered 900,000 dead and millions wounded.

The Vietnam war was just as illegal and immoral at the time of the Gulf of Tonkin affair, when the Senate voted 88 to 2 and the House 416 to 0 for a "mandate" for President Johnson to take "all necessary steps," as it is now generally admitted to have been. It is true that first press reports said that two United States destroyers had been attacked but had suffered no damage. It is true that a few faint voices said there had been no attack. (Even if there had been, did Johnson have the right to wage war without congressional action?) The investigation should have been made at once. The findings should have been published in a multimillion-circulation paper at once. The United States should not have been forced to wait for years for the truth about the Tonkin Gulf incident. (Wise, in "The Politics of Lying," concludes that the Tonkin Gulf attack was largely untrue. Robert L. Strout, in the *Christian Science Monitor,* agrees. So we had a war based on government say-so, if not government falsehood.)

For 30 years Herbert L. Matthews has been trying in books to correct the falsehoods that the correspondents with Franco published in his newspaper, the *New York Times,* reports for which the then managing editor and his assistants were to blame. Every correspondent in Madrid wrote that the Spanish war was Hitler's and Mussolini's preparation for a general war. The facts were so obvious that all correspondents in Madrid made the same statements; all tried to warn the nonfascist people that World War II was imminent.

No historian can say that the war could have been prevented, but many have since written that it would have been postponed, and had the writers from the Republican side been listened to—instead of being dismissed as spokesmen for the "Reds"—the democracies would have been prepared. Postponement and preparation would have resulted in a change in the character of the perhaps inevitable conflict; it would have saved millions of lives.

The press treatment of the news from Spain and of the career of Richard Nixon was similar. The press delayed printing the obvious facts, buried them, or ignored them.

In both historic instances there were reporters who knew the truth and tried to tell it. The failure was with mass means of communicating the truth.

The medium for mass communications proposed here needs nothing but a few million dollars to get going. Where will the money come from? (As the brilliant Henry Morgan once said, "Any man with ambition, integrity—and $10 million—can start a newspaper.") Every year hundreds of millions of dollars are given away for reactionary movements, for the spread of obscurantism, for the continuation of legends and falsehoods. Are there no multimillionaires on the liberal left with great ideas? Men like Alfred Nobel, who after inventing dynamite and making wars more horrible than ever before, left all his money to promote peace and goodwill among men? Or that German-born manufacturer in Manchester named Engels, whose bounty made possible the publication of Karl Marx's writings in newspapers and magazines and "Das Kapital?" The term millionaire Socialist has been applied to many men, but there is no record of anyone's establishing a newspaper instead of a foundation for doing good works.

The Ford Foundation has more than $2 billion. Through its Center for the Study of Democratic Institutions, it has published a series of pamphlets dealing with the mass media. In one of these Harry S. Ashmore advocated a continuous appraisal of the press, which he declared is presently "clearly irresponsible." Ashmore would make an excellent editor of any publication devoted to the continuous appraisal he suggests, and the Ford Foundation is the likeliest to endow it.

It has already made grants, as McGeorge Bundy states in a letter to the *Times*, to several publications, most of them struggling literary journals. But that is not enough. The Ford Foundation would not be inconvenienced for a day by the loss of $1.5 million such as Marshall Field III suffered with the greatest experiment in the history of a free press—and it could profit by learning the reasons for the tragic death of *PM*.

In reply to a letter I wrote the Ford Foundation regarding its enlarging the field of support for journalism reviews, as well as suggesting the ideal publication I have always had in mind, the foundation wrote that it was "taking another look in the general area of the rights and responsibilities of the press, which means that we will be considering the question of support for critical journalism reviews.... Your suggestions will certainly get careful attention in the process.... Thank you for taking the time to give us your thoughts on the [Columbia] Review and on the need for a 'yardstick' in the press."

If neither the Ford nor any other *pro bono publico* foundation, nor any billionaire not committed to reaction, has an interest in a "yardstick" newspaper, there could be group sponsors, such as the cooperatives and labor unions. This idea originated with George Addes, the secretary-treasurer of the United Auto Workers. Hardly had *In fact* begun to be a success, when Addes invited me to Detroit to discuss his plan. Although union men hate paying assessments, he said, he would propose a levy of fifty cents per annum, which would provide $3 million a year. Thus, a newspaper sponsored by the UAW could flourish, whether or not the general public or advertisers patronized it. If successful, a second and third paper would be started, and eventually he hoped the unions would have a chain of dailies from New York to California.

Addes asked me to write out a comprehensive prospectus and a statement; he guaranteed he would arrange for me to address the national convention of the CIO. But Pearl Harbor torpedoed this plan.

Failing sponsorship by foundations or rich and powerful organizations, I would propose a humble beginning, but not so humble as the four-page *In fact.* A small group, not necessarily rich but with some means, including persons of the stature of those who made up the Hutchins Commission, as many of the backers and sponsors of present critical publications as would be willing, and notably the Nader national and state organizations, could produce a national weekly newsletter of 50 to 100 pages. It could be sold by subscription or on the newsstands at a price below the usual magazine prices. I am sure it would be an instant success, and if it prospered, a daily could be considered. *In fact's* maximum circulation was 176,000. It was getting 3,000 subscriptions a week, one-third from union locals, and despite a boycott and universal silence (except when it was attacked by a coalition of enemies unsurpassed in American journalistic history, which in a few years scared away 120,000 subscribers), *In fact* prospered for eight of its 10 years at two cents and then four cents a copy. The sponsors I suggest would escape such an attack—even if McCarthy-era Redbaiting was ever revived. By presenting the facts as they are, to millions, they could influence thinking and actions. No one has ever doubted that *In fact,* with fewer than a million readers, was a force of considerable power.

The poet believed that truth, crushed to earth, would rise again. He didn't say when. A year after the election—as at the Watergate? Two centuries later—as in the works of numerous historians who are now rewriting the events of the American Revolution and for the first time telling it as it was? Long after an illegal and immoral war has wasted fifty thousand lives on a faraway battlefield—as in Vietnam? After a nation has been betrayed into fascist bondage—as in Spain? And will it rise and be effective or remain embalmed in doctoral theses and in journalistic memoirs? Is it not possible for truth to arise every morning—in the morning newspaper?

Some years ago I concluded a book (*1000 Americans*) with this paragraph: "Right or wrong, the present writer holds to his belief that in a nation and in a world where the means of mass communication are honest and free, when they function for the general welfare instead of private profits, there will be progress, because nothing will stop the march of an informed people."

The people of the United States were not informed about Vietnam, they were misinformed. They were lied to about the Tonkin Gulf incident, about the incursion into Cambodia, about the bombardment of Hanoi. The few knew and protested—the few are not the people. So because the millions were not informed, Vietnam goes into our history books as a disgrace and one of the great disasters.

Few people were truly informed about the actions of a politician named Nixon in the 1950's and 1960's and through the presidential campaign of 1972. When many people were told the facts in 1973 they took a step forward.

Voltaire, author of the Philosophical Dictionary, once wrote, "Humanly speaking, let us define truth, while waiting for a better definition, as a statement of things as they are." The idea of stating things as they are was first proposed, the written record shows, by Plautus in his Aulularia, circa 210 B.C., in the line "*Resipsa testiat*," and repeated by Terence in Adelphae "*Res ipsa indicat*" and similarly by Greeks and Romans whose sayings all translate liberally if not literally as "Let the facts speak for themselves."

Is this ancient idea outdated? Hohenberg, in his article previously quoted, seems to think so—he refers to "those old-fashioned journalists who still maintain that the way out of these predicaments is merely to print the news and let the public try to figure out what it means." In defense of such a policy I offer the conclusion Theodore White gives in his story of the downfall of a crooked president. He writes: "The tapes spoke for themselves."

Facts fairly and honestly presented. Facts speaking for themselves in this morning's newspaper are the history of our time—and the history books of the future. So if you believe that the history of civilization is itself an important means for furthering civilization, and if you believe that civilization has been and still is of some value, you must agree that this history—which even the gods cannot change—must be reported and recorded as truthfully (and quickly) as possible.